THE
STRATEGIC
CIO

THE STRATEGIC CIO

Changing the Dynamics of the Business Enterprise

Forewords by

Rob Carter
Chief Information Officer of FedEx Corporation

Filippo Passerini
Group President, Global Business Services and
Chief Information Officer, Procter and Gamble

PHIL WEINZIMER

CRC Press
Taylor & Francis Group
Boca Raton   London   New York

CRC Press is an imprint of the
Taylor & Francis Group, an **informa** business

AN AUERBACH BOOK

CRC Press
Taylor & Francis Group
6000 Broken Sound Parkway NW, Suite 300
Boca Raton, FL 33487-2742

© 2015 by Taylor & Francis Group, LLC
CRC Press is an imprint of Taylor & Francis Group, an Informa business

No claim to original U.S. Government works

Printed on acid-free paper
Version Date: 20140911

International Standard Book Number-13: 978-1-4665-6172-4 (Hardback)

Visit the Taylor & Francis Web site at
http://www.taylorandfrancis.com

and the CRC Press Web site at
http://www.crcpress.com

To my wife, Lynn, who has filled my life with love and kindness, and to our daughter, Danielle, her husband, Mike, and two precious grandchildren, Maxwell and Madeline, who forever give us joy, laughter, and love.

Contents

Foreword by Filippo Passerini

One Monday morning in October 2012, a colleague mentioned that Phil Weinzimer wanted to interview me for his book titled *The Strategic CIO: Changing the Dynamics of the Business Enterprise*. When I learned the book would focus on how CIOs transform their IT organizations into a more strategic and business-focused asset, I wanted to know more.

In my more than 30 years at Procter & Gamble, I've been focused on transforming IT into a competitive advantage for our company. What I've seen, particularly in the past 10 years, is CIOs undergoing a sort of identity crisis. The pervasiveness of technology has created an environment where some CIOs are completely focused first on *what to do with the technology* rather than on *creating value for the business* and *then* thinking about which technology will best help them achieve those goals.

Over the next few months, I shared with Phil my thoughts about the role of the CIO—what has worked for me and what I've seen work for others who are, first and foremost, business people and, second, technology experts. *The Strategic CIO* is a valuable resource for CIOs who want to improve the business value of their IT organizations. And what successful CIO doesn't want to do that?

During my tenure at P&G, I have held a variety of positions in both IT and line business, including marketing. One of the lessons I share is that the role of information technology is much more about helping business leaders make well-informed business decisions than using technology for technology's sake. Too many times IT organizations and their leaders lose sight of this goal.

Procter & Gamble is a consumer products company. With 84 billion dollars in sales reaching 5 billion people—approximately 70% of the world's population—we must continuously improve the value of our products. We have to be relevant and distinctive while meeting consumers' needs. This requires leadership at the executive level of the company and a wealth of talented people who execute with passion.

The Strategic CIO will help you transform your IT organization into a strategic asset for your company by following a four-phase transformation model, which focuses on the fundamentals of a strategic IT organization.

An important foundational step is to deliver basic services exceptionally well. Getting this right will earn the trust of the business so you can collaborate on projects that result in measurable business outcomes. The second phase is to understand the business, focus on user experiences, and improve business skills of IT personnel. We must speak the language of the business for the collaboration to be truly valuable. The third phase, focus on initiatives that drive business value, is the only path to take. After all, if we are not driving distinctive value, we are simply providing a commodity that could be delivered by any other service provider. The highlight of the transformation process is the fourth phase: Leverage technology strategically to innovate measurable value for the company. This is where true business value is achieved.

During my time at P&G, I've made decisions that reflect various steps in this model. When I began transforming the IT organization at P&G, we needed a new identity to emphasize our focus on the business and the role we knew we could play. We were suffering the same identity crisis I've since seen among CIOs. We changed the name of the IT organization to Information Decision Solutions (IDS). After all, information is our asset, and decisions are what we help business leaders achieve. Services are the pathway of delivering value to the business. When I became group president of Business Services and CIO, I merged IDS into the Business Services Group, a team responsible for providing a range of services, including people management, travel services, strategic sourcing, financial services, and business intelligence, required to operate the business every day. Our organization chart does not include the word *technology*. Instead, the focus is on providing services that add value to the business. These two major changes created a cultural shift focused on providing solutions, running Global Business Services as a business, and developing competencies and skills focusing on business first and technology second. This change of focus is what Phil addresses in the first and second phases of his transformation model.

The third phase of the transformation model is to focus on initiatives that improve business value. An example of this is the work our teams accomplished integrating Gillette into the P&G family. In 2005, P&G embarked upon the largest integration in the company's history—a mammoth undertaking by business and IT teams working collaboratively to integrate a multitude of applications, servers, data centers, and services. The integration, which included more than 1,100 projects in less than a year and a half, resulted in more than $1 billion in savings.

If you as a CIO can leverage technology to improve the speed to develop products, enter new markets, identify market trends, or improve customer value, you are innovating business value. This is the fourth phase of the strategic IT transformation and an area where we have made great strides at P&G.

Our business is complicated, and we recognized some time ago that executive and management teams had difficulty interpreting the data facing them when discussing a business problem. They had multiple databases of information, and not all of them were current. To make matters worse, teams could not efficiently analyze the data because of the clunky format.

Our Global Business Services teams addressed this by leveraging technology to develop a single source of real-time data called decision cockpits. The argument over different data sets and accuracy of information no longer exists. Our teams use *digital cockpits* at their workstations to display data in meaningful ways. P&G teams meet in specially designed conference rooms called *business spheres* with large flat screens that display real-time data using visual-based graphics and predictive analytics to help teams quickly analyze business problems. This dramatically speeds up the analysis time and improves decision-making.

Phil provides a number of other interesting examples of how CIOs are leveraging technology to innovate value. This is where CIOs have the power to influence the way business is conducted.

In this book, you will learn valuable lessons you can apply to improve business outcomes and drive value for your company. CIOs who focus on business results and create measurable value will succeed. Reading this book will elevate your thinking and help you identify the areas within IT that you should focus on to improve the value you provide the business. If you are a CIO who wants to improve the performance of your organization and help your company prosper and grow, *The Strategic CIO* should be at the top of your reading list. It will help change the dynamics of your business.

Filippo Passerini

Group President, Global Business Services
Chief Information Officer, P&G

Foreword by Robert B. Carter

I met Phil Weinzimer at the 2012 CIO100 Symposium & Awards Ceremony in Rancho Palos Verdes, California. We bumped into each other in the hallway following my talk about on how FedEx strategically leverages technology to enable its business units to compete collectively, manage collaboratively, and operate independently. Phil said that he wanted to interview me for his book because he recognized that what we accomplished at FedEx was changing the dynamics of the business enterprise, which is the main theme of *The Strategic CIO*. When we spoke, Phil shared with me his four-phase model that depicts how IT organizations transform into a strategic asset. I realized how relevant this book would be for CIOs, CEO's, or any other executive in the C-suite. It would also be valuable for a wide range of managers who are interested in understanding how IT can leverage technology to improve business outcomes. I found great insights from the 150 plus interviews Phil Weinzimer conducted with CIOs, business executives, and thought leaders.

From its very beginnings, in 1973, FedEx valued the importance of information and leveraging technology to improve business outcomes. Fred Smith, Founder of FedEx, always believed "the information about the package was as important as the package itself." At FedEx, we continuously leverage technology to enable this vision and strive to provide a superior customer experience with every FedEx interaction, which we call The Purple Promise, which is simply stated as, "I will make every FedEx experience outstanding." It is about business first and technology second.

Fred Smith's vision of leveraging information about the package required two fundamental building blocks. The first was to improve the internal processes. The second was to allow customer access for delivery information. What started as a process improvement initiative turned into a quality-driven management (QDM) program using 71 key metrics that measures service quality. We call this the Service Quality Index (SQI). Over the years, we leveraged technology to measure...measure...and measure all the critical points in the customer interaction process. In 1990, we won the Malcolm Baldridge award for our SQI quality initiative. The second component of Fred Smith's vision was to provide customers access to information, and we did that. In 1994, FedEx launched fedex.com, which was the first use of the web to allow customers to track package information. Today, we are a $45-billion-dollar global company that delivers over 10 million packages every day in 220 countries around the world.

Over the years, we have leveraged information technology and changed the dynamics of how FedEx conducts its business. At the strategic level, we completely revamped our infrastructure to support a more robust business model. At the product level, FedEx provides services to customers that provide package-level detail. SenseAware[SM] is one of these products. At the tactical level, our rotation technology enables sensors to scan six sides of a package moving at 400 feet per second. We never lose sight of providing a superior customer experience. We continuously strive to improve customer experience by applying information technologies strategically throughout the FedEx network and are changing the dynamics of our business enterprise. This is the main theme of *The Strategic CIO*.

I have been fortunate to work with dedicated people who focus on improving our customer experience and providing business value. FedEx has received numerous awards citing achievements in information technology. The awards are often presented to the CIO, as the leader of the organization. However, the real award winners are the dedicated FedEx team members who provide a superior customer experience in every FedEx interaction. We have been honored with Fast Company's 100 Most Creative People in Business award in 2010;

Information Week's Chief of the Year Award in 2000, 2001, and 2005; and CIO Magazine's CIO100 award 20 times since the award began in 1989. These are just some of the prestigious awards I was proud to accept on behalf of the FedEx IT team members. As a charter inductee into the CIO Magazine Hall of Fame, I have the opportunity to network with colleagues from around the world to share insights and learn from their successes.

Since joining FedEx in 1993, I worked in the IT organization as well as in its various business units. These assignments helped shape my thinking and management style. The journey has been very rewarding. However, good things do not happen overnight. When I became CIO in 2001, I realized that to improve the business by leveraging technology, we first needed to establish the credibility, trust, and support of the business. This is an obvious and important lesson Phil Weinzimer addresses in *The Strategic CIO* as the first and most important phase of transforming an IT organization. At FedEx, we achieved this goal over a six-year period. *The Strategic CIO* addresses this important transformation phase in a number of different ways. The case studies of Fox Entertainment and CSAA Insurance Group provide the step-by-step *how to* activities their IT executives utilized to establish the trust from the business units. The template models are useful for CIOs who strive to improve the trust-based working relationship with business units. Operational excellence and project governance models provide a solid framework you can easily use to improve these two core elements of IT success. The process for defining and measuring the business value of both commodity and business services is especially insightful and valuable.

I learned much about the business and the competitive environment during my assignments at FedEx. As a CIO, this is an absolute necessity. I would never have successfully added value during business meetings with C-suite colleagues without understanding the business. This is especially important for IT teams as well, since a solid understanding of the business provides a core foundation for working with business teams to focus on user experiences to improve customer interactions with FedEx. Additionally, our FedEx teams develop a set of skills that were customer- and business-focused, which complemented their technical skills. These themes represent the second phase of the four-stage transformation model in *The Strategic CIO*.

Weinzimer discusses, in a few chapters, the important components of understanding the business, focusing on user experiences to identify opportunities to improve value, and the three key competencies and associated skills required by a strategic IT organization. The competency and skills chapter is very insightful. It provides best-in-class examples of the nine key strategic skills and of how companies use these skills. This method brings to life the importance of these competencies and skills in building the knowledge base of your IT personnel. One of the examples I found interesting was that of Harry Lukens, CIO of Lehigh Valley Health Network (LVHN). He developed a workshop that every IT person attends. The workshop focuses on providing a solid understanding of the health care industry, competitive environment, LVHN business model, and business skills IT personnel require to interact with business teams. This is how CIOs transform their IT teams into business-focused teams.

I spend a lot of my time collaborating with the business to develop initiatives to improve it. Our goal within the information technology organization is to create business value, not just apply technology for technology's sake. This is the key theme in the third phase of the transformation model. Weinzimer provides examples from Randy Spratt, CIO at McKesson; Tom Grooms, CIO at Valspar; Clif Triplett, who was CIO at Baker Hughes; and Ann Wilms when she was CIO of Rohm and Hass; as well as others. The insights from these CIOs provide different perspectives as to how each succeeded at delivering business value. Tom Grooms, CIO at Valspar, developed a process to vet out project requests from the business. To be considered for approval, the project request must identify specific measurable business values. A simple process step that yielded remarkable business results.

The fourth phase of the IT transformation model in *The Strategic CIO* is to leverage technology strategically to innovate value. This is the fun part of being a CIO. This is where I can work with the business and identify technologies that are truly creative and change the course of the business. I can think of a number of initiatives we implemented at FedEx that were truly innovative. At the strategic level, we completely revamped our infrastructure to support a more robust business model. The model follows a concept I call "Four Horseman of Dominant Design," which I have spoken on frequently at symposiums. FedEx is pleased to be included along with Proctor & Gamble, Western Governor's University, Express Scripts, Lehigh Valley Hospital, CAI, Build-A-Bear Workshop, and others.

Phil Weinzimer provides great examples from many CIOs on how they transformed their IT organizations into a strategic capability. Some organizations are just beginning the journey, while others are in the process of implementing the other phases. Regardless of where you are on the transformation path, this book is for you. We, as CIOs, have a tremendous opportunity to change the dynamics of the business enterprise. You will definitely learn from all the CIOs who share their insights and experiences in this book. I know I have.

Robert B. Carter
Chief Information Officer of FedEx Corporation

Acknowledgments

Authoring a book is truly an educational experience. I met many people along this journey who shared their insights and experiences on the subject of the strategic chief information officer (CIO). Each provided me with nuggets of wisdom that together with my work experience form the content of this book. There are many people to thank.

Anyone who has written a book knows the impact it has on family members. Our daughter, Danielle, is grown and raising a family of her own, leaving my wife, Lynn, to cope with my writing, interviews, and research schedule. Lynn has been through this experience during the writing of my first book. When I told her about my desire to write a second book, she reluctantly agreed to experience all the same inconveniences that disrupt family life. As I wrote each chapter, Lynn was always there to read the drafts and, as delicately as she could, recommend improvements that made the words flow better. On days when I was in my home office writing from dawn to dusk, which was often, Lynn would bring me my breakfast, lunch, snacks, and, at times, dinner, making sure I was properly nourished. She was always willing to reschedule our social events when writing needed to take precedence. We first met in high school during our senior year. The moment I saw her, I knew she was my soul mate. To my dismay, at the time, I wasn't hers. However, after seven years of relentless pursuit, a trait many authors have, she finally realized I was her soul mate as well. She is my rock and the love of my life.

During the early phases of the book project, I sought council from four strategic executives—three CIOs, and one former McKinsey consultant—each of whom I have worked with and respect and helped formulate components of the book. Steve O'Connor, a friend for the past 12 years, shared his wisdom, insight, and experience, which were invaluable in developing the framework and content for this book. Hank Leingang, an experienced CIO and business executive, helped me think through and improve the strategic IT competency model. Bob Kaplan, whom I met at ITM Software, where he served as interim CEO, was very helpful in sharing his advice on the four-phase transformation model. Then there is my friend, the modest CIO. He knows who he is and I am forever thankful to him for sharing his book-writing experience, through countless phone calls and lunches.

I am honored to have two prestigious and well-recognized CIOs each write a foreword. Robert Carter, Chief Information Officer of FedEx Corporation, and Filippo Passerini, Group President, Global Business Services, and Chief Information Officer at Procter & Gamble, each well respected by their peers. They are also humble enough to recognize that their success results from the hard working personnel in their information technology organizations.

During the research phase of writing this book, I spoke to more than 150 CIOs, and business executives, as well as academic thought leaders, who were very helpful. Among them are a select group of executives who shared their wisdom and experiences, which appear in various chapters of the book. I am indebted to each of the following executives who were generous with their time and willing to share their knowledge to help others learn from their experiences. They are (in alphabetical order): Scott Blanchette, Dick Brandt, Tony D'Allesandro, Mark Egan, Jose Carlos Eiras, David Finnegan, Thomas Fruman, Steve Fugale, Tom Gill, Tom Grooms, Steve Heilenman, Terry Jacklin, Rebecca Jacoby, Stu Kippleman, Tony Lombardi, Harry Lukens, Debra Martucci, Mike McClaskey, Cynthia McKenzie, James McQuivey, Kevin Michaelis, Scott Millis, Ravi Naik, Ken Piddington, Calvin Rhodes, Perry Rotella, Sanjib Sahoo, Mark Settle, Wayne Shurtz, Gary Spears, Randy Spratt, Steve Tranquillo, Clif Triplett, Greg Valdez, Anne Wilms, and

David Zanca, as well as many others. You know who you are and I am forever grateful to you for sharing your experiences with me.

The academic community helps drive change through research, writings, and thought leadership. Lynda Applegate (Harvard), George Westerman (MIT), Rick Watson (University of Georgia), and Roger Nagel (the Emeritus Wagner Professor in Computer Science, Lehigh) were generous in contributing their knowledge and insights on the subject of the strategic CIO.

A complete listing of all executives interviewed appears in Appendix B.

I especially want to thank David Finnegan, CIO at Build-A-Bear Workshop, for sharing the wonderful history of the company and how his team transformed the physical animal stuffing activity into a digital wonderland experience that children and adults can enjoy. To really understand the digital experience, I had the opportunity to take my grandchildren to a local Build-A-Bear Workshop. Every grandparent should take the time to enjoy this experience with their grandchildren.

This book would not have been successful without the hard work of the Taylor & Francis Group/CRC Press publishing team. My special thanks to my editor John Wyzalek and project editor Todd Perry, who shepherded me through the acquisition and editing process as well as providing guidance and encouragement during the writing process. When it comes to book cover design, I relied on a colleague and friend: Richard Wood is a true artist and I am grateful for his hard work and diligence in designing a book cover that hits the mark.

While at ITM and BMC Software, I worked with two former CIOs, John Chambers and Dennis Waliczek. Each provided me interesting insights I incorporated in the book. I also worked with Marty Carty at BMC Software, an experienced IT professional and sales executive, who helped me think through possible titles for the book.

As I wrote each chapter, I always sought fresh eyes to review the material. I have to thank John Bowen, a current colleague and friend who reviewed some of the key chapters and helped point out key areas that needed clarification. I also wanted to gain an international perspective from CIOs. So, I want to thank Brian Donovan, my new friend in Australia, who helped me connect with a number of Australian CIOs and business executives.

Finally, I want to thank each of the 150 plus executives I interviewed for this book. Half are CIOs, the remainder are senior IT and business unit executives. Many of you shared your experiences in multiple interviews taking time away from your busy schedules. I congratulate each of you on your accomplishments in leveraging technology to improve business outcomes. Most importantly, your insights and experiences provide an excellent foundation for others to learn the value of how strategic CIOs are changing the dynamics of the business enterprise. I remain forever grateful for your knowledge and guidance.

I am anxious to hear from you as you embark upon the journey of transforming to a strategic IT organization. Please contact me and let me know about your successes as well as challenges. I look forward to hearing from you.

Phil Weinzimer
email: pweinzimer@gmail.com
twitter: @pweinzimer

1

INTRODUCTION

The Changing Role of the CIO

For the times they are a-changin'

Bob Dylan[1]

There is no better time to be a chief information officer (CIO). Just look around you! The consumerization of information technology (IT) is dramatically influencing the products and services your company provides to customers, vendors, logistic partners, and business personnel, across the entire value network, to create new markets and competitive opportunities. Some chief executive officers (CEO) and C-suite colleagues may understand the potential of leveraging information for strategic advantage and there is a larger group that does not. The challenge is how to accomplish it.

Your role as a CIO is changing from a technologist to a strategist. The consumerization of IT is revolutionizing how consumers shop, travel, and pay for services. The consumer experience is the focus. On the business side, IT is enabling almost every single business process, which drives and supports customer value. As a result, you, as a CIO, need to be more involved in business discussions than ever before. In fact, strategic CIOs collaborate with C-level peers to develop business strategies and innovate value. The role of a CIO is expanding, and those that truly add business value even oversee and manage key business functions.[2] Today, it is all about business outcome. You, as a CIO, are in the best position to participate and enable new information-rich products and services. The question is *are you and your IT organization up to the challenge?*

- Do you understand the business and competitive environment well enough to help the business achieve significant outcomes?

- Do your IT personnel have the necessary competencies and skills to effectively partner with and participate in business teams?
- Does your IT organization effectively collaborate with business unit executives and employ speed, agility, and quality in responding to their needs?
- Does your CTO understand how to apply the new and emerging technologies for competitive advantage?

You and your IT organization now have the opportunity to collaborate more effectively with your business peers than ever before. With the right strategy, your IT organization can have a significant influence to help your company create customer value, improve margin, and enhance shareholder wealth. You are not alone. Every CIO face the same challenge. With the right strategy, you and IT organization can have a significant influence to help your company achieve business success. To understand this dynamic, I interviewed over 155 CIOs, IT directors, and business executives. I captured their insights and experiences on the changing business landscape, leadership challenges, emerging technology challenges, and partnering opportunities. What I found is a compelling consensus on the following four critical success factors that CIOs must achieve to have a truly collaborative partnership with the C-suite and business unit teams to improve customer value, increase corporate revenue, and enhance shareholder wealth.

Build trust and confidence:

- Newly hired CIOs recognize they need to build the trust and confidence of business leaders by understanding their needs and execute flawlessly on delivering basic services.

Improve business skills:

- CIOs need to rebalance the skills within the IT organization because business unit leaders expect IT personnel to exhibit business skills if they wish to engage as part of business teams.

Partner with business teams to identify, analyze, develop, and implement opportunities that drive margin and optimize cost:

- IT personnel working as part of business teams is the best approach to identify business opportunities that leverage IT to drive top-line growth and cost optimization.

Leverage technology strategy to innovate new value:

- The CIO and IT personnel are in the best position to identify information-based opportunities and leverage technology to innovate new products and services for the business enterprise.

Numerous surveys on this subject address these critical success factor. The following are two examples.

The *Deloitte CIO Survey 2013*, in which 700 CIOs across 36 countries from the United States, Europe, the Middle East, Africa, Asia, and Australia were interviewed, supports these findings.[3] The survey found that *"Business focused and strategic skills"* are needed by IT personnel.

Successful CIOs proactively understand their business partner's objectives and views on technology.

CIOs have some way to go to improve their reputation as a credible partner to the business

The Economist survey of 536 C-suite executives also addresses the findings from my research[4]:

The ubiquity of mobile consumer devices such as smartphones and tablets is eroding the walls surrounding corporate IT environment and making it possible for companies to engage with staff and customers in new ways.

CIOs will need to play a new role or IT will change around them. The ability to change depends on IT addressing the C-suite's core needs and doing so through a language that clearly expresses the business value of technology investments

The impact of how consumers use technology will *"create opportunities for companies to develop innovative products and services to connect with customers in new ways, and to rethink traditional business processes.*

More than half of CIOs surveyed *do not believe that their IT function is considered a credible hub of innovation within their organization."* (ibid)

A number of recent books on the same subject also provide similar insights. *The Real Business of IT*, by George Westerman of MIT Sloan School of Management and Richard Hunter of Gartner Research, addresses how CIOs can transform the C-suite perception of IT from a *cost generator to value creator.*[5] *Digital Disruption*, by Forrester's James McQuivey Research, addresses how companies take advantage of the digital revolution to *get closer to customers and disrupt the usual ways of doing business.*[6] My first book, *Getting It Right*, explains the process of how to prepare a team-based workforce, perceive customer need, and provide new products and services to create sustainable value.[7]

There is no debate that the CIO plays an ever-more important role in today's global marketplace. CIOs are responding to help the C-suite leverage IT for strategic advantage. During my interviews, with CIOs and other business executives, I asked CIOs who have traversed the transformation process to explain how they moved up the curve from a technology provider to an effective business partner that collaborates with C-suite executives to create information-based products and services. There is a pattern to this success, and I have captured this process in, what I term, the strategic IT transformation phases (Figure 1.1).

This book is structured as follows:

- The four phases, which constitute the main sections of the book, represent a model CIOs navigate to improve their strategic impact on the business.
- Each section begins with a chapter that summarizes the section content: chapter objective, key points, examples, and templates used.
- Each chapter includes CIO case studies, templates, and lessons learned.
- Appendices at the end of the book includes a summary of each chapter as well as a list of the CIOs and other executives interviewed as part of my research.

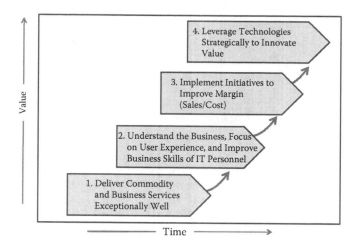

Figure 1.1 Strategic IT Organization Transformation Phases.

This book is not just for CIOs but also for board members, CEOs, and C-suite executives; IT directors, managers, and personnel; and business unit presidents, vice presidents, directors, managers, and personnel. We cannot leave out students, professors, and those in academia who need to understand the changing role of the CIO. A brief description of the value of this book for each of these constituents is included in Figure 1.2.

Following is an explanation of each book section to whet your appetite. I have developed a Book Reading Plan Template (Figure 1.3) to help you identify the sections and chapters you want to *Browse*, *Review*, or *Read in Detail*. The template provides a listing of chapter titles. You can mark *Browse, Review*, or *Read in Detail*, in the appropriate column, depending on your goal. Proactively developing a reading plan helps you manage your time. The template is found at the end of this chapter. Depending on your role, you may wish to focus on different sections of the book.

- A student who is interested in the importance of IT in today's dynamic marketplace should read each section diligently.
- A CEO who understands the need for IT to deliver basic services exceptionally well can quickly browse or review section one but spend more time reading the other sections in

---

Governance: Board of Directors

Understand the economic and strategic value of information and technology as part of an overall business strategy.

Chief Executive Officer and C-Suite Executives

Understand how strategic CIOs collaborate with other C-suite executives to strategically apply information and technology into the business model to drive customer value, profitability, and shareholder wealth.

CIOs, IT Vice-Presidents, Directors, Managers, and IT Personnel

CIOs:	Provide the vision, leadership, as well as demonstrate and communicate how the strategic value of information and technology can change the dynamics of the business enterprise.
VPs and Directors:	Learn how strategic CIOs think about, communicate, and apply the strategic value of information and technology in the business enterprise.
Managers and Personnel:	Learn how strategic IT organizations develop and exhibit business skills as they work within enterprise teams co-developing business solutions that drive bottom-line performance.

Business Unit Presidents, Vice-Presidents, Directors, Managers, Personnel

Presidents, VPs:	Understand how other company business unit executives work with the CIO in developing new product, service, and process strategies that drive strategic and economic value for the business enterprise.
Directors, Personnel:	Learn how other companies successfully develop enterprise-wide teams—composed of business unit and IT personnel—that work together to leverage information and technology strategically to innovate value and improve operating margin.

Academia: Students, Professors; Research Associates

Understand the growing and centric role of information and technology in the business enterprise and how it will help you succeed in your future career.

Figure 1.2   Book Value by Enterprise Role.

more detail to gain insight into how the CIO can enable business success.

- A CEO who recognizes that information and technology play an important role in developing an enterprise strategy but does not know how should read the whole book carefully.

Regardless of your role, there is much information that will help you succeed. The book reading plan is a guide for where to focus your reading time. Regardless of which sections you focus on, there are numerous examples, including insights, lessons learned, and templates from CIOs who have traversed the transformation phases.

The first section of the book, *Deliver Commodity and Business Services Exceptionally Well*, explores the foundation phase of the strategic IT transformation process. Every CIO knows that to build the trust and confidence of the C-suite, e-mail, phone systems, and applications that support the business processes must all work well each time employees access any of these services. It is comparable to you plugging a cord into an electric outlet. You always know that electricity will flow. This is the level of confidence business needs from the IT department. For those who think this is not difficult, speak to any IT person to explain the complexity of today's infrastructure. To help you understand the complexity of this phase, I include a number of chapters that provide you with the necessary methodology, tools, and case examples to build this capability for any IT organization.

Chapter 2, Section Overview: How to Deliver Commodity and Business Services Exceptionally Well, provides a summary of the chapters in the section.

Chapter 3, Business Value of Delivering Services Exceptionally Well, provides two examples of IT leaders who interacted with C-suite executives and business unit leaders to understand the services required to support their business needs.

Chapter 4, How to Excel at Operational Stability, discusses the importance of operational stability to ensure that commodity and business services are delivered exceptionally well. Included in this chapter are CIO examples, templates, and a framework for the effective governance of operational stability.

Chapter 5, How to Succeed at Project Governance, highlights the importance of project execution in light of increasing demands from the business. A framework for ensuring effective project governance provides an effective method for use in your IT organization. A case study of how a CIO and his IT team implemented an effective governance process will provide you guidance in how to ensure successful governance.

Chapter 6, How to Measure and Improve the Business Value of IT Services, provides an effective four-step process of how to measure and improve the business value of the services your IT organization provides the business. An IT process maturity grid tool and a case example will help you assess the business value as well as a process to improve the maturity of the business value you provide. Examples of CIO dashboards will help you better understand how you can effectively communicate the value of IT to the business.

The second section of the book, Understand the Business, Focus on User Experience, and Improve Competencies and Skills of IT Personnel, is a must-read for everyone, regardless of your role. If you, as a CIO, and your key IT leadership team do not understand how the business operates, the markets it competes in, and the value provided to customers, then it is game over. You will never be able to connect on a business level with the C-suite. Even if you, as a CIO, understand these critical components of the business, the challenge is to up-skill the competencies and skills of your IT leadership team who are probably well versed in technology but may not communicate with business personnel in a language they understand. Remember, it is all about IT and business personnel working in teams to identify solutions that achieve business outcomes and improve the company's competitive position. This can only be accomplished if team members, both IT and business unit personnel, can communicate effectively. One way is to focus on user experiences, which provides a common platform, just like a Rosetta stone.

This section of the book is, in my opinion, provides one of the most important lessons for CIOs. I have included a number of chapters on each of the key subjects.

Chapter 7, Section Overview—Understand the Business, Focus on User Experience, and Improve Business Skills of IT Personnel, provides a summary of the chapters included in this section as well as the importance in understanding the business enterprise and competitive landscape in order for your IT organization to serve the needs of the business.

Chapter 8, Why CIOs Need to Understand the Business to Succeed, explains why CIOs and the IT organization will not succeed without a well-based understanding of the business, the competitive environment, and the enterprise processes that operate the business. CIOs attain their role from different paths. Some are promoted from within IT or the business side. Still other CIOs attain their role from similar businesses or entirely different industries. Five examples of CIOs who attained their role from different paths provide insights into how they learned about the business. Also included is an example of an executive program that provides managers from different countries an opportunity to learn about various cultures and business practices, and to work with each other on a major project. Attendees learn about teamwork, working in different cultures, and how the training prepares them for their future business careers. A graduate of the program who pursued a path in IT explains how the program prepared her for success.

Chapter 9, The Importance of Understanding Your Organizational Culture in Building Effective Teams, explores the importance of organizational culture in the success formula of transforming into a strategic IT organization. The cultural orientation of your IT organization has a direct bearing on how successful you will be in your journey to transform into a strategic organization. It is important for you to understand the cultural framework, which includes four orientation cultures, each with its underlying characteristics that compete with one another and impact the behaviors of your IT personnel, in achieving your organization objectives. It is important for you to understand the importance of culture, how to measure culture, and what you can do to leverage your organization's cultural orientation. It is an important component in transforming your IT organization into a strategic powerhouse.

Chapter 10, Key Competencies and Skills of a Strategic IT Organization, focuses on the four strategic competencies and associated skills IT personnel need to exhibit if they are to work effectively in business teams collaborating on identifying, analyzing, developing, and implementing solutions that achieve significant business outcomes. Understanding the business is the main competency required to work effectively in business teams. Additionally, IT personnel need to have a competency to understand the market, competitive environment, and value gaps the company can leverage to achieve competitive advantage. On the technology side, the third competency, IT personnel need to leverage their technology skills with an understanding of the basic technology strategy, the need for organizational agility, and the need for strategic project capabilities to enhance project throughput with a high degree or quality and value. These three competencies form the core competencies. The fourth competency cuts across the other three, and thus, I name this cross-competency skills. These include the ability to share and communicate a vision with business teams as well as provide leadership when engaging with business teams on the power of information and associated technologies.

Examples from eight corporations on how IT organizations use each competency and associated skills in working with business teams provide real insight and lessons learned that you can apply in your IT organization.

Chapter 11, How to Measure and Improve the Maturity of the Competencies and Skills of Your IT Organization, focuses on how you can measure the strategic maturity of your IT organization using a five-step process. A template and case example provide you guidance in how to use the template to identify the maturity gaps of the strategic IT competencies and skills that need to be improved in your organization. Included are suggested scenarios of how you can use the maturity assessment for different IT teams and suggested techniques to improve the strategic maturity skills.

The third section of the book, Implement Initiatives to Improve Margin, builds on the first two sections. Delivering services exceptionally well and improving the business skills of your IT personnel enable your IT teams to work collaboratively as part of business teams on initiatives that result in real business value for your company. Case study examples of CIOs who implemented initiatives that resulted in improved sales and/or reduced costs provide you with real insight into how strategic CIOs think and collaborate with C-suite executives to drive change.

Chapter 12, Section Overview: Implement Initiatives to Improve Margin, provides an overview of this section. The focus is on how important it is for your IT personnel to work collaboratively with business teams to identify initiatives that improve business revenue and/or reduce cost in line with your company business strategy.

Chapter 13, How Strategic CIOs Focus on Initiatives to Improve Margin, provides case examples of five CIOs from a variety of industries—chemical, pharmaceutical, gas and oil explorer, IT services provider, and banking—who drove initiatives and partnered with C-suite executives to form IT/business teams that implemented significant initiatives to improve their company performance. The insights from these CIOs will help you better understand how they successfully leveraged their trust-based relationship and IT personnel business skills to partner collaboratively to achieve business outcomes.

The fourth section of the book, Leverage Technology Strategically to Innovate Value, will take you through the journey of seven CIOs who used their business knowledge, C-suite relationships, and IT personnel business skills to leverage information and associated technologies to drive innovative and measurable value for their company. The section starts with a chapter that explores the significance of leveraging technology strategically and examples of where information and associated technologies seamlessly weave into our daily lives. With this foundation, we highlight seven CIOs, in subsequent chapters, who have successfully leveraged technologies strategically to innovate value.

Chapter 14, Section Overview: Leverage Technologies Strategically to Innovate Value, provides an overview of how this phase of the IT strategic transformation model leverages the prior three phases as well as a review of the forthcoming chapters.

Chapter 15, Why Leveraging Technologies Strategically to Innovate Value Is a Game Changer will help you understand the significance of leveraging technology strategically. Included are examples of where information and associated technologies seamlessly weave into our daily lives.

Chapter 16, How FedEx Leverages Technology Strategically to Innovate Value, provides in-depth examples of how the CIO, his IT leadership team, and IT teams work with business teams to create a competitive advantage for the company. How the CIO, Rob Carter, and his IT organization dramatically changed the way business units use IT is a great example of how IT leads the charge to change the business model. Additionally, you will learn the process Carter used to convince the CEO that the IT organization could help the business provide a more information-rich business model to enable business units to more effectively work together but still maintain their independent structure. A perspective from the business unit CIO of FedEx Freight is an equally good example of how technology is leveraged to create unique business value. A third example of a business unit CIO's leveraging technology to create a new service offering will help you perceive how IT leaders think about driving new value for the company. Additional examples of leveraging technology will provide you with interesting and valuable insights.

Chapter 17, How Procter & Gamble Leverages Technology Strategically to Innovate Value, provides a different view from the most senior IT executive of the company. Filippo Passerini is passionate about helping business leaders make well-informed business decisions. He and his team digitized information and implemented data analytics across Procter & Gamble to enable employees, managers, and executives understand the implication of customer and market data and make the necessary business decisions with reduced risk. His strategic initiatives to leverage technology are heralded by the industry. His CIO Lifetime Achievement Award from Berkeley's Haas School of Business speaks to his results. This chapter is a must-read for everyone who wants to get inside the brain of a strategic CIO.

Chapter 18, How Five CIOs from Different Industries Leverage Technology Strategically to Innovate Value, will help you understand how CIOs from different industries tackle the challenge of overcoming the chasm between IT and business units. Each does so by focusing on providing business value through leveraging technology strategically. You will learn how the CIO of Build-A-Bear Workshop changed the physical in-store model of customers, creating stuffed animals into a digital experience that broadens the reach to customers throughout the entire shopping experience. The CIO of Penske Corporation shows us how to leverage technology across a myriad of businesses in different industries. The CIO of Express Scripts collaborates with business leaders to help customers improve health outcomes by enabling technologies that also improved business results—a win for the customer and a win for the company. The CIO of Verisk not only applies technology strategically to innovate value in the insurance risk business but also leads a newly developed business unit to help companies manage risk along their supply chain. The CIO of Lehigh Valley Health Network innovates value in providing health care through integrating technologies with patient services that results in saving lives.

Chapter 19, Section Overview: How to Measure the Strategic Maturity of Your IT Organization, includes an assessment template, process, and guidelines to measure the strategic maturity of your IT organization. The process identified in this chapter will help you develop a transformation roadmap based upon your analysis of the assessment. Guidelines are also provided to conduct a 360-degree process across the business enterprise.

The book concludes with Chapter 20, Final Thoughts: An Executive Challenge, which discusses an ongoing challenge for C-suite executives. Every day, personnel across the enterprise make business decisions that could adversely impact the company revenue, profitability, and even survival. Remember JPMorgan's London Whale scandal of 2012! The challenge is how to proactively identify and mitigate potential risk areas for major business processes. An information-based enterprise solution that captures process history, adverse impacts to the business, and mitigating actions becomes a "coach and mentor" to personnel throughout the enterprise and provides management with "early-warning" indicators of potential problems. Think of this as having a coach sitting on your shoulder providing you with warnings, guidelines, and actions that can avert potential risk areas.

Final Thoughts

Buckle up and get ready to take a journey that will accelerate your career. Learn from CIOs who successfully collaborate with C-suite executives to drive improved business value and transform their IT organizations into business savvy teams. Use this journey to develop your roadmap to become a strategic CIO. Read, learn, apply, and, most of all, have fun.

Following is the Reading Guide Template to plan your journey (Figure 1.3).

Develop Your Book Reading Plan

Instructions:
1. Below is a template you can use to develop a checklist for your book reading plan; which chapters to browse, review, or read in detail
2. Read the definitions, in italic, for each category (browse, review, read in detail).
3. Read the statement below each description to determine, based upon your reading goals, where to focus.

Reading Plan

Reading Plan Categories	Browse	Review	Read in detail
Category Description	*Read through the chapter quickly to gain a sense of the content*	*Review the chapter with focus on the process, activities, and case studies*	*Read the chapter in detail to understand, learn, and apply the process, activities, and case studies to my company*
Determining Where to Focus	Determining which chapters to browse, review, or read in detail *(Read the statement and place a check mark ( ) in the column that best describes your goal)*		
	I understand the concept of the book section but am always interested in learning how other companies achieve this goal	I understand the concept of the book section but don't know how other IT organizations achieve this goal	I realize that this is an important concept but don't understand its value or how it is executed
Book Section/Chapters			
Foreword 1: Rob Carter—Executive Vice President, Information Services and Chief Information Officer-FedEx Corporation			
Foreword 2: Filippo Passerini—Group President, Global Business Services and Chief Information Officer, Procter & Gamble			
1. Deliver Commodity and Business Services Exceptionally Well			
1. Introduction			
2. Section Overview: Deliver Commodity and Business Services Exceptionally Well			
3. The Business Value of Delivering Commodity and Business Services Exceptionally Well			
4. How to Excel at Operational Stability			
5. How to Succeed at Project Governance			
6. How to Measure and Improve the Business Value of Commodity and Business Services			
2. Understand the Business, Focus on User Experience, and Improve Business Skills of IT Personnel			
7. Section Overview: Understand the Business, Focus on User Experience, and Improve Competencies and Skills of IT Personell			
8. Why CIOs Need to Understand the Business to Succeed			
9. The Importance of Understanding your Organizational Culture in Building Effective Teams			
10. Key Competencies and Skills of a Strategic IT Organization			
11. How to Measure and Improve the Maturity of the Strategic IT Competencies and Skills of your IT Organization			
3. Implement Initiatives to Improve Margin (Sales/Cost)			
12. Section Overview: Implement Initiatives to Drive Margin			
13. How Strategic CIOs Focus on Initiatives that Drive Margin			

Figure 1.3   Book Reading Plan Template.   *(Continued)*

14. Section Overview: Leverage Technologies Strategically to Innovate Value			
15. Why Leveraging Technology Strategically to Innovate Value Is a Game Changer			
16. How FedEx Leverages Technology Strategically to Innovate Value			
17. How Procter & Gamble Leverages Technology Strategically to Innovate Value			
18. How Five CIOs From Different Industries Leverage Technology Strategically to Iinnovate Value			
19. How to Measure the Strategic Maturity of Your IT Organization			
20. Final Thoughts: An Executive Challenge— Can CIOs Impact How Companies Manage the Business Enterprise in the 21st Century to Minimize Decision Risk			
21. Afterword: James A Stikeleather, Executive Strategist and Chief Innovation Officer, Dell			

Figure 1.3 (Continued)   Book Reading Plan Template.

Citations

1. *The Times They Are a-Changin'* by American singer-songwriter *BobDylan*, released in January 1964 by *ColumbiaRecords*.
2. Where Process is King: Phil Weinzimer, *CIO Magazine*, July 1, 2013.
3. *The Deloitte CIO Survey 2013: Reconnect. Rebuild. Reimagine. Redeliver.* Deloitte Touche Tohmatsu; http://www.deloitte.com/assets/Dcom-Australia/Local%20Assets/Documents/National%20Programs/CIO/Deloitte_CIO%20Survey_2013.pdf.
4. *The C-Suite Challenges IT: New Expectations for Business Value*; Written by Economist Intelligent Unit; *The Economist*; Sponsored by Dell Services; http://i.dell.com/sites/doccontent/business/solutions/whitepapers/en/Documents/final-study-the-it-challenge-dell-economist-report.pdf.
5. *The Real Business of IT: How CIOs Create and Communicate Value*; Richard Hunter and George Westerman; Harvard Business Press, Boston, MA; Gartner, Inc. and George Westerman.
6. *Digital Disruption: Unleashing the Next Wave of Innovation*; James McQuivey; 2013, Forrester Research, Inc. Published by Amazon Publishing, Las Vegas, NV.
7. *Getting It Right: Creating Customer Value for Market Leadership*; Philip Weinzimer; 1998, John Wiley & Sons, Inc, New York, NY.

2

Section Overview

How to Deliver Commodity and Business Services Exceptionally Well

Every chief information officer (CIO) will tell you that delivering services exceptionally well is an important foundation component in building a trust-based working relationship with C-suite executives and business teams. This foundation component is the first phase of the four phase IT strategic transformation model depicted in Figure 2.1. Each of the CIOs I interviewed say the same thing: "It's basic blocking and tackling." When each took on their CIO role at their current company, one of the first priorities was to gain a good understanding from the business how well commodity and business services are delivered. Many found that improvements were required. One would think that this is a no brainer and each IT organization delivers services exceptionally well. This is not the case. Ask Rob Carter from FedEx. Many of the CIOs I interviewed told me that it takes two to six years to develop a trust-based relationship.

Today's information-based marketplace is very complex. It's not the same as it was 10 years ago. More third-party solutions, everyone bringing their own devices, and security challenges create an environment where delivery of basic commodity and business services is more complex.

Those of you who are about to embark on a new role as CIO should find this section valuable as it demonstrates the important steps in developing an excellent service delivery model. Examples of CIOs who have successfully accomplished this phase of the transformation will help you embark on the journey.

If you feel your organization is delivering services exceptionally well to the business, you may want to review the material as a refresher and reassess how the business perceives the delivery of services. You may

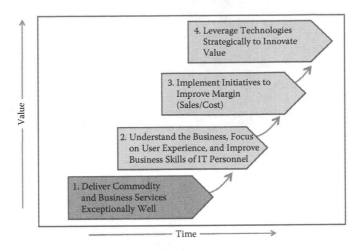

Figure 2.1   Strategic IT Organization Transformation Phases.

find the results interesting and will be able to head off some potential delivery issues.

Following are the questions each chapter will answer.

Delivering Services Exceptionally Well: Chapters 3 through 6

Chapter 3: Business Value of Delivering Services Exceptionally Well

- How did two CIOs succeeded in delivering exceptional services?
- How will a *seven-step process* help you improve the delivery of services you provide the business?
- What are the types of templates and third party solutions you can use manage service delivery excellence?

Chapter 4: How to Excel at Operational Stability

- Why is *operational stability* important in the delivery of services to the business?
- What is an *effective governance framework* that you can use to manage operational stability?
- What should you *measure* to achieve operational stability?
- How did *two CIOs achieve operational stability* within their respective companies?

Chapter 5: How to Succeed at Project Governance

- Why is *project governance* important to the success in managing your project portfolios?
- What is an example of a *framework* you can use to successfully govern your project portfolios?
- How did a CIO and the IT organization successfully improve project success?

Chapter 6: How to Measure and Improve the Business Value of IT Service

- Why is it important to *communicate the business value* of services delivered to the business?
- What is *the four-phase process* to help measure the business value of IT services?
- How can a Process/IT Service maturity grid help you assess the business value of the services you provide the business?
- What is an *excellent example of a CIO Dashboard* that communicates the value of IT services?
- What are *some examples of how CIOs* improved the value of IT services to the business?

3

BUSINESS VALUE OF DELIVERING SERVICES EXCEPTIONALLY WELL

You will never partner or build credibility with the business if the IT organization delivers services to the business that disrupt daily work activities.[1]

Mike Hedges
CIO, Medtronic

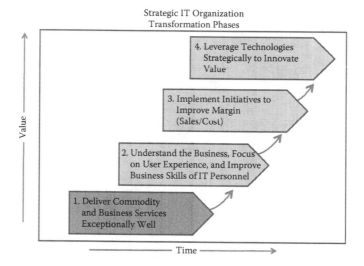

Strategic IT Organization
Transformation Phases

Every transformation starts with a first step. In the case of transforming into a strategic information technology (IT) organization, the first step is to deliver basic services exceptionally well. Included in this chapter is a step-by-step roadmap, with examples, to help you improve services to users in the enterprise. Two great examples of strategic chief information officers (CIOs) whose IT organization excel at delivering basic services are included with artifacts to help you and visualize the process. If you do not get this first step right, you will never be able to partner with the business. This first step is a basic element for every CIO who strives to become a strategic partner with C-level executives in their company. Following is a high-level overview of the chapter objective, key points, and case examples.

A. CHAPTER OBJECTIVE

1. Explain the importance of delivering basic services exceptionally well in developing a trust-based relationship with C-suite executives and business management personnel.
2. Provide a seven-step framework CIOs utilize to achieve excellence in delivering basic services (commodity and business services) to the business (Figure 3.1).
3. Share insights and experiences from two CIOs in implementing processes to achieve superior delivery of basic services to the business.

B. KEY POINTS

1. Delivering basic services exceptionally well is *table stakes* for building a trust-based relationship with C-suite executives and business personnel.
2. Delivering basic services without disruption builds trust and credibility for the CIO and the IT organization.
3. Assessing, analyzing, and improving the delivery of basic services is a process.

C. EXAMPLES INCLUDING TEMPLATES USED

- CSAA Insurance Group
- Fox Entertainment Group
- University of Pennsylvania

Delivering basic services exceptionally is the first step in building a trust-based relationship with business executives, especially if you are a CIO who wants to solve business challenges and achieve outcomes that drive customer value, increase revenue, and enhance shareholder wealth. Tony D'Allesandro, CIO of Rogers Corporation, is an experienced CIO who truly understands the importance of delivering basic services to users: "Today, it's table stakes. If you want to sit at the executive table and help the business solve problems, you have to deliver basic services very well. Otherwise, you will never have the business conversation with other business executives."[2]

Business personnel were more tolerant of minor disruptions when these specialized business services first appeared in the marketplace. However, today, these sophisticated business systems must always be available for use and considered basic services. Stuart Kippelman is CIO of Covanta Energy, the 1.7 billion dollar global operator of energy from waste (EfW) and renewable energy products. Kippelman recognizes that cloud computing, smartphones, mobile, social intelligence, and other potential revenue generation projects are all key IT initiatives and good things to work on. He tells his CIO colleagues "don't forget about the core stuff like data centers, email, and telephony. You cannot ignore the processes that support the business every day. Be on alert so you don't take your eye off the core IT projects that must be maintained and delivered flawlessly."[3] The lesson learned here is that you cannot ignore basic commodity services.

Kippelman is not alone in advising CIOs that you cannot ignore basic services. Ernst and Young conducted a study of 300 CIOs in 2012 titled "The DNA of the CIO." In that study, Benoit Laclau, a partner within the UK Advisory practice and a former CIO, said, "if your IT systems are fine in the morning then this is just okay, because it's what users are expecting. But anything that deviates from that is terrible."[4]

Mike McClaskey, CIO of Dish Network (recently promoted to EVP-Human Resources), groups basic services into two distinct categories. The first is commodity services, which include e-mail, telephony, and help desk, etc. The second is business services, which include enterprise resource planning (ERP) systems, financial systems, human resource (HR) systems, customer service systems, etc.[5]

Business users constantly press CIOs to maintain exceptionally good service. This is because they base their expectation on their personal experiences. Adults and children of all ages use smartphones, tablets, electronic games, and other devices with the ease of adults. They turn on these devices and connect instantaneously and seamlessly. They tweet, use Facebook, and text, with nimble fingers that move at a rapid pace and glide over the keyboard quickly and with ease. Think about it! When you plug a cord into an electric outlet, you expect the electric connection to work all the time. Coffee makers prepare your morning java and toasters crisp your bread, bagel, or muffin, all using preset programmable timers. When you shop using the Internet, the experience is seamless and without any disruption. Everything works all the time.

Every day, you turn on your smartphone, computer, or tablet. You look at pictures on your smart phone, check e-mail, listen to music, as well as connect with other applications. You perform these actions seamlessly. You fill up the car with gas, shop for groceries, and buy clothes at the local mall, all with a swipe of your credit card and without any. Performing all these activities is simple. It's intuitive. As they say, "it's Apple Simple." You want the same level of service in the business environment. You don't want any disruptions in service to the applications you use. It does not happen in your personal life, as you use your iPhone or other smart devices. So why shouldn't you experience the same seamless and efficient service in your business environment?

It should not surprise you that business personnel you interact with every day experience seamless service of technology in their personal lives. The consumerization of IT is great for the consumer but could have negative effects for the IT organization.

Each day, personnel all over the globe enter customer orders, check inventory status, analyze monthly sales, measure manufacturing performance, analyze sales metrics, prepare monthly budgets, etc. E-mail, telephony, order entry, shipping, finance, and other applications that support the business need to operate efficiently. Business personnel want these systems up and running all the time. The expectation is that there should be no disruption to service.

We all recognize today that business runs on IT. As a result, we expect flawless delivery of basic services. Unless your IT organization can achieve this level of service, you will never have the opportunity to work with business peers in a collaborative way to focus on initiatives that will drive successful business outcomes. As the CIO, it is up to you to lead the charge and communicate this message to the IT organization. More importantly, you need to make sure that IT personnel exhibit competencies and skills that reflect the goal of exceptional service delivery (this is covered in more detail in Chapter 10). When service disruptions occur at the office, they call you, the CIO, and ask, "Why can't your applications work just as well as the technologies I use in my personal life?" Believe me when I tell you that it will only get worse in the future. Tolerance for service disruptions diminishes for the younger generation of workers—the digital generation—who are more technologically proficient.

If you think they will tolerate any outages or downtime, you are clearly mistaken. Listen to what Stuart Kippelman told me when he was on his way shopping with his 9-year-old daughter:

> I was taking my nine-year old daughter to the store one Saturday morning. She loves to listen to music on my iPhone. Every time she enters the car with me, I give her my iPhone so she can listen to music using the Bluetooth capability in the car. It takes about 10 seconds for me to reach for my keys, start the car, and activate the Bluetooth. During this 10-second period, my daughter tries to listen to music but the Bluetooth hasn't kicked in yet. She shakes the phone and loudly screams, "Daddy, it isn't working." This happens every single time my daughter is in the car with me.[3]

CIOs who get it realize that delivering basic services exceptionally well is the foundation for building a trust-based working relationship necessary to collaborate with the business. SanDisk Corporation is the leading manufacturer of flash memory cards for imaging, computing, mobile, and gaming devices. When Ravi Naik joined SanDisk as CIO, he met with business unit heads and learned that "some of the basic IT services weren't working as well as the users required. We spent the next six months improving the basic services to build the trust of my colleagues."[6]

Every CIO recognizes that delivering basic services is the key necessary to maintain daily business activities, across the entire enterprise value chain. Steve O'Connor, CIO CSAA Insurance Group, an AAA insurer, says it best: "As a CIO, you want to help the business. However, you will never be able to have a business conversation with any of the business unit executives if you do not do the basics well."[7] Every successful business executive will tell you that the first objective to addressing a major issue is to develop a plan, which usually involves a set of process steps. Many of the CIOs I interviewed apply

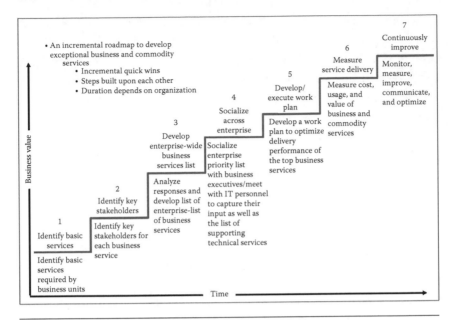

Figure 3.1   A Common Process to Improve Delivery of Services.

the same general process in addressing the issue of improving the delivery of basic services. The process involves the following seven steps (Figure 3.1).

A more in-depth view into each of these process steps, along with examples, is useful for those of you who want to improve the delivery of basic services.

Identify Business and Commodity Services Required by Business Units

CSAA Insurance Group provides automobile, homeowners, and other personal lines of insurance to AAA members through partnerships with AAA clubs in 23 states and the District of Columbia. It is the 16th largest personal lines property and casualty insurance group in the United States and is rated A+ by A.M. Best. The customer base was growing rapidly and the company leadership recognized that IT was a key to the future success of the company. The company was experiencing a growth spurt and was looking for the right CIO to lead the IT organization. One of the board members recommended a CIO who possessed the business acumen, leadership skills, and technical competence that could effectively work with the executive team to enable the anticipated rapid growth of the company. In April 2011, the CEO hired Steve O'Connor as the CIO. The choice was easy. O'Connor had the right experience. General manager for IT business management for BMC Software, cofounder of ITM Software, and CIO and vice president of information services for Silicon Graphics, Inc., O'Connor held various IT leadership and management positions within Sun Microsystems and Cullinet Software. On top of his business experience, O'Connor also had a JD degree from Suffolk University in Boston and a BS in Computer Science from Boston College. With a successful record of accomplishment in IT and business, coupled with a law degree, Mr. O'Connor was the perfect candidate for the CIO job.[7]

Prior to accepting the CIO position, O'Connor met with the board to listen to their perspective of what the business needed, in terms of IT, to achieve their strategic goals. What he heard was not a surprise, based on his vast IT experience. One of the board members mentioned that the number one IT issue was numerous outages of basic services supplied to the business by IT. (ibid)

To address this issue, O'Connor spent his first 60 days on the job meeting with leaders of the marketing, sales, and finance and other key business leaders to understand the business and the competitive marketplace. One of the areas he focuses on was service delivery. O'Connor's approach followed his philosophy on IT:

> IT is a business, and as a business, CIOs need to provide the enterprise with the services required to achieve corporate business objectives.[8]

Strategic CIOs who want to improve the delivery of basic services follow a process. Although some perform different types of activities, there is a common pattern (see Figure 3.1). Whether you are a newly appointed CIO through a promotion or job search or currently in a CIO role, you can utilize this process. Depending on the maturity of basic service, you may begin at different stages of the process. Regardless of your status, the process will be beneficial.

O'Connor scheduled meetings with every business unit VP and key staff members to understand what they did, the major categories of work, and the information needs to support the key activities used in the creation and delivery of products and services to internal personnel at CSAA Insurance Group as well as customers and agents. His objective was twofold. The first was to send a clear message to the business leaders that the IT organization was there to serve their needs. The second was to understand the activities and supporting information technology required for the business to succeed.

Send a Clear Message to the Business Leaders That IT Was There to Serve Their Needs

Too often, the IT organization is thought of as *those technical people who write code* or *IT is not part of the business.* The reality is that business units define the services IT delivers. Yet business leaders believe that IT defines the IT needs of the business. This is not true. In fact, IT defines the IT strategy. The information needs to support the business are defined by the business unit executives. The IT organization translates these information needs in the applications they develop to support business processes. The major disconnect here is that IT organizations do not appropriately communicate the linkage of the IT services to the business activities in a way business leaders will understand. It is the age-old issue of business speak versus IT speak.

O'Connor's goal was to reverse the false impression of IT. The way he accomplished this was to engage in a business dialogue with the business leaders to understand their work activities and the information needs required by the organization to succeed. O'Connor wanted the business VPs and all employees of CSAA Insurance Group to view the IT organization as part of the business and not an isolated cost center that does the work no one understands. As part of the overall goal, O'Connor moved to the next phase of the process.

Understand the Activities and Supporting Information Technology Required for the Business to Succeed

To demonstrate to the business leaders that IT is there to support their needs, O'Connor wanted to make sure that he understood the major categories of work and associated activities performed by each business unit. Each of these activities required a business service that provided the enabling technology for personnel to perform their jobs. O'Connor knew that IT was required to enable each of these activities.

He did not engage in an IT discussion. He focused the conversation on the business activities and needs of the business unit leaders. He asked the business unit executives and staff to explain what they did, how they did it, and the associated challenges encountered in performing their jobs:

> I asked open-ended questions that started with what, why and how. This type of question provoked an explanation and dialogue. I never went into solution mode. My focus was to listen, learn, and understand what the business did and needed to be successful.[9]

When O'Connor completed the round of discussions with business unit VPs and their staff, he summarized his notes and developed a list of the major categories of work for the company. His summary included the processes and activities that the business units performed to achieve their business mission. He then worked with his IT team to identify the business services that supported the main activities of CSAA Insurance Group.

One of the business unit executives O'Connor met with was the VP of business strategy. The business strategy to plan administration was one of the major processes of his organization. The VP identified the activities his organization performed as part of this process. One activity was the development of the corporate strategy. Another was gathering intelligence from the marketplace and competition. A third was the development of the strategic plan. The VP identified others' work activities as well. When complete, O'Connor had a listing of the major work activities performed by the business strategy organization as part of the business strategy to plan process.

When O'Connor completed his first round of discussions, he met with his IT team to identify the business services that supported the business strategy organization. The list included corporate strategy, corporate intelligence, and a few others (see Figure 3.2).

O'Connor and his IT team followed the same process for all the processes and work activities identified by each of the VPs and their staffs. The next step of the process was to revisit with each of the VPs to validate the list of business services, identify key stakeholders for each business service used, and prioritize the business services in order of importance to the organization.

CSAA insurance group
Portfolio—Business strategy to plan administration
–Corporate strategy
–Corporate intelligence
–Plan strategy
–Set goals
–Align organization
–Align plan

Figure 3.2   CSAA Insurance Group: Business Strategy to Plan Administration Portfolio.

Identify Key Stakeholders and Priority for Each Business Service

O'Connor scheduled a second round of individual meetings with each VP and their staffs. The first objective of the meeting was to validate the list of business services O'Connor's team identified to support the business processes identified by the VP and staff. The second objective was to identify the level of importance for each business service in supporting the business processes performed by each organization.

For example, the business strategy VP validated the list of business services identified by O'Connor's team and identified the key stakeholders for each business. During the meeting, O'Connor's team completed the template they used to capture stakeholder information (Figure 3.3. *Names omitted for proprietary reasons*).

Develop Enterprise List of Business Services

To help the VPs identify the level of importance for each business service, O'Connor's team provided a list of questions to help facilitate the discussion. O'Connor knew from his experience that providing a list of questions in advance of the meeting is always a better way to prepare individuals for the information requested and enables them to develop succinct and quality responses.

The questions focused on the importance of the service to the mission of the organization, as well as questions around the type of information the business unit required to improve the service. These questions are similar to questions asked by all strategic CIOs to understand the information needs of the business. Figure 3.4 includes a set of basic questions you can ask your business users to

CSAA information technology business services	Executive customer	Executive owner	Business owner	Product manager
Corporate strategy				
Corporate intelligence				
Plan strategy				
Set goals				
Align organization				
Align plan				
Executive customer	Executive responsible for the business unit receiving the service			
Executive owner	Executive accountable for the business unit activity (Corporate Strategy is an activity that supports Business Strategy Plan Administration)			
Business owner	Business Unit individual who is responsible for the business activity			
Product manager	Information Technology manager responsible for the business activity			

Figure 3.3   CSAA Insurance Group IT Business Services Portfolio.

Examples of basic questions for business users regarding business services

Instructions: During our next meeting would you please provide the following information for the business services utilized by your business unit

Guidelines: *It's important that the meeting be face-to-face so you can have a face-to-face dialogue*

1. Prioritize the business services in an order that represents, from high to low, the services that are the most important in the creation of products and services for your internal as well as external customers.
2. Rate the level of service provided by IT for each service on a scale of 1–10 (*1 for poor service 10 for Exceptional Delivery of Services*), as well as rationale for the scoring.
3. Describe the level of service required by your Business Unit for each of the business services it uses (*a scale representing service level agreement metrics*)
4. Identify any additional information that would help improve the value your business unit provides the business enterprise in achieving its strategic goals?

Figure 3.4   Some Basic Questions for Business Users Regarding Business Services.

understand their specific information needs. Notice that the questions focus on improving the organization's business outcomes. The discussion is business based, not IT based. You can certainly add additional questions as you deem necessary. This list is a good starting point.

At the conclusion of each meeting with the business unit VPs and their staffs, O'Connor and his team reviewed their notes, completed the template columns as to the priority of the service, and added any additional comments that were relevant to understanding the value of the business service provided. O'Connor reviewed the completed template with the VPs and made modifications as required. *(Figure 3.5 is an example using the business strategy organization data. Details are omitted due to the propriety of the information.)*

When O'Connor's team completed all the meetings with the business unit VPs, he was ready for the next step in the process. They populated the key stakeholder template listing with the data collected from the meetings with all the business units. Figure 3.6 is a representation of the template. Key data are omitted for proprietary reasons.

To help business users, CSAA developed a service portal for internal users. The portal provided basic information. Shadi Ziaei, IT service center manager for CSAA Insurance Group, takes pride in the evolution of the service portal. By providing a service catalog, the service providers can also track all the work that comes into their areas, identify demand, and provide the appropriate response.

> The objective of the Service Catalog is to provide one single portal for all employees to request services. This eliminates unnecessary runaround and hand offs in determining where to go for service requests. Instead of emailing or calling someone, who may or may not be the right person, employees know where to go to make requests. Expectations are set in advance with the user. We already know who fulfills the request and what the turnaround times are. The process is a lot more efficient. Everyone is happy.[10]

Implementing a new service portal overcame many of the issues resulting from a manual, time-intensive process. PMG is the process automation company that implemented the automated service portal. Caesar Fernandez, director of product and business solutions for PMG, led the 90-day implementation:

> CSAA Insurance Group had a homegrown ticketing system. Business users would make requests and the manual process caused delays. Additionally, users were not sure what to request. Our team went in and

CSAA Insurance Group: IT Business Services Portfolio

CSAA information technology business services	Executive customer	Executive owner	Business owner	Product manager	Priority #	Additional comments
Corporate strategy						
Corporate intelligence						
Plan strategy						
Set goals						
Align organization						
Align plan						
Executive customer	Executive responsible for the business unit receiving the service					
Executive owner	Executive accountable for the business unit activity (corporate strategy is an activity that supports business strategy plan administration)					
Business owner	Business Unit individual who is responsible for the business activity					
Product manager	IT manager responsible for the business activity					
Product manager	Importance the business unit has on the overall achievement of the business unit objective					
Additional comments	Additional information to help understand the value of the business service					

Figure 3.5 Example of Aligning Key Stakeholders to Business Strategy to Plan Administration Process.

CSAA Insurance Group: Information Technology Business Services Portfolio

Information technology business services	Executive customer	Executive owner	Business owner	Product manager	Priority #	Additional comments
Business strategy to plan administration						
Corporate strategy						
Corporate intelligence						
Plan strategy						
Set goals						
Align organization						
Align plan						
Business intelligence and analytics administration						
Enterprise analytics (Business Scorecards)						
Corporate intelligence analytics						
Product management analytics						
Member—customer analytics						
Sales analytics						
Club/agency analytics						
Marketing analytics						
Web analytics						
Policy analytics						
Billing analytics						
Payment analytics						
Claims analytics						
Fraud analytics						
Claims litigation analytics						
Finance analytics						
Audit analytics						
People and performance analytics						
Staff development—Training Analytics						
Real estate analytics						
Information technology analytics						
Supplier analytics						
Other analytics						
Channel services administration (WEB Portal Administration)						
Employee portal administration (Internal)						
CSAA insurance group						
Business to policy holder administration						
Business to club administration						
Business to business portal administration						
Business to supplier administration						

Figure 3.6 Business Services Portfolio: Example of Key Stakeholder Template (Partial List of Services). *(Continued)*

Product management administration						
Product design administration						
Product development administration						
Product administration						
Rating administration						
Marketing administration						
Brand administration						
Inventory administration						
Campaign administration						
CRM administration						
Customer administration						
Prospect administration						
Lead administration						
Sales administration						
Quote administration						
Binding administration						
Sales compensation administration (Commission)						
Insurance operations administration						
Policy administration						
Automated underwriting administration						
Billing administration						
Insurance operations document management administration						
Claims administration						
Claims administration						
Claims document management administration						
Fraud administration						
Claims litigation administration						
Financial administration						
Insurance payment administration						
Disbursements administration						
General ledger administration						
Purchasing administration						
Accounts payable administration						
Accounts receivable administration						
Fixed assets administration						
Billing (inter-company billing and allocations) administration						

Figure 3.6 (*Continued*)   Business Services Portfolio: Example of Key Stakeholder Template (Partial List of Services).   (*Continued*)

Expense administration						
Financial budgeting, planning and analysis administration						
Tax administration						
Audit administration						
Project and portfolio management administration						
Cash, investment, risk management administration						
Human resource administration						
Human resources administration						
Talent acquisition administration						
Talent management administration						
Performance management administration						
Payroll administration						
Benefits administration						
Employee relations administration						
AAA university administration						
Real estate administration						
Real estate portfolio administration (arcibus)						
Security administration						
Facilities administration						
Corporate affairs administration						
Legal administration						
Matter management (prolaw)						
Prolaw document management administration						
Legal forms administration (contract image) (hummingbird)						
Ethics hotline administration						
Special network environment administration						
eDiscovery administration						
Information technology administration						
Service costing administration						
Supplier management administration						
Demand and resource management administration						
ITSM administration						
Data exchange administration						
Interfaces administration						
Data exchange 3rd party administration						
Data management administration						

Figure 3.6 (*Continued*) Business Services Portfolio: Example of Key Stakeholder Template (Partial List of Services).

implemented our service catalogue, identified and deployed the crucial 100 services that enabled IT to deliver services more quickly. Over the following months we deployed 200 additional services. We integrated to their front end ticketing system and users now have an improved shopping experience...This was a win-win situation for both the service provider and the user of the service. Our service Catalog has optimized many ad hoc processes since its inception.[11]

The portal contains categories such as IT internal services, computers and accessories, new hire, human resources, request for new services, and a host of other services. It has evolved over the years.

Socialize across Enterprise

When O'Connor and his team completed all the individual meetings with each VP, they needed to socialize the complete list of enterprise business services to the CSAA Insurance Group executive team. O'Connor scheduled a meeting with the executive team to present the results of his interviews. His objectives for the meetings were the following:

1. Gain an understanding by the executive team of the business services required to support the major processes of the company.
2. Share the level of service the business requires in meeting its goals as well as their perception of the level of service provided by IT for the business services.
3. Gain consensus from the executive team as to the priorities the IT organization should focus on.
4. Gain an understanding by the executive team that the IT organization is an integral part of the business team and focused on supporting the business needs of the organization.

O'Connor accomplished his goals at the meeting and developed a plan, agreed to by the executive team, to focus on a number on commodity and business services that needed improvement. The executive team was completely involved in the process and recognized that they drove the information needs of the business:

- Share with his direct reports the information gathered from each of the business unit VPs and their staffs.
- Identify the IT technical services required to support each of the business services *(e.g., data center services, security, network, desktop, help desk).*

One of O'Connor's objectives was to change the way IT personnel think about the work they do each day. It is not about writing code. It is about how the business uses IT applications, projects, and supporting activities each day. After the executive team agreed to the list of processes and supporting business services, O'Connor worked with an IT team to develop a mapping of the business services to the supporting technical services. This helped IT personnel change the way they think about the work they do. Every project, every activity, and every task are associated with a business service that drives value to CSAA Insurance Group customers.

Transforming the way IT personnel think about their work is a major cultural change and is a challenge for any CIO.

Another major accomplishment for O'Connor was gaining the trust and respect of the executive team. CSAA Insurance Group developed a team-based approach to improve services for the company. O'Connor and his IT team were now ready to develop a detailed plan to improve delivery of basic services.

O'Connor was a newly hired CIO with no knowledge of how CSAA Insurance Group conducted its day-to-day business activities. Therefore, O'Connor had to start his process from the beginning. Other CIOs use different techniques to improve delivery of basic services. Some CIOs even have the opportunity to build a service organization from scratch. Such is the case with Cindy McKenzie at Fox Entertainment. Let us examine how McKenzie improved delivery of basic services using steps one through four of the common process to improve delivery of basic services (see Figure 3.1).

When Cindy McKenzie led the enterprise application services at Fox Entertainment Group, her group provided application shared services for Fox business units. Although Cindy McKenzie did not have the CIO title, her role as Senior VP of the Enterprise Application Services Group enabled her to perform as if she was the CIO of the group. As a separate IT organization, the enterprise application services provided a host of shared services to Fox companies, which include Fox Filmed Entertainment, Fox Entertainment Group, Fox News, Twentieth Television, Fox International Channels, and other divisions. Shared services include financial, human capital management, legal affairs, litigation, tax, treasury, audit, risk, corporate security, content security, corporate Intranet, and royalties.

In 2006, Fox executives decided to create a shared services organization and asked McKenzie to define the overall operating and governance model, as well as the detailed service catalog and service-level agreements for each service. McKenzie understood the need for delivering basic services exceptionally well:

> In today's business environment it's a given that basic services have to be delivered exceptionally well. We have to meet our Service Level Agreements (SLA) all the time. Our added value to the business is the speed and agility of our delivery capability. The marketplace is changing quickly and we have to adapt with agility to the changing needs of the business.[12]

Since joining Fox in 2001, McKenzie led the enterprise technical systems group for Fox Filmed Entertainment, which was the foundation for the newly formed enterprise application services (Cindy McKenzie joined PricewaterhouseCoopers as managing director in April 2013). With 20 years of senior IT leadership experience in the financial and entertainment industries, McKenzie was the perfect candidate for the job. (ibid)

Already part of a Fox business unit (Fox Filmed Entertainment) for 5 years prior to leading the consolidation of shared application services in 2006, McKenzie knew the executives as well as the key stakeholders using basic services from other Fox business units. Her challenge dealt with business units losing control over services they previously managed.

A shared services organization can have its challenges if it did not originate as part of the initial organization structure of the company. In McKenzie's situation, the applications supported by her organization were part of each Fox business entity. The consolidation of common services into a single enterprise application shared services group certainly caused some natural resistance due to the perceived loss of control. The way to counter any perceived resistance due to loss of control is to show users of these services the value they receive.

In Steve O'Connor's situation, he had to follow each of the common process steps to improve the delivery of basic services. Remember, when he accepted the CIO position, he knew from conversations with the board that service delivery was a major issue for CSAA Insurance Group. In McKenzie's situation, the challenge was consolidation and value. Each of the Fox business units could deliver the service themselves or purchase basic services from external vendors. This meant that McKenzie had to show value to the Fox business units to ensure that her organization would provide these services. McKenzie had a number of factors in her favor. Since McKenzie was already familiar with the services, executives, and key stakeholders, her first task was to develop a list of business services available to all the Fox business units. She consolidated steps one through four (previously described at the beginning of this chapter: a common process to improve delivery of basic services, Figure 3.1): identify basic services, identify key stakeholders, develop enterprise list of services, and socialize across enterprise.

McKenzie is all about business. "You have to communicate to the business in a language they understand."[11] To help the business units understand the shared services provided by her organization, McKenzie developed a service catalog that defined, in business terms, the services available for each of the service categories (see Table 3.1). For example, financial management services, in the first column, is a category of work performed by the financial organization. The services McKenzie's organization provides (second column) include general ledger, project cost, procurement, and billing. The various business units utilizing these services are FG, TTV, FFE, etc. (third column).

To help users understand the value of each of the services, McKenzie also provides the business units with more detailed information about each service offering. For the financial services organization, the service catalog also provides additional information for each of the services. In Figure 3.7, you can see the services, description, and sample features for three services. You will notice that the description and sample features are in business speak and provide the user information they will understand. For example, the project cost service description says, "Project Cost enables users to track and manage project activity. Project Cost is the central repository for detailed

Table 3.1 EAS Service Catalog: Summary

SERVICE CATEGORIES	SERVICES	ENTITIES
Financial management services	• General ledger	• XXX • XXX
	• Project cost	• XXX • XXX
	• Procurement	• XXX
	• Billing	• XXX
	• Accounts receivable	• XXX
	• Accounts payable	• XXX
	• Accounts payable imaging	• XXX
	• Expenses	• XXX
	• Asset management	• XXX
	• Cash management	• XXX
Human capital management and other HR services	• HR / eProfile	• XXX • XXX
	• Benefits / eBenefits	• XXX • XXX
	• Payroll / ePay	• XXX • XXX
	• HR, benefits, and payroll portal	• XXX
	• Onboarding	• XXX
	• Merit administration	• XXX
	• Electronic learning management	• XXX
	• Performance management	• XXX
	• HR contract management	• XXX
	• Time collection/HTG	• XXX
	• Talent acquisition	• XXX
	• Bonus administration	• XXX
Legal applications management services	• Matter management	• XXX
	• Contract management	• XXX
	• IP management	• XXX
Enterprise tools	• Document management/Records Management/Document portals	• XXX
	• Document collaboration (SharePoint)	• XXX
	• eRoom	• XXX
	• Workflow development Tool	• XXX
	• Enterprise reporting	• XXX
	• Business intelligence	• XXX
Other application management services	• Corporate intranet	• XXX
	• Provisioning	• XXX
	• Tax management	• XXX
	• Treasury cash management	• XXX
	• Investigative case management	• XXX
	• Visitor and Parking Management	• XXX
	• Physical access control	• XXX
	• Real estate lease management	• XXX
	• Crisis communication	• XXX
	• Royalties	• XXX

Fox Shared Application Services

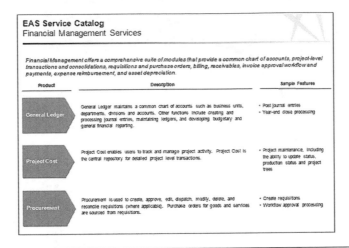

EAS Service Catalog
Financial Management Services

Financial Management offers a comprehensive suite of modules that provide a common chart of accounts, project-level transactions and consolidations, requisitions and purchase orders, billing, receivables, invoice approval workflow and payments, expense reimbursement, and asset depreciation.

Product	Description	Sample Features
General Ledger	General Ledger maintains a common chart of accounts such as business units, departments, divisions and accounts. Other functions include creating and processing journal entries, maintaining ledgers, and developing budgetary and general financial reporting.	• Post journal entries • Year-end close processing
Project Cost	Project Cost enables users to track and manage project activity. Project Cost is the central repository for detailed project level transactions.	• Project maintenance, including the ability to update status, production status and project trees
Procurement	Procurement is used to create, approve, edit, dispatch, modify, delete, and reconcile requisitions (where applicable). Purchase orders for goods and services are sourced from requisitions.	• Create requisitions • Workflow approval processing

Figure 3.7   Financial Management Services.

project level transactions." The sample features are *project maintenance, including the ability to update status, production status, and project trees.*

To socialize across the Fox companies (step four of the *common process*), the shared application services group works with each business unit to provide enhanced services. McKenzie and her team meet regularly with business units to discuss their business needs for improved services. The Fox business units and the shared application services group work together to develop projects that meet the needs of the business units.

One of the socialization vehicles McKenzie's organization provides is an application map of the shared application services for each of the following 10 major business processes:

1. Acquire
2. Produce
3. Market
4. Sell
5. Distribute
6. Broadcast
7. Studio
8. Finance
9. HR, benefit, and payroll
10. Legal

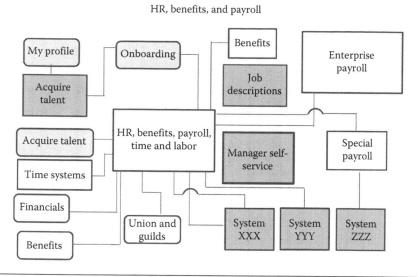

Figure 3.8 Application Mapping to Key HR, Benefits, and Payroll-Example.

The benefit of providing the application map is that it provides an enterprise view of shared services for all the Fox business units. Additionally, it reflects the complexity of the services provided that most business personnel do not understand. Figure 3.8 is an example of the HR, benefits, and payroll application mapped to the associated key processes. McKenzie's achievements were well recognized. In 2013, Price Waterhouse hired McKenzie as Managing Director in the US Entertainment Media and Communications (EMC) practice.

Develop/Execute Work Plan

At CSAA Insurance Group, Steve O'Connor's team, comprised of IT and business personnel, developed a work plan. The executive team reviewed and approved the plan. One of the major projects resulting from this exercise was the development of a new claims processing system. The business VPs identified this as the single most important capability that needed to be improved. O'Connor needed an experienced project manager who successfully managed large multimillion dollar projects. He hired Mark Jacobson to manage the claims processing project. He worked with Mark in previous companies and was confident that he was the right person to manage the project. The implementation consisted of IT and business personnel. The project completed 3 months ahead of a 12-month schedule, and project expenses were under budget. Delivering the first major project under O'Connor's leadership was a grand-slam win; on time and under budget, external customers loved it, and CSAA Insurance Group personnel found the system more efficient. More importantly, the IT organization gained new credibility with the business. The relationship between the IT organization and the business transformed from a cost center to a business partner.

At Fox, McKenzie's shared application services group provides regular status updates through regularly scheduled meeting and published documents to provide the business units on project status. Following is an example of a status report on capital projects for a Fox business unit (Table 3.2).

To share accomplishments, the shared application services group provides an annual summary of all activities by service catalog item as well as an overall view of accomplishments (Figure 3.9).

McKenzie spends much of her time interacting and communicating with the business. In addition to providing regular updates, McKenzie updates on the latest technology trends in the industry. Her objective is threefold:

1. Project updates: McKenzie updates the business units on project status, issues, and mitigation plans. This proactive approach helps build a trust-based relationship with the Fox business units.
2. Thought leadership: Updating Fox business units on the latest technology trends provides insight and thought leaderships. To be proactive, McKenzie's organization develops some applications, as a proof of concept, to show the Fox business units how they could improve their productivity, for example.

We noticed that many executives used iPads for email, web access, and calendaring. We build a crisis management prototype that worked on the iPad securely to provide key information. Instead of looking in their wallets or purses for a small printed card with phone number or URL information, designated personnel now click on an icon for key communication updates. We also found a web application that uses a document management application that would

Table 3.2 Open Capital Projects

NAME	START DATE	END DATE	COST	STATUS	COMMENTS/ISSUES
Directory enhancements ●●●	MM/DD/YY	MM/DD/YY	$XXX.XX	In progress	xxxxxxxxxxxxxxxxxxxxxxxxxxxxxxxxxxxxxxxxxxxxxxxxxxxx xxxxxxxxxxxxxxxxxxxxxxxxxxxxxxxxxxxxxxxxxxxxxxxxxxxx
PeopleSoft financials for Turkey ○	MM/DD/YY	MM/DD/YY	$XXX.XX	Phase III in progress	xxxxxxxxxxxxxxxxxxxxxxxxxxxxxxxxxxxxxxxxxxxxxxxxxxxx xxxxxxxxxxxxxxxxxxxxxxxxxxxxxxxxxxxxxxxxxxxxxxxxxxxx
Film and TV amortization for tax ●	MM/DD/YY	MM/DD/YY	$XXX.XX	In progress	xxxxxxxxxxxxxxxxxxxxxxxxxxxxxxxxxxxxxxxxxxxxxxxxxxxx xxxxxxxxxxxxxxxxxxxxxxxxxxxxxxxxxxxxxxxxxxxxxxxxxxxx
PeopleSoft financials and Expenses 9.1 upgrade ●	MM/DD/YY	MM/DD/YY	$XXX.XX	In progress	xxxxxxxxxxxxxxxxxxxxxxxxxxxxxxxxxxxxxxxxxxxxxxxxxxxx xxxxxxxxxxxxxxxxxxxxxxxxxxxxxxxxxxxxxxxxxxxxxxxxxxxx

● Open key issues prevent the project from completing on schedule.
○ Some open issues, project is at risk of delaying but can still be corrected.
● No key open issues, project is on schedule.

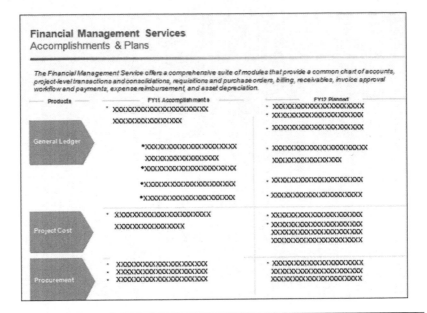

Figure 3.9   Financial Management Services: Accomplishments and Plans (*data removed*).

publish anything on an iPad. One example of a potential usage is for a sales executive who previously would have to peruse numerous emails to find daily sales data can now click on an iPad icon to get the latest data in one place.[12]

3. Building a trust-based relationship: McKenzie's goal was simple. The focus of her organization is to provide value to FOX business units: "If I can show value to the business units for the services of our organization, then I have done my job well." [13]

Measure Service Delivery

Measuring service delivery is important if you want to ensure that the services are providing value to the business. Steve O'Connor is a stickler about measuring application performance and maintains a set of key metrics. Cindy McKenzie is also a stickler at about ensuring that the applications Fox employees use on a day-to-day basis are up and running all the time.

The Fox Enterprise application services group was moved from the business unit it supported into a separate Fox business unit. When it was established, in 2006, Fox executives allowed Fox business units to choose between McKenzie's organization and external vendors for enterprise application services. This places additional pressure on McKenzie: "I have to maintain a low cost structure while at the same time provide value. Therefore, I have to measure costs and communicate those costs as well as value to the business." (ibid)

The financial ERP system used by the Fox Enterprise applications shared services group provides visibility of costs for each of the shared services at a business unit level. We have all been involved in discussions with business unit executives about IT service costs. Most business executives believe that IT costs are too high. To combat this perception, McKenzie provides per unit costs for each of her services, such as the cost per invoice and cost by paycheck that can be compared to the costs of outside services. McKenzie also uses these data to show the cost of new services or enhancements to existing services. The business then can use these data to ensure that they agree with the return on investment before approving any expenditure.

McKenzie works hard at maintaining the cost data and benchmark data she shares with business units: "Using accurate cost data and benchmark data enables us to have meaningful conversations with the business. It helps the business make informed decisions about new requests or changes based on return on investment." (ibid)

To improve the delivery of basic services as quickly as possible, O'Connor started from the ground floor to build an effective service capability. O'Connor measured service delivery at the root level. His philosophy is simple: "I want to get at the root problem for every service disruption. If you solve the root problem, the disruptions will not reoccur."[6] O'Connor measures every service disruption. He initiated a process to reduce disruptions. To help him achieve the goal of resolving disruptions by eliminating root causes, he initiated the following process[7]:

1. Every IT director will own a service and be accountable for managing service disruptions.
2. IT directors will document all service disruptions in a daily log.
3. IT directors will prepare a monthly uptime report for each application (see Table 3.3).
4. Each IT director is accountable for identifying the root cause of the disruption.
5. CIO chairs daily service disruption status meeting.

Table 3.3   Monthly Uptime Report: Example

CSAA INSURANCE GROUP
UPTIME REPORT FOR TOP APPLICATIONS : JANUARY 20XX

APPLICATION NAME	APPLICATION VENDOR NAME	IT OWNER	TARGET		AVAILABILITY INDEX		SERVICE AVAILABILITY INDEX	
			DAYS	MIN	UNAVAILABLE (MIN)	AVAILABILITY (%)	UNAVAILABLE (MIN)	AVAILABILITY (%)
1	xxxx	xxxx	31	41,640		100.0		100.00
2	xxxx	xxxx	31	41,640		100.0		100.00
3	xxxx	xxxx	31	41,640		100.0		100.00
4	xxxx	xxxx	31	41,640	83	99.9		100.00
5	xxxx	xxxx	31	41,640		100.0		100.00
6	xxxx	xxxx	31	41,640		100.0		100.00
7	xxxx	xxxx	31	41,640	483	98.92	483	98.92
8	xxxx	xxxx	31	41,640		100.0		100.00
9	xxxx	xxxx	31	41,640		100.0		100.00
10	xxxx	xxxx	31	41,640		100.0		100.00

11	xxxx	xxxx	31	41,640	431	98.07		100.00
12	xxxx	xxxx	31	41,640	491	98.18	491	98.18
13	xxxx	xxxx	31	41,640		100.0		100.00
14	xxxx	xxxx	31	41,640		100.0		100.00
15	xxxx	xxxx	31	41,640		100.0		100.00
16	xxxx	xxxx	31	41,640	83	99.81	83	99.81
17	xxxx	xxxx	31	41,640		100.0		100.00
18	xxxx	xxxx	31	41,640		100.0		100.00
19	xxxx	xxxx	31	41,640		100.0		100.00
20	xxxx	xxxx	31	41,640		100.0		100.00
21	xxxx	xxxx	31	41,640		100.0		100.00
22	xxxx	xxxx	31	41,640		100.0		100.00
23	xxxx	xxxx	31	41,640		100.0		100.00
	Totals			XXX,XXX	XXX.XX	XX.XX%	XXX.XX	XX.XX%

6. Service owners (IT directors) are accountable to identify remediation of root cause for each service disruption.
7. CIO must be convinced that remediation will eliminate root cause problem prior to the removal of service disruption from service disruption log.

To understand the value of a service, you need to understand its cost. Spending more money to develop and support a service than the value it provides does not make much business sense.

Ron Weber is a problem management consultant at CSAA Insurance Group. Weber's role is to identify and initiate service improvement programs focused on improved IT performance. These improvements result from reductions in business disruption and support costs, greater business and IT transparency, and improved partnerships and communications. Weber tracks the top 40 applications. He measures the days and times the service is available, the duration of any service disruptions, and a host of other metrics. The following is an example of the type of report Weber uses to determine uptime for any given month. He also runs a year-to-date report, which he reviews with application and operations teams.

With this type of data, Weber and the team can calculate the total cost of an incident compared to the cost for IT to remediate the root cause. This not only helps the business but helps the IT organization eliminate repetitive issues that take time and money and disrupt the business. In addition, Weber also tracks the impact to the business of a service disruption. Let us look at the following hypothetical example:

1. Let's assume the sales order entry application processes, on average $100,000 of orders per day.
2. The application needs to be available 24 hours per day.
3. The average sales entered each minute is equal to $69.44, (100,000 divided by 24 hours, divided by 60 minutes).
4. Every minute that the application is unavailable to the business has a potential impact of approximately $70 in lost sales.

Tracking this information helps the IT organization measure the business impact of downtime and helps build a culture focusing on business value.

O'Connor's uptime goal for each service is 100% and IT directors' compensation package includes this metric as one of the parameters. O'Connor does not think a 100% target is unreasonable: "If existing customers cannot access our customer service portal, to increase policy coverage, for example, it impacts our ability to service them."[8]

Measuring service delivery helps you accomplish three main objectives. First, it provides quantitative data that avoid discussions based upon opinions. Second, it enables you to compare your IT organization's service cost against benchmark data. Third, it enables you to use these data to determine the value of the service to the business (see Chapter 5). Measuring the cost, usage, and value of commodity and business services is necessary have for any CIO who wants to enable the business to succeed.

Continuously Improve

Every successful executive knows that implementing a continuous improvement program is a smart thing to do. This is an excellent method for improving performance. To be successful, a continuous improvement program needs to monitor, measure, improve, communicate, and optimize.

McKenzie approached continuous improvement driven by business requirements. Her organization monitors performance metrics on a regular basis and always measures service levels against agreed-upon service levels and benchmark data. Additionally, McKenzie's team seeks feedback regularly from business and IT personnel. Reviewing IT performance data regularly with business executives uncovers improvement opportunities. These monthly updates to the business units provide status on projects as well as a forum to receive feedback on performance through a set of dashboard reports.

These meetings allowed the business unit executives to review requests for enhanced or additional services across all business unit services by the shared services organization. It also provides a forum where the executives can review all the requests to determine if they are still valid and/or they need modifications based upon new data (Figure 3.10).

During these update meetings, McKenzie also provides an update on key current and planned initiatives (see Figure 3.11). Her goal is

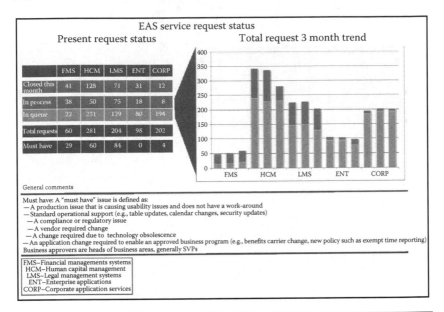

EAS service request status

Present request status   Total request 3 month trend

	FMS	HCM	LMS	ENT	CORP
Closed this month	41	128	71	31	12
In process	38	50	75	18	8
In queue	22	231	129	80	194
Total requests	60	281	204	98	202
Must have	29	60	84	0	4

General comments

Must have: A "must have" issue is defined as:
— A production issue that is causing usability issues and does not have a work-around
— Standard operational support (e.g., table updates, calendar changes, security updates)
   — A compliance or regulatory issue
   — A vendor required change
   — A change required due to technology obsolescence
   — An application change required to enable an approved business program (e.g., benefits carrier change, new policy such as exempt time reporting)
Business approvers are heads of business areas, generally SVPs

FMS–Financial managements systems
HCM–Human capital management
LMS–Legal management systems
ENT–Enterprise applications
CORP–Corporate application services

Figure 3.10   EAS Service Request Status.

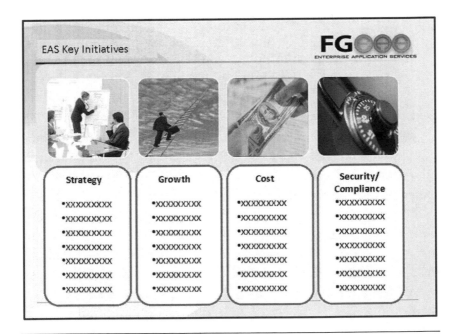

Figure 3.11   Enterprise Application Services.

to capture input and feedback from the users of the services: "It is not about what I think is required. It is about what the business believes they need. I can add insight and thought leadership on technologies but the business defines the needs."[12]

Steve O'Connor is a very proactive executive. He spends more than 50% of his time meeting with business unit executives and management. He consistently seeks input on service performance. His goal is to monitor, measure, and improve service delivery. He communicates on a regular basis to all levels within his IT organization.

O'Connor meets regularly with the board to update them on his plans. His strategic plan is about continuously improving value to CSAA Insurance Group customers. O'Connor identified 10 key improvement initiatives (see Table 3.4) after his first 100 days on the job.

Notice that the number one priority is operational stability. This is in line with the major service delivery issue. His list of 10 initiatives is the key to his communication plan. He always updates personnel in town hall meetings and the board on the same 10 initiatives.

There are many different approaches to continuous improvement. Regardless of the approach you take, make sure you follow the following five basic principles:

1. *Monitor IT activities from a 360-degree perspective*: Capture feedback from key IT and business stakeholders for the services you are monitoring. This provides a realistic assessment of the value of the service from all personnel involved.

2. *Measure service delivery on a regular basis*: We are constantly reminded by management gurus that *you can't manage what you can't measure*. Identification of key metrics and measurement techniques and analysis of data are key to identifying areas for improvement.

3. *Improve processes and services based upon feedback and goals*: Utilize feedback from users and IT personnel to identify activities focused on improving service delivery. Capturing feedback without acting on it sends the wrong message to the business.

4. *Communicate on a regular basis to all levels of management as well as key personnel*: Communication is the key to maintaining a

Table 3.4 CSAA Insurance Group IT Business Priorities

	IT BUSINESS PRIORITIES	
	PRIORITY	DRIVERS
Must-have	1. Operational efficiency	• Revenue, customer sat, protect brand
	2. Separation	• Core biz strategy for growth
Business basics	3. Policy administration system	• Req. to play across clubs and states
	4. Single claims platform	• Req. to play across clubs and states
Competitive advantage	5. Web and mobile	• Changing consumer behaviors, demographics
		• Effective marketing profitable products
	6. Business analytics	• Competitive pricing
		• Marketing effectiveness
Risk and operational efficiency	7. Compliance	• Reduce risk, protect brand
	8. HR platform	• Replace legacy platform w/no roadmap
	9. IT cost competitiveness	• Align resources to core investments
	10. IT financial systems	• Adequate patch now, replace later

common understanding of service performance and improvement plans.

5. *Optimize performance of service delivery to achieve business outcomes that drive company success*: Focus on optimizing performance by setting aggressive targets. You will never optimize performance if you look for simple incremental improvements.

Delivering services exceptionally well is the mantra for every chief information officer (CIO) who takes on the leadership role of an information technology (IT) organization. Every CIO knows this is the foundation for building a trust-based relationship with the business. Whether your company is involved in manufacturing, services, logistics, engineering, or academia, it just does not matter. You have to focus on delivering services exceptionally well. If not, your successor will have the opportunity to take on this challenge.

There are many interesting scenarios where CIOs take on the leadership role in a company without knowledge of the industry. There are two major challenges in this scenario. The first is learning about the business and the second is assessing the value IT delivers to its customers through its services. The CIO then has to develop a plan to learn about the business as well as improve service delivery.

Such was the case for Tom Murphy in February 2013, when the University of Pennsylvania appointed him vice president for IT and university CIO.

Murphy has 30 years of deep IT and business experience and is regarded by many as more of a business leader and strategist. His successes at multibillion dollar companies such as Marriott, Royal Caribbean Cruise Lines, and AmerisourceBergen Corporation (ABC) provided Murphy with the opportunity to build his strategic, communication, and leadership skills. As with his move to ABC, this role in academia was a new industry for Murphy, and his challenge was to learn quickly how information and technology are applied in a university environment. And this he did. University structures encourage independence and entrepreneurship. When it comes to IT, there are some universities, such as Princeton, that have a more centralized structure. However, at the University of Pennsylvania, the IT structure is highly decentralized, and the challenges for delivering IT services exceptionally well present some interesting opportunities.

The University of Pennsylvania was founded in 1740 and is located in Philadelphia, Pennsylvania. It is one of the most prestigious universities in the world. Twelve schools with 5,000 researchers and faculty provide education to approximately 25,000 students in the fields of arts and sciences, medicine, law, business, engineering, and other disciplines. Each school has evolved over the years as an independent entity that also includes its own IT organization and unique IT services. Of the approximately 900 IT personnel on campus, 275 work for Murphy's Information Systems and Computing organization (ISC) that provides core administrative information systems, voice, data, video networks, data center, storage, and other basic services for the university. In addition, his team offers project management, development, video production, classroom technology, and consulting services. His organization operates as a service to Penn, and each school can choose to use some, all, or none of those services. Murphy has no authority or governance over IT in the schools. The remaining 625 work for the various university schools providing IT services that are in some cases redundant to those offered by the ISC and in other cases very specific to the needs of the school. For instance,

Wharton's Executive MBA team needs customer relationship management (CRM), which is not a tool used by other schools. The life science schools (med, vet, nursing, and dental) have specific regulatory requirements and applications they use that are unique to their schools. All the schools have their own first-level break/fix teams that cater to the needs of the faculty, students, and staff.

Murphy's mission is to "provide technology leadership through collaboration for today's solutions and tomorrow's innovation."[1] Murphy's approach to achieving his mission "is to improve the collaboration across the University schools by leveraging technology products in an innovative way to facilitate new ways of teaching and learning."[2] Sounds like a sound objective. However, there are numerous challenges in a university environment where a culture of independence and innovation is fostered and encouraged, especially at a university founded almost 300 years ago. Take a simple IT service such as an e-mail. Today, e-mail is a common electronic service used to communicate. Over the years, university schools developed their own e-mail systems. Today, there are 24 independent e-mail systems across university schools. Murphy's organization supports some of them and the schools support others. One would think that communication and collaboration would be much more effective if there were a single e-mail system across various university schools, a scenario that also exists at other university institutions. Murphy says that this scenario exists in other universities as well. This is one example of an opportunity for improving the delivery of basic services. Murphy views his role as a facilitator to help promote innovation and learning across the university, and he is starting with focusing on delivering basic services exceptionally well. His three-point plan reflects a strategy founded in years of business, communication, teaming, and leadership experience.

Collaborate Effectively

Murphy wants his organization to be the "hub of collaboration and doing smart IT." How is he doing it? Murphy explains that he wants to "improve IT's role in university decision making and coordination by being the hub of collaboration." Murphy organized an IT roundtable comprised of university IT leadership teams. "My role is to facilitate change." One of the subjects the group addresses is communication.

"I challenged the group to address the communication issue and develop a solution." The way he is accomplishing this is through basic leadership principles. He asked the group, "Could we develop a set of unique requirements for a communication system that would satisfy the need of each University School? If we can, then we could reduce the 24 e-mail systems to a much smaller number; perhaps one or two." As the facilitator, Murphy does not control the group; he helps them discover, analyze, and develop a solution that will benefit the entire University. (ibid)

Organize for Efficiency

When Murphy arrived at the University of Pennsylvania, he discovered an "IT department organized around the traditional structure. It was technology based and not customer based. The Systems Engineering & Operations, Network & Telecom, and Administration Information Technology groups all worked autonomously and had little inter-team interaction. Each group managed client relationships differently, with various outreach efforts and no coordination." This lack of interteam interaction resulted in tremendous duplication in tools, platforms, and architectures just in the ISC. For example, Murphy discovered that there were over 900 tools used in the IT organization to perform their activities. He is reorganizing IT into a customer-focused organization that provides technology-based services. The center of the organization is client services, which includes a formal relationship management organization, as well as a central intake team (there were at least 19 areas of intake previously), and a campus technology team focused on helping the schools' IT organizations. The other IT groups all operate in service to the client service group. Technology-based organization models create silos of communication as well as redundant technologies. Reorganizing IT to a customer-focused organization will not only result in efficiencies but also more importantly provide a superior level of service to university schools. (ibid)

Measure and Communicate Value of IT Services

The university funds 30% of the ISC budget. The remaining 70% is funded through direct billing to the university schools for the IT services provided by the ISC. However, like relationship management, each group within the ISC bills the clients for services they offer, and those bills are difficult to decipher and they all come at different times. Some IT bills detail servers, data center costs, and other infrastructure technology costs without relating it to the services provided. As a result, the university schools do not really understand IT costs and how they relate to the service provided. "I have twelve people preparing and administering bills. This is very inefficient," says Murphy. This is not unique to the University of Pennsylvania. This is a common problem experienced today by many technology organizations.

Fortunately, new companies are emerging that address this challenge with solutions that focus on capturing, analyzing, reporting, and communicating IT costs as service costs, in a language the user can understand. Murphy's organization is evaluating a number of different providers for such a solution, and the result will be an improved billing process and, more importantly, improved delivery of basic and commodity services. As Murphy noted, if the client can't understand and doesn't trust what they're paying for today, why would they consider purchasing more services from ISC in the future? When implemented, the relationship between IT and the user community will change. The new relationship model will enable IT to provide bills in a language the user can understand; Murphy will then be able to have a more meaningful dialogue with university schools about the service provided, its cost, and the value received. The dialogue will be completely different. The following are two examples of a conversation where the user wants to reduce the cost of a service and a conversation where the user wants to improve the quality of the service:

> I see that video services cost my school 'x' dollars. This is more than I thought I would spend. Could we do something about reducing the amount of video services provided to my school?
>
> Video services really help the school and we need more of it. Do you know of any new technologies we can use that will improve the quality of the video but also improve the costs associated with the service?

The entire tone of the conversation will change. Murphy's organization will begin to have meaningful conversations with university schools about how to improve learning and collaboration with improved technologies.

Murphy is a bright and articulate CIO who understands the lay of the land and knows that facilitating change is not easy. At AmerisourceBergen, he led a 4 year SAP project that required over a thousand business and IT personnel to work together in teams and deliver the implementation on time and within budget. The project was successful because he "involved business personnel who had leadership roles as well as a great team of business and IT professionals that communicated effectively." The SAP implementation was regarded as a watershed moment for AmerisourceBergen. The implementation of SAP, as painful as it was at the time, enabled the company to attract large new customers like Walgreens that changed the entire landscape of the industry and would not have been possible prior.

Murphy sees his role as one where he focuses on leadership helping organizations understand the power of leveraging information and technology to improve performance. He said it best during an interview with the University of Pennsylvania's *The Current*, where he talked about his role as CIO:

> The issue is not one of either control or decentralization. It's a question of uniting people into a team and creating an environment conducive to sharing ideas and opinions openly, and establishing common ground from which to start rather than using differences as the starting point. I visualize Mt. Everest when I think about what success will look like. Finding our common ground as an IT community and working together to drive the most value possible on behalf of the University while respecting the uniqueness and independence of each operating unit—that's what I see as our Mt. Everest.[1]

Murphy is 16 months into the transformation of IT at the University of Pennsylvania. His focus is on leveraging information and technology to facilitate learning and collaboration. His starting point is delivering services exceptionally well. In an interview with the Penn Current, he said, "I think Computerworld Magazine once called me a renaissance CIO." Look out world, the renaissance at the University of Pennsylvania has just begun.

Chapter Summary

Identify Basic Services for Each Business Unit

The IT organization develops applications or acquires vendor-developed applications, based upon the requirements of the business, to support almost every business process in the enterprise. These applications form a portfolio of commodity services (e-mail, telephony, help desk) or business services (financial, HR, legal). If you are a newly hired CIO, or promoted into the role, you need to follow a process to identify the key basic services the business requires to achieve their objectives:

1. You need to meet with the leadership team of each business unit to understand what they do, how they do it, and any issues they have with the supporting IT applications that enable their business processes.
2. Once you have gained sufficient knowledge of how each business unit operates, you can meet with IT personnel to identify the IT services that support each business unit's processes.
3. You then need to validate that list with the leadership team for each business unit.

This basic step forms the foundation of your services delivery capability.

Identify Key Stakeholders

Identifying key stakeholders for each service is necessary if you are to manage service delivery as a project. You need to capture data, provide updates, and include them in all communications relative to the service. Following is a list of key stakeholders, as a minimum, you should identify.

Executive customer	Executive responsible for the business unit receiving the service
Executive owner	Executive accountable for the business activity (corporate strategy is an activity that supports business strategy to plan administration)
Business owner	Business unit person who is responsible for the business activity (change wording on graphic from *individual* to *person*)
Product manager	IT manager responsible for delivery of the business service

Develop Enterprise-Wide Business Services List

The IT organization supports the business through a number of applications they develop or acquire from vendors. A listing of these services, which includes a definition of the service, the business activities they support, and the value provided, in business terms, is a critical component for every IT organization. The process of developing an enterprise-wide services portfolio includes the following steps:

1. Identify business activities for each business unit, the associated services that support the business unit activities, and the key stakeholders for each business service.
2. Develop an enterprise-wide list of business services. This list of services includes both commodity services and business services.
3. Validate with business units and modify as necessary.
4. Update services portfolio listing on a regular basis, using a service portal accessible to all personnel.

Socialize across Enterprise

Socializing the enterprise list of services is important to validate the data and modify accordingly. Following are some key tips to help you:

1. Socialize enterprise list of services with business executives and their staffs.
2. Review the services list to ensure accuracy and alignment to business unit needs.
3. Provide communication artifacts (service portal tutorial, word documents, slides, etc.) to help inform and educate company personnel.

Develop/Execute Work Plan

Improving the delivery of basic services—commodity and business services—is a project and in some cases a portfolio of projects that form a program. So, execute this activity as a project and manage it carefully. More importantly, IT personnel need to understand the importance of this project to the success of the business. Incorporate regular project update meetings for all IT personnel to share the status of the project, successes achieved, and business value delivered. Some key tips are as follows:

1. Create a project charter for each project, which includes a plan of activities, key milestones, communication plan, and key metrics.
2. Assign IT managers to every service and hold them accountable for accomplishing key metrics.
3. Review project with IT personnel as well as key business unit executives on a regular basis.
4. Communicate status of services improvement program to all company personnel.
5. Solicit feedback from all company personnel to capture issues, trends, and suggestions for improvement.

Measure Service Delivery

Make sure business personnel measure IT delivery performance of basic services based upon facts and not perceptions. To do so, you must develop a set of meaningful metrics that measure cost, usage, and value of the commodity and business services. Remember, you cannot manage what you do not measure. Following are some guidelines in developing a set of meaningful measures:

1. Identify the level of service the business requires to accomplish their goals.
2. Codevelop a set of easily measured metrics and associated service-level agreements.
3. Report service-level results versus service-level agreements on a regular basis.
4. Work with business unit executives to monitor services to ensure alignment to business objectives.

Continuously Improve

Always strive to improve the performance of service delivery. In addition, do not forget to set stretch goals that appear hard to achieve. Do not ignore the five key principles to continuous improvement:

1. Monitor your performance.
2. Measure the results.
3. Improve delivery.
4. Communicate at all levels throughout the company.
5. Optimize for success.

Diane Burkert, Enterprise Service Desk side services executive at CSAA Insurance Group, provides a perspective on the need to deliver services exceptionally well that all IT personnel should embrace:

> The biggest challenge seems to be immediacy and transparency. We are all 'users' of services as consumers. When those same users come into the office, they expect everything to be available immediately.[16]

If you are a CIO striving to transform your IT organization to be strategic, heed the advice from Stuart Kippelman, CIO at Covanta:

> It is important we all remind ourselves that IT has two jobs to do. We have fought for many years for that seat at the table with our business partners, and we deserve to be there. However, that seat was built with credibility gained from delivering basic services exceptionally well and managing and running the business of IT. If you haven't thought about that lately, it's time for a refresher.[17]

We used two diverse examples to show the process strategic CIOs use to deliver services exceptionally well. In the case of Fox Enterprise application shared services, Cindy McKenzie developed a service delivery capability from the ground up. Steve O'Connor, on the other hand, as a newly hired CIO, needed to improve an existing IT organization to become strategic. His first step was to determine how to deliver services exceptionally well. Each CIO followed a fundamental process. What we did not discuss was the underlying methodologies used by strategic IT organizations to ensure operational stability and successful execution of projects. These are the two foundation components for delivering basic services exceptionally well. This is the subject of the next chapter.

Citations

1. Mike Hedges, CIO Medtronic/Phil Weinzimer Interview, January 29, 2012.

2. Tony D'Allesandro, CIO Rogers Corporation/Phil Weinzimer Interview, April 18, 2013.

3. Stuart Kippelman, CIO Covanta Energy/Phil Weinzimer Interview, March 13 and 20, 2012.

4. The DNA of the CIO; *Opening the Door to the C-Suite*, Ernst & Young 2014, p. 10. http://www.ey.com/Publication/vwLUAssets/DNA_of_the_CIO/$FILE/DNA_of_the_CIO.pdf.

5. Mike McClaskey, CIO Dish Network/Phil Weinzimer Interview, December 20, 2012.

6. Ravi Naik, CIO Sandisk/Phil Weinzimer Interview, April 5, 2012.

7. Steve O'Connor, CIO CSAA Insurance Group/Phil Weinzimer Interview, August 20, 2012.

8. Steve O'Connor, CIO CSAA Insurance Group/Phil Weinzimer Interview, September 25, 2012.

9. Steve O'Connor, CIO CSAA Insurance Group/Phil Weinzimer Interview, November 20, 2012.

10. Shadi Ziaei, IT Service Center Manager/Phil Weinzimer Interview, April 29, 2013.

11. Caesar Fernandez, PMG Director of Product and Business Solutions/Phil Weinzimer Interview, May 15, 2013.

12. Cindy McKenzie, Sr. Vice President Fox Enterprise Application Group/Phil Weinzimer Interview, September 19, 2012 (Cindy McKenzie joined Price Waterhouse Coopers as Managing Director in April 2013).

13. Cindy McKenzie, Sr. Vice President Fox Enterprise Application Group/Phil Weinzimer Interview, October 21, 2012 (Cindy McKenzie joined Price Waterhouse Coopers as Managing Director in April 2013).

14. Staff Q&A with Tom Murphy, Penn Current. University of Penn News, Maria Zankey, September 12, 2013; http://www.upenn.edu/pennnews/current/2013-09-12/interviews/staff-qa-tom-murphy.

15. Tom Murphy, Vice President for Information Technology & University Chief Information Officer/Phil Weinzimer interview; June 27, 2014.

16. Diane Burkert, Enterprise Deskside Services Executive as CSAA Insurance Group/Phil Weinzimer Interview, April 20, 2013.

17. Stuart Kippelman, CIO Covanta Energy/Phil Weinzimer Interview, March 13, 2012.

4

How to Excel at Operational Stability

Succeeding at operational stability has enabled us to work with the business and focus on improving processes that have saved billions of dollars.

David Kepler
*Corporate Vice President of Shared Services and
Chief Information Officer of The Dow Chemical Company*

Understanding the importance of delivering basic services is a first step in working with your business peers to establish credibility for your information technology (IT) organization. Delivering services exceptionally well requires a well-tuned IT infrastructure that achieves operational stability, the subject of this chapter. We will explore a framework that can help you improve the operational stability of your IT infrastructure. Following is a high-level overview of the objective, key points, and examples used in this chapter.

A. CHAPTER OBJECTIVE

1. Reinforce the importance of operational stability as a foundation for delivering basic services exceptionally well.
2. Share a framework chief information officers (CIOs) can utilize to achieve operational stability (Figure 4.1).
3. Explore how two CIOs ensure operational stability within their respective companies.

B. KEY POINTS

1. As the CIO or IT Director, your number one issue needs to be the operational stability of the business services you provide the enterprise.

2. A well-thought-out and sound architecture is required to support the business strategy.

3. Don't get caught building an architecture that resembles the physical architecture of the Winchester Mystery House in San Jose, California (see Figure 4.3).

4. Implement an effective change management process.

5. Measure what's important: ensure that uptime, abnormal terminations, performance issues, and defects meet or exceed the service level agreements (SLAs) your business peers require.

C. EXAMPLES

- CSAA Insurance Group
- Fox Entertainment Group

D. KEY TEMPLATE

- See Figure 4.1.

GOVERNANCE FRAMEWORK—OPERATIONAL STABILITY

Guiding Principles

Less is more	Sound architecture	Change management process
Having fewer servers, routers, cables, hardware vendors, service providers, contracts, etc., to manage will lower your risk for a malfunction and/or failure to occur.	IT infrastructure is a complex array of equipment, wiring, hundreds of business applications, and other components that have to work in harmony for the business to run efficiently without disruption.	IT personnel want to do the right thing. But sometimes haste makes waste. A simple 5 minute fix on a production system without going through a rigorous change management process to test any changes can result in many days of unnecessary downtime.

Measure What's Important

Uptime	Abnormal terminations	Performance issues	Defects
The time applications are available and functional within the parameter of the Service Level Agreement (SLA) (*measured in minutes/week or month.*)	The number of occurrences that an application terminates abnormally over a specific time *period (blue screen, application shutdown, etc.)*	The number and associated details of when a user is not experiencing the performance expected from the application (*delay in populating data, screen refresh time, etc.*).	The number and associated details when an application isn't performing as advertised (*missing data, incorrect calculation, etc.*)

Operational stability remediation processes

Rigorous processes and oversight to mitigate operational stability issues and meet and/or exceed service level agreements

Services Portfolio

Business Services (*examples*)

Product development applications	Engineering applications	Sales/marketing applications	Customer support applications	Manufacturing applications	Logistics applications

Support/technical services (*examples*)

Help desk	E-mail	Telephony	Network	Data center

Figure 4.1 Governance Framework—Operational Stability.

Operational Stability

Operational stability is one of the major challenges encountered by any IT organization. As discussed in the previous chapter, business personnel do not want any disruption to computers, telephone systems, or the business applications they use each day. Think about it! Customers place orders, pay bills, and check on inventory status. Companies use business systems that interact with their suppliers, distributors, and customers across their entire value chain. These business systems need to be operational, and any disruption affects sales, profitability, and customer relationships.

Operational stability is about ensuring that applications and all services are available to users. In today's global environment, companies operate in multiple locations around the world. Procter & Gamble (P&G), for example, operates in 180 countries. The sun never sets on a P&G location. Therefore, service availability is required 24/7. There are many other companies like P&G. So, as the CIO of global company, you can never lose sight of the fact that operational stability is an important objective.

We have all experienced service disruptions. When that happens, we call the IT help desk. The usual response is *the service is down and we are working on the problem.* Somewhat annoying, isn't it? Disruptions to services caused by infrastructure issues have financial impacts to the business enterprise. Disruptions can affect sales revenue, customer and internal user satisfaction, and employee productivity. A customer facing an order system that cannot accept customer orders is devastating to a company as it will have a negative impact on customer satisfaction. We have all experienced moments when there were issues with accessing an application. It disrupts our work cadence. One study, by Dave Laurello, the president and CEO of Stratus Technologies, says that "a number of industry analysts firms peg the cost of an hour of IT system downtime for the average company at well above $100,000."[2] A white paper by Tripwire says that Gardner estimates that 70%–80% of all changes performed to applications by IT personnel are accidental or unintentional. In one instance, a technician, not following procedures, made an error in changing a router that took 22 hours to fix.[3]

Trying to solve operational stability issues through tactical efforts is only a temporary band-aid. A well-thought-out governance process provides the boundaries and associated processes necessary to ensure the optimal performance of the services you deliver to the enterprise. Figure 4.1 represents a governance framework that can help IT organizations optimize operational stability through incorporating guiding principles, metrics, and remediation processes to their services portfolio.

Every governance model requires a framework. The operational stability governance framework is no exception. To understand this governance framework, we will begin with a definition for each of the four major framework components, followed by an in-depth analysis of the activities in each component of the framework.

Guiding Principles

Every organization should have a set of guiding principles that drive their business activities and behaviors. For example, Figure 4.2 reflects the guiding principles for Blackstone—a premier global investment and advisory firm. These guiding principles provide a foundation for how employees behave in conducting their daily business activities.[4]

In the context of operational stability, the guiding principles in the model depicted in Figure 4.2 are less is more, sound architecture, and change management process.

Blackstone Guiding principles
Accountability Our capital and reputation are always on the line
Excellence Anything less is never acceptable
Integrity Leadership demands responsibility
Teamwork Always makes us better
Entrepreneurship Using creativity to find opportunities overlooked by others

Figure 4.2   Example of Guiding Principles.

Less Is More

You can significantly improve your operational stability by having fewer servers, routers, and other technical components. When I was a young boy in 1960, I worked at my father's gasoline station in the Bushwick section of Brooklyn New York. At 8 years old, I was able to fix a flat tire, change the oil, tune-up an engine, and replace brakes. Cars were simple back then. When I opened the hood of a customer's car, there was an engine block, battery, regulator, carburetor, electric coil, and a few other mechanical and electrical devices. Only a few items would malfunction. Today automobiles are complicated machines. If you don't believe me, open the hood of a current-year automobile and see if you can identify any of the components. My friend has a BMW. When he opens the driver's door, he can hear the *click* of the computer hard drive engaging. Today's automobiles are complicated computer-controlled machines. Each one of the components under the hood and throughout the automobile has a potential for failure. Now think about a data center and all the complex array of servers, routers, cables, etc., in your company. There's even more chance of failure as you contract with multiple vendors who provide a variety of support and consulting services. The more components you have, the more the chance for failure. There are fewer chances of failure if you have fewer components.

For an IT organization, this means that you should strive for fewer hardware vendors, service providers, and vendor contracts to manage. Doing so will result in less of a chance for a malfunction and/or failure to occur. Doing so requires an aggressive and effective partnership strategy that requires oversight, trust, and an ongoing relationship. So remember, less is more.

Sound Architecture

A sound architecture is a necessity for all the IT to work both effectively and efficiently. Some key advantages of a sound architecture are as follows:

- IT is a critical ingredient of the products and services of your enterprise.

- IT provides the enabling technology to support the enterprise processes across the entire value chain. As such, it is a mirror image of the business.
- A well-designed IT architecture provides a powerful competitive advantage in delivering products and services to all internal users and external customers.
- IT requires a well-designed architecture just like a well-constructed building.

Without a sound architecture, operational failures can occur, systems may not operate efficiently, and the business could experience difficulty in conducting everyday business activities. Let us look at two examples of architectures that do not involve IT. Technical speak is easy for those who work in IT or really understand the technologies of IT. However, those that are not conversant in *Technology Speak* can relate to the issues by comparing examples in one's personal life. Sometimes, it is a lot easier to use nonbusiness examples. I know a number of strategic CIOs who, when speaking to a business group, or even the board of directors, use nontechnical examples to clarify their main points.

Dysfunctional Architecture   A great example of a dysfunctional architecture is Winchester Mystery House in San Jose, California. It was used by a CIO to explain the necessity of an effective architecture for the business. Around 1890, Sarah L. Winchester, a wealthy eccentric, commissioned the architect Chris Gounalakis to build a house. The project took almost 40 years to complete as Sarah Winchester changed designs very often. The house appears very elegant when you look at it from the outside. However, when you go inside, you begin to realize that the architecture is very dysfunctional. The sprawling mansion contains 160 rooms with 2,000 doors, 10,000 windows, 47 stairways, 47 fireplaces with 17 chimneys, 13 bathrooms, and 6 kitchens. There are windows that are built into the floor, staircases lead to nowhere, doors open onto blank walls, and there are upside down posts. There is even a staircase that rises only nine feet. It has 44 steps with each step only 2 inches high. Imagine living in a house like this. Each room, staircase, and door are beautiful examples of workmanship, but together, they do not function as effective living quarters (Figure 4.3).[4]

Figure 4.3 The Winchester Mystery House. (From Winchester Mystery House used in CIO presentation.)

Sound Architecture   Λ CIO friend of mine told me about his company's new corporate headquarters. When the board decided it needed a new corporate headquarters, an architect was hired. The architect met with the board and executive team to understand what they desired in a building. He asked the board of directors a set of questions. The answers provided the architect with some of the major requirements.

1. The building should have four floors.
2. The building should house approximately 250 people comfortably.
3. The elevator banks needed to be in a central location to make it easy for people to navigate the building.
4. Every floor required a kitchen with a microwave, industrial size refrigerators, and a plenty of countertops and storage areas.
5. Restrooms should be conveniently located.
6. Conference rooms and offices should have glass walls to evoke an open air environment.

7. Sufficient electrical outlets and circuit breakers needed to be installed to handle multiple devices.
8. Backup generators are required in case of storms or electrical disruptions.

There were other items identified as well. The objective was to make the workplace as comfortable as possible to the employees as well as provide an open-air environment to foster teamwork.

The architect drew up a plan and reviewed it with the board and executive team. The final drawings included the board's recommendations. Before the excavation of a single shovel of dirt, the architecture drawings were finalized and agreed to by the board, executive team, and an employee team representing all the employees. Everyone agreed that the well-thought-out plan included input from all interested parties.

When the building was finished and company personnel moved in, everyone was just astonished. Everything was perfect. Employees felt as part of a team. The glass walls of the conference rooms and offices conveyed an open environment and enabled effective teamwork. Everyone thought that a kitchen on every floor was a great idea and it proved to be a great informal meeting place. The building, as a number of employees stated, was "just the perfect place to work." This is a perfect example of planning a sound architecture—making sure all the pieces fit together logically.

Lessons Learned The lesson learned from the Winchester House example is that on the surface everything looks fine, but once you are inside the house, all the functioning elements—rooms, windows, staircases, and fireplaces—don't make any sense. The good news is that today the house is a tourist attraction and a famous landmark in San Jose, California. The second example of a newly constructed corporate headquarters represents a perfect example of why developing an architecture plan is so important before any construction begins.

A sound architecture for your home or office is important. The same rule applies to the technology architecture of your business enterprise, which includes a complex array of technology platforms that include a variety of equipment, wiring, hundreds of business applications, and other components that have to work in harmony for the business to run efficiently without disruption. The IT architecture is no more than a mirror image of how the business operates. What do you think would happen if business units do not have a sound business model that reflects a set of seamlessly integrated processes that create value for its customers? The result is that the IT organization ends up supporting a variety of business processes with applications and other business services that do not connect, just like the hallways of the Winchester Mystery House. As an IT leader, you can take the initiative to help the business understand that an effective IT architecture requires the business look at its business processes to make sure that they align with and support the business strategy.

Effective Change Management Process

In today's technology-driven marketplace, business applications, which support the day-to-day processes that operate the business, are very complex. Therefore, IT organizations need to make sure to apply a rigorous set of practices to any application modifications. In the context of operational stability, we define change management to include configuration management, application changes, and problem management. Configuration management deals with configuration settings for all applications, application changes address any coding modifications, and problem management identifies and records changes to systems resulting from problem/incident tickets.

An effective change management process minimizes service disruptions, which can be very annoying to users. We all have experienced the scenario when a business application stops functioning because a well-intentioned engineer or developer had a great idea and said, "I can get this done real quickly. All I have to do is change a couple of lines of code." Well, guess what? Good intentions sometimes lead to unfortunate disasters. Following is an example.

A few years ago, I managed the implementation of a major project suite for a Fortune 500 company. Our implementation team, working with the client's IT personnel, spent 4 months installing, configuring, and testing before we released the solution to production where 2000 employees could manage their expenses. Three days into production release, one of the client's junior IT engineers had a great idea. Some of the users experienced a lag time when entering certain data into the application. Instead of following the change management process—testing the fix on the developmental platform, then on the test platform, and then documenting and obtaining the approval for implementation on production system—the junior engineer thought that he could fix the problem quickly by just changing some code on the production system. Well, you can guess what happened. The 5-minute fix brought down the entire application suite for 3 days. It was a mess.

The consulting and client implementation team conducted a lessons learned meeting upon the successful completion of the fix. We discussed what happened. The rules were simple. Do not blame any team member. Focus on diagnosing the problem, understand the root cause, and develop a permanent fix. The team did just that. They modified the change management process to add some additional checks and balances to avoid any direct code change to a production system without a set of escalating signed-off approvals.

Computer glitches happen all the time. Some even make national news. On April 17, 2013, *The Wall Street Journal* published a lead article in the Marketplace section about a computer glitch that resulted in the cancellation of *880 flights and delayed 1,070 flights*. You can imagine the financial impact on American Airlines, let alone the customer goodwill. One family returning to their home in San Francisco from vacation could not claim their luggage when their flight was canceled after a 1-hour delay on the tarmac before returning to the gate. When the family tried to reschedule their flight on a different airline, American Airlines personnel weren't able to redirect the luggage to the flight as the application could not be accessed due to a performance issue. The very frustrated passengers said that *they were being held captive by their luggage*.[7] United Airlines had a similar mishap during the merger with Continental Airlines in March 2012. As part of the merger, United Airlines integrated the frequent flyer programs and backend computer systems. Unfortunately, someone goofed. There were *rampant flight delays and lingering customer-service frustrations for passengers*, said Jeff Smisek, the chief executive of United Continental.[8]

In 2007, when US Airways and America West merged airlines, US Airways made the fatal error of integrating their computer systems to the smaller systems at America West. Disaster struck. Check-in kiosks crashed across the country. Tom Horton, American Airlines (AMRs) chief executive, said in an interview with *Sky News* that *it is important to adopt the systems and processes.* The smaller IT organization at America West did not have mature change management systems.[9]

Caveat emptor is the lesson (*Let the Buyer Beware*). Put more simply, never travel during airline computer upgrades, conversions, or integrations during mergers.

Companies with global customers need to be very careful. In October 2011, 70 million Blackberry users experienced a blackout that lasted up to 3 days for some users. This is an example event people never forget.[10] Unfortunately, these events occur, but most are avoidable by following prudent change management practices. The lesson learned is to implement and follow a rigorous and well-tested change management process. Developers and engineers want to do the right thing. They have the right intent and right heart, but they will inadvertently change things, out of their zest for speed. Moreover, things break. So make sure you follow a proven change management process.

Measure What's Important

Cindy McKenzie and Steve O'Connor are examples of strategic CIOs who are very focused and keen on details. Both are sticklers; they ensure the availability of both commodity and business services for use by employees on a day-to-day basis. What they both have in common is that they only measure what is important and communicate it to the business on a regular basis. Following is a report prepared by the IT organization at CSAA Insurance Group. It represents the uptime for an application at USAA Insurance Group. The report tracks total hours in the day, uptime hours, and downtime hours and provides specifics about downtime events.

O'Connor's team uses this report to measure uptime and percentage downtime, as it helps the team focus on the key metrics to measure success. The objective was to start capturing uptime metrics for key business services. Steve O'Connor used this process for educating the IT personnel on the importance of measuring uptime metrics (Table 4.1).[11]

I've spoken to a lot of CIOs about the types of metrics they use to measure the effectiveness and efficiency of applications. Following are the four of the most commonly used in measuring operational stability.

Table 4.1 Uptime Metrics Report: Example

	Date	Total	Jan-12	Feb-12	Mar-12	Apr-12	May-12	Jun-12	Jul-12	Aug-12	Sep-12	Oct-12	Nov-12	Dec-12	DATE
							PAS APPLICATION MONTHLY / YEARLY UPDATE METRIC								
Days in month		304	31	28	31	30	31	30	31	31	30	31	30	31	
Hours application required		4:00 am PST to 10:00 pm PST													
Total hours per day		18 hours	18	18	18	18	18	18	18	18	18	18	18	18	
Total hours per month		5,472	558	504	558	540	558	540	558	558	540	558	540	558	
Total gross minutes per month		394,200	33,480	30,240	33,480	32,400	33,480	32,400	33,480	33,480	32,400	33,480	32,400	33,480	
Total minutes per month system available		392,402	33,459	30,240	33,480	31,860	33,285	31,873	33,417	33,215	32,400	33,293	32,400	33,480	
Total minutes per month system unavailable		1,798	21	0	0	540	195	527	63	265	0	187	0	0	
Incident—Intermittant Outage	Jan 27, 12	21	21	0	0	0	0	0	0	0	0	0	0	0	4:11 pm to 4:32 pm = 21 minutes Outage/Cause time difference on SSO Servers Versus PAS Servers
No Outages February	Feb 12	0	0	0	0	0	0	0	0	0	0	0	0	0	No Outages February
No Outages March	Mar 12	0	0	0	0	0	0	0	0	0	0	0	0	0	No Outages March
Incident—Phoenix Data Center Outage	Apr 9, 12	360	0	0	0	360	0	0	0	0	0	0	0	0	Network Outage (Said from 2:21 to 4:11 - Can't confirm) Listed as 360 Minutes
Incident—PAS Outage—Unable to Quote	Apr 26, 12	180	0	0	0	180	0	0	0	0	0	0	0	0	7:58 to 10:58 Users Unable to QUOTE/ PAS = 3 hours = 180 minutes - Application/Server/Database Connection Issue

Incident	Date	Total	1	2	3	4	5	6	7	8	9	10	11	Notes
Incident—PAS Outage—Users **Multiple errors on login**	May 20, 12	195	0	0	0	195	0	0	0	0	0	0	0	9:15 to 12:30 Users not in PAM repository/404 error – changed URL/PAS not allow Agents to sell with multiple risk state role
Incident—PAS Outage—Auditors Running Reports	Jun 1, 12	11	0	0	0	0	11	0	0	0	0	0	0	Auditors Running Reports
Incident—Saeed Database Connection Outage	Jun 7, 12	46	0	0	0	0	46	0	0	0	0	0	0	Database Connection problem
Incident—Ent\Client\Ext	Jun 18, 12	313	0	0	0	0	313	0	0	0	0	0	0	Ent\Client\Ext – user ID's Deleted 18th & 19th/18:47 to 16:29 – Estimated 313 minutes out (Wed night – Thursday morning)
Incident—Cant take credit card through PAS	Jun 23, 12	58	0	0	0	0	58	0	0	0	0	0	0	Credit card through PAS - Salesforce. COM Issue – URL?
Incident—Cant take credit card through PAS	Jun 27, 12	15	0	0	0	0	15	0	0	0	0	0	0	Server Patch incident – 10 in morning rather than at night
Incident—Saturday—Server Hung—Batch Job Running	Jun 30, 12	84	0	0	0	0	84	0	0	0	0	0	0	Batch Job running during day/ Consumed Connections
Incident—Tuesday—PAS Address Validation	Jul 3, 12	63	0	0	0	0	0	63	0	0	0	0	0	Load Balancer Partial Failure - Manual rollover
Incident—August release—Extended Maintenance—Sunday	Aug 5, 12	265	0	0	0	0	0	0	265	0	0	0	0	
Incident—October—Lost DB Connection = Root Cause?/Tuesday	Oct 9, 12	43	0	0	0	0	0	0	0	0	43	0	0	
Incident—October—Sunday Extended Deploy Window 144 minutes	Oct 28, 12	144	0	0	0	0	0	0	0	0	144	0	0	
		0	0	0	0	0	0	0	0	0	0	0	0	
Percentage uptime	NA	99.54%	99.94%	100.00%	98.33%	99.42%	98.37%	99.81%	99.21%	100.00%	99.44%	100.00%	100.00%	
Percentage downtime	NA	0.456%	0.06%	0.00%	1.67%	0.58%	1.63%	0.19%	0.79%	0.00%	0.56%	0.00%	0.00%	

Uptime

This metric measures the time applications are available and functional within the parameter of the service level agreement (SLA) established with the business. Let us look at an example. The established SLA for a customer service application (CSA) is 100% availability, 24 hours a day, 365 days per year, or 10,080 minutes per week (24 hours × 60 minutes × 7 days). The SLA for most customer-facing applications falls in the range of 96%–98%. Let us assume, for this example, that your sales organization requires the CSA be up at least 98% of the time. This converts to 10,584 minutes per week (98 × 10,800 minutes). Your IT organization should try to achieve this goal.

To achieve a 100% uptime metric is very costly. You might need a second instance of the application or a backup data center and/or additional hardware and software. These are management decisions that the business needs to agree to. These decisions are based upon the investment required to achieve the 2% differential of a 98% and a 100% uptime SLA. Regardless of the percentage agreed to, uptime needs to be measured, documented, and communicated to the business on a weekly basis.

One of the most significant challenges for the CIO is how to communicate the business value that the IT personnel provide to the business. It is not just writing quality code. It's about enabling the business to create value. A value metric most people understand is sales dollars. Therefore, you might want to consider measuring uptime not only in minutes but also in the sales dollars generated through the use of the application. This is a great example of how you can communicate the importance of maintaining the uptime of applications to your IT personnel.

You also should consider developing a *lost revenue* metric that measures the sales revenue lost as a result of the application not being available to users. This is not a difficult metric to calculate. You start with the revenue generated by the CSA for a designated time, say, the last 12 months, and divide it by the uptime SLA metric as measured in minutes. Following is an example:

- Your company's online sales for the last 12 months were 480 million dollars. The average monthly value of sales generated through the online CSA is 40 million dollars (480/12).

- Your uptime SLA metric for the CSA is 98%, which calculates to 10,584 minutes (as described earlier).
- If you divide the 40 million dollars by the monthly uptime metric of 10,584 minutes, your result, rounded to the nearest dollar, is $3,780 of sales revenue per minute.

For every minute the CSA is available for use, it will generate, on average, $4,000 in sales revenue. The converse is also true. For every minute the CSA is *not* available, your company could potentially lose $4,000 in revenue. When customer-facing applications are down, customers will sometimes move on to a different company's website to order a product. Your company loses revenue. More importantly, you may even lose the customer forever. Remember, the goal of the IT organization is to work with the business to achieve business outcomes; in this example, it is about generating sales revenue, which is very important to the company. In fact, I know some CIOs who base a major portion of their IT directors' bonus compensation on achieving uptime SLAs.

Abnormal Terminations

This metric measures the number of occurrences that an application terminates abnormally over a specific time period. We all know someone who has experienced the infamous *blue screen* phenomenon on his or her computer, or we ourselves would have experienced it when we attempted to log in to an application. These are examples of abnormal terminations. This is the most frustrating experience for users. These events must be measured, diagnosed, and fixed so they never happen again. The best way to do this is to escalate these events to the CIO. This visibility gets everyone working to eliminate abnormal terminations. I even know of one CIO who keeps a file of abnormal terminations and has the application owner report on the root cause analysis and remedial action taken. In addition, the application owner has to provide the CIO the proof that the particular cause of the abnormal termination will never occur again. This is not a punishment but a method to change the behaviors of your personnel to get at the root cause of a problem and mitigate it so that it doesn't occur again.

Performance

Performance issues occur when a user does not experience the performance expected from the application. A customer accesses your website to inquire about product information, and the system *hangs* for about 2–3 seconds before the web page materializes. It is the longest 2–3 seconds one has ever experienced! We have all been there and it is very frustrating. The analogy to this is watching a news broadcast on your television. Imagine at the beginning of the 6:30 pm news, the newsperson does introduces him/herself and then hesitates, not moving a muscle, and just stares at the camera for 2–3 seconds before saying another word. This is not very entertaining. In fact, it is unacceptable and very frustrating.

What do some CIOs do to eliminate performance issues? They set up performance and tuning teams to pound away at an application to test its performance based upon the functionality parameters of the application.

Performance issues need to be logged, investigated, tested, and remediated. The key to eliminating performance issues is to test them constantly under different use conditions. So make sure you have a rigorous process in place, which includes performance issue documentation, root cause analysis, remediation plans, and quality assurance testing. In addition, make sure you report regularly to the business community as to the status of performance issues and remediation plans to mitigate such future occurrences.

Defects

When an application isn't performing as advertised, then there is a defect. Let us look at an example. A customer calls your customer service representative for some product information and at the same time wants to place an order. The customer service representative logs in to the order entry application and enters the customer name. The application functionality was designed to automatically populate the account number, address, and other information so that the customer service representative doesn't have to type the information that the database already has recorded from previous transactions. In this example, not all the data have been prepopulated correctly.

The shipping and associated logistics routing information is missing. Therefore, the customer service representative has to ask the customer for the information and enter the data. Upon completing the order entry process, the customer service representative logs a ticket to the help desk to report the functionality issue. This is frustrating not only for the customer service representative but also for the customer who has to provide the same information communicated during previous calls. This results in customer relationship issues. So now, you have a sales VP having a very unpleasant conversation with the IT director or even the CIO, depending on the customer, to figure out how the IT organization is going to solve this customer satisfaction issue.

Performance testing is a means to minimizing defects. I am sure you have ever seen the automobile commercial where you see a car inside a enclosed room with its windshield wipers operating while rain and wind pound the vehicle. This is an example of performance testing. Business applications must go through the same rigorous testing process. The metric for measuring the performance should be "0" performance issues. However, the reality is that with the complexity of systems today, performance issues always occur. The goal is never have the same performance issue repeated.

A defect remediation process needs to be in place within your IT organization. The teams need to analyze the issue, determine the root cause, and eliminate the defects. Do not forget to report defects and resolution to the business community. The worst mistake you can make is not communicating the status of defects to the business community. Remember, communication and expectation setting are key to building and maintaining a good working relationship with your business peers.

Services Portfolio

The subject of Services Portfolio was discussed in Chapter 3.

Chapter Summary

As the CIO or IT director, your number one issue needs to be the operational stability of the business services you provide the enterprise. This is the most critical issue that IT organizations face today and in the future. The business utilizes the services you provide each day to provide products and services to your company's customers and business partners across the entire value chain. These services need to be operational and stable.

Many service management solutions address operational stability. CISCO, BMC Software, Computer Associates, and IBM are some of the well-known companies that provide solutions in this area that could meet the needs of your company. Make sure that the solution you choose incorporates the principles of the Information Technology Infrastructure Library (ITIL), which a universally accepted bellweather methodology. In the 1980s, the British Government developed a methodology they could use to improve the quality level of IT services. Later known as ITIL, the methodology is a series of documents that support the planning of consistent, documented, and repeatable processes to improve service delivery to the business. ITIL is a well-recognized and respected methodology used globally by many companies. It has evolved over the years to incorporate more breadth and depth that spans all the organizations of a business enterprise. A certification concept, similar to Six Sigma, includes three different certifications (Figure 4.4).[12]

The pace of change in today's rapidly changing marketplace results in services redefined, eliminated, and reinvented. Regardless of the business services the IT organization *provides* the business, you still need an effective governance model to ensure flawless delivery of the services. So remember the following three guiding principles and four key metrics that will enable you to provide operational stability for the services you provide to the business.

Foundation certificate
Foundation certificate enables people to understand the terminology used within ITIL. It focuses upon foundation knowledge with regard to the ITIL Service Support and Service Delivery sets as well as covering generic ITIL philosophy and its background.

Practitioner's certificate
Qualification on the specific disciplines within the ITIL Service Support or Service Delivery set, including customer and IT organization communication.

Manager's certificate
Aimed at experienced professionals, who will be involved in the management of service management functions.

Figure 4.4 ITIL Certification Types.

Guiding Principles

1. Less is more: The fewer the components, hardware vendors, service providers, and contracts you have to manage, the less chance of operational failure.
2. Sound architecture: IT architecture is a complex array of technology platforms that include equipment, wiring, hundreds of business applications, and other components that have to work in harmony for the business to run efficiently without disruption.
3. Effective change management process: Developers and engineers want to do the right thing. They have the right intent and right heart, but they will inadvertently change things. Remember, things break. So make sure you follow a proven change management process.

Metrics

Measure what's important: ensure that uptime, abnormal terminations, performance issues, and defects meet or exceed the SLAs your business peers require.

So remember, if you have an effective governance model, you will earn the trust and respect of your C-level peers. You will also be able to partner with them to discuss their challenges and together develop solutions that achieve specific business outcomes that create customer value, increase revenue and return on investment (ROI), and enhance shareholders' wealth.

Citations

1. David Kepler, Corporate Vice President of Shared Services and chief information officer of the Dow Chemical Company/Phil Weinzimer Interview, November 26, 2013.
2. Behind the nines: An examination of uptime solutions, Dave Laurello, September 18, 2012; http://slashdot.org/topic/cloud/behind-the-nines-an-examination-of-uptime-solutions/.
3. What's good for security is good for operations, TGripwire, 2012; http://i.zdnet.com/whitepapers/Tripwire_Security_and_Ops.pdf, p. 3.
4. Blackstone   Website;   http://www.blackstone.com/the-firm/guiding-principles.

5. Winchester Mystery House; http://www.winchestermysteryhouse.com/.
6. Winchester Mystery House used in CIO presentation. Photograph used in Steve O'Connor presentation to the USAA Insurance Group Board.
7. Outage Snarls American Air Flights; *Wall Street Journal*; Wednesday, April 17, 2013, Section B, p. 1.
8. United Continental CEO: Still fixing bugs in new computer system, April 19, 2012, Gregory Karp, Tribune reporter; http://articles.chicagotribune.com/2012-04-19/business/chi-united-continental-ceo-still-fixing-bugs-in-new-computer-system-20120419_1_seats-or-access-frequent-flier-united-fliers.
9. Glitch with kiosks forces US Airways passengers to wait; Associated Press, March 5, 2007; http://www.post-gazette.com/stories/business/news/glitch-with-kiosks-forces-us-airways-passengers-to-wait-474944/#ixzz2QqHVVexU.
10. BlackBerry Blackout Latest Trouble for RIM, CNBC.com, October 1, 2011; http://www.cnbc.com/id/44914502.
11. Steve O'Connor, CIO, CSAA Insurance Group/Phil Weinzimer Interview, September 25, 2012.
12. ITIL Central Website; News and Information for ITIL Library; http://itsm.fwtk.org/FAQ.htm.

5

HOW TO SUCCEED AT PROJECT GOVERNANCE

As the stewards of taxpayer dollars, we need to manage project risk through a well-defined and proven governance process.[1]

Calvin Rhodes
CIO, State of Georgia

In the previous chapter, we discussed operational efficiency as a basic element for delivering services exceptionally well. A second element is project governance. Why is this important? Think about it! Every activity performed by personnel in your information technology (IT) organization is part of a project. Following is the objective, key messages, and examples used in this chapter.

A. CHAPTER OBJECTIVE

1. Discuss the importance of project governance in providing an effective oversight and governance process for all projects and associated portfolios in the business enterprise.
2. Provide a project governance framework CIOs can use to provide an effective governance process within the IT organization.
3. Share a case study of an IT organization that uses an effective governance process tool in managing a diverse set of project portfolios.

B. KEY POINTS

1. A well thought of project governance process will minimize project risk and improve project success.
2. Bad communication, lack of planning, poor quality control, missing interim deliverables, poor budget, and project management contribute to project failures.
3. Your project governance process should include guiding principles, project excellence governance processes and metrics, project portfolios, and a project portfolio management (PPM) tool.
   a. Guiding principles include visible leadership, defined tactics, effective communications, project excellence, and metrics.
4. Project portfolios should be organized by categories and viewable across different categories, characteristics, and strategic alignment. Sustain, operational, and strategic is one category grouping.

C. EXAMPLES

- State of Georgia—Georgia Technology Authority (GTA)

D. FRAMEWORKS

- Governance Framework—Project Excellence

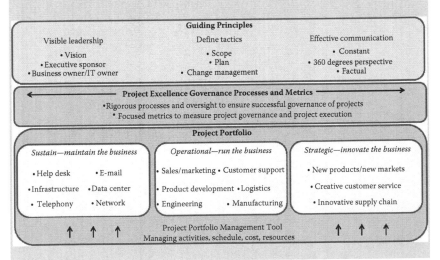

Guiding Principles		
Visible leadership	Define tactics	Effective communication
• Vision • Executive sponsor • Business owner/IT owner	• Scope • Plan • Change management	• Constant • 360 degrees perspective • Factual

◄——— Project Excellence Governance Processes and Metrics ———►
• Rigorous processes and oversight to ensure successful governance of projects
• Focused metrics to measure project governance and project execution

Project Portfolio

Sustain—maintain the business	*Operational—run the business*	*Strategic—innovate the business*
• Help desk • E-mail • Infrastructure • Data center • Telephony • Network	• Sales/marketing • Customer support • Product development • Logistics • Engineering • Manufacturing	• New products/new markets • Creative customer service • Innovative supply chain

↑ ↑ ↑   Project Portfolio Management Tool   ↑ ↑ ↑
Managing activities, schedule, cost, resources

Your IT and business teams work on large projects, which include the development of sales applications, financial applications, human resource applications, and order entry applications for internal users. They also develop applications for customers, such as customer service applications, as well as logistic applications for your channel partners. These teams also work on smaller projects such as application enhancement releases, help desk issue, and incident resolution. Even the activities associated with an outsourced or purchased application is a project. There are always data center projects to improve efficiency or install new equipment. The point here is that most work activities are indeed part of a project and need to be managed through a governance model to ensure successful outcome.

IT organizations manage many projects. Whether big or small, these projects always have risks and project managers (PMs) always want to minimize risk. Project plans are perfect the moment they are developed. Once the project clock starts, subsequent events influence project schedules and costs. Resources with the required skills might not be available resulting in errors or increased work effort. Incorrect or expanded scope requirements extend project schedules. Improper testing results in rework. Each of these risk areas affects the ability of the IT organization to optimize project throughput—the number of projects executed during the fiscal year. When schedules extend beyond planned dates, or costs exceed budget, fewer projects complete in a fiscal year, and potential business benefits of projects not able to be implemented are deferred to a future point in time.

If you think about projects only in terms of cost, schedule, and resources, then you need to change your focus. You need to realize that projects provide business benefits in terms of customer value, improved revenue, reduced cost, and shareholder wealth. Once you do this, your perspective on the importance of project success will change beneficially. Now, let us get back to some basic issues that affect successful project delivery.

A Gartner survey in 2012 cited that large IT projects "are more likely to fail than small projects...due to functionality issues and substantial delays." Projects with budgets greater than $350,000 exceeded budgets 25% of the time. The failure rate of projects greater than one million dollars was *almost 50% higher than projects with budgets*

Table 5.1   Project Failure Statistics

BULL SURVEY	
CATEGORY	%
Bad communication	57
Lack of planning	39
Poor quality control	35
Missing interim deliverable	34
Poor budget management	29
Poor project management	20

below $350,000.[2] The survey cited the following six key issues that led to project failure:

- Functionality issues
- Substantially late
- Quality issues
- High cost variance
- Cancelled after launch
- Rejected or not implemented for other reasons

Not much changed over the years. An earlier Bull survey in 2008 identified the following failure categories and the associated percentage attributed to project failure.[3] Although worded differently from the Gartner study, there are parallels (Table 5.1).

As you can see, six major categories attributed to project failure. The survey also found that 53% of project cost exceeded the original estimates by 189%, and 31% of projects were cancelled before they were completed. How could this be? You would think even the most basic PPM solutions would yield improved results.

Many companies struggle with managing projects because they fail to realize that it is a process, not just a set of activities. What's more significant is that you have to employ a consistent set of processes to achieve project execution success. A McKinsey article in 2011 states that "standardized work practices is the foundation for continuous improvement...."[4]

Most PPM-type solutions provide capabilities to track project activities, schedules, cost, and resource availability. Some even provide alerts based upon exceeding specified parameters. What they do not provide are the governance guidelines and processes necessary to ensure successful project execution.

Following is a real example of a vacation not properly planned. You may know someone who had the same experience.

Michael, a neighbor and friend, was planning a family vacation. With a stressful job, working overtime, as well as weekends, he could not properly plan the family vacation. He could not find the time to plan and told me that he is stressed out over it. One day at the office, Michael was having lunch with John, a close colleague. Michael mentioned to John that his wife and three children, ages 12–18, were forever reminding him to find a resort and plan the vacation. It was getting close to summer, and the longer he waited, the harder it would be to find room availability. John recommended a resort that Michael and his family would enjoy. Michael called the resort later that afternoon, asked two or three questions, and made the reservation. The resort was within driving distance. Although it was 550 miles from their home, he and his wife would share the driving duties. Michael was worried about navigating the drive since the resort was located in an area he had never traveled to before. He did not want to start his vacation with driving issues. Therefore, he purchased a GPS system from the local electronics store to help him navigate the trip. The GPS had the following major capabilities:

- Large screen display
- Flexible entry of destination address or intersections
- Turn-by-turn voice and map directions
- Traffic congestion alerts
- Fuel and food locations
- Save feature and easy retrieval of route directions

Michael thought this would solve the major risk of his family vacation. However, he was wrong. Three weeks later, Michael and his family started their drive to the vacation resort. A day after his return, we saw each other from adjoining lawns. I asked him about his family vacation. He said, "the drive was great but the vacation was terrible." He cited the following top five reasons:

1. The room was too far from the pool.
2. The resort lacked adequate children and teenage activities.

3. The staff-to-guest ratio was inadequate.
4. The quality of the food was inconsistent and the variety for our kids was poor.
5. Some of the features advertised on the resort website were unavailable during our stay.

What Michael failed to do was investigate the resort, ask the right questions, and take the necessary time to plan the vacation. He decided that he alone would be responsible for planning the entire vacation.

What Michael failed to realize is that planning the family vacation is a project. Michael focused on the tool, the GPS technology, to help him navigate to the vacation resort. What he neglected were the other planning activities. The lesson learned is that it is not just about the technology but the governance process in place to manage the boundaries, guidelines, and oversight necessary for successful execution of a project.

In today's highly competitive marketplace, change occurs rapidly and IT organizations receive many more project demands than they can deliver with the existing resources and capital budgets. To stay competitive, business executives always seek ways to improve customer retention, improve revenue, and reduce costs. Any project affecting shareholder net worth is a prime project for consideration. The challenge for every IT organization is to successfully deliver as many successful projects as they can given the resource and budget constraints. To achieve this, IT organizations need to manage project risk and do this proactively, not reactively.

PMs primarily focus on cost, schedule, and resources. They focus on areas that may appear to reflect a well-run project, when in fact other events are brewing that will affect project risk in the near future. The PM may not know about it until it happens.

We have all heard for many years that failure occurs in 20%–25% of projects. You would think that with all the PPM solutions in the marketplace the statistics would improve. If your IT organization has a project portfolio of 40 million dollars this fiscal year resulting in 8–9 million dollars of wasted investments due to project failure, the CEO and other executives would not consider this a job well done. This scenario occurs repeatedly in companies all over the world.

Why does this happen? The answer is simple. You do not have an effective governance model to oversee project execution. The best way to ensure consistent project success is to employ a project governance framework that provides the boundaries, guidelines, and process to ensure project success, regardless of the PPM solution used.

Governance Framework

The following graphic depicts a best-practice governance framework your IT organization can use for achieving project excellence. It incorporates best practices from many IT organizations I observed during my career. The four main categories of the framework are guiding principles, project excellence governance processes and metrics, project portfolio, and project portfolio management tools (Figure 5.1).

Following the explanation for each of the major components of the governance framework is an example of how the Georgia Technology Authority (the IT organization for the state) uses a governance process to ensure success of projects executed across the 119 state agencies.

Guiding Principles: As described in the previous chapter, guiding principles drive business activities and behaviors. For governing

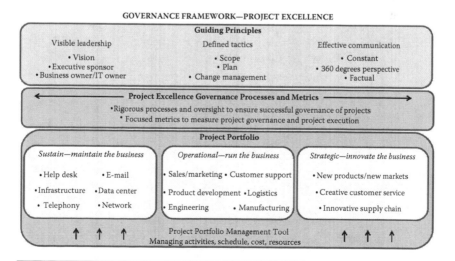

Figure 5.1 Governance Framework: Project Excellence.

projects, there are three guiding principles that provide the impetus for the organization to succeed at executing projects. These are visible leadership, defined tactics, and effective communication.

Visible leadership focuses on the three key roles that are required for effective project governance: executive sponsor, business owner, and IT executive.

Vision

Every organization needs a vision of success. This is the role of the organization's leadership. The vision should define the accomplishments of the organization, using clear and concise wording, which guide the organization's actions:

- Define the accomplishments the organization must achieve to be successful
- Clear and concise language
- Guides the organizations activities

Executive Sponsor

Every major project needs an executive sponsor. This executive cannot be a figurehead role. The executive sponsor

- Must have the authority, accountability, and responsibility for the overall success or failure of a project
- Must have decision making at the macro level, rewarded when the project is successful, and penalized—in some fashion—if the project does not succeed
- Works with the business owner and IT executive to govern the projects in a team-based environment
- Is the definitive decision maker

Business Owner/IT Executive

Business owner: Every IT project that impacts a business process needs a business owner. If not, the project will fail:

- Make sure you assign a business executive who is directly impacted by the project results. Otherwise, he or she does not have a vested interest in the success or failure of the project. The process owner is a perfect candidate for this role.

- Choose a business owner with a successful track record of accomplishment, works effectively in teams, communicates well, and deals with conflict resolution in a positive way.
- The business owner is accountable and responsible for all aspects of the program on a day-to-day basis. The questions the business owner asks are: Do we have the right vision and requirements? Do we have the right financial support? Is the plan realistic and on track? Do we have a good handle on issues and risk?
- Make sure the business owner works closely with the IT owner.

IT executive: Every IT project that impacts a business process needs an IT executive who manages the IT components of the project. The IT executive

- Responsible for all the technology components of the project
- Works with the business owner and business/IT teams to translate the business requirements into IT speak
- Accountable and responsible for the architecture, infrastructure, development, quality assurance, release management, change process, etc., required for project success
- Releases the project major deliverable to the business owner after successful user acceptance testing
- Works closely with the business executive and executive sponsor

Georgia Technology Authority

The Georgia Technology Authority (GTA), the technology arm for the state of Georgia, is a great example of how a strategic organization pursues project success with an effective governance process.

We begin with some background followed by details that explain the governance process used by the GTA.

Background

Calvin Rhodes was appointed CIO at the GTA in 2011. The state organization consists of 120 state agencies, which execute hundreds of IT projects each year. Each agency operates as independent divisions, similar to a federated model, with its own IT professionals that focus on the agency.

The GTA tried, on several occasions, to implement a uniform Project Portfolio Management (PPM) tool across all state agencies. It was difficult to gain consensus since each agency operates as an independent business unit. As a result, each state agency selects a PPM tool of their own choosing to manage the projects. Even though each agency chose their own PPM tool, there were projects that failed and experienced major risk and affected Georgian citizens.[6]

The GTA encountered a number of challenges in monitoring the hundreds of projects executed by the state's agencies. They included the following six major challenges (Figure 5.2).

1. Gathering project data from agency project managers (PMs) is cumbersome and preparing monthly dashboard reports using Excel is time consuming.
   a. Every month, PMs complete a manually generated Excel spreadsheet, with numerous tabs, which provides status for each project indicator (schedule, budget, business objectives, risk, issues, organizational readiness, etc.) as well as project financials.

---

1. Gathering project data from agency project managers is cumbersome and preparing monthly dashboard reports using excel is time consuming
2. Project data is prepared by the project manager and doesn't represent input from key stakeholders
3. Access to data is limited
4. Lack of predictive project behavior limits risk assessment to current and past project activities
5. Lack of an adequate issue management capability prevents proper mitigation of project risk
6. Project requests from agencies do not capture pertinent data to rationalize investments decisions

---

Figure 5.2 GTA Project Governance Challenges.

    b. The collection of data from PMs and consolidated in a presentation package requires about 80 person-hours of effort.

    c. Qualitative data, in the form of comments, provided by the PM, represent the PM's view of the project.

    d. The project data are imported into a GTA spreadsheet that drives green, yellow, or red status.

    e. The GTA spreadsheets are consolidated into an overall document that is used by each critical project review (CPR) panel member during the monthly CPRs.

2. Project data are prepared by the PM and don't represent input from key stakeholders.

    a. Data, which are provided by each PM, represent best efforts as to the project status. However, it is only the view of the PM. Lack of input from key stakeholders masks potential issues and increases potential for project risk.

3. Access to data is limited—it is a push, not a pull, limiting access to only those involved in preparing and reviewing the monthly data. It is not shared across the agencies to foster learning and continuous improvement.

    a. Data are captured in Excel spreadsheets and therefore are static. It is also not available to everyone. Data are pushed to users rather than pulled from a web-based application.

4. Lack of predictive project behavior limits risk assessment to current and past project activities.

    a. A picture only portrays current activity when capturing quantitative data. Projects behave in mysterious ways. A green project can turn into a red project overnight. We have all experienced this.

    b. The ability to use current and historical data to predict project risk greatly improves the governance capability and more importantly helps PMs improve their skills in project management through developing risk mitigation strategies.

5. Lack of an adequate issue management capability prevents proper mitigation of project risk.

    a. The current system is cumbersome to use in capturing project issues.

    b. Lack of ability to easily record and assign tasks to mitigate issues increases project risk.

6. Project requests from agencies do not capture pertinent data to rationalize investments decisions.

    a. The current process for capturing project request data is manual and doesn't provide adequate information to assess risk, business alignment, and an overall opportunity.

    b. Lack of business case and associated data didn't allow for proper analysis and comparison of multiple projects.

Georgia Technology Governance Process Guiding Principles

Guiding Principles: Visible Leadership

Calvin Rhodes-CIO has an extensive business background in private investment and industry. He established Paladin, a private investment firm, and was executive vice president at Fulton Paper Company, where he held a number of executive positions in operations and IT. With a technology and business background, his vision for the State of Georgia is to "connect Georgians to their Government by leveraging technology... It's all about enabling citizens to access government services more easily."[3] One quickly learns after speaking with Rhodes that he views the State of Georgia's IT organization as a business by "providing value to its customers."[5]

Rhodes has three main strategies for the GTA:

1. Consolidate state agency IT infrastructure and network services into an enterprise shared services model to enable improved efficiencies.
2. Implement a full IT governance structure, providing transparency across state agencies so everyone can see anything relative to spend.
3. Enable agencies to provide online services, which improve value and empower the citizen.

The GTA is responsible for providing oversight for all IT projects. The goal is for all projects to be delivered on time, within budget, and achieve their business goals. This is the responsibility of the enterprise governance and planning group (EGAP), directed by Tom Fruman, a business focused executive and experienced in project management. Fruman, who reports to Rhodes, bases his governance philosophy on his business, project management, and IT experience: "I believe people want to do the right thing, but sometimes need guidelines, training, and oversight to help them improve their skills, reduce project risk, and ensure a successful project outcome."[6]

The GTA also identifies a business owner and IT owner for each state agency project. The complement of the state CIO, governance office director, state agency business, and IT owner, for each project, provides the visible leadership required to govern project execution among the state agencies.

Guiding Principles: Defined Tactics

Defined tactics address the boundaries of the project, the execution/control activities, and stakeholder acceptance of business environment changes. The three components are scope, plan, and change management.

Scope Scope provides the boundaries that define the objectives, requirements, deliverables, timelines, budget, etc. If the project scope is not properly defined, the project will expand in time, dollars, and resources. Following are some key tips to ensure that project scope is properly addressed:

- Document the scope of the project in detail.
- Clearly define the scope so that all constituents understand it.
- Make sure there is no *wiggle room* for people to interpret the scope differently than intended.
- Define the scope with the minimum, necessary, and sufficient boundaries to achieve the project objectives. This will help to protect the company's investment and avoid duplication and unnecessary expenditures.
- Ask two qualifying questions to test the necessary of investing in the project. Do I have this capability today? If the answer is *yes*, you might not want to invest in this project. If I do not

add this now, will I lose customers or market share? If the answer is *no*, then put it on the wish list for the future.

- Ruthlessly define the scope.

Plan   Every IT project requires a plan to define the specific day-to-day activities, financials, and resources to be successful. Some key tips in ensuring a successful plan are the following:

- Make sure you have the following key areas well defined: activities, timeline, budget, resources, risk, issue management, risk management.
- Do not approve any project for which budget dollars are not available and/or do not have all required project approvals. Do not fall into the trap of *we have 2/3s of the money and we'll get the rest later.* The project will fail.
- Codevelop the plan with a team knowledgeable in each of the key areas: requirements, design, development, test, change management, quality assurance, release phases, etc.
- Include business teams in the plan development.
- Include milestone reviews and issue mitigation reviews on a regular basis.
- Ruthlessly review the plan and gain agreement from all the key stakeholders.
- Utilize *tiger teams* to review the plan at various timelines to obtain an objective view of the status.
- Document the project plan in a formal document that is signed by all key stakeholders indicating their approval.
- Review the plan on a regular basis with key stakeholders to address status, deviations, and mitigation plan to address any project issues.

Change Management   Change management addresses two key areas that most dramatically impact project success. Every project plan, prior to the start of the first activity, is perfect. Every activity is identified, resources assigned, and costs allocated. Once the clock starts to click away, things happen: requirements are added or modified or moved to other projects. New *rush* demands are placed on the IT organization, budgets scrutinized, and project funding impacted.

Every project needs an effective change management process to provide oversight for any deviations from the original project plan. The second area that impacts project success is the acceptance by key stakeholders and users for the changes in business activities impacted by the project. It is imperative to obtain buy-in from the stakeholders to ensure project success. Some key tips on each of these two areas are as follows:

Changes impacting scope, resource, financial, and timelines

- Utilize a change management process that is well defined, agreed to by all stakeholders, and rigorously enforced.
- Ruthlessly review the plan and gain agreement from all the key stakeholders.
- Document and maintain a change management log that captures all changes, their impact, and resolution activities.

User acceptance of changes for business activities impacted by project

- Include stakeholders in the requirements definition process who will be impacted by the project changes. They provide good input, are a reality check, and can become the goodwill ambassadors for the project.
- Include stakeholders in project reviews to provide status, capture their input, and add reality check to project execution.
- Include stakeholders in process reviews and all testing activities to capture their input. Remember, never ignore the user in project activities. It's the key element that will make or break the successful implementation of the project.

The defined tactics used by the GTA to govern the projects across the 120 state agencies include the establishment of the critical panel review (CPR). The CPR attendees include the state CIO, governance director, state agency business, and IT owner. Project identified as complex and/or critical is reviewed on a monthly basis. The CPR has a defined scope, plan, and change management process that provides the boundaries to identify proactively potential project risk (see the section on "Project Excellence Governance Processes and Metrics" for more detailed explanation).

Guiding Principles: Effective Communication

Effective communications is probably the most underutilized component in executing projects. It is important for communications to be constant, incorporate a 360-degree view of the project, and be realistic. These three components result in effective communication. Also, remember to clearly identifying the benefits that result from successful implementation of the project. Remember, it is all about achieving business outcomes, the common thread everyone latches onto.

Constant   Communications must be constant to be effective. The more you communicate, the more informed your organization. Constant communication helps ensure project status is available to all stakeholders and employees, expectations are set, and issues and mitigation plans are visible to all:

- Develop a communication plan that details the types of communications and timeline used during the project.
- Include a variety of communication techniques including newsletters, e-mail, webinars, town hall meetings, brown bag lunches, and project website. There's no such thing as too much communication.
- Celebrate small victories and include all key constituents. There is nothing better to stimulate additional adrenaline for future activities than to share accomplishments with the core and extended team.

360 Degrees   Communications should include more than just the project team. Many more constituents are affected by the project. Do not forget to make communications bidirectional. Communications is a two-way street. Listening is as important as informing. Make sure you identify the key constituents and include them in the appropriate communications material that keeps them informed:

- Communication is a two-way process. Develop a communication process that provides for 360-degree feedback and includes a listening process to capture feedback from all stakeholders.
- Identify the key constituents and include them in all communications. These include the company executive and

management team, business unit head, department managers, and users of the business processes impacted by the project.

- Include supply chain partners impacted by the project. They have a vested interest if they are impacted by the project.

Factual Successful communications must be realistic. There is nothing worse than surprises. They can deteriorate morale and cripple the momentum of a project:

- Communications should provide complete visibility and transparency for all project-related activities.
- Communicate the mitigating actions to resolve the issue. A problem without a solution sends the wrong message.
- No one will blame you for issues that arise during projects. Issues occur all the time. The way you manage issues is important. Effectively managing issues provides confidence to the project team and stakeholders that project issues will be addressed and resolved.

The critical project review (CPR) panel provides a formal and effective 360-degree communication process for the governance of projects executed by Georgia's state agencies. A more detailed explanation is included in the next section "Project Excellence Governance Processes and Metrics." In addition, there is a governor's panel that reviews those projects deemed to be at risk and most critical in impacting the citizens of Georgia.

Project Excellence Governance Processes and Metrics

Project excellence governance processes and metrics provide the guidelines and metrics used to oversee and manage the governance and execution of projects. Sometimes known as project management, this requires documented processes, which need rigorous administration to be successful (*project management is discussed in more later in this chapter*). If not, the chances for a successful project will diminish. You should also develop a set of governance and execution metrics that provide quantitative measurements. A set of metrics that focus on issue management measures both dimensions. Developing a set of metrics that measure the number and types of issues identified, the number of repetitive issues, and issue mitigation times is a key indicator of process adherence and project execution.

The tactical organization within Tom Fruman's EGAP organization responsible for the day-to-day oversight and governance of projects is the Enterprise Portfolio Management Office (EPMO). Teresa Reilly is the director of this group. Her team's focus is to assist state agencies to achieve project success.

When asked about the objective of the EPMO, Reilly said the following:

> *Our objective is to ensure IT project success and improve the maturity of our project management practices through portfolio management, project assurance, and the development of policies, standards, guidelines. We also provide consulting, education and training in support of our core mission.*[7]

Reilly summarizes her project assurance philosophy as follows: (ibid)

- Project management is a defined discipline, but you need a balanced view of how the project is progressing.
- We need to provide a level of discipline in managing projects to reduce project risk.
- We need to help PMs become more proactive in responding to risks.
- Capturing views of the project from key stakeholders provides a more realistic view of potential project risks.

To achieve their goal, the EPMO employs the following four-step process to provide governance for state agency projects:

1. Capture high-level data for the portfolio of projects identified by agencies as projects for investments.
   a. Agencies provide information on projects they are considering for investment *(project name, objective, investment summary, benefit, business case, etc.)*.
2. Evaluate and identify the subsets of projects and associated data, reviewed by the CPR on a monthly basis.
   a. The CPR provides oversight for projects that are complex and/or critical:

      i. Projects greater than 1 million dollars

     ii. Projects with significant business risk that would impact the citizens of the state, regardless of project cost

  b. The GTA CIO (Calvin Rhodes) is the chair for the monthly CPR.

  c. Attendees include:

      i. GTA Personnel: Calvin Rhodes (Chair), CIO; Tom Fruman, director EGAP; Teresa Reilly, director EPMO

     ii. State agency personnel: state agency PM, state agency business owner, and the vendor PM, if there is one

    iii. A representative from the governor's office

    iv. The independent verification and validation (IV&V) vendor (the GTA contracts with independent consultants (vendors) to conduct project reviews and recommend specific actions to improve project success), a representative from the governor's office

  d. Teresa Reilly's team (EPMO) prepares a projects review book that includes key information for the projects reviewed by the CPR.

  e. Each project team (PM, business owner) presents the project status to the CPR (*approximately 20-minute sessions*).

  f. Projects identified with significant risk are forwarded for a CPR review by the governor's office.

3. Provide education and training to state agency personnel to improve their skills in managing IT projects.

  a. Teresa Reilly's organization (EPMO) includes highly experienced project management personnel who provide training to state agency project teams on the art of project management.

4. Advise state agencies of industry frameworks and best practices to ensure successful project execution.

  a. EPMO personnel have extensive project management experience and provide project teams with a variety of templates and best practices to minimize project risk and improve skills.

  b. Conduct project audits via the IV&V program.

The governance processes instituted by GTA provide the boundaries, processes, and oversight necessary to ensure successful governance of projects. More importantly, this is a proactive versus reactive approach to governance, which identifies potential risk areas predicatively enabling the project teams at the agency and state level to take the necessary actions to mitigate and minimize the impact of project risk.

Project Portfolio

Project portfolio includes all projects executed in the IT organization. The portfolio of projects at the GTA are similar to those of other organizations and can be categorized into three common buckets:

- Sustain projects maintain the business *(help desk, mail, data center, etc.).*
- Operational projects run the business *(applications that support sales, marketing, manufacturing, engineering, finance, human resources, etc.).*
- Strategic projects innovate the business, providing new products and services that drive margin and ROI *(new customer service portal, new product, revamped logistics supply chain, etc.).*

Project Portfolio Management

PPM tools manage the activities, financials, schedules, and resources of the project. There are many *PPM* tools on the market today. Make sure you chose a solution that fits best with your organization's culture, provides the flexibility to effectively manage your projects, and can be easily configured for use. Following are some attributes that should be included in the solution you use (Table 5.2).

Project management is a critical component for project success. It is more important today than ever before. Why? Business units develop new products, services, and processes at a faster pace than ever before. As a result, the IT organization is the recipient of many project requests that need to be vetted for strategic alignment, prioritized, and executed with minimal risk. This is where project management skills take on a more important role than in

Table 5.2   Key PPM Solution Requirements

1. Provide governance for the portfolio of projects regardless of the project management tools used by the state agencies.
   - Each agency selects the tool they use for managing projects. To maintain the federated model used in the state, the GTA needed to find a tool, which would easily provide governance for the state agency projects by easily capturing, analyzing, and displaying data in a dashboard.
2. A solution that isn't overkill for the governance team and agency project management personnel.
   - Initial implementation accomplished in approximately 30 days with configuration occurring in the following 30–60 days.
   - Solution is intuitive and easy to use.
   - Training is not complicated and can be accomplished by company personnel.
3. Web-based solution that provides data to anyone, anywhere, and at any time.
   - Ability to access project and governance data by all personnel from any desktop at any time and from anywhere.
4. Captures qualitative data from key stakeholders to provide 360 degree project perspective.
   - Ability to capture quantitative data from project management tool supplemented with capture of *soft* data from key stakeholders provides a more realistic view of the project and potential risks.
5. Easily import project data into the governance solution.
   - Automated data import from state agency project management tools would eliminate manual and cumbersome effort.
6. Provides effective Issue Management Capability.
   - Capture issues in automated environment, assign issues to owners, and provide issue status updates for all stakeholders to review.
7. Identifies key risk indicators and provide predictive risk scores based upon quantitative and qualitative data.
   - Provide summary metric for key project indicators.
   - Provide the predictive metric regarding future risk based upon quantitative and qualitative data.
8. Improves project manager's skills through self-learning and 360 degree feedback.
   - Project assessments, which measure the key project indicators through a set of questions with a set of answer choices to provide insight to the project managers and implementation teams of the potential areas of risk.
   - Over time these assessment questions become intuitive and part of the daily activities performed by project managers in the execution of projects.
   - Provide the predictive metric regarding future risk based upon quantitative and qualitative data.
9. Displays dashboard metrics of key project indicators and automated reporting.
   - Display key project indicators in dashboard.
   - Provide for qualitative comments for each key indicator.
   - Provide for flexible reporting on key project data.
10. Captures key data for project requests and analyze data based upon business need and potential risk.
    - Easily capture project request data in automated environment to properly analyze investment opportunity for risk and value.

the past. In the past, business units submitted projects to the IT organization. The projects were reviewed and, if approved, executed under the watchful eyes of PMs. IT organizations used a variety of project management tools to provide schedule, cost, and resource information to monitor project status. The role used to be tactical. Today, PMs that are part of a strategic IT organizations partner with business teams. The basic technical skills of project management are table stakes. The real value of a PM today is to work with business teams from the ideation phase through project execution to ensure that the projects, aligned strategically to the business, are successfully implemented and achieve the intended value the project. Following are four key points relative to the role of a PM in a strategic IT organization:

1. The role of the PM is extremely important in today's rapidly changing and information-rich marketplace.
2. The marketplace is changing quickly and companies constantly pursue new opportunities to create and improve customer value and develop new products, as well as new and enhanced services.
3. Today, business units place increased demands (project requests) on the IT organization that need to be executed quickly and successfully.
4. PMs need to develop a set of business skills (business knowledge, process knowledge, communication, vision, and leadership) to effectively partner with business teams from the ideation phase through project execution and value realization. Chapter 10 (Key Competencies and Skills of a Strategic IT Organization) discusses these in detail.

Succeeding at Project and Portfolio Governance

The skill sets required by PMs have expanded to include a whole set of business skills. Just ask Frank Schettini, CIO of the Project Management Institute (PMI). PMI is the world's largest not-for-profit membership association for the project management profession. PMI's professional resources and research empower more than

700,000 members, credential holders, and volunteers in nearly every country in the world to enhance their careers, improve their organizations' success, and further mature the profession. PMI's worldwide advocacy for project management is reinforced by globally recognized standards and certification program, extensive academic and market research programs, chapters and communities of practice, and professional development opportunities.[8]

Schettini speaks frequently on the topic of project management and how PMs need to enhance their skills to become a high-performing PM. Schettini spoke about this at one of the national conferences on program management:

> So, what does a high-performing project manager look like? Technical project and program management are no longer good enough. They're now table stakes. Without a clear understanding of the organizational and business strategy and excellent leadership skills to apply to the myriad of challenges often faced in organizations, a project manager isn't even in the game. They are looking for project managers to help drive the strategy and provide business value to the process, not just administer it. Today's executives are demanding a focus on skills that support their strategy for the next three to five years—not fix the issues of the past one to two years. Looking back makes you only as good as you should have been in the past—similar to what business management guru, Tom Peters, says about benchmarks. Aligning your skills to what your organization needs for the future prepares you to add value going forward.[9]

PMI has a Global Executive Council made up of senior executives, CIOs, and IT personnel from large, Global Fortune 100 companies. Schettini summarizes what the council, other organizations, and governments from around the world identified as the most important skills for today's PM, in addition to technical skills of managing project budget, scope, and schedule:

- Alignment to project objectives to the business strategy
- Integrity
- Ability to influence stakeholders
- Negotiation skills

- The ability to inspire
- The ability not only to understand the objectives and how they map to the business strategy but to communicate it to the entire project team
- Ability to tangibly measure business benefits to ensure realization of those benefits when the project is delivered

Schettini also talks about a Korn Ferry survey that identified the following additional set of critical skills PMs require: (ibid)

- The ability to deal with ambiguity
- Creativity
- The ability to manage innovation
- Strategic agility
- Planning skills
- The ability to motivate others
- A talent for building effective teams
- Being able to manage vision and purpose

When Schettini speaks at conferences, he communicated the importance of these skills using the following graphic (Figure 5.3).

PMs certified by PMI need to complete a prescribed amount of education and training each year to maintain their credentials. PMI certifies courses, seminars, webinars, etc., that PMI members can participate in to maintain their PMI credentials. Schettini says, "during the past few years we are seeing PMI members improving their communication, leadership, and strategic skills to a greater degree

Figure 5.3   Talent Triangle.

than ever before, proving that PMI certified Project Managers are seeing the light." (ibid)

PMI does an excellent job of surveying the business landscape of executives to identify skills needed by PMs. They communicate on a global level to PMI members through regional chapters as well as national and international conferences. Having a PMI certification is an achievement and sends a clear message to the business leadership that PMI-certified PMs today understand that technical project management skills need to be supplemented with business skills if IT and business teams want to partner to successfully execute projects and achieve the business value projected.

Chapter Summary

Projects fail for many reasons. I have identified some at the beginning of this chapter. Most everyone will agree that a 20%–30% project failure rate is not out of the norm. Major causes of project failures are bad communication, lack of planning, poor quality control, etc. To minimize risk and increase the probability of project success, you need an effective governance framework.

An effective governance framework has four components:

1. Guiding principles
2. Project excellence processes and metrics
3. Project portfolio
4. PPM solution

Guiding Principles

Guiding principles provide the overall guidelines for managing projects:

- *Visible leadership* focuses on the following three key roles that are required for effective project governance: executive sponsor, business owner, and IT executive.
- *Defined tactics* address the boundaries of the project, the execution/control activities, and stakeholder issues resulting from changes to business processes. The three components are scope, plan, and change management.

- *Effective communications* is probably the most underutilized component in executing projects. To be effective, communications needs to be constant, incorporate a 360-degree view of the project, and be realistic. Make sure you clearly identify the business benefits that are linked to the project. Remember, it is all about achieving business outcomes. Everyone will latch onto this common thread.

Project Excellence Processes and Metrics

Project excellence processes and metrics provide the guidelines and measurements used to oversee and manage the governance and execution of projects. Make sure the processes are rigorously defined and administered. Utilizing the best PPM tool could influence project success if not governed by project excellence processes. You should also develop a set of governance and execution metrics to provide quantitative measurements to ensure process adherence and successful project execution.

Project Portfolio

Project portfolio includes all projects in the IT organization and is categorized into three distinct buckets: sustain projects maintain the business; operational projects run the business; and strategic projects innovate the business, providing new products and services that drive margin and ROI.

Project Portfolio Management Tools

PPM tools manage the activities, financials, schedules, and resources of the project. There are many *PPM* tools on the market today. Make sure you chose the one that fits best with your organization's culture, provides the flexibility required to effectively manage your projects, and is easily configured for use.

More detail on the solution used by the GTA to provide an enabling tool to effectively govern their complex project portfolios across 119 state agencies is provided in the following text.

GEORGIA TECHNOLOGY AUTHORITY GEMS SOLUTION

Overall Value

The value of implementing a governance process, enabled with the CAI solution, provided the State of Georgia with strategic and operational value for managing the portfolio of projects executed by state agency personnel:

- The monthly update process is easier than the previous Excel-based scorecard.
- Projects can be evaluated through the proposal stage.
- Projects are evaluated from several project roles versus just the PM.
- Dashboard KPI dials are driven by qualitative and quantitative data.
- Issue tracking automates the reporting, resolving, and closing of issues.
- The tool greatly enhances communication since the PM receives and assesses input from several roles.
- Stage gate questionnaires enhance process compliance.

Data Gathering of Project Data for Governance Analysis

One of the major challenges faced by Reilly's team was the time to capture data, prepare project dashboards, and properly display project status. The CAI solution overcame those challenges. For example, the 80 person-hour manual process of collecting project data from the PMs and consolidating into a presentation package for the CPR now takes only about 4 hours of effort.

PROJECT DASHBOARDS

The project dashboard (see the following figure) provides visual representation of the quantitative and qualitative data that drive the key project indicator gauges to reflect ranges within red, yellow, or green, a benefit they never had before. "Visually displaying the range within each key indicator helps

the project managers and Critical Project Review Panel interpret the degree of risk more effectively than the previous process," says Reilly.

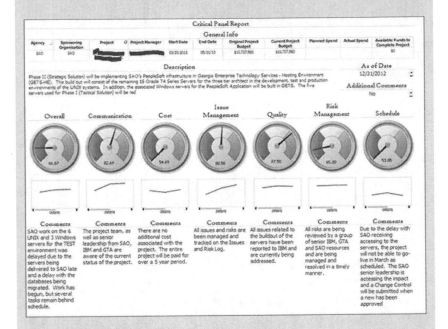

PREDICTIVE ANALYSIS

The CAI solution uses a set of algorithms based upon completed
assessments to predict the potential risk of the project for each
key project indicator. This single capability makes the solution
a proactive process of anticipating risk and taking mitigating
actions prior to the risks occurring.

IMPROVING PROJECT MANAGER SKILLS

Governance is more than just oversight. It should involve improving the skills and capabilities of PMs. People truly learn from
experience. The assessment questionnaires, which focus on risk
categories, are completed by key project stakeholders, providing
a 360-degree view of the project. Over time, PMs intuitively
behave in a manner that addresses these potential risk areas in a
proactive way.

QUANTITATIVELY ANALYZING PROJECT REQUESTS

One of the major benefits is the process of reviewing and analyzing the business value for project requests. An enterprise pipeline report for requested projects was manually prepared using Excel spreadsheets and very time consuming (see the following example):

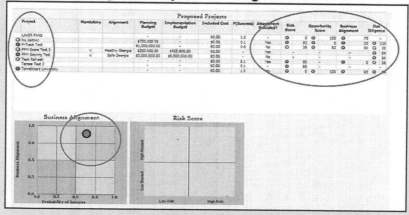

The CAI solution automated the process to prepare. Now the CAI solution provides dashboard data for these requested projects and provides an analysis grid to display the business alignment and risk score for the portfolio of requested projects.

SUMMARY

Georgia's state agencies are reaping the benefits of the CAI solution named GEMS (Georgia Enterprise Management System by the Georgia Technology Agency). Now, project data are imported into GEMS and dashboard data as well as a detailed information are available for all to view in real time. Analysis of key project indicators is available to the critical panel for review of all the complex and critical projects. Most importantly, the solution uses algorithms to predict the degree of potential risk for each key indicator. This feature makes the solution a more proactive versus reactive solution.

The GEMS project dashboard provides visual representation of the quantitative and qualitative data to drive the key project indicator gauges to reflect ranges within red, yellow, or green, a benefit they never had before. Knowing the range within each color helps the PMs and critical review panel interpret the degree of risk more effectively than the previous process.

With an average of 200–450 million dollars of projects to govern each year, the state can now look at ways to improve project success. They now have a solution that can minimize risk, improve governance, and improve project success.

Therefore, if your organization is experiencing project assurance and portfolio governance challenges and is not willing to accept a 25%–35% project failure rate as an acceptable norm, heed the lessons learned from GTA. Learn how they applied a solution to minimize risk, improve project management skills, achieve project success, and most importantly provide value to the citizens of the state.

Citations

1. Calvin Rhodes-CIO, State of Georgia/Phil Weinzimer Telephone Interview, February 4, 2013.
2. Gartner Survey Shows Why Projects Fail, Analyst: Lars Mieritz. Published: June 1, 2012, ID:G00231952/http://thisiswhatgoodlookslike.com/2012/06/10/gartner-survey-shows-why-projects-fail//June 10, 2012.
3. Project Failure Statistics and Facts, Michael Wood, September 26, 2008, PM Hut./http://www.pmhut.com/project-failure-statistics-and-facts.

4. Bensemhoun, D., Chartrin, C., and Kropf, M. Tackling the roots of underperformance in IT, Copyright 2011 McKinsey & Company; http://www.mckinsey.com/insights/business_technology/tackling_the_roots_of_underperformance_in_banks_it.
5. J.C. Penney Apologizes in Ad Developed Under Former CEO. Bloomburg News; By Matt Townsend May 2, 2013; http://www.bloomberg.com/news/2013-05-01/j-c-penney-apologizes-in-ad-developed-under-former-ceo.html.
6. Calvin Rhodes-CIO, State of Georgia/Phil Weinzimer Telephone Interview, March 5, 2013.
7. Tom Fruman, Director of EGAP/Phil Weinzimer Telephone Interview, February 11, 2013.
8. Teresa Reilly, Director, Enterprise Portfolio Management Office (EPMO).
9. PMI Website; http://www.pmi.org/About-Us.aspx.
10. Frank Schettini, CIO, PMI Institute/Phil Weinzimer Interview, December 19, 2013.

6

How to Measure and Improve the Business Value of IT Service

Improving the value of services is all about understanding what the business is trying to accomplish and express it in business terms everyone can understand. It's not about the technology of the service, but the value the service provides the business[1]

Rebecca Jacoby
CIO, CISCO

Improving the business value of IT services is a goal every CIO strives to achieve. Accomplishing this objective requires a process to assess, analyze, improve, and monitor the business value IT services provide the enterprise. Following are the objective, key points, and examples used in this chapter.

A. CHAPTER OBJECTIVE

1. Reinforce the importance of providing business value through the delivery of IT services
2. Share a framework and associated process for assessing the business value of IT services delivered to the business
3. Examine a process IT organizations can use to assess and identify the maturity of the business value for IT services you deliver to the business

B. KEY POINTS

1. CIOs must communicate the business value IT services provide the business.
2. CIOs need to assess how well IT services provide business value as well as measure how efficiently each IT services is executed.
3. There is a process CIOs can use to measure the effectiveness and efficiency of IT services.

C. EXAMPLES

• Synopsys, Cisco, American Financial

D. TEMPLATES

1. Strategic Framework to Improve Business Value of IT Services

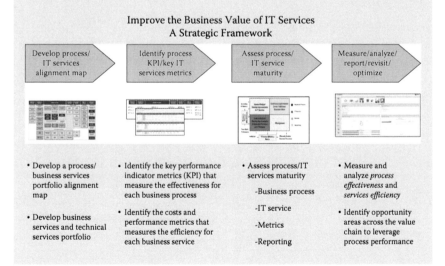

Improve the Business Value of IT Services
A Strategic Framework

Develop process/ IT services alignment map	Identify process KPI/key IT services metrics	Assess process/ IT service maturity	Measure/analyze/ report/revisit/ optimize
• Develop a process/ business services portfolio alignment map	• Identify the key performance indicator metrics (KPI) that measure the effectiveness for each business process	• Assess process/IT services maturity	• Measure and analyze *process effectiveness* and *services efficiency*
• Develop business services and technical services portfolio	• Identify the costs and performance metrics that measures the efficiency for each business service	-Business process -IT service -Metrics -Reporting	• Identify opportunity areas across the value chain to leverage process performance

Business unit executives cringe every month when they receive their monthly statement from the information technology (IT) organization, in the form of IT bill or chargeback, which identifies the information costs associated with their business unit. The statement usually arrives via email or in hard copy and consists of many pages of data, usually represented in columns and rows, using terms such as router costs, data center costs, server costs, maintenance costs, terabytes, virtual servers, all of which business people don't understand very well. It is difficult for business executives to align these cost items to the services they receive and business processes they perform, let alone the value they generate. Most executives recognize that IT is a necessary cost of business and just accept the charges without much fanfare. As one business unit vice president said to me, during one of my book interviews, "It's just not worth the time to discuss this. I'm going to get hit with this charge anyway."[2]

If your business peers view your IT organization as a techno-centric cost center, and not as the value based provider of services, you need to pay close attention to the rest of the chapter. This can really help you transform the way the business views IT. Communicating the value of IT services to business unit vice presidents is a key component for building a trust-based relationship with your business peers. Unless you can accomplish this, your IT organization will forever be viewed as the cost center where technical stuff happens versus a strategic partner where IT personnel partner in business teams to create significant and measurable business outcomes. If your IT organization enables business value and you cannot communicate in a way that business personnel understand the value, your IT organization will be misperceived as a cost center. The challenge is to communicate value in business terms. The objective of this chapter is to define a process you can use to communicate and improve the business value of the IT organization.

Many business units managers view IT organizations as cost centers and not the value generators, which they really are. This is the challenge for every CIO. One CIO from a Fortune 500 company said to me, "The business just doesn't understand that the information technology organization supports the business processes that drive the company. The business defines the business processes; IT enables the processes leveraging information technology."[3] What is a CIO to do in order to change the misconception of the IT organization? The answer is simple. The objective is to change the perception of IT from a technology provider to that of a services-oriented organization that helps the business create sustainable value. The pathway to accomplish this is to clearly map the IT services, associated costs, and value derived by the business units in performing their activities, across the enterprise value chain.

The first step is to educate the business community about how IT supports the business. How does a CIO handle this challenge? During a quarterly update meeting with business unit executives, Tom Grooms, the CIO of Valspar, reviewed the quarterly IT activities and the goals and objectives for the remainder of the fiscal year. One of the first slides was on IT challenges. There was only one bulleted sentence. It read as follows:

• Educate the Business in How IT Services Provide Business Value

The next slide identified the ways IT provides business value (Figure 6.1).[4] As you read the slide, think about how generic the statements are and how you can use this to help communicate the various ways your IT organization provides value to the business.

Communicating the intent to help the business understand the value of the IT organization is a good beginning. Actually demonstrating how IT services provide value is an entirely different challenge.

Valspar, the global coatings company with 10,000 employees in 25 countries, hired Tom Grooms as the new CIO in January 2012. Grooms had a challenge. The business viewed IT services as a free service. IT costs were included in the coprorate cost pool that was allocated to the business. The business never thought about IT as a cost, but just a department ready to serve the needs of the business.

How IT Services Provide Business Value	
Business environment	• Business Processes Across the Enterprise Value Chain Create Customer Value, Drive Revenue/Margin, Enhance Shareholder Wealth • Key Performance Indicators Measure the Effectiveness of Business Process
IT environment	• IT Provides a Set of Business and Technical Services that Support Business Processes • Key IT Service Metrics Measure the Efficiency of Business Services
Challenge	• How to Measure the Impact that Business Services Have on Adobe Business Processes • How do Analyze Process and Business Service Performance to Identify Opportunities for Improvement that Drive Business Outcomes

Figure 6.1   How IT Services Provide Value.

IT received numerous requests, always exceeding the supply of resources to perform the work. The culture in the IT organization was to figure out a way to get it done. IT personnel would never say *no*. It was the rule for IT. Of course, other work had to shift, and the daily routine in IT was trying to figure out what to work on first, what to move into the future, and how to satisfy the increasing demands from the business.

Grooms changed all that. With a strong experience-based philosophy on collaborating with the business and providing value-based solutions, he embarked on a program to change the mindset of how the business viewed the IT organization. He realized that he needed to figure out a way for the business personnel to view IT as an enabler of business value and that the services IT provided to the business have to provide measurable value at a designated cost. In other words, just like any other business investment, IT expenditures require a business case. His objective was to help the business understand how the IT supports and enables the business processes that drive value to Valspar customers. In order to do that, Grooms, and his IT teams, continuously worked with the business to understand the business value of the requests for IT services. This meant developing a business case for each IT request. In addition, Grooms needed to make sure that business requests benefited the company as a whole and not just a single business unit. For example, a division manager requested an enhancement to a service used to support a process used by his plant in Chicago. The sister plant on the West Coast was fine with the current process. In the past, IT would approve the request from the Chicago plant. Grooms conducted some research and found that the enhancement would only benefit the Chicago plant, and not any of the other sister plants manufacturing the same products. So Grooms said *no* to the Chicago general manager, explaining that there was no overall Valspar value to the enhancement.

Slowly, the business began to understand that IT services link to the supported business process. Grooms started asking a set of questions when the business requested enhancements or new services: "Why is the investment necessary? How will this help Valspar? Are you committing to the savings/revenue projected in your business case?" These were all perfectly legitimate questions. Slowly, the business started to think differently about IT. They realized that these were legitimate *business questions* and that Grooms' organization was trying to help ensure that IT investments for services required by the business were viewed as any other corporate investment, thereby enhancing the process and business performance.[4]

Methodology Framework to Improve the Value of IT Services

Following is a framework you can use to develop a strategy to improve the value IT services delivered to the business.[5] The methodology consists of the following four phases. Each of the four phases are explained in more detail following the graphic depicted in Figure 6.2.

- Develop process/IT services alignment map
- Identify process KPI/key IT services metrics
- Assess process/IT services maturity
- Measure/analyze/report/revisit/optimize

Develop Process/IT Services Alignment Map

In an earlier chapter, we discussed the need to develop a portfolio of business services to deliver basic services exceptionally well. To help your business leaders understand the value of the IT services delivered to their business units, you need to map the IT services to the business processes their organization utilizes to perform their

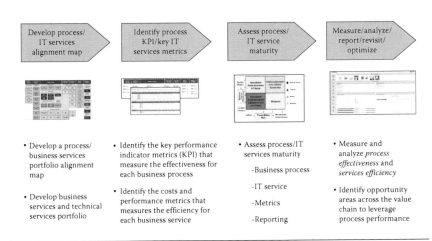

Figure 6.2   Improve the Business Value of IT Services—a Strategic Framework.

work activities. Following is a process you can apply and modify as appropriate.

The process is simple.

1. Revisit the working documents you used during the process of developing IT services where you met with the business unit executives and their team.
2. Schedule a follow-up meeting with each business unit team to review and identify the work activities, by major process, performed by the business unit.
3. Review the list of business services provided to the business units and map the services to the business process. You can accomplish this in a working session with a whiteboard and flip charts.
4. Document the working session results and send it to the business unit team to validate.
5. Consolidate the mappings from each business unit team into an enterprise process/IT services map. Review for duplications and errors and modify accordingly.
6. Meet with business leaders, and their teams, to review the consolidated mapping and modify as necessary.

Figure 6.3 is an example of a process/IT services alignment map.

Identify Process KPI/Key IT Services Metrics

How often have you heard the phrase, *you cannot manage what you do not measure?* How effective a process and a service perform is no exception. You cannot objectively evaluate the performance of a process or a service if you do not have any measurements goals. The measurements can be based upon the effectiveness (business value derived) or efficiency (How quickly the service is delivered). However, each provides a different dimension of performance. The performance of a business process is all about achieving a defined outcome. The performance of an IT service is how efficiently the service performs.

Key performance indicators (KPIs) are quantifiable measurements you can use to measure the performance of a business process.

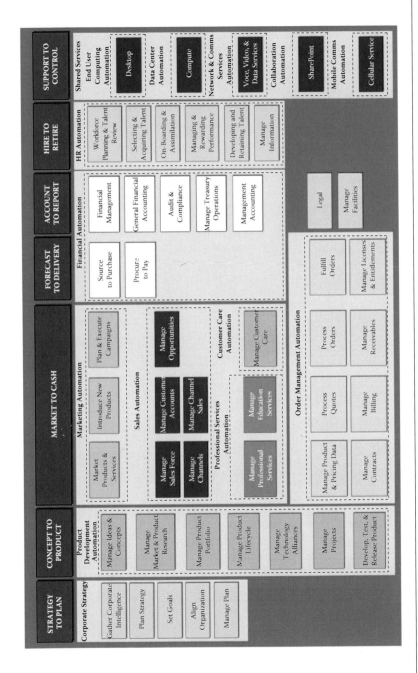

Figure 6.3 Key Processes Aligned to Business Services—Example.

STRATEGY TO PLAN	CONCEPT TO PRODUCT	CONCEPT TO CASH	FORECAST TO DELIVERY	ACCOUNT TO REPORT	HIRE TO RETIRE	SUPPORT TO CONTROL
KPI A-1	KPI B-1	KPI C-1	KPI D-1	KPI E-1	KPI F-1	KPI G-1
KPI A-2	KPI B-2	KPI C-2	KPI D-2	KPI E-2	KPI F-2	KPI G-2
KPI A-3	KPI B-3	KPI C-3	KPI D-3		KPI F-3	KPI G-3
		KPI C-4	KPI D-4			KPI G-4
			KPI D-5			

Figure 6.4 Key Processes and Associated KPI—Template.

Service metrics measure the performance of the technology that supports the process. Let us look at a customer order process as an example (Figure 6.4).

The objective of a customer order process is to enable customers to order your company's products or services. Customer satisfaction, ease of use, and flexibility of entering orders are examples of business process outcomes. Number of incidents, downtime, problems, wait times, and mean time to repair are measures of how well the technology supports the process.

Metrics can measure time, quality, quantity, cost, and customer satisfaction. Following are a few simple guidelines to follow when choosing metrics:

1. Choose metrics that make business sense.
2. Don't choose a metric that you can't measure.
3. Keep it simple.
4. Develop metrics that follow the SMART principles (specific, measurable, actionable, relevant, and timely).
5. Don't be a slave to the metric. That is, do not expend more effort to collect the metric than the value it provides.

Figure 6.5 (Monthly Financial Summary Report—Data Center) is an example of a report that measures monthly performance metrics of the data center. The report shows, by month, the planned versus

Summary | Financial Summary | Chargeback | Cost Model | Direct Cost

Fiscal Year: [FY2010 ▼]   Export

Cost Summary

	January	February	March	April	May	June	July	August	September	October	November	December	Year to Date Total	Total
Cost Model	Data Center Facility Cost Model #01	Data Center Facility Cost Model #01	Data Center Facility Cost Model #01	Data Center Facility Cost Model #01	Data Center Facility Cost Model #01	Data Center Facility Cost Model #01	Data Center Facility Cost Model #01	Data Center Facility Cost Model #01	Data Center Facility Cost Model #01	Data Center Facility Cost Model #01	Data Center Facility Cost Model #01	Data Center Facility Cost Model #01		
Planned Cost	$297,148.31	$297,148.31	$297,148.31	$297,148.31	$297,148.31	$297,148.31	$297,148.31	$294,648.31	$297,148.31	$297,148.31	$297,148.31	$297,149.54	$594,296.62	$3,565,280.95
Actual Cost	$308,538.90	$295,587.90	$298,038.90	$298,373.90	$296,908.90	$297,913.90	$297,938.90	$297,766.90	$296,888.90	$295,528.90	$299,388.90	$281,567.90	$604,126.80	$3,564,442.80
Variance	($11,390.59)	$1,560.41	($890.59)	($1,225.59)	$239.41	($765.59)	($790.59)	($3,118.59)	$259.41	$1,659.41	($2,240.59)	$15,581.64		

Consumption Summary

Unit of Measure	January Named Users	February Named Users	March Named Users	April Named Users	May Named Users	June Named Users	July Named Users	August Named Users	September Named Users	October Named Users	November Named Users	December Named Users	Year to Date Average
Planned Consumption	435	440	446	456	462	462	473	475	478	480	488	495	437.5
Actual Consumption	433	0	0	0	0	0	0	0	0	0	0	0	216.5
Variance	2	440	446	456	462	462	473	475	478	480	488	495	

Unit Cost Summary

	January	February	March	April	May	June	July	August	September	October	November	December	Year to Date Average
Planned Unit Cost	$683.10	$675.34	$666.25	$651.64	$643.18	$643.18	$628.22	$620.31	$621.65	$619.06	$608.91	$600.30	$679.22
Actual Unit Cost	$712.56	$0.00	$0.00	$0.00	$0.00	$0.00	$0.00	$0.00	$0.00	$0.00	$0.00	$0.00	$356.28
Variance	($29.46)	$675.34	$666.25	$651.64	$643.18	$643.18	$628.22	$620.31	$621.65	$619.06	$608.91	$600.30	

Figure 6.5 Monthly Financial Summary Report—Data Center.

actual costs, consumption, unit cost, and variance. This is a summary report. Supplemental reports provide more detailed information about the business units usage history. These types of reports provide a basis for a business dialogue between IT and the business units as to the usage and value derived from the data center. A business service should have a financial profit and loss (P&L) statement. You need to measure the planned versus actual costs since IT costs are part of an overall budget.

There are many sources available to help identify the right metrics your organization should use. ITIL is a good place to begin.[6] There are also many websites that provide helpful information.[7]

Assess Process/IT Service Maturity

Once you have identified the business processes and mapped them to their relevant services, you can assess the process and the service based upon the metrics identified. The process to accomplish this is simple (Figure 6.6):

1. Form a team comprised of IT and business unit personnel to develop an assessment instrument you can use to capture the objective data, as well as the subjective data from service stakeholders for each IT process as well as the IT services group that supports the process.
   a. For each process you want to measure, develop a set of three to five questions that assess the effectiveness of the process.

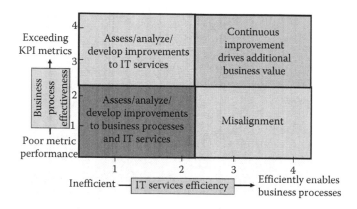

Figure 6.6 Process/IT Services Maturity Grid.

The scoring would be 1–5. A score of 5 reflects a high effectiveness in terms of KPI's being achieved and a score of 1 would reflect a process where the KPI's are on the low end of the scale. Similarly, you would develop a set of three to five questions to measure the efficiency of the process on a scale of 1–5. A score of 5 would indicate that the process is very efficient and a score of 1 would indicate that the process is very inefficient.

I would suggest that the assessment be performed by IT personnel as well as business personnel so you have a 360° view of the process. It will be interesting to see the disparity between how IT personnel rate the process and how business unit personnel rate the process.

2. Use weighted algorithms to develop a score for each process questions as well as IT service questions.
3. Plot the scores on the maturity grid.

Following is an example of results plotted on the maturity grid for a customer order process (Figure 6.7):

a. The total weighted average for the questions measuring the process is 2.8.
b. The total weighted average score measuring the efficiency of the IT services is 0.9.

As you can see from the scoring, the process scored fairly well but the IT service scored very poorly. The implication is that the customer

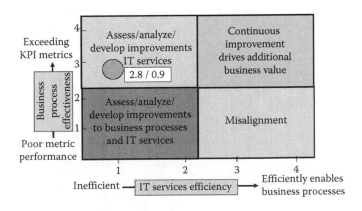

Figure 6.7   Process/IT Services Maturity Grid—Example.

order process works. The process exceeds the KPIs established. However, the delivery of the service is very inefficient, as indicated by the score of 0.9. The IT organization needs to meet with the business process owner to understand the issues that create the inefficiency. Perhaps the customer service screens are overly complicated, creating some confusion when servicing customers. Perhaps customer service representatives may be spending more time than necessary servicing a customer. Whatever the issues, it is important to understand them, analyze them, and improve them.

Measure/Analyze/Report/Revisit/Optimize

The maturity grid provides an initial indication of the process effectiveness and process efficiency. To truly understand the issues associated with the process and/or service performance, you need to peel back the onion and analyze the process and the service in more detail.

Saama Technologies is a services company headquartered in Campbell, CA, that provides data science solutions focused on solving the data management and advanced analytics challenges of the world's leading brands. For CIOs, they provide dashboard solutions using their opsSENSE solutions suite that portray data in meaningful ways. Figure 6.8 includes some examples of dashboards Saama has created. The data are for demonstration purposes and do not reflect any client confidential information. "CIO dashboards presented in a meaningful way can really influence business results," says Jitender Nankani, the principal for Solutions at Saama Technologies.[8]

One of their clients, a global e-commerce business, was challenged to reduce transaction costs and grow topline performance. To analyze their business required intense manual efforts to provide the visibility for executives into health initiatives, budget forecasts, project roadmaps, and other data to ensure an alignment with engineering operations. Many different data sources and systems required individual interfaces to retrieve raw data, which was subsequently massaged and aggregated manually. "There was no real-time analysis, historical reference checks, ease of use interface, or an integrated system to provide actionable insights," says Murali Krishnam, practice area leader for Big Data Solutions at Saama Technologies.[9]

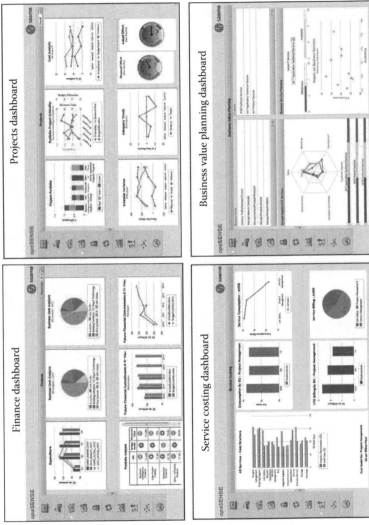

Figure 6.8 Saama Technoloiges CIO Dashboard Example.

Saama implemented their opsSENSE solution framework to measure, monitor, manage, and optimize the clients' engineering operations. The goal was to enable decision makers at various levels, from knowledge workers to executives, to get the right visibility into day-to-day operations to drive, prioritize, and rationalize the strategic decisions toward improving the company level KPIs.

Saama cites impressive results that were achieved by the implementation of opsSENSE:

- Reduced run and managed cost of maintaining engineering operations analytics by 50%
- Increased speed of decision making by 33%
- Improved financial clarity by providing visibility from an initiative to project level
- Enabled confident decision making by leveraging a validated and trustable data set
- Faster time-to-value for operational excellence through automation
- Interfaced with nine different data sources, validated, integrated, and fed information into the leadership dashboard

Debra Martucci is the CIO and vice president of Information Technology for Synopsys, the two billion dollar plus company, located in Mountain View California. It is a market leader in electronic design automation (EDA), providing products and services that accelerate innovation in the global electronics market. Martucci spends a lot of time analyzing data and trends associated with financials, IT expenses, operations, staff projects, and security. "The data was all over the place. I needed a single source to capture pertinent data and display it in a way that provides trend analysis to highlight where I need to focus for any area that was out of acceptable range."[10] Martucci contracted with Saama Technologies to design and build a CIO dashboard. "The 42-inch Monitor is prominently displayed on the wall outside Martucci's office for everyone to see," says Mark Sutherlin, the senior IT analyst involved in the project.[11] The digital dashboard displayed outside Martucci's office is a visible reminder for all personnel of the key IT metrics. Accessible online personnel from across the company can access the dashboard. "It's really helped us gain the trust of the business," says Sutherlin. (ibid) The dashboard includes six tabs for each of the key

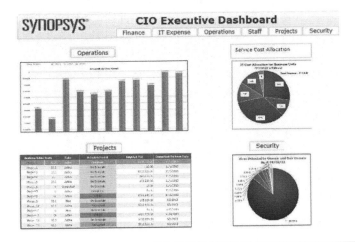

Figure 6.9   Synopsys CIO Dashboard—Example (Data Sanitized).

areas Martucci considers key to the success of IT. They are finance, IT expenses, operations, staff, projects, and security (Figure 6.9).

Martucci attends an executive staff meeting every week. One of the documents she brings to the meeting is the weekly report of key data from the dashboard. At the meeting, she updates the key executives on the IT performance and the value provided to the business. The weekly report is also provided to IT management, who share it with their IT teams. Martucci is pleased with the dashboard approach to communicating IT value. "It helps me in three ways. First, it enables me to spot trends and areas I need to focus on immediately that otherwise would slip through the cracks. Second, it provides complete transparency of IT across the business. Third, it improves our relationship with the business in numerous ways through open communications. Our goal is to support the business and help business teams create products and services that innovates value for our customers."[10]

As discussed earlier in the chapter, it is important to develop a process/service alignment mapping in order to measure the cost of IT services as they relate to the business processes they enable. One of the biggest challenges facing CIOs today is to measure the value of IT and communicate that value to business leaders in a language they understand. Most IT organizations measure the technical aspects of IT: servers, MIPS, data center costs, networks, etc. Financial reports capture these costs, which are then allocated to the business using a variety of methods. Unfortunately, business leaders don't understand these costs as they relate to the business units they manage. As a result, they reluctantly accept these charges and continue to ask, "What is the value of IT to my business unit?" The problem is that IT does not correlate these metrics into business language.

Simply stated, key business processes are the vehicle that provides business value. Information and technology enable these business processes to function properly. Order entry processes capture order data, logistics processes move materials throughout the value chain, customers use customer service processes to interact with the company representative, Internet and mobile processes communicate with customers, etc. Information and technology are the enablers of business processes, and a method to measure how information and technology provide value to the business is necessary in today's information-centric enterprise.

Up until a few years ago, there was no solution available on the market that IT could use to communicate the business value of IT from a services perspective. A few companies tried their hand in developing a solution for this issue. The one that seems to lead the pack now is Apptio.

Sunny Gupta and Paul Mclachlan cofounded Apptio in 2007. McLachlan, the CEO of Apptio, was named Ernst & Young Entrepreneur of the Year in 2012 and had 20 years of enterprise software experience with roles in general management, strategic marketing, product management, and business development. McLachlan, the CTO of Apptio, had 15 years of software architecture experience, prior to cofounding Apptio, and spent more than a decade building performance and troubleshooting tools for Java and .NET, first at Compuware and NuMega Technologies and more recently at Mercury Interactive and HP, where he was the chief architect of the Diagnostics Component of Business Availability Center and LoadRunner.

Apptio is the independent software-as-a-service leader in technology business management (TBM), a new category, and discipline backed by global IT leaders that helps clients understand the cost, quality, and value of the services they provide to the business users. Apptio created the category (TBM) and is the clear leader because of their comprehensive approach.

The Apptio TBM Suite provides an integrated set of cloud-based applications enabling IT leaders to run the business of IT. Clients who use Apptio TBM solutions achieve deep visibility into the total cost of IT services and can communicate the value of IT to the business through an interactive Bill of IT™, strategically aligning the planning, budgeting, and forecasting processes. Apptio's TBM solutions play a critical role in helping companies understand and drive chargeback, virtualization, cloud, and other key technology initiatives (Figure 6.10).

Chris Pick is the chief marketing officer (CMO) for Apptio. He understands marketing, especially for software solutions. Prior to joining Apptio in 2009, he was an operating partner in Austin Ventures' CEO-in-residence program where he focused on identifying new growth strategies and defining disruptive business models. He was also the CMO and vice president of products at NetIQ for 8 years and ran Ernst & Young's Global security practice for 4 years.

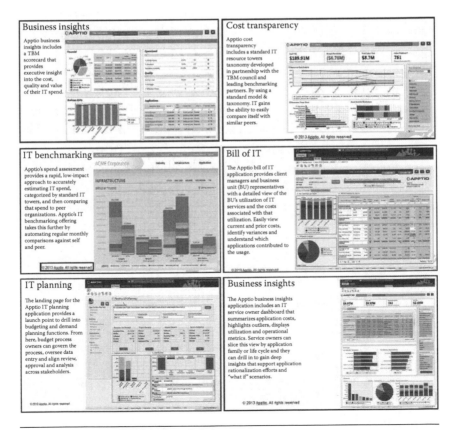

Figure 6.10   Apptio TBM Solution—Overview.

Apptio walks the talk. With 175 customers served in the Fortune 1000 space, Apptio is well on its way to becoming the business management solution of choice among CIOs. Cisco, Bank of America, Conway Freight, Exxon, First American Financial, J.P. Morgan Chase, Farmers Insurance are just a few of the recognizable names Apptio has as clients. The following two client examples show how using Apptio TBM solutions provided clear measurable value in a few short months[12]:

> Cisco's CIO, Rebecca Jacoby was having *"...difficulty in categorizing associated with assembling technologies together to deliver a capability to the business"* and also *"...wanted to show how that cost related to the value we were delivering to the business."* By implementing one of Apptio's solutions Cisco's top 25 service owners prepare and present a balanced scorecard to the business users. As Jacoby describes it, *"this has changed the value conversations regarding technology at Cisco."*

> Larry Godec is Senior Vice President and CIO at First American Financial. Godec was aware that *"...the firm's IT portfolio was beginning to swell with redundant systems, but he couldn't identify the specific unnecessary applications."* Using Apptio's TBM solution enabled Godec and his team to have visibility into IT costs and performance. Now, Godec can communicate the value of First American's core title and escrow system that runs on a single database instance. Godec says, Apptio's TBM solution *"helped me break down the cost by division and show them the value of the core system."*

Meeting the needs of its customers is an important strategic objective. To achieve this goal, Apptio established a TBM council, with Pick as president, to ensure that CIOs have a voice in identifying requirements to run IT as a business. The council, created in 2012, includes 500+ members focused on creating the professional discipline, standards, and industry benchmarks required to run IT as a business. The council is documenting the discipline in a TBM book that will help facilitate benchmarking by business technology leaders against those practices.[14]

Larry Godec, the CIO of First American Financial, summarizes the need to communicate the business value as follows: "Our business partners must understand what they are consuming, how much it costs, and what choices they have to better balance cost, performance, risk and other qualities?" (ibid)

Chapter Summary

Improving the business value of IT services, and communicating its value to the business, is a critical component for a strategic CIO to succeed in gaining credibility with the business. In this chapter, we have

- Identified a four-step framework for assessing, analyzing, measuring, and communicating the business value of IT services
- Reinforced the need to measure the maturity of your key business processes
- Discussed the use of an assessment framework to help you measure the effectiveness of business processes as well as the efficiency of how well IT delivers services to enable those processes
- Highlighted a CIO dashboard used by Synopsys as well as a solution from Apptio that addresses Technology Business Management (TBM), a new discipline created by Apptio

The key messages of the chapter are as follows:

- CIOs must communicate the business value IT services provide the business.
- CIOs need to assess how well IT services provide business value as well as measure how efficiently each IT services is executed.
- There is a process CIOs can use to measure the effectiveness and efficiency of IT services.

Citations

1. Rebecca Jacoby, CIO Cisco/Phil Weinzimer Interview, December 7, 2012.
2. Anonymous Business Unit VP/Phil Weinzimer Interview, December 14, 2013.
3. Anonymous CIO/Phil Weinzimer Interview, April 12, 2013.
4. Tom Grooms, CIO-Valspar/Phil Weinzimer Telephone Interview, April 26, 2013/Modified slide from CIO presentation to business unit vice-presidents, quarterly update.

5. Developed by Phil Weinzimer, Strategere Consulting; 2013.
6. ITIL website; http://www.itil-officialsite.com.
7. Various websites where you can research various metrics your organization can use to effectively measure monthly performance. http://www.itil-officialsite.com/, http://www.on-demand-itsm.com/ITSM-Metrics-That-Matter_8-13-09_v2.pdf, http://simplicable.com/new/ITIL-guide (November 2012), http://www.prosci.com/metrics.htm, http://www.klipfolio.com/resources/kpi-examples-top-call-center-metrics.
8. Jitender Nankani, Director-Consulting, Saama/Phil Weinzimer Telephone Interview, February 28, 2013.
9. Murali Krishnam, Practice Area Leader, SaamaTechnologies/Phil Weinzimer Interview, March 6, 2013.
10. Debra Martucci, CIO Synopsys/Phil Weinzimer Interview, November 1, 2013.
11. Mark Sutherlin-Senior IT Analyst, Synopsys/Phil Weinzimer Interview, November 4, 2013.
12. Chris Pick-CMO, Apptio/Phil Weinzimer Interview, December 12, 2013.

7

SECTION OVERVIEW

Understand the Business, Focus on User Experience, and Improve Business Skills of IT Personnel

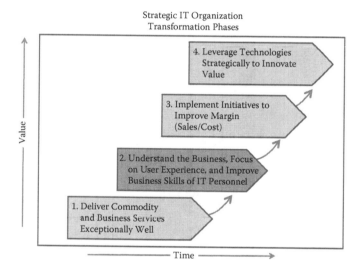

Strategic IT Organization
Transformation Phases

Newly appointed CIOs, who are hired from outside the company, will tell you that assessing service delivery, understanding the business, and IT personnel competencies and skills are three of the most important to-dos for the first 100 days on the job. As stated in Chapter 1, the first two phases of the IT Strategic Transformation Phases are most often implemented in parallel.

It is extremely important for CIOs and key IT executives to have a keen understanding of how the business operates on a day-to-day basis, the competitive environment, and where value creation occurs across the value network, which encompasses customers, distribution channels, company personnel, sourcing partners, etc. With this knowledge, CIOs and key IT personnel can identify potential value creation opportunities. For CIOs, it is equally important to assess the organization culture, as well as the competencies and skills of IT personnel to determine gaps that would inhibit the effective partnering with business teams in analyzing, identifying, and implementing solutions that achieve business outcomes.

Following are the key questions each chapter will address.

Understand the Business, Focus on User Experiences, and Improve Competencies and Skills of IT Personnel: Chapters 8 through 11

Following are the key questions each chapter will answer:

Chapter 8: Why CIOs Need to Understand the Business to Succeed

- Why is *understanding the business* important to the success of the CIO?
- How will *knowledge of enterprise business processes* help the CIO partner more effectively with C-suite executives?
- What are the *different ways CIOs learn about the business*? (Six CIO examples)

Chapter 9: The Importance of Understanding Your Organizational Culture in Building Effective Teams

- What is *the importance of organization culture* to the success of the IT organization?
- What are *the differences between the four orientation cultures*: collaboration, control, create, and compete?
- Is there a *right or wrong culture* for your organization?
- How can you *assess the organization culture* of IT personnel?

Chapter 10: Key Competencies and Skills of a Strategic IT Organization

- What is the *difference between a competency and a skill*?
- What are the *four key competencies and associated skills* of a strategic IT organization?
- *Why are these competencies and skills important* in building a collaborative and trust-based relationship with business executives and business teams?

Chapter 11: How to Measure and Improve the Maturity of the Strategic IT Competencies and Skills of Your IT Organization

- Why is it important to *measure the strategic competencies and associated skills* for your IT organization?
- How to use a *four-step process to measure* the strategic competencies and skills of your IT organization?
- What are the *various types of maturity assessments* you can use for your IT organization?
- What is an *example of an IT strategic maturity assessment, with templates,* that can be used to measure the strategic maturity of your IT organization?

8

WHY CIOs NEED TO UNDERSTAND THE BUSINESS TO SUCCEED

CIOs need to understand the needs of the business if they are to truly leverage technology in innovative ways.

James Schinski
Vice President and CIO, PP&L Corporation

Every strategic CIO will tell you that knowing how your company operates on a day-to-day basis is a prime requirement if you want to be successful. Your company, as well as others, operates across a complex value chain composed of business processes that include company, customer, supplier, and distribution channels. Each of these channels involves one or more process activities that develop, market, manufacture, deliver, and service the products and services your company provides customers. If you are a CIO who wants a seat at the executive table, you must understand the activities associated with business processes across the entire value chain, their interrelationships with complementary processes, and the associated information touch points. If you do not, you will fail. It is as simple as that!

Following are the objective, key messages, and examples used in this chapter.

A. CHAPTER OBJECTIVE

1. Reinforce for CIOs and key IT personnel the need to understand how the business operates, the value provided to customers, the competitive market, and industry trends.

B. KEY POINTS

1. A strategic CIO will not be successful without a well-based understanding of how the business operates.
2. The depth of understanding includes knowledge of the key processes across the entire value enterprise.
3. CIOs move into the role from the business, within IT, from other companies, in similar or dissimilar industries.
4. CIOs learn about the business in different ways, depending on experience.

C. EXAMPLES

1. CIOs and IT directors share their experiences in learning about the business.
   - Mike McClaskey, CIO, Dish Network
   - Scott Blanchette, CIO, Vanguard Health
   - Steve O'Connor, vice president and CIO, CSAA Insurance Group
   - Niel Nickolaisen, CIO, Western Governor's University
   - Kevin B. Michaelis, vice president, Global IT, and CIO, Air Products and Chemicals
   - Greg Lewis, IT director, Ironclad
2. Training Tomorrow's business leaders and CIOs
   - Dick Brandt—Director, Iacocca Institute—Global Village

Strategic CIOs attain the role from different paths. One path could be from within the company either from the IT organization or from one of the business units. Other paths could be from a company within a similar industry or different industries, with or without an extensive IT background. Regardless of the path, the CIO needs to understand the company business strategy, competitive market, and industry trends. How CIOs gain business knowledge, depending on their background and path to their current role, is the subject of this chapter. Following is a brief summary of how the CIOs discussed in this chapter learned about their company.

Mike McClaskey, CIO at Dish Network, has deep technical knowledge, which he fine-tuned at Perot Systems. Dish was looking for a CIO with strong technical skills, and McClaskey was a good fit. McClaskey hit the ground running when he joined Dish Network as part of a working team focused on reengineering business processes. His orientation into the Dish business model and associated activities, via the reengineering project, provided a solid understanding of the business activities across the entire value chain. McClaskey was recently promoted to Executive Vice President, Human Resources at Dish Network.

Scott Blanchette, CIO at Vanguard Health, learned IT through self-study and a variety of senior IT positions, leading up to the CIO role, at various companies in the health care industry. Vanguard hired Blanchette because his vision to transform health care companies from a sick-care to a well-care provider was exactly what executive management desired. However, Vanguard's business model was different from the companies Blanchette had worked for previously. Blanchette held in-depth meetings with management teams from all the business units to learn how business is conducted on a day-to-day basis.

Steve O'Connor, CIO at CSAA Insurance Group, is a highly technical and experienced CIO. With a background of working for software development companies, O'Connor developed a four-step process for learning about the insurance business at the company as well as gaining knowledge in the insurance industry, an area in which he had had no prior experience.

Nick Nickolaisen, former CIO Franklin Covey is a rare breed of business executives that attain the CIO role because they complain so much about IT that the CEO appoints them as CIO to stop the nagging and complaining. The CEO's strategy, in this scenario, is to provide the business executive the opportunity to lead the IT organization and fix the IT problems the business complains about. This is exactly what happened to Niel Nickolaisen, when he was vice president of operations at Franklin Covey, later promoted to CIO after much complaining. The challenge facing Nickolaisen was an IT organization who knew that he constantly complained about IT. Additionally, IT personnel never interacted with the business, so Nickolaisen needed to help IT personnel transform IT into a business-focused organization.

Kevin Michaelis, vice president of Global IT and CIO at Air Products and Chemicals, Inc is a new breed of CIO who was promoted to the role from the business. His career at Air Products spans 20-plus years and his experience leveraging his chemical engineering degree in various positions within the business, leading to vice president of the Liquid Bulk and Generated Gases business in Europe. Tapped as the CIO in 2012, Michaelis already knew the business but had no line experience in IT. He understands the need to provide superior customer service based upon his previous business unit roles. In his new role as CIO he initiated a global initiative to provide an improved experience for Air Products customers by leveraging IT.

Greg Lewis, IT Director, Ironclad Performance Wear, is a bright young database expert, with good interpersonal skills and business acumen, who helped Ironclad emerge from an archaic information systems infrastructure into a more modern information-based business. Start-ups with nonsoftware development products face a difficult IT challenge. With limited funds, these companies focus on investing in products, sales, and marketing. IT investment is limited. Even as they grow, there is minimal investment in IT. Such is the case with Ironclad Performance Wear, founded in 1998, which is a leader in developing task-specific worker gloves. Their IT infrastructure was outsourced. They hired an IT director in 2011. Previously, the company hired outside consultants, who built a series of independent databases, developed custom reports based upon management requirements, and never really understood the business. Lewis needed to learn about the business as quickly as possible so he could help improve the inefficiencies that hampered the growth of the company.

Another avenue for the CIO role is the young college educated graduate who is early in his/her working career and has a desire to work hard and one day be promoted to a role in the C-Suite. Today's college graduates, who start their careers at the bottom of the hierarchical ladder, are the future CFOs, CEOs, COOs, and CIOs. Learning about business during their early years in business is invaluable in developing the business skills that will propel them to successful professional careers. The Iacocca Institute at Lehigh University, in Bethlehem Pennsylvania, recognizes the need to train our future leaders of business and industry. The Global Village program is an intense five-week program where approximately 100 interns (young managers from companies all around the world) learn about business. Started in 1997, the program graduated over 1600 participants from over 50 countries. The program is unique, inspiring, and promotes a camaraderie among participants through a worldwide network of Global Village graduates.

The methods used by IT leaders to learn about business vary. Each of the examples used in this chapter provides insight into how IT leaders learned about the business. For CIOs to be strategic, they need to understand how the company operates on a day-to-day basis. These examples are a great source for those who might still be struggling with concerns about taking on the role and challenged with how they will learn about the company's day-to-day business operations. Each of these examples provides a successful process for learning about the business. Read on, enjoy the read, and leverage the learning.

Mike McClaskey: Dish Network

Sometimes, a company is looking for a seasoned CIO who has deep-rooted technology experience in turning around IT departments with archaic and unaligned architecture and arm-length relationships with the business. This was the scenario for Dish Network when they were looking for a new CIO in 2007. Dish was in the middle of a customer relationship management (CRM) implementation that was not going well. The IT infrastructure was a mess and the credibility of the IT organization with the business was not good. Mike McClaskey was the perfect candidate. Dish Network hired him as CIO in 2007. Not only did he fit in culturally, but also had the perfect technology background. McClaskey spent the prior 12 years at Perot Systems as the vice president of Infrastructure Solutions and CIO. His responsibilities included IT strategy and managing the operating customer-facing data centers. At Perot Systems, outsourcing was the main service provided to clients. During his time at Perot Systems, McClaskey always worked with client infrastructure environments that were generally not in good shape.

In the outsourcing business, it's like dealing with sick patients in the emergency room. You have to develop a quick response triage process. In IT parlance, we had to rapidly evaluate the client infrastructure and provide an environment that will perform to the service levels identified by the client.[2]

The IT environment that existed at Dish was not one many strategic CIOs would want to encounter. However, for McClaskey, it was perfect. "I wasn't afraid of what I would find. I had the experience and brought with me a set of diagnostic capabilities I developed at Perot Systems. I had experienced these types of environments for twelve years previously." (ibid)

When McClaskey arrived at Dish Network, he needed to quickly diagnose the infrastructure problem, understand the Dish business, and succeed at some quick wins. His strategy was "…to accomplish this quickly so I could build a ladder of trust with the Dish management team." (ibid)

To address the infrastructure problem, McClaskey applied the similar triage process he used at Perot:

1. Rapidly evaluate infrastructure
2. Evaluate personnel in IT to identify triage team
3. Assess infrastructure, applications, and processes to identify challenges, gaps, and opportunities

McClaskey and his triage team focused on identifying the infrastructure issues that disrupted business operations and created an atmosphere of distrust between the business and the IT organization. "We identified some major issues, focused our energies on the problem, and addressed the major problems."[5] The IT organization moved to a service-oriented IT architecture, improved the release process of application enhancements to provide value to customers more quickly, and dramatically improve operational stability of the infrastructure that reduced downtime, help desk calls, and rework. McClaskey built the first few rungs of his *trust ladder*.

In parallel to the basic blocking and tackling activities to improve the infrastructure issue, McClaskey also needed to learn about Dish: How the business operated? How Dish interacted with customers? How customers interacted with Dish? What were the competitive market issue and challenges? These and other questions needed answers if McClaskey was to develop an IT strategy that would leapfrog Dish to the front of the competitive marketplace.

McClaskey found the perfect source for discovering how Dish Network conducted business on a day-to-day basis: his COO. One of the COO's first major efforts was a business simplification initiative. McClaskey describes the initiative as follows:

> Our COO wanted to analyze the business from different perspectives across the value chain and dig into the business processes, rules around flows, acquiring customers, performing services for a customer, etc. The scope of the business simplification initiative involved all the major work processes at Dish. We conducted deep dives on existing business rules and processes, resulting in changes and cleanups to the processes and associated rules with the goal of simplifying, often through consolidation, sometimes but not always requiring IT changes.[3]

The COO wanted McClaskey to be part of the business simplification team. The reason was simple. IT enables most all of the business processes. Involving IT as part of the process made business sense. McClaskey's timing was perfect. Here he was, just starting out at Dish and figuring out ways to find out about the business. Of course, he met with business unit heads and other Dish employees to learn about how Dish conducted its day-to-day business operations. At that level, you only get the 20,000-foot view. You do not have the time to dig into the process details. McClaskey wanted to understand the business at a more granular level. As a member of the business simplification team, he could roll up his sleeves, get his hands dirty, and understand all the business processes that made the Dish Network tick.

Personnel from marketing, sales, service, IT, and other areas of the company participated in the working sessions. The business simplification teams analyzed business processes from across the value chain. These processes included those encompassing the back office, customer service, marketing, sales, and other organizations. Everyone participated on an equal level, regardless of position or title. The team members dissected the processes using whiteboards, sticky notes, and a variety of other techniques to identify opportunities that would result in a more simple process and still provide value to the business.

The initiative was a 2-year effort but continued afterward using continuous improvement to tweak and improve processes.

> I learned a huge amount about the business. We spent grueling hours, which encompassed days and weeks of effort, getting into the details of how business processes work, how data is captured, recorded, processed, and reported. It was a painful but very rewarding process. (ibid)

In parallel with the business simplification initiative, Mclaskey was actually experiencing customer processes. He experienced three different processes in real time.

> I spent days in a call center wearing a headset and listening in on customer service calls sitting aside a customer service agent. I also spent days in a truck with an installation technician, including a snowy, below-zero day watching our technician install the satellite dish atop a customer's roof and interact with the customer during the installation process. In addition, I spent time at our satellite uplink installation where our giant 10-meter dishes link to satellites distributing the video products customers receive through their dishes. (ibid)

The ability to experience the processes firsthand and interact with customers by spending time with customer service representatives, sales personnel, and service technicians was invaluable. He participated in sales meetings and was able to observe firsthand the sales process at a potential customer's home. When he accompanied a sales person to a potential customer's home, he participated in conversations discussing Dish products and services and was able to listen to the questions asked by the prospective customer as well as observe the body language. "There is nothing that replaces experiencing an actual customer interaction. It creates a visual that can never trump the written word," says McClaskey. (ibid)

The business simplification initiative enabled Dish to improve their business processes, one-at-a-time, using a methodical approach. About halfway through the 2-year initiative, it was evident that some of the customer-facing applications as well as workforce applications were disjointed, inefficient, and hindered the company's growth plans. This was the birth of McClaskey's business transformation initiative, which included a complete overhaul of the billing, customer care, workforce management, and telephony systems. He developed credibility with the management team, through his involvement and contribution to the business simplification project, and was confident the project would be successful. The multiyear project encompassed hundreds of business and IT personnel and logged over 1.5 million hours. The most critical moment of the project was when Dish had to cut over to the new system. McClaskey did hold his breath for a few minutes as they flipped the switch on the evening when 14 million subscribers moved onto the new platform without any major issues. This major initiative was delivered on time and within budget.

The business transformation initiative would not have been successful had McClaskey not learned about the business from the ground up, as part of the business simplification project. Not only did Dish management applaud his efforts in leading the initiative, but he was also recognized by the Enterprise CIO Forum as Transformational CIO of 2012 and by the Denver Business Journal as CIO of the Year in 2013, in addition to numerous recognitions for his team.

Scott Blanchette: Vanguard Health

I am sure you often hear the expression "Experience is the best teacher." I remember a conversation with my brother, Mel, six months after he graduated with a master's degree in electrical engineering and started his first job at an aerospace company. After 4 years of study at Brooklyn Polytechnic Institute, in Brooklyn, New York, for his undergraduate degree in electrical engineering and 2 years of study for his master's degree, he was amazed at how little he really knew when it came down to applying his learning in designing radar systems. Mel said, "The electronic technician I work with knows so much more than me. However, after thinking about it, I realized that the technician had 15 years practical experience working with electronic missile systems." My brother realized that improving skills occurs only when you complement your education with practical experiences.

In business, experience is the best teacher. The wisdom of experience is the path Scott Blanchette decided to pursue, and it paid off handsomely. Blanchette is CIO of Vanguard Health and the MIT Sloan CIO Symposium winner of the 2013 CIO Leadership Award.

Blanchette pursued a career in the military until he suffered an injury in 2000. "When I left the military, I did not know what I wanted to do. I had an undergraduate degree in history with a minor in engineering, and a master's degree in military history and operations management. I was well-educated but poorly skilled."[4] To help him apply the practical experiences from the business world, Blanchette started as a consultant for a professional services firm and worked on a variety of projects that focused on IT in the health care industry. This experience provided him with a foundation for experiencing the practical side of business and seeing how people from different companies address day-to-day challenges. After a few years of consulting, Blanchette wanted to learn more about the health care industry, so he took a position at Stanford Medical Center in the IT organization. With a focus on learning through practical experience, he quickly took on more responsibility in security, infrastructure, and operations. He also had the opportunity to work with the CEO on IT issues. It was during this period that he improved his technology skills as well as a practical knowledge about the health care industry. It was obvious to him that one of the major issues facing the health care industry was their focus. Health care providers were focusing on sick care versus well care. So in 2006, Blanchette moved to Healthways as CTO. Healthways, Inc, with headquarters in Nashville Tennessee, provides a variety of well-care solutions to health care providers. In 2007, Blanchette moved into the CIO role where his IT organization applied analytics to identify health risks from the 100 million filed claims. The goal was to "improve the health and well being of people by proactively identifying recommended courses of action to improve health. As a result, we worked with business teams to developed 22 products, which identified a variety of well being health recommendations health care providers can use to recommend well care to their subscribers based upon their medical profiles." (ibid)

In 2010, Blanchette worked on a Healthways–Vanguard Health team to pursue joint ventures. Vanguard Health operates over two-dozen acute care and specialty hospitals and complementary facilities and services in the metropolitan areas of Chicago, Illinois; Phoenix, Arizona; Detroit, Michigan; San Antonio, Texas; and Boston,

Massachusetts. Both companies thought synergies could be achieved by working together. The executives at Vanguard were so impressed with Blanchette that they offered him the CIO job in 2011. The key executives at Vanguard wanted to fundamentally change their focus from sick care to well care, and they needed a visionary who could work with their management team to turn their vision into reality. It was a perfect fit for Blanchette and Vanguard.

When Blanchette arrived at Vanguard to take on the CIO role, he needed to accomplish three major objectives. The first was to understand how Vanguard conducted business on a day-to-day basis. The second was to evaluate the basic services delivered to the business and determine if the business was satisfied with the level of service provided by the IT organization. The third was to start working with business executives to help transform the vision of the executive management team from a sick-care to a best-in-class well-care provider.

To accomplish his first two objectives, understanding how Vanguard operated on a day-to-day basis, and assess IT services, Blanchette scheduled meetings with the business unit vice presidents and their direct reports. He would start each meeting by explaining his background and his vision for health care. He went on to ask three questions to begin a dialogue. What are the major business processes and underlying activities performed? How do personnel in your business unit interact with other business unit personnel in performing their jobs? How well satisfied are you with the performance of the IT organization in supporting the needs of your business unit?

Business unit executives and their key staff provided Blanchette with a detailed explanation of how their business unit operated on a day-to-day basis and how their personnel interacted with other business unit personnel. In most cases, multiple meetings were required to provide Blanchette the level of detail he wanted. After about two months of meetings, he gained a great deal of knowledge about Vanguard's day-to-day operations.

Blanchette was pleasantly surprised about the reaction of the business leaders to his third question as to the level of services provided by the IT organization. Most business units were not very happy with the level of service from IT. Help desk support was poor. Application downtime was unacceptable, and business unit personnel felt as though the IT organization did not really care that much about providing quick, accurate, and quality service. However, although the business unit executives and key personnel were very dissatisfied with the level of service, they were delighted that the executive responsible for the IT organization was speaking to them about the level of service from the IT organization. "They told me that this never happened before." (ibid) Although disappointed that the level of service required his immediate attention, Blanchette was pleased that his first interactions with business unit executives and managers were positive and he was building a solid beginning of trust-based relationship.

During the time Blanchette was meeting with business leaders, he also worked closely with his executive manager, Bradley Perkins, MD, chief strategy and transformation officer at Vanguard, to understand the business strategy. Perkins joined Vanguard in 2009 from the Center for Disease Control, where he served as chief strategy and innovation officer. Perkins's role, as described on the company's website, was to "accelerate Vanguard's transformation to compete more successfully in the rapidly changing health and health care environment."[5] Blanchette and Perkins shared a common vision. They could complement their industry knowledge and health care backgrounds to help reshape Vanguard to adapt to the changing health care competitive landscape. As a result of working with Perkins, he understood Vanguard's vision and roadmap for changing the culture, underlying values, and path the company needed to pursue to reshape the health care industry. It was a perfect fit for each of them.

Blanchette was positioned for success. He had a good working knowledge of how Vanguard operated as a business. He understood, through his meetings with Perkins, Vanguard's business vision and strategy. He knew what he had to fix in IT to provide dramatically improved service to the business units. He could now begin to fix IT and accomplish his third objective, working with business executives to leveraging IT and transform Vanguard from a sick-care to a best-in-class well-care provider.

Moreover, he did succeed. The MIT Sloan CIO Symposium Awards Committee presented Scott Blanchette with the 2013 CIO Leadership Award. Dr. George Westerman of MIT's Center for Digital Business, cochair of the Award Program, said, "Scott distinguished himself from a very strong group of finalists by his exceptional leadership and vision, and his stewardship over a wide range of achievements, from the IT back office to new IT-Driven, to improve the speed and quality of health and health care services."[6]

Steve O'Connor: CSAA Insurance Group

Sometimes, a CIO takes on the role with a company in an industry that he/she has no experience in. Such is the case with Steve O'Connor when he accepted the role of CIO at CSAA Insurance Group. The company sells automobile, home, and life insurance products to AAA members in 23 states.

The CEO was looking for a CIO with deep and broad technology and business experience who could leverage IT to improve business performance and support a rapid growth strategy. O'Connor had the right experience. His technical experience included holding almost every role within IT. He is one of those leaders who are not afraid to roll up his sleeves and work with his IT teams to get things done. He is not a micromanager. He manages boundaries effectively, leading IT teams to accomplish the tasks. He has a great reputation as a leader, coach, mentor, and business partner. He held various IT leadership and management positions at Sun Microsystems, Cullinet Software, and Silicon Graphics. He was also the founder of ITM Software. When BMC Software acquired ITM, O'Connor managed the IT business management product line. He attained a JD degree after college to improve his communications and logic skills. The CEO and the board believed O'Connor was the perfect candidate for the CIO position.

O'Connor knew that he needed to learn about the insurance industry in a methodical manner. Prior to his current role, most of his background was in software products sold to a variety of companies in different industries. He never worked for an insurance company before, and if he was going to make a significant impact on the company, he needed to develop a process for learning about the company as well as the insurance industry. O'Connor realized that his learning would not be a 90-day event. Rather, it would be a continuum.

There is no short cut to learning. You have to dedicate a substantial amount of time in learning. If you did not take on the CIO role from the business side, there is no short cut to investing time. Knowledge about the company and insurance business is a puzzle. There are puzzle pieces that have to fit together to create the body of knowledge I need to be productive in this position.[7]

After some thought, O'Connor developed the following four-step process for acquiring knowledge about the company and the insurance industry:

1. Meet with business unit executives and key staff to understand how they conducted business as well as identify the IT services provided by the IT organization.
2. Dedicate time, on a regular basis, for self-learning through literature and industry journal subscriptions.
3. Learn about the industry from subject matter experts.
4. Understand the rules used in the IT systems that support the business processes.

*Meet with Business Unit Executives and Key Staff to
Understand How They Conducted Business as well as Identify
the IT Services Provided by the IT Organization*

O'Connor scheduled meetings with the vice presidents of each business unit, including their staff. His goal was to "Introduce myself to each business unit vice president and key staff members. Understand the major business process they perform. How their mission aligns with the overall business strategy. Find out what services they utilized from the information technology organization, and how the value of the services supported their business unit goals and objectives." (ibid)

The meetings were valuable not only to O'Connor but also for the business unit executives and their staff. Understanding the business processes provided a foundation for how personnel from each business unit worked with each other to create value for its customers. Listening to the business unit goals and objectives and their alignment to the overall company strategy helped O'Connor piece together how each business unit contributed to the overall business strategy. When asked about the services each business unit uses from the IT organization, some of the answers were interesting. One business unit vice president said, "I don't use any of your stuff." O'Connor followed

up with the following question. "Do your personnel use computers, email, voice mail, video conferencing, etc.?" The vice president
responded, "Sure we do." In response, O'Connor said, "Well, these
are all IT services that we provide your organization. I'm interested
in understanding how effective these services are and if you have any
suggestions on how to improve them." O'Connor needed to educate
the business units so they could understand some of the basic services
provided by IT that keep the business running day after day. (ibid)

The business unit meetings helped O'Connor understand the business, learn about the improvements in IT services the businesses
need to improve their performance, and begin building a relationship
and partnership with business leaders to work together to grow the
business.

*Dedicate Time, on a Regular Basis, for Self-Learning through
Literature and Industry Journal Subscriptions*

The second piece of the puzzle was self-education. O'Connor blocks
out three hours per week to self-educate. He reads publications, books,
blogs, and other materials to help him learn about the insurance
industry. He also subscribes to the NACD Weekly Reader (National
Association of Corporate Directors). The association helps executives
expand their knowledge on board matters by updating subscribers on
emerging issues, new policies, and leading board practices, all with
the goal of improving the board performance. O'Connor also reg-
isters for webcasts that provide information on the insurance industry. One such webcast was J.D. Power's, The Changing State of the
Insurance Industry, which focused on auto insurance. As O'Connor
says, "self-education is a discipline. You have to be focused, persistent,
and continue to devote the time to it. There are no short cuts." (ibid)

Learn about the Industry from Subject Matter Experts

One of the executives at CSAA Insurance Group is a career insurance executive. "He has probably forgotten more about the insurance
industry than I'll ever know. Before each meeting, I prepare a set of
questions to help me gain a broader and deeper understanding of our
business and the insurance industry specifically. He provides great

insight based upon his experience to help me understand the nuances of the business." (ibid)

O'Connor also recognizes that the insurance industry is part of the financial services sector. He meets with the CFO on a regular basis. Insurance companies invest the premiums they collect. The interest and gains on these investments supplement the insurance claims paid and provide a source of income for the business. "Understanding how we make money on the insurance premiums we collect is an important element of learning the financial levers that drive our business." (ibid)

O'Connor also meets with industry subject matter experts whenever he can to increase his knowledge about the insurance business. Gaining insights of these experts provides valuable lessons, based upon their experiences, which you do not acquire from publications and textbooks.

Understand the Rules Used in the IT Systems that Support the Business Processes

Another perspective of the learning continuum is to delve into the IT application that supports the business processes. Using the knowledge attained during the meetings with business unit executives and their staff, O'Connor spends time each week digging into these applications. The process he uses is to roll up his sleeves and work with the IT teams to help him understand the business rules used by the application to support the business processes. "This process really helps me understand the business processes. For example, the policy administration and claims administration application embeds all the rules of how the insurance industry operates." (ibid) Following this method for all the major applications helped O'Connor learn about the business and the insurance industry.

When you do not have any experience in the industry, learning about a business is a painstaking process, but necessary if you want to succeed. O'Connor followed his four-step process to learn about CSAA Insurance Group as well as the insurance industry. With an understanding of the business, he could then begin working with his C-level peers to improve IT services and begin the planning process to enable the aggressive growth plan for the company. After about six months, O'Connor developed an IT strategy for the company. When asked about the discipline it takes to learn about the business, he says, "As a new CIO, if you didn't come from the business side, there is no short cut to investing the time needed to learn about the company, the industry, and the competitive market." (ibid)

Niel Nickolaisen: Western Governor's University

Johann Wolfgang von Goethe (1749–1832) is the most famous for writing *Faust*, the famous German play. What most may not know is that he also authored the phrase "Beware of what you wish for in youth, because you will get it in middle life."[8] Over the years, people have modified the phrase to "Be careful for what you wish for, you just might get it." Niel Nickolaisen started his career on the business side and was appointed CIO after complaining about the inefficiencies of the IT organization to the CEO at Franklin Covey, where he was vice president of operations.

Nickolaisen served in the US Navy from 1983 to 1991. During his service, he obtained his BS in physics from Utah State University and a master's degree in engineering from MIT. In 1991, he embarked on his journey in private enterprise with a position as an engineering manager at GE. This is where he worked on many process improvement projects and learned about how business operates on a day-to-day-basis. His next job was as vice president of operations at Franklin Covey. His focus was on process improvement. He observed that many systems supporting the business were homegrown and very inflexible. "I did everything to optimize processes without systems support. I informed management that I could further improve processes if we had the support of the information technology organization."[9]

Nickolaisen recalls the day he had a very frank discussion with the CEO.

> I reiterated my frustration with the IT organization and its lack of support in improving business processes. I said that to him, "you have to do something about IT." The CEO responded with "I just did" I then asked him what he meant by that. And he said, " I just made you CIO." (ibid)

Nickolaisen faced three very difficult tasks as the new CIO. First, he had 100 IT employees who probably hated him. Second, he needed to learn about IT. Third, he needed to understand how IT supports the business. His first order of business was how to deal with the IT staff, which was aware of his criticism of their organization. He realized that one of the basic principles of management is that most people want to do a good job. One major obstacle confronting personnel is they may not have the skills and competencies needed to perform the job. Another obstacle is that some people are great technicians and promoted to a manager position, which they cannot perform effectively. In addition, others may not excel at their technical skills but have great communication and interpersonal skills. Nickolaisen approached the problem as follows: "I didn't know what they did. I didn't know anything about IT. I decided that I'm going to assume I was wrong about them and I'm going to prove they are wrong about me." His first order of business was to communicate this to them in a series of meetings with his staff as well as IT town hall meetings. (ibid)

His next order of business was to educate the IT staff on how Franklin Covey operated the business.

The IT organization was always very isolated and never interacted with the business. Nickolaisen is a very process centric manager. He started taking his staff to meetings with all the key business unit heads and staff. His objective during these meetings was to have the business unit identify any issues with the services delivered by IT, as well as to identify the services required by the business unit to improve their performance. These meetings were very successful.

> The business unit managers and staff were brutally honest about the service they received from IT. This was the first time IT personnel met with their internal customers. It was an enlightening experience for them. It shook them up a bit and softened them. I told them after the meetings, we blame and fix processes, not people. Our task is to fix the processes and I'll help you succeed. So, let's get better at fixing the processes. (ibid)

During the next few months, Nickolaisen worked with the IT teams to improve the services the business identified as critical to their performance. During that period, he made some personnel changes. In the past, technical performance was the basis for promotion.

Unfortunately, some of these managers did not have the managerial skills for the job. Niel Nickolaisen created two career paths in IT with appropriate financial compensation. The first was the technical route and the second was the managerial path. "I took people from the middle of the IT organization and made them leaders because they had skills. People displaced from leadership roles, were bruised and unhappy, but realized, after a period, that they performed better in their technical role." (ibid)

During his role as CIO at Franklin Covey, Nickolaisen learned much about managing an IT organization and bridging the gap between the business and the IT organization. IT personnel learned about the business by interacting on a regular basis, the business found value in the IT organization, due to its improved performance, and IT personnel realized that Nickolaisen was a good manager. In fact, of the 100 IT staff Nickolaisen inherited, only four left the company.

Kevin B. Michaelis: Air Products and Chemicals, Inc.

Air Products and Chemicals is a global $10 billion chemical and gas company with 22,000 employees headquartered in Allentown, Pennsylvania. It provides gases, chemicals, equipment, and services to a vast array of industries around the globe. It is the world's largest supplier of hydrogen and helium. The company has built leading global supply positions in growth markets such as semiconductor materials, refinery hydrogen, coal gasification, natural gas liquefaction, and advanced coatings and adhesives.

Kevin Michaelis is vice president of Global IT and CIO at Air Products and Chemicals, Inc. He is a veteran Air Products executive. With a BS in chemical engineering and MBA in finance, he started his career in Air Products as an engineer and quickly moved up the ranks through the business leading to his role as vice president of the Liquid Bulk and Generated Gases in Europe.

Air Products prides itself on a management team that is well versed in all aspects of the business. This is achieved through a management rotation program where key personnel manage different areas of the business. Michaelis was tapped to become CIO from his European assignment running the Liquid Bulk and Generated Gases business after the previous CIO, also a business leader, moved into another role. Management wanted to continue the practice of IT leadership with a business-oriented executive. Michaelis explains this management strategy. "The advantage of having a businessperson lead IT is that it provides business input and tightens the gap between IT and the business. This helps Air Products executives better understand IT and helps bridge the gap between IT and the business."[10]

As vice president of the Liquid Bulk and Generated Gases business in Europe, Michaelis understands the need to provide superior customer service through every interaction. Bulk gases are delivered to customer sites. One of the first business initiatives supported by Michaelis is the Enterprise Platform Renewal program.

The objective is to provide a "richer customer experience leveraging technology." (ibid) When bulk gases are delivered to the customer, the initial point of contact is the truck driver. Previously, the driver delivered the gas and moved on to the next delivery. Now the role is completely different. The driver becomes the point of contact with the customer and provides a 360-degree view of the customer user experience.

When the driver transfers the bulk gas from the truck to the customer, he or she uses a handheld mobile device to initiate a number of transactions:

- Transfers the inventory from finished goods to the customer
- Automatically triggers the accounts payable function and prints the invoice on site
- Communicates a service request for a valve leak, tank leak, and repair request directly to a customer service representative
- Automatically triggers a message to the sales person for the account

The advantage for the customer is one point of contact. "The customer doesn't have to hunt through his rolodex to find the number for sales, customer service, or repair. Everything is handled through the delivery driver. The drivers are now effectively our extension of our customer service department." (ibid)

Part of the rollout included extensive training for the drivers to take on the new role. Interacting with customers is an important role, and Air Products wanted to help the drivers interact with customers providing a one-touch-point experience. Michaelis says, "Customers reaction has been positive and pleased with the higher level of service." (ibid)

IT and business teams working together to provide a superior customer service experience improves customer satisfaction, improves customer retention, and drives business growth. This is a great example of innovative executives and employee teams working together and leveraging technology to create new business value.

Gregg Lewis: Ironclad Performance Wear

Emerging product consumer companies sometimes do not have the financial resources to invest in a full-blown IT organization. They invest in product development, marketing, and sales as their core and outsource their IT needs. Such is the case with Ironclad Performance Wear, the brand leader in technical task-specific performance work gloves. The company, founded in 1998, is headquartered in El Segundo, California. Ed Jaegar, the founder of Ironclad, developed the idea of task-specific work gloves, while on a job site in 1998.

> I noticed that each person had very expensive task-specific tools that they needed in order to get the job done, but also realized that none of these people were wearing gloves. Being curious, I asked the guys around the jobsite why they weren't wearing gloves and all of their answers were similar. "I can't use the gloves that are available because they're too bulky. Sure they protect my hands, but they are hot, I can't feel my tools, they only come in one size and they basically get in the way of me doing my job."[11]

The idea of developing task-specific worker gloves was born when Jaeger realized he used motorcycle gloves when he worked at construction sites. Jaeger grew up riding motorcycles and the industry designed gloves for specific bike types (dirt bikes, road bikes, off racing, etc.). Motorcycle gloves "fit snug and are basically an extension of your hand. I realized that there was a huge disconnect between the worker and their most important tool-their hands. They needed a glove that protected their hands and helped them get the job done." Jaeger's idea was to "...build a glove that offered protection and performance, but sacrificed neither. I also wanted to create a brand that these guys could be proud to wear, a brand that would stick with them through thick and thin, and a brand that was built solely for them." (ibid)

Today, Ironclad sells about 80 distinct types of gloves all over the world. The gloves "...cater to the specific demands and requirements of industrial, construction, do-it-yourself, and sporting goods consumers, including carpenters, machinists, package handlers, plumbers, welders, roofers, oil and gas workers, mechanics, hunters, gardeners and do-it-yourself users."[12]

Ironclad imports all its products from Asia. As a result, IT needs to focus mainly on supply chain components (vendor orders, order status, shipping information, shipment receipts at US ports, warehouse, distribution, etc.), sales channels, customer orders, and company financials. The entire infrastructure is outsourced, and the information systems used to manage the business, prior to 2012, were a set of databases, which were not connected. A part-time information systems consultant managed all the information needs. When the sales manager needed a specific report, he would sketch out the requirements and ask the systems consultant to generate the report. The systems consultant, although technically competent, did not have an understanding of the business and provided everything asked for. The consultant never engaged in a dialogue with the managers concerning what they needed or why they needed it. As you can imagine, there were a plethora of reports, based upon individual requests from management personnel. The business grew rapidly, and in 2011, management recognized they needed a full-time employee with business and technical skills to direct the IT needs. In June 2012, Ironclad hired Greg Lewis as its full-time IT director.[13]

Lewis graduated from UCLA in 2000 and learned about IT and business during the next several years while working for a variety or companies. Lewis honed his technical skills and learned about managing people and understanding business processes at Docufide, a leader in electronic transcript (eTranscript) exchange, which enable individuals and educational institutions to collect, promote, and share their education credentials in simple and secure ways. As operations manager, Lewis coordinated and supervised automated processing of customer documents, including handling all failures and exceptions. At Perr & Knight, an actuarial consulting firm, he was manager—competitive intelligence—and used his database, technical, and business skills to help double division sales and increase productivity by 25%. While at the Housing Authority of the City of Los Angeles (HCLA), he managed a quality control department and property listings department. His team revamped some of the business processes to improve productivity by integrating pen and paper audit processes with a proprietary online database system.

Lewis employed a three-step strategy upon taking on the IT role at Ironclad. He wanted to *observe* to learn and understand the business; *analyze* the business processes, enabling technology and systems to determine alignment to business needs; and *implement* a plan to leverage IT to improve business performance.

During the first few weeks, Lewis met with the CEO, COO, CFO, and VPs of sales, marketing, and R&D. Each provided him with an overview of the business, how they operated their organizations, and the information needs required to fuel the projected rapid growth of the company. His next step was to dig into the various databases to determine what information is captured, how information is stored, the relationships of the various databases, and the variety of reports generated for the business.

As part of the *observe* and *analyze* phases, Lewis identified a number of interesting anomalies:

> … many of the department managers asked for specific report that the IT consultant would develop custom reports accessing different databases. When managers requested additional reports, the IT consultant would again, develop custom reports. The sales vice-president wanted special reports on sales. The Marketing vice-president wanted his version of customer reports. This was the same scenario with the other manager. All reports requests were unique, individually customized, by accessing separate databases that did not integrate. (ibid)

Lewis also found that many of the reports missed key information that would be helpful to management. Logistic reports did not reflect inventory information. Vendor order reports were unique for a specific country, regardless of product. Additionally, the data lacked graphical representation of data. The reports displayed data in a table format.

When Lewis conducted a second round of interviews with the business executives and managers, he brought examples of reports each of the executives had requested in the past. He would ask each, "Why did you run this report? Why is this important to you? What business problem are you trying to solve? How will it help the business?." (ibid) Lewis's objective was to engage each executive in a business discussion so he could better understand the business issues they were addressing each and every day. These meetings helped him gain a sound understanding of the business, challenges, and opportunities where he might be able to leverage technology to improve business outcomes. These meetings enabled him to formulate a plan to leverage technology for Ironclad. He implemented a number of major initiatives.

One major initiative was to help the quality control department proactively plan for the inspection of vendor shipments. Previously, shipments would arrive, and the quality control department would queue the products for inspection. It was a painful process. Personnel did not know when products were scheduled to arrive. In addition, the type of products created backlog issues and, sometimes, customer problems due to delayed shipments to customer stores. Lewis believed that by providing vendor-shipping information to the quality control department ahead of time, the department could plan inspections. Personnel could prioritize inspections based upon customer order ship dates, high-margin versus low-margin products, and inventory levels. The solution was an application that integrated databases to provide a quality control planning system for the company. The result was proactive versus reactive planning, smoother flow of products through the quality control organization, improved productivity, and greater customer satisfaction.

Another major initiative was the development of a customer order system that provided integrated information relative to customer orders, inventory availability, factory orders, and inbound logistic information from vendors, as well as information regarding shipments to customers. Previously, a customer would call and the sales person, or customer service representative, would have to access separate databases to find inventory information, vendor order status, and logistic information. It was time consuming, onerous on ironclad personnel and frustrating for the customer. Now, a single system accesses all the data necessary to provide the customer a response immediately.

Lewis initiated other programs to leverage IT to improve business performance. He integrated the databases and improved the ability to access information more efficiently. Websites improvements resulted in a more user-friendly experience. Lewis developed a sales margin analysis system that enabled the management to identify margins by account, as well as other information to support sales personnel. In addition, other improvements leveraged IT. However, none of this would have been possible if Lewis had not taken the initiative to understand the business at a practical level. More importantly, he took the time and asked the right questions to find out the business issues, challenges, and opportunities managers faced on a day-to-day basis. This enabled him to leverage information that improved operational efficiencies and support Ironclad's aggressive growth path.

Dick Brandt: Lehigh University Iacocca Institute: Global Village for Future Leaders of Business and Industry

Many companies operate in multiple continents. Understanding how your business operates on a day-to-day basis is difficult enough but even more complex in an international arena. Different cultures apply varying work practices and business relationships in how they conduct business. Executives today need to be not only business savvy but also internationally astute in how business is conducted in different parts of the world. For example, relocating data centers from Germany or the Netherlands to the United States is not as simple as handing out layoff notices, shutting down a facility, and moving, selling, or buying new equipment. It just does not work this way in Germany or other European countries. There are rules and regulations governing the reduction of personnel as well as severance pay. Therefore, if you do not understand how your business operates in different countries, your in store for some interesting and painful lessons.

The Iacocca Institute at Lehigh University, Bethlehem, Pennsylvania, started the Global Village program in 1997 to prepare future business leaders. Dick Brandt is the director of the program. He describes Global Village as "an intense five-week program that provides attendees from around the world a cross-cultural experience discussing business issues, solving real business problems, and learning how different businesses operate."[14] Brandt is on the faculty at

Lehigh, teaching courses in business, negotiations, and accounting ethics. His broad business background includes vice president positions at AT&T and Lucent Technologies where he had global responsibility for sales, projects, and technical support. His experience is a perfect fit for his role in Global Village.

Each year, the program enrolls approximately 100–120 people, most of whom are from outside the United States. Since its inception, the program has graduated 1650 people from 130 countries. The majority of graduates are in their twenties when they enroll in Global Village. Brandt explains the benefits of attending the program. "The attendees, referred as interns, develop international management skills early in their careers, as well as a global network of Global Village graduates around the world they can leverage in their careers." (ibid) They also develop teaming and entrepreneurial skills. An important element of the program is to attain global business knowledge and understanding of different cultures. Brandt talks about how "…many of the attendees are still figuring out their career paths and the Global Village experience provides them an opportunity to interact with others in different roles." (ibid)

Why is this important? The business landscape today is global and to prepare future C-level executives requires a solid understanding of how different companies from different parts of the world conduct business. Some of the graduates are now in the CIO role. Others may end up as a CIO. Regardless of their role, the graduates develop business skills by working in teams on challenges a company needs to address.

The program includes a variety of business courses, field trips to local companies to see, first hand, how they conduct business, and practical experience working on real international projects identified by global companies. The most intriguing part of the program is the practical experience. The 100 plus program participants are divided into approximately 15 teams of 6–8 people, each mentored by an experienced global executive. Global companies identify projects for each of the teams. Each team does research, interviews people, and presents a findings report to the sponsoring company executives. One interesting project was a major consumer company that wanted to expand to China. The team researched the market, the company, and historical and forecasted data. They concluded that expanding to China at that time was not the right choice. As a result, the executives scrapped their expansion plans.

To help each program participant understand the global marketplace, each Global Village participant presents their background, the company they work for, an overview of the products and services produced, and the markets they compete in. They also provide information on how their companies work with other companies in different countries. This helps each participant gain a better understanding of how others do business in different countries and markets. There are also interactive panel discussions of international business executives. During these sessions, the executives talk about different international business issues and challenges they faced, and participants can ask questions of the panel members.

The project component of the Global Village program presents the greatest challenge for the interns. Each team has to research, analyze, and develop solution scenarios in six weeks. This is in addition to the other Global Village activities. None of the team members know each other, as this is the first time they meet. Even more interesting is the fact that team members are from different countries and English is not their primary language. There is a lot of pressure. An executive mentor who is well experienced in business coaches each team. John Bowen, is one of the mentors, and has been involved with Global Village for the past few years.

John Bowen is director of Global Partnerships for Computer Aid, Inc., responsible for expanding CAI's international business presence. In this role, he has led CAI's international growth in Asia, Latin America, Europe, the Middle East, and North Africa. Before joining CAI, he served for nearly 10 years as CIO of PPL Global, the international division of PPL Corporation. In that role, he was responsible for IT management and operations in eight companies in five countries in Latin America and Europe and lived for several years in Argentina and Chile. He has more than 35 years of IT experience, including executive leadership, technology management, strategic planning, and large-scale system implementation.[15]

John is also founder and president of Management Envision LLC, a research and consulting company focused on innovation in effective presentation of complex issues in process, project, and program management.

John is a magna cum laude graduate of DePauw University with degrees in mathematics, computer science, and symbolic logic. He has taught international business, information engineering, and project management for MBA programs at eight universities. He has authored an acclaimed project management methodology and established project management offices in multiple companies in the United States and Latin America. (ibid)

When Bowen first started participating in the Global Village program in 2010, he recognized that the teams needed some coaching in how to manage a project, especially when there is a tight deadline, as is the case with the Global Village program. The teams had some challenges in organizing as a team, resolving team issues, handling conflicts, and generally organizing a project. Over the next 2 years, based upon Bowen's recommendation, the program placed more emphasis on coaching the teams and the team mentors in managing and organizing their projects. In fact, for the 2013 Global Village program, Bowen conducted a project management workshop for all the Global Village attendees as well as the executive mentors. During his two-hour workshop, he devoted a lot of time to discuss how teams form, bond, deal with conflict, resolve conflict, etc. By setting this expectation with the interns, they were better prepared to handle team formation issues during the following weeks of working on their projects. Bowen stresses that "one of the most common failures of a project team is to deal with the subjective project challenges, the greatest one being team formation and working together on a tight schedule" (Figures 8.1 and 8.2). (ibid)

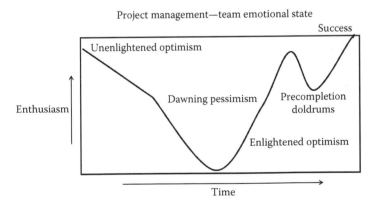

Figure 8.1 Global Village Project Management Workshop: Team Emotional State Cycle.

Project managment–team formation

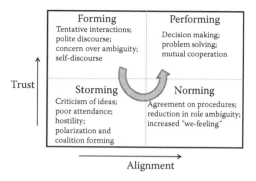

Figure 8.2 Global Village Project Management Workshop: Team Formation Cycle.

This training helped the teams as well as the team mentors. When Bowen observed the interim project status updates, he noticed that "the quality of the project deliverables improved, communication was more effective, team conflict was resolved more amenably. The entire project experience really helped the interns develop project skills they will use for the rest of their careers." (ibid)

The interns found the workshops valuable. Following is an email Bowen received from an intern from Spain. This email is representative of over a dozen he received praising the value of the workshops he conducted.

Hi John,

One month after the end of the GV I'm thinking what a wonderful experience I have lived. The project group, your aid, and availability have been very important and I want to thank you for having contributed to my growth.

At the beginning I had some problems with the English language because I wasn't so fluently speaker, and it didn't not allow me to express my potential one hundred percent, but now I've improved a lot, and I'm happy for that. The GV experience had a strong impact in me, so now I'd like to have new experiences, improve my English more, find a job opportunity abroad, etc.

Good luck John, and thank you again for all your suggestions.

Bye,

Amedeo

Bowen adds significant value to the Global Village program. Brandt speaks very highly of him:

> John is a dedicated professional with tons of international experience. His advice to my management team in a recent meeting, has caused us to rethink the project management part of our training to prepare our teams for working together on the 15 consulting projects for outside companies and NGO's. We look forward to introducing this additional project management training in the 2014 Global Village Program.[14]

The Global Village program has helped many up and coming executives prepare them for the future. I was able to locate an alumnus from the 2004 Global Village program. My objective was to find out how Global Village benefited her career. Her story is interesting. Ameya Vanjari is currently the global head of delivery in the business and IT architecture consulting practice at Tata Consultancy Services in Mumbai, India. When she attended Global Village, she only had 5 years of working experience in the technology aspects of IT across different countries and wanted more responsibility in leading and managing various functions in the consulting practice. Vanjari knew that as she rose through the ranks in the IT organization at Tata or other companies, she needed to experience interacting with people from different countries. Her role at Tata recently changed. She was to work on a global team, and the exposure to global cultures was an important component she needed to address. So when presented with the opportunity to attend Global Village (GV), she immediately jumped on the opportunity.

> My manager introduced me to Global Village. At that time, I was looking for a program on leadership and management. Global Village would provide me with an exposure to global cultures in a seven-week program. The program was a perfect fit for me.[16]

Her experience was very beneficial. It really helped her experience the interaction with other team members from other countries in planning a project. She explains the experience as follows:

> The program was a world-class-example of how to plan and execute any project, work with a passionate team to develop a detailed plan for a company project. I had been to a few countries before

Global Village (GV) -stayed in US, UK and visited a few other countries around Europe. Still, GV provided me with the opportunity to understand variety of cultures and build relations, friendships with the most lively and interesting people from across the globe! Today, when I travel for work across the globe, I am so comfortable just having friends to reach out to in any place I visit. (ibid)

How has the Global Village program helped Vanjari in her career since she attended Global Village?

It helped me very much. In the last 8 years, I have set up and led the enterprise architecture consulting practice in TCS. As part of this role, I have executed multiple engagements to define IT Strategies and architectures, helping enterprises make the right investments in technology & maximize value to the business from these. Today, we are a global team of 150+ consultants - and I am part of the leadership team. I have also had an opportunity to be an interim CIO for a mid-sized retailer in India. I would never have achieved the skills I have today without attending Global Village. (ibid)

The Iacocca Global Village program helps managers understand the international business community by working in teams comprised of people with different cultures, backgrounds, and management experience. Brandt talks about one of the key areas of the program. "The focus is on teaming and teamwork and presentation skills, key components of successful executives. The experience is life changing."[13]

Chapter Summary

This chapter is about the absolute necessity for CIOs to understand the business environment. This includes

- The value the company provides its customers
- How the value is created
- Working knowledge of the day-to-day key business processes used by company personnel
- Market environment
- Competitive market and associated opportunities and challenges

Key Points

1. A strategic CIO will not be successful without a well-based understanding of how the business operates.
2. The depth of understanding includes knowledge of the key processes across the entire value enterprise.
3. CIOs move into the role from the business, within IT, from other companies, in similar or dissimilar industries.
4. CIOs learn about the business in different ways, depending on experience.
5. Six strategic CIOs and an IT director shared their experiences in learning about the business:
   - Mike McClaskey, CIO, Dish Network
   - Scott Blanchette, CIO, Vanguard Health
   - Steve O'Connor, vice president and CIO, CSAA Insurance Group
   - Niel Nickolaisen, CIO, Western Governor's University
   - Kevin Michaelis, vice president, Global IT, and CIO at Air Products and Chemicals
   - Greg Lewis, IT director, Ironclad
6. Future business leaders need to learn about business and different operating cultures early in their career. The Global Village at the Iacocca Institute in Lehigh University accomplishes this objective.
   - Iacocca Institute—Global Village

Citations

1. James Schinski-VP and CIO-PPL Corporation/Phil Weinzimer Interview, September 18, 2012.
2. Mike McClaskey, CIO Dish Network/Phil Weinzimer Interview, December 27, 2012.
3. Mike McClaskey, CIO Dish Network/Phil Weinzimer Interview, January 29, 2013.
4. Scott Blanchette, CIO Vanguard Health/Phil Weinzimer Interview, June 30, 2013.
5. Vanguard Health Website: http://www.vanguardhealth.com/vanguard-leadership, July 5, 2013.

6. Press Release MIT Sloan: http://www.marketwatch.com/story/mit-sloan-cio-symposium-names-winner-of-the-2013-cio-leadership-award-2013-05-22.
7. Steve O'Connor-CSAA Insurance Group/Phil Weinzimer Interview, July 9, 2013.
8. The Works of Johann Wolfgang Von Goethe by Johann Wolfgang Von Goethe, Dana Estes-publisher, Copyright Francis A. Niccolls & Co., 1902.
9. Niel Nickolaisen-CIO WGU/Phil Weinzimer Interview, July 3, 2013.
10. Kevin B. Michaelis, Vice President Global IT and CIO at Air Products and Chemicals, Inc./Phil Weinzimer Interview, December 4, 2013.
11. Greg Lewis, Director IS/Phil Weinzimer Interview, May 15, 2013.
12. Reuters Profile; Ironclad Performance Wear (ICPW.PK); Corporate Overview; http://in.reuters.com/finance/stocks/companyProfile?symbol=ICPW.PK
13. Greg Lewis, Director IS/Phil Weinzimer Interview, June 12, 2013.
14. Dick Brandt, Director Global Village Iacocca Institute-Lehigh University/Phil Weinzimer Interview, June 13, 2012.
15. John Bowen, Founder, and President of Management Envision LLC/Phil Weinzimer Interview, October 14, 2013.
16. Ameya Vanjari, Global Head of Delivery: Business and IT Architecture Consulting Practice at Tata Consultancy Services in Mumbai, India/Phil Weinzimer Interview, September 1, 2013.

9

THE IMPORTANCE OF UNDERSTANDING YOUR ORGANIZATIONAL CULTURE IN BUILDING EFFECTIVE TEAMS

See what you're doing wrong, laugh at it, change and do better.

Spencer Johnson
Who Moved My Cheese?[1]

Organizational culture is a complex subject. Just ask Sniff, Scurry, Hem, and Haw, the four characters in the infamous book *Who Moved My Cheese?* by Spencer Johnson, M.D. The four characters, two mice and two little people, traverse a maze to find cheese that keeps moving. How each responds to the moving cheese and how each character helps the other navigate change is a lesson in organizational culture we should all learn. The parable is a great example of how personnel in an organization develop behaviors, sometimes conflicting, in performing their jobs. The book helps readers understand key concepts in changing organizational culture. If you are a C-suite executive, business unit executive, director, or manager, you need to understand the key concepts of organizational change. The culture of your organization derives from the underlying values and behaviors personnel exhibit as they work in teams, or independently, on programs, projects, and individual work assignments. Therefore, as a CIO, it is imperative for you to understand what organizational culture is, why it is important, how you measure it, and how you can change it. Following are the chapter objective, key messages, and examples used.

A. CHAPTER OBJECTIVE

1. Understand how the culture of your organization derives from the underlying values and behaviors personnel exhibit as they work in teams, or independently, on programs, projects, and individual work assignments.
2. Understand what organizational culture is, why it is important, how you measure it, and how you can change it.

B. KEY POINTS

1. A company's business strategies have a direct bearing on the cultural orientation required by the IT organization as well as other business units.
2. To achieve company goals, personnel work together on projects that align to business strategies.
3. Understanding the various cultural orientations, and how they compete with one another, is an important element in successfully achieving desired business outcomes.
4. There are four orientation cultures: collaboration, control, create, and compete.
5. Each dimension includes a set of underlying characteristics exhibited by the organization. The orientation and underlying characteristics compete with one another to achieve specific outcomes. If your organization has an internal focus, such as manufacturing, then the underlying characteristics focus on collaboration and control. If your organization has an external focus, such as marketing or product development, then the underlying characteristics focus to create value and compete effectively.

6. There is no right or wrong culture orientation. You need to define the one that aligns best with your organizational goals. What is important is to know what your organizational culture orientation is today versus what it needs to be, in order to make the necessary cultural adjustments to successfully deliver business outcomes as defined by your company strategy.

C. EXAMPLES

Four Different Organizational Types

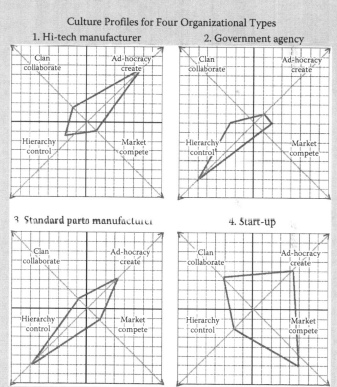

Culture Profiles for Four Organizational Types

D. TEMPLATES

1. Competing Values™ Framework

Collaborate

Focus: Values

Situation: A community united by shared beliefs, competency is closely linked to unique abilities, strong identification with a lifestyle

Purposes: Community and knowledge

Practices: Building teams and developing communities, training, and coaching, creating shared vision and values, harmonious work environment

People: Build trust, helpful, resolves conflict, empowering, good listener, encourages participation

Environment: Harmonious atmosphere, collaborative workplace, informal communication, shared values

Measures: Employee satisfaction, employee turnover, training per employee, competency peer review

Create

Focus: Vision

Situation: Differentiation creates significantly higher margins, a new methodology changes the game, an industry is situated around blockbuster invention

Purposes: Innovation and growth

Practices: Encouraging radical thinking, launching new ventures, specializing emerging opportunities, launching change initiatives, destroying the old way of doing things

People: Visionary, optimistic, generalist, enthusiastic, quick thinker, expressive

Environment: Stimulating projects, flexible hours, free from everyday constraints, diverse workforce

Measures: Diversity of experiments, new market growth, adoption rate, revenues from new products and services

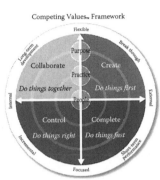

Control

Focus: Process

Situation: Organization has large and complex scope and scale, government regulations and standards determine business practices, failure is not an option

Purposes: Efficiency and quality

Practices: Implementing large scale technology and systems, applying continuous improvement processes, complying with regulations, adhering to standards

People: Organized, methodical, technical, practical, objective, persistent

Environment: Clear roles, logical objectives, structured work, cohesive work processes

Measures: Budget adherence, milestones achieved, number of failures, regulatory compliance

Compete

Focus: Goals

Situation: Shareholder demands are the primary driver, aggressive competition, markets change from mergers and acquisitions, investors demand quick results

Purposes: Profits and speed

Practices: Managing performance through objectives, investing for increasing rates of return, quickly starting and killing initiatives, quickly confronting problems

People: Goal oriented, assertive, driven, accountable, decisive, competitive

Environment: High pressure, fast moving, quantifiable results, pay for performance

Measures: Gross profit, time to market, return on investment, operating income

2. Organizational Culture Assessment Template

1. Dominant characteristics	Now	Preferred
A. The organization is a very personal place. It is like an extended family. People seem to share a lot of themselves.	25	25
B. The organization is a very dynamic and entrepreneurial place. People are willing to stick their necks out and take risks.	5	25
C. The organization is very results oriented. A major concern is with getting the job done. People are very competitive and achievement oriented.	15	25
D. The organization is a very controlled and structured place. Formal procedures generally govern what people do.	55	25
Total	100	100

2. Organizational leadership	Now	Preferred
A. The leadership in the organization is generally considered to exemplify mentoring, facilitation, or nurturing.	60	25
B. The leadership in the organization is generally considered to exemplify entrepreneurship, innovation, or risk taking.	5	25
C. The leadership in the organization is generally considered to exemplify a no-nonsense, aggressive, results-oriented focus.	15	25
D. The leadership in the organization is generally considered to exemplify coordinating, organizing, or smooth-running efficiency.	20	25
Total	100	100

3. Management of employees	Now	Preferred
A. The management style in the organization is characterized by teamwork, consensus, and participation.	10	25
B. The management style in the organization is characterized by individual risk taking, innovation, freedom, and uniqueness.	5	25
C. The management style in the organization is characterized by hard-driving competitiveness, high demands, and achievement.	15	25
D. The management style in the organization is characterized by security of employment, conformity, predictability, and stability of relationships.	70	25
Total	100	100

4. Organizational glue	Now	Preferred
A. The glue that holds the organization together is loyalty and mutual trust. Commitment to this organization runs high.	35	25
B. The glue that holds the organization together is commitment to innovation and development. There is an emphasis on being on the cutting edge.	5	25
C. The glue that holds the organization together is the emphasis on achievement and goal accomplishment.	5	25
D. The glue that holds the organization together is formal rules and policies. Maintaining a smooth-running organization is important.	55	25
Total	100	100

5. Strategic emphasis	Now	Preferred
A. The organization emphasizes human development. High trust, openness, and participation persist.	20	25
B. The organization emphasizes acquiring new resources and creating new challenges. Trying new things and prospecting for opportunities are valued.	5	25
C. The organization emphasizes competitive actions and achievement. Hitting stretch targets and winning in the marketplace are dominant.	10	25
D. The organization emphasizes permanence and stability. Efficiency, control, and smooth operations are important.	65	25
Total	100	100

6. Criteria of success	Now	Preferred
A. The organization defines success on the basis of the development of human resources, teamwork, employee commitment, and concern for people.	20	25
B. The organization defines success on the basis of having the most unique or newest products. It is a product leader and innovator.	25	25
C. The organization defines success on the basis of winning in the marketplace and outpacing the competition. Competitive market leadership is key.	10	25
D. The organization defines success on the basis of efficiency. Dependable delivery, smooth scheduling, and low-cost production are critical.	45	25
Total	100	100

Instructions:

The purpose of the Organizational Culture Assessment Instrument is to assess six key dimensions of organizational culture. In completing the instrument, you will be providing a picture of the fundamental assumptions on which our organization operates and the values that characterize it. There are no right or wrong answers for these items, just as there is no right or wrong culture. Be as accurate as you can in responding to the items so that our resulting cultural diagnosis will be as precise as possible. For our purposes, "organization" is AAA Northern California, Nevada & Utah Insurance Exchange.

The OCAI consists of six dimensions. Each dimension has four alternatives. Divide 100 points among these four alternatives, depending on the extent to which each alternative is similar to our organization. Give a higher number of points to the alternative that is most similar to our organization. For example, on Dimension 1, if you think alternative A is very similar to AAA Northern California, Nevada & Utah Insurance Exchange, alternatives B and C are somewhat similar, and alternative D hardly similar at all, you might give 55 points to A, 20 points each to B and C, and 5 points to D. Just be sure your total equals 100 for each Dimension.

Note that responses in the NOW column mean that you are rating our organization as it is *currently*. Complete this rating first. Once you have finished, think of our organization as you think it should ideally be in the future in order to be spectacularly successful. Complete the instrument again, this time responding to the items as if we had achieved extraordinary success. Write these responses in the PREFERRED column. Your responses will thus produce two independent ratings of our organization's culture—one as it currently exists and one as you wish it to be 2–3 years from now.

There are four basic concepts you need to know about organizational culture.

1. *Organizational culture exists throughout the company.*
   Personnel throughout the company develop an organizational culture that adapts to the behaviors of the organization. Personnel in a start-up company must be innovative, work well in teams, and perform different roles. Personnel in a large consumer products company need to understand that there are processes, rules, and structure that everyone must adhere to for the company to prosper.

2. *Organizational culture can differ by organizational unit.*
   Organizational units within a company perform different tasks with different goals. Personnel in the marketing department always look for new ways to advertise and connect to customers. The culture in marketing is creative. Personnel in the manufacturing department maintain a schedule and ensure quality work. The culture in this environment is structured.

3. *Organizational culture is composed of underlying characteristics that can complement and/or compete with the characteristics of other types of organizational cultures within a company.*
   Organizational culture is the outcome of group behavior and norms, which represent the rules that govern the group behavior. Personnel turn off cell phones in meetings as a sign of courtesy to fellow attendees, respect the opinions of others during group discussions, and encourage open communication. These are all behaviors that groups of people accept as rules that govern the work environment. Sometimes, group norms can be in conflict. Encouraging creativity and innovative work habits may be acceptable in the advertising department but conflicts with the activities of the medical laboratory environment that processes blood samples. Each of these group norms is acceptable behavior, but not conducive to the specific work environment.

4. *Organizational culture must be measured—both current and desired state.*
   Measuring your organization current versus desired state is important because it will identify any potential gaps that can impede your organization's ability to perform work effectively.

For example, you need to identify some alternative scenarios for developing an application enhancement for the sales organization. You ask a group of developers to meet and discuss the requirements with a group from the sales organization. Together, they together, identify a few scenarios based on risk, cost, and schedule. If the underlying behavior characteristics in your development team include a work environment that is isolated from the business and is a very structured and controlled environment, then it would be difficult for the developers to work in a collaborative environment with business teams. If you do not measure the current state as well as the desired state of your organizational culture, you will never know what roadblocks are ahead of you when implementing new strategies.

These are the four concepts that we will analyze in this chapter. Understanding these four concepts will help you determine the appropriate strategic IT competencies and skills your IT teams and other business unit teams require to be successful in implementing your company business model, the topic of the next chapter.

Many of the CIOs I interviewed acknowledged that to transform an introspective technology-focused organization to one that focuses on customer value and business outcomes requires an understanding of organizational culture and strategic IT competencies and skills. They also acknowledged that the "people" component of the transformation formula is the most difficult to understand, analyze, and execute. Developing competencies and skills is an important component for a strategic IT organization. However, if you do not understand the current culture in your organization, or the desired culture, you will have difficulty leveraging IT strategic competencies and skills. Your journey will be difficult and fraught with many roadblocks and failures.

Therefore, to begin, we need to understand more about organizational culture by answering the following four questions before we proceed with a discussion on IT strategic competencies and associated skills, which is discussed in Chapter 10:

1. What is organizational culture?
2. Why is it important?
3. How do you measure it?
4. What actions can you take to change organizational culture?

What Is Organizational Culture?

Each of us has a unique DNA (deoxyribonucleic acid) that contains the basic building blocks that make each of us who we are. IT organizations, as a whole, have DNA that drives their culture and associated behavior. Left unchanged, IT organizations will develop a set of characteristics and behaviors that form the basis of how they perform and interact with other company personnel. What is organizational culture? John Kotter, the Harvard professor and chief innovation officer, is a well-regarded thought leader on the subject of leadership and change. In a *Forbes* article, Kotter writes, "Culture consists of group norms of behavior and the underlying shared values that help keep those norms in place."[2] The culture of an organization impacts the way employees are treated, customers are treated, and business is conducted and a host of other behaviors. The culture of an organization also affects the productivity of the workforce: how people work together creating new products, how personnel communicate, and how personnel work together in teams. Stated in simple terms, organizational culture is cultivated from the behaviors personnel exhibit as they perform their jobs.

Many times, the founders define organizational culture. Walt Disney, Microsoft, and Wal-Mart are good examples of this. Other times, market conditions force companies to make changes to products, the roles personnel perform, and the processes used by personnel in their daily work activities. Sometimes, entire organization units are consolidated or eliminated. Look at the auto industry. The major competitors in the United States have completely changed how automobiles are manufactured, their relationships with supply partners, and their focus on the customer. General Motors, Chrysler, and Ford have completely reshaped their organizations. They even changed the way personnel work together. In today's global marketplace, you can be guaranteed that complacency will not help your competitive position. Regardless of the cause, companies in today's environment recognize their focus must encompass customer needs and value-based experiences. A company that recognizes the need to be more customer focused requires a change in how personnel work together to develop products and services, how they think about customers, as well as how company personnel interact with customers. Organizational culture will have to change. Personnel will have to learn or leverage different competencies and skills. It is not as simple as turning a light switch on. It requires much thought, good planning, and focused execution.

CIOs who need to transform their IT organization to become more strategic need to first gain a basic understanding of organizational culture and the process of changing behaviors of personnel in their organization. Change is not easy for anyone. Kotter says, "People change what they do less because they are given analysis that shifts their thinking than because they are shown a truth that influences their feelings."[2]

Let us look at personal and business examples to clarify Kotter's point. How many smokers do you know that have never been able to break the cigarette habit because of someone giving them statistics indicating smoking is bad for one's health and can cause cancer? Most just nod their heads and continue the habit. The ones that do stop smoking decide to change their behavior because they internalize the reasons why smoking is bad for their health and, as a result, they think and feel differently. In a business environment, the same process applies. I recall early in my career when I attended an organizational-wide meeting where the company executives presented their annual plan and initiatives that "would drive the company revenue and profitability." New initiatives would require that personnel put in much hard work. After the meeting, a group of us met and discussed the meeting. We all came to the same conclusion. We could not see the "what's in it for me?" piece of the formula. Kotter calls this message analysis-think-change[3] These company-wide announcements usually end up with personnel walking away, shaking their heads, and not changing their behaviors. People do not change their behavior easily. Forcing people to change is not a good long-term strategy. However, if management would convey a message that personnel could relate to, behavior change would be easier. Kotter calls this type of message see-feel-change.[3]

Later in my career, I worked for a Fortune 500 information services company. During my second week of employment, I attended a town hall meeting where the executive team announced a change in corporate strategy. Instead of just telling the employees about it, they personalized the message. They explained why the new strategy was important to clients, what changes were required for the organization, changes to business processes, and how the changes would affect employees. New training would be initiated that would help develop required skills and result in each of us growing professionally, whether we remained at the consultancy or moved on to another company. I was able to visualize the reasons why the company strategy needed to change. More importantly, I could see how I would grow professionally and how this would help my career path. I felt that the changes articulated by the management were important and that I needed to be part of the change. As Kotter says, change is most effective if it is based on the *see-feel-change* process versus the *analysis-think-change* process.

Why Is Organizational Culture Important?

Organizational culture is an important component to the success of any business strategy, especially one that involves the IT organization. Companies today operate in a complex network of business processes across an enterprise value chain that extends from customers to suppliers. Each of these processes is enabled by leveraging information technology. As the competitive environment becomes more intense, companies modify their strategies, which can affect almost every person in the company, sometimes very dramatically. Product development life cycles shorten every year. Every year, 3M Corporation increases the percentage of revenue target from newly developed products. As a result, people need to work smarter, harder, and faster. Understanding how to build an organizational culture that manifests itself in these behaviors is important. If you do not, your successor will figure it out. Therefore, organizational culture is important in the transformation of any IT organization that wants to become strategic.

Organizational culture can take many different forms. There is not one right form or wrong form. The culture embodied within a company is dependent on the industry the company competes in, marketplace forces, and the organizational DNA required for achieving success. Apple, Google, Samsung, and high-tech manufacturers represent companies with an organizational culture that fosters innovation and creativity. At the other end of the spectrum are heavy-duty manufacturing companies, spare parts manufacturing companies, or even government agencies, where control and consistency of product or service is very important.

Personnel in every organization possess a set of competencies and skills they use each day. Aligning them to accomplish business strategies is a key to the success of a strategic CIO. A person who is very structured, doesn't think out of the box, or requires much hand-holding and supervision is not an ideal candidate for employment at innovative companies like Apple or Google. Alternatively, a person who is very creative and innovative and does not like to be constantly supervised or work in a structured environment is not the ideal candidate for a job in federal agencies or heavy-duty manufacturing companies, where discipline and a set of strict processes and work values are required. Employees who have a work culture that fits into one of the previously mentioned categories will be successful. It is important to align an organization's work culture with a person's work style, skills, and behaviors. Otherwise, conflict will occur and organizational objectives will be difficult to achieve.

How Do You Measure Organizational Culture?

There are many books and papers published on the subject of measuring organizational culture. If you research the subject, you will find that one of the most popular and time-tested approaches to measuring organizational culture is the *Competing Values*$_{TM}$ Framework developed by Kim S. Cameron and Robert E. Quinn.[4,5] Before we delve into measuring organizational culture, we need to understand the framework that identifies the underlying characteristics of organizational culture.

Competing Values Framework

The Competing Values Framework is based upon the following assumptions:

1. Different cultures operate within an organization.
2. Each culture represents different organizational interrelationships that can complement or conflict with an organization's goals.
3. Organizational culture falls into two distinct dimensions.
   a. The first, measured vertically along the X-axis, is individual flexibility at one end of the scale (Microsoft or Nike) and stability and control at the opposite end of the scale (New York Stock Exchange or Coca-Cola).
   b. The second dimension, measured horizontally along the Y-axis, is internal capabilities (Dell-way or HP way) at

one end of the scale and external market positioning on the other end of the scale (Toyota and Honda).[4]

4. The two dimensions from four quadrants represent opposite and competing organizational characteristics.[4]

5. Measuring the degree to which your organization exhibits characteristics along each of the two dimensions and associated quadrant is important because it helps management determine the alignment of the organizational culture to the achievement of company strategies. It also helps personnel within the organization understand how their behaviors and orientation drive specific organizational outcomes. Measuring organizational culture also provides a *sense-see-feel* approach to help personnel understand why organizational behavior change, current state versus desired state, is necessary to achieve business strategies and associated goals.

In the center of Figure 9.3 you see a circle that reflects a basic view of the two dimensions and the four quadrants.[4] Each of the four quadrants is characterized by an organizational form and orientation that provides insight into the cultural orientation of the organization.

- The upper two quadrants, collaborate and create, focus on flexibility and energy. The lower two quadrants focus on stability and control.
- The two quadrants on the left, collaborate and control, focus on internal capabilities. The two quadrants on the right focus on external capabilities.
- The characteristics represented in each quadrant compete with those in the diagonal quadrant. Characteristics in the upper right quadrant, create, are the exact opposite of those in the lower left quadrant, control. The same holds true of characteristics in the upper left quadrant, collaborate, versus the lower right quadrant, compete.

Now look at Figure 9.1 but focus on the four rectangle shapes outside the circle, which provide more characteristics for each of the four dimensions (Collaborate, Control, Create, and Compete). This will

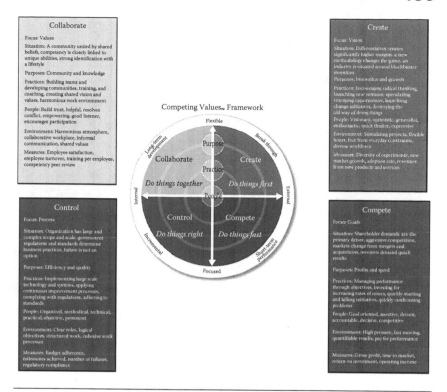

Figure 9.1 Competing Values_{TM} Framework. (From *Competing Values Leadership: Creating Value in Organizations*, Kim S. Cameron, Robert E. Quinn, Jeff DeGraff, and Anjan V. Thakor Edward Elgar, Edward Elgar Publishing Limited, 2006/: pdf overview of book and first chapter; http://competingvalues.com/competingvalues.com/wp-content/uploads/2009/07/A-Process-for-Changing-Organizational-Culture.pdf/.)

provide you with more insight and a better understanding of the organizational culture characteristics for each quadrant. Spend a few minutes reviewing the graphic and think about organizations you have worked for, have worked with, or have heard about, and I am sure you will be able to associate the organizational culture with the quadrant characteristics described in the Competing Values_{TM} Framework.[4]

By examining the characteristics of each quadrant, you should notice the following:

- The upper quadrants, collaborate and create, focus on flexibility and energy versus the lower quadrants, control and compete, which focus on stability and control.

- The two quadrants on the left, collaborate and control, focus on internal capabilities versus the two quadrants on the right, which focus on external capabilities, create and compete.
- The characteristics represented in each quadrant compete with those in the diagonal quadrant. Characteristics in the upper right quadrant, create, are the exact opposite of those in the lower left quadrant, control. The same holds true of characteristics in the *collaborate* quadrant versus the *compete* quadrant.

Measuring Organizational Culture Using the Competing Values Framework

Now that you have a basic understanding of the framework, we will discuss how you can measure the cultural orientation within your company. The creators of the Competing Values Framework developed an effective and widely used assessment instrument to measure the organizational culture for your organization. Figure 9.2 is an examples of the Assessment Instruments

1. Six distinct dimensions and related characteristics align to the four quadrants of the Competing Values Framework.
2. There is no right or wrong answer. The responses measure an individual's assessment of the organizational culture characteristics.
3. Each respondent performs two assessments using the same instrument. The first is based on the current state of the organization culture (now), and the second is based on the desired state of the organization culture (preferred).
4. Each dimension consists of four statements. Each statement represents the characteristics of one of the four quadrants.
5. The respondent identifies a score, from 1 to 100, for each statement. The score indicates the respondent's perception of the degree to which the organization represents the characteristic. The greater the degree of similarity of the organization to the assessment question characteristic, the higher the score. For example, a score of 25 indicates low similarity, whereas a score of 75 indicates high similarity to the question. The scores for the four questions of each dimension must equal 100.

1. Dominant characteristics	Now	Preferred
A. The organization is a very personal place. It is like an extended family. People seem to share a lot of themselves.		
B. The organization is a very dynamic and entrepreneurial place. People are willing to stick their necks out and take risks.		
C. The organization is very results oriented. A major concern is with getting the job done. People are very competitive and achievement oriented.		
D. The organization is a very controlled and structured place. Formal procedures generally govern what people do.		
Total	100	100

2. Organizational leadership	Now	Preferred
A. The leadership in the organization is generally considered to exemplify mentoring, facilitation, or nurturing.		
B. The leadership in the organization is generally considered to exemplify entrepreneurship, innovation, or risk taking.		
C. The leadership in the organization is generally considered to exemplify a no-nonsense, aggressive, results-oriented focus.		
D. The leadership in the organization is generally considered to exemplify coordinating, organizing, or smooth-running efficiency.		
Total	100	100

3. Management of employees	Now	Preferred
A. The management style in the organization is characterized by teamwork, consensus, and participation.		
B. The management style in the organization is characterized by individual risk taking, innovation, freedom, and uniqueness.		
C. The management style in the organization is characterized by hard-driving competitiveness, high demands, and achievement.		
D. The management style in the organization is characterized by security of employment, conformity, predictability, and stability of relationships.		
Total	100	100

4. Organizational glue	Now	Preferred
A. The glue that holds the organization together is loyalty and mutual trust. Commitment to this organization runs high.		
B. The glue that holds the organization together is commitment to innovation and development. There is an emphasis on being on the cutting edge.		
C. The glue that holds the organization together is the emphasis on achievement and goal accomplishment.		
D. The glue that holds the organization together is formal rules and policies. Maintaining a smooth-running organization is important.		
Total	100	100

5. Strategic emphasis	Now	Preferred
A. The organization emphasizes human development. High trust, openness, and participation persist.		
B. The organization emphasizes acquiring new resources and creating new challenges. Trying new things and prospecting for opportunities are valued.		
C. The organization emphasizes competitive actions and achievement. Hitting stretch targets and winning in the marketplace are dominant.		
D. The organization emphasizes permanence and stability. Efficiency, control, and smooth operations are important.		
Total	100	100

Figure 9.2 Organizational Assessment Template.   (*Continued*)

6. Criteria of success	Now	Preferred
A. The organization defines success on the basis of the development of human resources, teamwork, employee commitment, and concern for people.		
B. The organization defines success on the basis of having the most unique or newest products. It is a product leader and innovator.		
C. The organization defines success on the basis of winning in the marketplace and outpacing the competition. Competitive market leadership is key.		
D. The organization defines success on the basis of efficiency. Dependable delivery, smooth scheduling, and low-cost production are critical.		
Total	100	100

Instructions:

The purpose of the Organizational Culture Assessment Instrument is to assess six key dimensions of organizational culture. In completing the instrument, you will be providing a picture of the fundamental assumptions on which our organization operates and the values that characterize it. There are no right or wrong answers for these items, just as there is no right or wrong culture. Be as accurate as you can in responding to the items so that our resulting cultural diagnosis will be as precise as possible. For our purposes, "organization" is AAA Northern California, Nevada & Utah Insurance Exchange.

The OCAI consists of six dimensions. Each dimension has four alternatives. Divide 100 points among these four alternatives, depending on the extent to which each alternative is similar to our organization. Give a higher number of points to the alternative that is most similar to our organization. For example, on Dimension 1, if you think alternative A is very similar to AAA Northern California, Nevada & Utah Insurance Exchange, alternatives B and C are somewhat similar, and alternative D hardly similar at all, you might give 55 points to A, 20 points each to B and C, and 5 points to D. Just be sure your total equals 100 for each Dimension.

Note that responses in the NOW column mean that you are rating our organization as it is *currently*. Complete this rating first. Once you have finished, think of our organization as you think it should ideally be in the future in order to be spectacularly successful. Complete the instrument again, this time responding to the items as if we had achieved extraordinary success. Write these responses in the PREFERRED column. Your responses will thus produce two independent ratings of our organization's culture—one as it currently exists and one as you wish it to be 2–3 years from now.

Figure 9.2 (*Continued*) Organizational Assessment Template.

6. The organizational assessment template in Figure 9.2 consists of six dimensional characteristics. There are four statements for each dimension. Score each statement and total the results for all four questions. The maximum total is 100. You can weight the maximum score for each dimension question if you wish but the total for the dimension cannot exceed 100.

7. Add the total scores for each dimension (maximum score is 600) and divide the results by 6, the number of dimensions. The result is the average score.

8. Plot the organizational averages using a spider graph to depict the visualization of the scores.

Examine the assessment template shown in Figure 9.2.[6] Following is an example.

There are six organizational dimensions. Each dimension has four statements (A,B,C,D) that represent a unique characteristic of the organization. As you read each characteristic for a dimension, you should be able to map the response to one of the quadrants.

If you were completing this assessment for your organization, you would read each of the four characteristics for each domain and determine the degree to which your organization exhibits this characteristic. For example, look at the third domain, 3.0 Management of Employees, and the first question A, *The management style in the organization is characterized by teamwork, consensus, and participation.* If the management style of the company strongly depicts this characteristic, then you would give a high score, say, 75. Now move on to the other questions. You would probably score these lower. If, however, your organization's management of employees is more similar to characteristic D, *The management style in the organization is characterized by security of employment, conformity, predictability, and stability of relationships,* then you would score it high, and you would score the other choices lower. When you complete the current state assessment, you then use the same instrument but focus on the desired state of the organization. You should score each dimension characteristic based on how you believe the organization would demonstrate these characteristics in the desired state (Figure 9.2).

Viewing Results of the Organizational Culture Assessment

A radar chart, also referred to as a spider chart, is the best method for reviewing these types of assessments and is the recommended method in the assessment instructions. The assessment administrator adds all the scores for each dimension-associated characteristic and enters the results in the summary excel sheet. An average score is calculated for each domain and characteristic and is plotted on the radar chart, using the excel graph option. The advantage of a radar chart is that it plots the values for each characteristic across the different dimensions. Low scores show in the center of the chart while greater scores extend from the center to the outer ring. The visual is very effective. Figure 12.3 is an example of four organizational types resulting from an assessment. Each type strongly represents one of the quadrant profiles. Let us look at each assessment type and summarize the organizational characteristics to provide you with a better understanding of how the assessment provides a good perspective of the organizational culture (Figure 9.3).

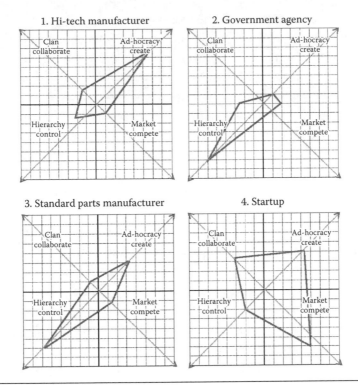

Figure 9.3   Culture Profiles for Four Organizational Types.

High-Tech Manufacturer

High-tech companies design, develop, manufacture, and service complex products and services using a combination of electronics, mechanics, optics, and other technologies.

Apple, Samsung, and LG are representative of high-tech manufacturers who face global competition and shorter product development cycles. As a result, the companies have a strong external focus, as represented by a high score in the upper right quadrant. At the same time, these companies also require control of production and quality across a complex supply chain. However, the volatile global marketplace forces these companies to constantly improve these controls to meet the ever-changing enhancements to their products and services. Therefore, the scoring represented in the lower left quadrant, control, is low, and the overall focus is greater externally than internally.

Government Agency

Government agencies have a very strong emphasis on focusing internally, especially by controlling processes and underlying activities with a tight reign. Think of the US Postal Service. The challenge is to maintain consistent execution of processes to ensure delivery of millions of pieces of mail six days a week. This is a massive undertaking. The only method to ensure success is to have consistency of process and ensure that employees work together to execute efficiently. As you see from the radar chart, there is a high degree of control with a high score in the lower left hand Control quadrant very little external focus resulting in very low scores in the upper and lower right hand Create and Compete quadrants.

Standard Parts Manufacturer

Standard parts manufacturers face global competition. As a result, these companies focus constantly on new markets and customers while at the same time maintaining a strong focus on internal controls to ensure consistency of quality.

The automotive industry is a good example. Denso Manufacturing is a global automotive supplier of advanced automotive technology, systems, and components operating in 33 countries with approximately 120,000 employees. Their customers include Toyota, Honda, General Motors, Chrysler, Ford, Fiat, Subaru, and Mitsubishi. Denso has a strong internal focus on quality and cost, as represented by a high score in the lower left quadrant, control. The company also has a strong external focus to remain competitive. Denso invests about 8% of consolidated net sales into research and development. Their investment pays off handsomely. Denso has over 30,000 active patents. Standard parts manufacturers have to maintain a stronger focus on consistency of quality through rigorous process controls while at the same time focus to a lesser degree, externally, on new markets and competitive pressures.

Global standard parts manufacturers also need to maintain a collaborative behavior across all of the facilities to ensure consistency. This is represented by the score in the collaborative quadrant located in the upper left section of the framework.

Start-Up Companies

The initial focus for start-up companies is on growth versus profitability. As a result, start-up companies have an external orientation. The objective is to obtain a growing customer base during the initial stages. ITM Software, founded in the late 1990s, is a good example. A group of CIOs having dinner discussed some of their major challenges. One was just like the cobbler who was so busy repairing shoes for customers that he did not have time to fix the shoes of his children. CIOs constantly maintain and develop applications for marketing, finance, sales, and other business units but never have time to manage the business of the information technology organization. They all agreed that IT needed a business solution. They researched the market and could not find a viable solution. They decided to build one and founded ITM Software to help CIOs manage the business of IT. The suite of solutions was called IT Business Management. I joined the company in 2003 as managing principal in the consulting organization. Our focus was building a leading-edge solution suite that filled a gap in the market of CIO-oriented business solutions. Our teams focused externally on developing and building solutions quickly, and being first to market with our solution suite. The external focus was very strong. This is why the organizational culture scores for start-ups are high on the two right quadrants. We were always meeting with prospects, customers, and research organizations to be ahead of the curve and rapidly respond to external forces. At the same time, we also needed to collaborate with our team members in developing new functionality and new solutions. You will notice that the scores for the upper left quadrant, collaborate, are almost as high as for the create quadrant. Internal controls around the process were not as important as we had to be flexible and agile to respond quickly to changes. Processes changed quickly. This is why scores in the lower left quadrant, control, fell low for start-up companies.

Changing Organizational Culture

Changing organizational culture is not easy. It is a complex subject. Go to the library and you will find shelves of books on the subject. What you should always remember is that the organizational culture that is most aligned with your company's vision and strategy will successfully deliver results. In my consulting career, I have often spoken to executives about the importance of people as part of the success formula. We often cast personnel into groups of A, B, C, and D players. A players are smart and flexible, communicate well, and do what is needed to get the job done. B players are also smart and flexible and communicate well, but need some direction and leadership. C players need constant direction and leadership and must be mentored and trained. D players are the laggards and either must improve or find another job. The challenge is to develop a team of A, B, and C players with an organizational culture that is best aligned to achieve the business results desired. There are many examples of teams composed of A, B, and C players, which demonstrate an organization culture that will transform poor strategy and mold it to a new one that achieves the ultimate vision and goals. Hence, we often hear the phrase—*an A strategy with a C team will always fail, but an A team with a C strategy will always turn that strategy into one that succeeds.* Determining the organizational culture that is the best fit for your organization to succeed is a critical component to achieving the desired business results.

In this chapter, we have defined organizational culture, why it is important, and how to measure it. The hard part is changing it to fit the needs of your business. Sometimes, it requires major changes in leadership and personnel or some degree of education, training, and mentoring. In most cases, it is a combination of both. The focus of this chapter is to provide you with a foundation for understanding organizational culture. The process of changing organization culture, as previously stated, is a complex one and the subject of other books. A good resource to get you started is *Diagnosing and Changing Organizational Culture* by Kim Cameron and Robert Quinn.[5] This book will guide you through a well-thought-out process that will achieve results.

Chapter Summary

Your company business strategies have a direct bearing on the cultural orientation required by IT organization as well as other business units. To achieve company goals, personnel work together on projects that align to the business strategies. Understanding the various cultural orientations, and how they compete with one another, is an important element in successfully achieving desired business outcomes.

Following are the key messages:

- The *Competing Values*_{TM} Framework is an example to help you understand the various cultural orientations within organizations. The basic premise is simple. There are different dimensions of organizational culture. In the example used in this chapter, there are four. Each dimension includes a set of underlying characteristics exhibited by the organization. The orientation and underlying characteristics compete with one another to achieve specific outcomes. If your organization has an internal focus, such as manufacturing, then the underlying characteristics focus on collaboration and control. If your organization has an external focus, such as marketing or product development, then the underlying characteristics focus on creating value and competitive markets.
- There is no right or wrong culture orientation. You need to define the one that aligns best with your organizational goals. What is important is to know what your organizational culture orientation is today versus what it needs to be, in order to make the necessary cultural adjustments to successfully deliver business outcomes as defined by your company strategy.
- We also defined a method to measure your organization's current organizational culture as well as the desired state. The gap provides you with the necessary information required to develop a plan to mitigate the gap and reorient your organization to exhibit the desired behaviors.

The next chapter focuses on the competencies and skills required by a strategic IT organization.

Citations

1. *Who Moved My Cheese?*; Spencer Johnson; 1998, G.P. Putnam's Sons, New York.
2. The Key to Changing Organizational Culture: *Forbes Magazine*, September 27, 2012; http://www.forbes.com/sites/johnkotter/2012/09/27/the-key-to-changing-organizational-culture/.

3. *The Heart of Change: Real-Life Stories of How People Change Their Organizations*; John P. Kotter and Dan S. Cohen; Copyright 2002, John Kotter and Deloitte Consulting.

4. *Competing Values Leadership: Creating Value in Organizations*; Kim S. Cameron, Robert E. Quinn, Jeff DeGraff, and Anjan V. Thakor Edward Elgar; 2006, Edward Elgar Publishing Limited, 2006/: pdf overview of book and first chapter; http://competingvalues.com/competingvalues.com/wp-content/uploads/2009/07/A-Process-for-Changing-Organizational-Culture.pdf/.

5. *A Process for Changing Organizational Culture*; Kim Cameron/Abstract for chapter to be included in The Handbook of *Organizational Development*, 2004; Micahel Driver; http://competingvalues.com/competingvalues.com/wp-content/uploads/2009/07/A-Process-for-Changing-Organizational-Culture.pdf.

6. *Diagnosing and Changing Organizational Culture: Based on the Competing Values Framework*, 3rd edn; Kim S. Cameron and Robert E. Quinn; March 2011, John Wiley & Sons.

10

KEY COMPETENCIES AND SKILLS OF A STRATEGIC IT ORGANIZATION

People make us successful. They need to exhibit the right skills if we are to succeed at collaborating with the business to achieve our corporate goals.[1]

Ravi Naik
CIO—SanDisk

When you speak to strategic CIOs, it is very clear why they succeed. The conversation is all about business. Whether it is Randy Spratt from McKesson, Filippo Passerini from Procter & Gamble (P&G), or Rebecca Jacoby from Cisco, the message is loud and clear. Today's CIOs need to focus on solving business outcomes. They need to understand how the business works, its financial structure, and a focus on achieving results that drive business success. However, CIOs cannot do it alone. They need an organization that can think, act, and behave as business people. To accomplish this requires a clear understanding of the organizational culture as well as the business competencies and associated skills necessary for a strategic information technology (IT) organization to be successful. We discussed organizational culture in the previous chapter as a foundation to a discussion of key competencies and skills required for a strategic IT organization. Following are the objectives, key points, examples, and templates included in this chapter.

A. CHAPTER OBJECTIVE

1. Understand the difference between competencies and skills
2. Identify the competencies and skills required by a strategic IT organization

B. KEY POINTS

1. There is a difference between competencies and skills:
   a. Competencies are the effective applications of skills. It is more of an umbrella term that also includes behavior and knowledge.
   b. Skills are specific learned activities that may be part of a broader context.
2. There are 4 competencies and 12 associated skills

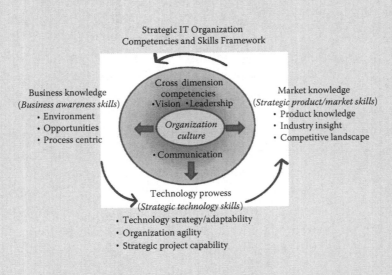

Strategic IT Organization
Competencies and Skills Framework

Business knowledge
(*Business awareness skills*)
• Environment
• Opportunities
• Process centric

Cross dimension competencies
•Vision •Leadership
Organization culture
•Communication

Market knowledge
(*Strategic product/market skills*)
• Product knowledge
• Industry insight
• Competitive landscape

Technology prowess
(*Strategic technology skills*)
• Technology strategy/adaptability
• Organization agility
• Strategic project capability

   a. *Business knowledge competency*
      a1. *Business knowledge and environmental skill*
      a2. *Opportunities and challenges skills*
      a3. *Process-centric skills*

    b. *Market knowledge competency*
      b1. *Product knowledge skills*
      b2. *Industry knowledge skills*
      b3. *Competitive landscape skills*
    c. *Technology prowess competency*
      c1. *Technology strategy/adaptability skills*
      c2. *Organization agility skills*
      c3. *Strategic project capability skills*
    d. *Cross-dimensional competency*
      d1. *Vision, leadership, and communication skills*

C. EXAMPLES

1. CIO and IT executive examples for each competency and associated skills
   - Randy Spratt—CIO/CTO, McKesson
   - Harry Lukens—CIO, Lehigh Valley Health Network
   - Steve O'Connor—CIO, CSAA Insurance Group
   - Rosa Sibilsky—business process director, CSAA Insurance Group
   - Debra Martucci—CIO, Synopsys
   - Ravi Naik—CIO, SanDisk
   - Grace Liu—director of finance and human resource (HR) IT, SanDisk
   - Calvin Rhodes—CIO, Georgia Technology Authority (GTA)
   - Sanjib Sahoo—CIO, OptionMonster Holdings

D. TEMPLATES

Strategic IT organization competencies and underlying skills

1. Strategic IT Organization Competency and Best Practices Skills Matrix (Figure 10.1)

STRATEGIC COMPETENCY	ASSOCIATED SKILLS/BEST PRACTICE		CROSS COMPETENCY SKILLS
BUSINESS KNOWLEDGE Business Awareness Skills	1. Business Environment	IT Personnel Understand and Articulate the Enterprise Business Strategy, Objectives, Culture, and Internal Environment	**1. Vision** IT Vision that Aligns with Corporate, Business Units, and IT Organization
	2. Opportunities/ Challenges	IT Organization Understands the Enterprise Business Opportunities to Enhance Customer Value, Revenue, Profitability as Well as Challenges that Impact Enterprise Growth.	
	3. Process Centric	IT Organization Understands How IT Services and Underlying Technologies Align and Enable Enterprise Business Processes that Create/Support Customer Value	**2. Leadership** CIO Guides the IT Organization in Developing the Skills/ Competencies/Knowledge to Enhance and Develop the IT Services Aligned to Business Needs and Effectively Collaborates with Business Peers to Achieve Business Vision/Financial Objectives/ Market Strategies
MARKET KNOWLEDGE Strategic Product/Market Skills	*MARKET*		
	1. Product Knowledge	Knowledge of How Customer Value is Derived from Enterprise Products/Services	
	2. Industry Knowledge	Understanding of Industry Landscape and Upcoming Trends and their Alignment to Enterprise Products and Services	
	3. Competitive Landscape	Insight into Competitive Environment and the Associated Customer Value Gaps and Opportunities	
TECHNOLOGY PROWESS Strategic Technology Skills	*TECHNOLOGY*		
	1. Technology Strategy/ Adaptability	Incorporates a Technology Strategy that Integrates Emerging and Existing Technologies into New and/or Enhanced Customer Value and Revenue Streams.	**3. Communication** IT Personnel Effectively Communicate and Team with Business Personnel to Understand/Uncover Opportunities to Drive Revenue /Reduce Cost
	2. Organization Agility	Combined IT/Business Teams Rapidly Respond to Changing Business Needs Utilizing Enabling Technologies to Develop/Enhance Customer Products and Services	
	3. Strategic Project Capability	Increase Capacity to Implement Strategic Project by Reducing Run & Maintain/Enhancement Project Costs/Execution time and Improving IT Personnel Technology/Business Skills	

2. Strategic IT Organization Competencies and Skills Framework (Figure 10.1)
3. Transformation Path to Optimize IT Performance (Figure 10.5)

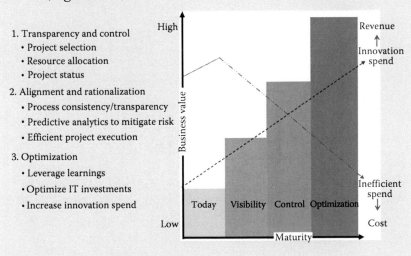

1. Transparency and control
   • Project selection
   • Resource allocation
   • Project status
2. Alignment and rationalization
   • Process consistency/transparency
   • Predictive analytics to mitigate risk
   • Efficient project execution
3. Optimization
   • Leverage learnings
   • Optimize IT investments
   • Increase innovation spend

Pat Blake is executive vice president and group president of Technology Solutions at McKesson. He is responsible for the businesses within the Technology Solutions Division that provide software, automation, services, and consulting for hospitals, physician offices, imaging centers, home health-care agencies, and payers. The IT component for the Technology Solutions Division is a huge and critical component for its success.[2] Blake speaks highly of Randy Spratt, who is CIO as well as chief technology officer (CTO) of McKesson. "What Randy does really well is embed his technology people into the cadence of the way we run our business."[3]

Spratt understands the McKesson business, the culture of the IT organization, and the competencies and skills personnel need to drive business outcomes. When mobility became a real hot topic, Spratt organized an IT team to meet with business teams to better understand their business needs and share that knowledge across the organization. The objective was to develop the baseline knowledge for a mobility strategy. This would not have been successful if Spratt and his IT organization did not embody a collaborative culture and understand how the business operates, its competitive value, and how technology could enable or improve current McKesson products and services.

Strategic CIOs recognize that to succeed in today's competitive environment, business competencies and associated skills are a basic requirement for the CIO and more so for the IT personnel, in addition to technical skills. The IT organization will never succeed at collaborating with the business if they do not have a set of business competencies and skills. How many meetings have you participated in with one or more of the participants sitting quietly and never participating? Alternatively, have you been in meetings that include business and IT personnel, where the IT person tries to contribute but has no real knowledge of how the business functions? I remember during my early consulting career when I was at Xerox Professional Services, I was invited to participate in a meeting with a health-care provider. I was young and naive about how the health-care business operates. During the meeting, I was fascinated at the discussion of health-care issues and their challenges. Unfortunately, I could not contribute to the meeting. I felt ignorant and nonproductive. At the end of the meeting, I realized that

I did not have the right competencies and skills to contribute value during the meeting. From that moment, I promised myself that I would not participate in any future meetings unless I understood the business issues, competitive market, and some success stories that would make me a credible member of a meeting. So what are the key competencies and skills required for a strategic CIO and IT organization?

When I interviewed one of the CIOs for this book, I related the experience at Xerox Professional Services. Since I was open and honest about my shortcomings during my early career, he decided to share an experience as a programmer at a software company. He was 23 years old at the time and had an MBA to supplement his computer science degree. He knew he had the right education to help him move up the corporate ladder quickly. He knew that his technical skills were good. He received accolades from his managers for the great work he did. During one of his earlier annual reviews, his manager told him that he was very good at his technical skills. He also told me that "I had some basic business skills but I needed to improve them." He said, "during meetings with business personnel you tend to discuss all the technical issues but don't discuss them in business terms." The CIO responded to his manager by saying, "I know how business works, I learned all that stuff during my MBA courses." My manager told me that knowing the basic skills is great but demonstrating them in a meaningful manner is the true test. "I had some basic business skills. I did not have the experience to apply those skills in a way that would allow me to demonstrate that I could speak in business terms instead of technical terms."[4] The CIO told me that from that moment on he focused on gaining as much experience as possible when discussing technology solutions from a business perspective. Over time, he developed the ability to apply his business skills to communicate to his business peers in the language of business. This was one of the most important lessons learned that helped him to be a successful CIO.[4]

The Difference between Competencies and Skills

The CIO in the previous example stated that he had the business skills but he didn't have a competency in dialoguing in business terms.

He just didn't have the experience. What is the difference between a competency and a skill?

Some people interchange the terms *skills* and *competencies*. They are not synonymous. A competency is more of an umbrella term that also includes behaviors and knowledge, whereas skills are specific learned activities that may be part of a broader context. By looking at several examples of both competencies and skills, the difference may become clearer. Let us look at a simple example. Just because you know how to use a hammer to pound a nail into a piece of wood or know how to use a screwdriver doesn't make you carpenter. Using a hammer and screwdriver is a skill. Being a carpenter is a competency because you are applying the skills in an effective manner. Competencies are the effective application of skills. Building knowledge and applying that knowledge to develop a set of strategic IT competencies and skills is an imperative today. So, what are the strategic IT competencies and associated skills? Read on, and find out more.

Competencies and Skills of a Strategic CIO and IT Organization

The journey for a strategic CIO to transform the IT organization requires a focus on four critical strategic competencies. These are business knowledge, market knowledge, technology prowess, and cross-dimensional competencies, as depicted in Figure 10.1. You will notice that at the center of the figure is organizational culture, which we discussed in the previous chapter. The type of organization culture

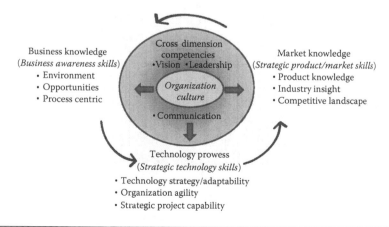

Figure 10.1 Strategic IT Organization Competencies and Skills Framework.

required in your IT organization will determine the extent to which each of the competencies and skills need to be exhibited.

Each competency is comprised of three underlying skills used to develop the business behaviors of a strategic IT organization. The fourth competency, cross dimension, includes three skills utilized across each of the other three competencies. The competencies and underlying skills are a must-have for CIOs and IT organizations who want to embark on the transformational journey to become an effective strategic IT organization that creates customer value, increases revenue, and enhances shareholder wealth.

Each of the underlying skills associated with the corresponding strategic competency is important for IT personnel to understand and apply. Figure 10.2 provides a best-in-class description of how these skills should be applied in a strategic IT organization. Take a few minutes to review the table. The next section of this chapter discusses each competency and associated skills in more detail.

Business Knowledge Competency

Business knowledge is all about developing an awareness of your company's business environment. If you, as the CIO, want to be a strategic partner to the business, you need a solid knowledge base of your company's business environment. Otherwise, you or your IT personnel cannot effectively communicate and partner with business teams to address company objectives. The three skill areas required for this competency are business environment, opportunities/challenges, and process centricity.

Business Environmental Skills

Developing business environmental skills will enable your IT personnel to understand and articulate the business enterprise strategy, objectives, culture, and internal environment. Understanding the business is fundamental if you want your IT organization to align services to the needs of the customer. The focus in the IT organization is no longer IT value: it is the business value measured by business outcomes.

CIOs are beginning to realize that they need to build strategic IT organizations with personnel that have a service-oriented philosophy

STRATEGIC COMPETENCY	ASSOCIATED SKILLS / BEST PRACTICE		CROSS COMPETENCY SKILLS
BUSINESS KNOWLEDGE — Business Awareness Skills	1. Business Environment	IT Personnel Understand and Articulate the Enterprise Business Strategy, Objectives, Culture, and Internal Environment	**1. Vision**
	2. Opportunities / Challenges	IT Organization Understands the Enterprise Business Opportunities to Enhance Customer Value, Revenue, Profitability as Well as Challenges that Impact Enterprise Growth.	IT Vision that Aligns with Corporate, Business Units, and IT Organization
	3. Process Centric	IT Organization Understands How IT Services and Underlying Technologies Align and Enable Enterprise Business Processes that Create / Support Customer Value	**2. Leadership**
MARKET KNOWLEDGE — Strategic Product/Market Skills	*MARKET*		CIO Guides the IT Organization in Developing the Skills / Competencies / Knowledge to Enhance and Develop the IT Services Aligned to Business Needs and Effectively Collaborates with Business Peers to Achieve Business Vision / Financial Objectives / Market Strategies
	1. Product Knowledge	Knowledge of How Customer Value is Derived from Enterprise Products / Services	
	2. Industry Knowledge	Understanding of Industry Landscape and Upcoming Trends and their Alignment to Enterprise Products and Services	
	3. Competitive Landscape	Insight into Competitive Environment and the Associated Customer Value Gaps and Opportunities	**3. Communication**
TECHNOLOGY PROWESS — Strategic Technology Skills	*TECHNOLOGY*		IT Personnel Effectively Communicate and Team with Business Personnel to Understand / Uncover Opportunities to Drive Revenue / Reduce Cost
	1. Technology Strategy / Adaptability	Incorporates a Technology Strategy that Integrates Emerging and Existing Technologies into New and/or Enhanced Customer Value and Revenue Streams.	
	2. Organization Agility	Combined IT/Business Teams Rapidly Respond to Changing Business Needs Utilizing Enabling Technologies to Develop/Enhance Customer Products and Services	
	3. Strategic Project Capability	Increase Capacity to Implement Strategic Project by Reducing Run & Maintain / Enhancement Project Costs/Execution time and Improving IT Personnel Technology/Business Skills	

Figure 10.2 Strategic IT Competencies and Associated Skills-Best Practices.

and embody both business and technology skills. Some CIOs believe they need to take drastic actions to remake their IT organizations. The 2011 PA/Harvey Nash international Survey of 2500 CIO's identified business skills as the most important for CIO's to develop.[5]

An IDGE survey in 2012 reported that 27% of CIOs would remake their company's IT departments from scratch, if they could. Bill Weeks, CIO at SquareTwo Financial since 2010, did exactly that. Weeks believes business skills is a must for IT personnel. The IT organization Weeks inherited focused internally and didn't interact with the business, except for a few directors. In fact, his predecessor didn't want IT personnel speaking with any business personnel. The CIO and the few IT directors told the IT organization what they needed to do. Weeks needed to change the culture. He needed a *combination of tech skills and collaboration skills.* With a growth spurt in progress, IT would never support the needs of the business by exhibiting silo behaviors. Weeks began a communication program with IT personnel to educate them on the need to *understand what our business needs to be successful.* His development teams, led by business analysts, worked with business teams. Underutilized business analysts got the message but many of the other IT personnel were not comfortable *interacting with the business* and left the company. Over time, Weeks replaced almost 70% of IT personnel.[6]

Opportunities and Challenges Skills

If you and your IT team can develop opportunities and challenges skills, then they will be more effective in working with business teams. Knowing what business opportunities exist as well as challenges provides your IT personnel with the ability to work in business teams to identify IT solutions that can enhance customer value, revenue, and profitability.

A hospital environment is a good example of where IT personnel can benefit from understanding the opportunities and challenges. Lehigh Valley Health Network (LVHN) is a thousand-bed magnet-designated hospital in Allentown, Pennsylvania. IT personnel's work is a fast-paced environment. Patients' lives are on the line every minute of every day. Applications that support the physicians, nurses, laboratories, and administrative functions have to be available all the time.

Backup systems need to be in place in case of service disruptions, due to power outages, or system malfunction. IT personnel constantly focus on maintaining these systems and developing new or enhanced applications to support the hospital's medical needs.

Harry Lukens, CIO at LVHN, strongly believes that IT personnel need to know what the hospital business opportunities and challenges are in order to understand the value they provide to the health network. To accomplish this, Lukens started a curriculum of courseware, workshop-led, that provides all IT personnel with a foundation of the health industry, the competitive market of the LVHN, and a sound understanding of the business processes that support the hospital delivery of medical services. "This is the only way our IT personnel can understand our business and the opportunities that exist for us to help improve health outcomes," says Lukens.[7]

Process Centric Skills

Building a set of *process-centric skills* is a key foundation skill that every CIO and key IT personnel require to work effectively with the business. The business enterprise consists of numerous processes across the value chain supported by IT. Understanding these enterprise processes and how they align to customer value is critical in effectively working with business personnel to achieve business outcomes for company challenges and opportunities. The good news is that IT personnel are in an excellent position to have this knowledge since IT enables most business processes. The trick here is to be able to articulate how business processes work using business speak and not technological speak.

With process-centric skills, IT personnel can work with business teams to understand the value of each business process and the associated value of the technology supporting the process. IT personnel can also work with business teams to reengineer or reinvent processes to achieve improvement. In addition, enhancements to applications, revising Service Level Agreements (SLAs), and revisiting enabling technologies, among others, are part of a toolkit IT personnel can also utilize to improve business processes through IT, if applicable.

In April of 2011, the CSAA Insurance Group hired Steve O'Connor as the new CIO. As O'Connor became familiar with the business, he realized that there was no formal process mapping of the company's business processes. One of O'Connor's information strategies was to improve the flow of information to add value to customers. He could not accomplish this without understanding what the business processes were. O'Connor met with the CEO and discussed with her the need for the company to document its business processes. He explained its importance in improving the applications that support the business processes, as well as a baseline for improving the processes themselves. O'Connor volunteered to set up a team within the IT organization to inventory the existing processes and work with the business to facilitate the documentation of the processes. O'Connor was insistent that the ownership of the processes belongs with the business but he would take the first step to document them. Once documented, his team would work with the business to identify improvements that would support and facilitate the company's aggressive growth strategy. The CEO gave O'Connor the green light to proceed.

O'Connor chose a talented IT professional with both business and technology experience to lead the project. He chose Rosa Sibilsky as the business process director. Sibilsky began working with the business to document for the first time the business processes of the company. Sibilsky's plan was to *identify the process owners, and then work with each area to make sure they have the processes clearly documented.*[8] Over a few months after meeting with business personnel, Sibilsky accomplished her first major task: developing a value chain of the key business processes that drive the company (Figure 10.3).

Once Sibilsky and her team identified the key processes, they needed to drill down a few levels to understand how the processes worked, documents are utilized, people are involved, and interaction with other business processes. The methodology chosen was to utilize workshops to capture the information needed for each key business process. The workshops included Sibilsky's team as well as business personnel from the various organizations involved in the process. Sibilsky chose an IBM tool, Blueworks Live, to capture the key information for each of the business processes. Sibilsky's team facilitated the workshop and used the tool to capture the information.

One of the workshops was to identify key information for direct mail campaign approvals. There were eight business personnel in the workshop. "It was eye opening for them. Everyone talked about the

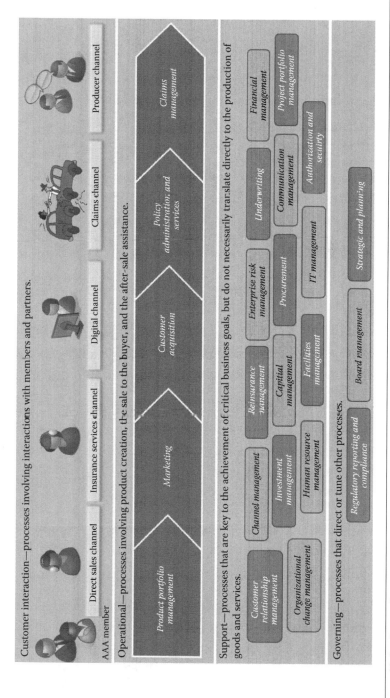

Figure 10.3 Process Framework: Insurance Value Chain.

process, what he, or she did or did not know. It was a surprise for a lot of them because they are used to working in silos. One of the attendees said that the 'workshop was awesome' because they now understood the upstream and downstream activities." (ibid) At the end of the workshop, the group populated the tool with the information needed. Following is an example of the approval activities captured in the workshop. The tool also captured detailed information about all the activities such as process owners, personnel involved, and documents utilized (Figure 10.4).

Developing process-centric skills is a real asset for personnel in the IT organization. It is the only way to support the business properly. Remember, the enterprise value chain is a set of business processes that create value to customers, supplier networks, business personnel, and anyone involved in the creation of the company's products and services business.

Market Knowledge Competency

Having a competency in market knowledge will provide you and your IT organization with a keen understanding of the market and competitive environment. Every business has challenges, as well as opportunities. Meetings occur every day around the world where business teams discuss challenges and identify opportunities that will enable the company to grow and prosper. Unfortunately, if you, as the CIO, or your leadership team does not understand the market environment, you will sit idle in these meetings just listening. Eventually, you will not be invited to any more of these meetings.

If you are satisfied with being the recipient of directives from your C-level peers with guidance on how your IT organization can support the business, then you are not a strategic CIO. If, however, you want to improve you stature and involvement with your C-level peers in addressing business issues and collaboratively address business challenges and opportunities, you need to improve your knowledge about your company's competitive market.

Debra Martucci (CIO at Synopsys), Ken Piddington (CIO at Global Partners), Wayne Shurts (CIO at Sysco Foods), and Sanjib Sahoo (CIO at OptionMONSTER) have developed market knowledge skills they use every day in meetings with their C-level peers.

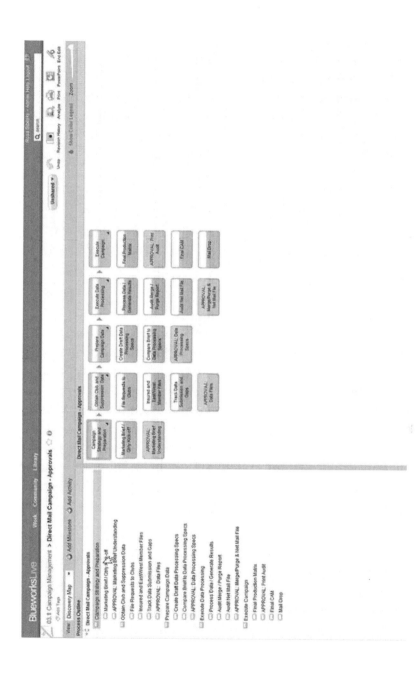

Figure 10.4 Capturing Key Processes and Associated Activities: Example.

Because they understand the market their company competes in, they can actively contribute in business discussions and enable business outcomes. The three skill areas of this competency are product knowledge, industry insight, and competitive landscape. Each of these skills complements one another to form a market knowledge competency. Having knowledge just about your company's products, or just about industry insight, or just about the competitive landscape isn't enough to form the market knowledge competency. You need all three skills. For this competency, I will define each of the three skills and then provide two CIO examples that demonstrate the market knowledge competency.

Product Knowledge Skills

Gaining knowledge about the products and services your company provides to customers and value chain partners is necessary for any CIO who wants to become a strategic partner with the business. How do you expect to understand the business challenges if you do not know your company's products and services? You cannot. Knowledge about the products and services provides the context for participating in business discussions about the company challenges and opportunities.

Your IT organization designs, develops, or acquires solutions to support the company business processes. As a result, you are aware of all the information intersects where value is created. As the CIO, you and your IT teams are in a perfect position to identify the value opportunities for your company's products and services, across the entire value network. These *value points* represent opportunity areas for business/IT teams to work together and identify new opportunities to create and enhance new products and services. Spending time with product marketing personnel as well as with sales executives conducting sales calls is a great way to learn about your company's products and services.

Industry Knowledge Skills

Understanding industry trends will enable you to work with marketing, sales, product engineering, and other organizations responsible for designing, developing, manufacturing, selling, and supporting your company's products and services. Having this knowledge will make you an active participant in discussions with your C-level peers and other business personnel in discussing company challenges and opportunities.

The best way to gain these skills is to spend time with the business areas and the appropriate personnel. There is no substitute to learning than experiencing the activity. Spend time with sales executives visiting clients to understand their issues and challenges. Work with marketing personnel to understand industry history, current trends, and future activities, which will impact the industry as a whole. With industry knowledge skills, IT personnel are in position to understand the industry landscape and how it aligns to the products and services of the enterprise.

Competitive Landscape

When you and your key IT personnel have a comprehensive understanding of the competitive landscape, you and they are better informed and capable of identifying the associated issues and opportunities that your company needs to overcome. You need to be able to understand the competitive landscape, the companies you compete with, and the value that differentiates your company from your competitors. Think about it. You are participating in a meeting with the C-level executives from marketing, sales, and manufacturing. The group is discussing new product ideas and working to complete a two-by-two grid that identifies the positives and negatives of each new product idea. You cannot participate in this discussion if you don't understand the competitive environment and what makes your company products and services valuable to customers.

The best way to learn about the competitive landscape is to work with personnel in the marketing, sales, distribution, and customer support organizations so you can hear first hand from people who live in the competitive landscape each day. This is the same process described in the other two skill areas of market knowledge.

CIOs that truly have market knowledge skills can provide invaluable help in matching IT solutions to business opportunities. Following are two examples of strategic CIOs who helped their company achieve business outcomes.

Debra Martucci is CIO and vice president of IT for Synopsys. The 2 billion dollar plus company, located in Mountain View California, is a market leader in electronic design automation (EDA) by providing products and services that accelerate innovation in the global electronics market. "Their products help engineers design computer chips that are about 6 atoms wide, and when you are at the atomic level we are enabling the efficient design of some interesting products," says Brian Beattie, CFO at Synopsys.[9] Synopsys is a very sophisticated engineering company and is heavily dependent on the IT organization to support their product development needs. Who better to lead the IT organization than an engineer? Martucci has a master's degree in physics and a stellar background in software automation with experience at NASA in the Space Shuttle Division. She also managed teams responsible for developing code for very large-scale real-time, embedded microprocessor and database generation systems for advanced aircraft radar simulation.

Martucci not only understands how engineers design the Synopsys products, she also understands the industry and competitive environment. Martucci utilizes these skills every day as she leads the IT organization and collaborates with engineers and other business units the design, development, manufacture, and support of Synopsys products and services.

Because Martucci understands the product, industry, and competitive environment, she is very effective in understanding the challenges and opportunities Synopsys engineers have in developing and enhancing new products. Following is one example as explained to me by Martucci:

> My team worked with the engineering department to understand a design issue that prevented them from more efficiently designing products. We developed a tool engineers could use to overcome the issue and improve the efficiency of the design. It worked so well, that we now sell that solution to our customers.[10]

Because Synopsys products are so heavily dependent on engineering, the IT organization needs to work very closely with the engineers. Unfortunately, not all IT personnel are well versed in business skills.

To overcome this challenge, Martucci hires MBAs from top schools—such as Kellogg School of Management and Wharton

School of the University of Pennsylvania—to mentor her IT staff in marketing, finance, modeling, and other business skills. "The MBA's help drive thought leadership and encourage the rest of her team." Martucci describes her next step, which was to reorganize her teams to work more closely with the business. "I reorganized so I can leverage my teams to work more closely with the business and drive business applications and solutions for finance, marketing, product design, and other business units."[10] To help disperse business and market knowledge throughout the organization, she instituted role rotations and assigned new responsibilities to help broaden team skills. "I recently took a super star who was running infrastructure and made him responsible for networks and collaborative web tools."[10]

Martucci also implemented a 360-degree program to help IT personnel understand that the skills they need to succeed in the future are not the same skills they have today. "I also have a group of our midlevel managers and high-potential technical personnel involved in training programs."[10] Martucci spends a lot of time and energy focusing on career development of IT personnel and engagement with the business. "We've made huge investments in improving the skills of our people. These are the next leaders of our company."[10] Martucci sees the results as her teams engage with the business and apply their competencies and skills on achieving business outcomes that support the growth of the company.

Technology Prowess Knowledge

Technology prowess addresses the strategic technology skills required by your IT organization to leverage and align IT solutions to the needs of the business. Remember the times you have left your home and 5 minutes later ask yourself, "Did I close the garage door?" Well, now you can use your Craftsman remote control that allows you to monitor and operate your garage door from anywhere with your Internet-enabled smartphone, cell phone, laptop, or tablet. You can check status, close the garage door if you have left it open, or even open it for friends or deliveries when you aren't home.[11]

While some IT organizations leverage their internal IT personnel, a number of CIOs are thinking outside the box and engaging their vendors in leveraging their market, competitive, and technology skills to collaborate with the IT organization and the business to focus on achieving the company's business objectives. P&G's CIO, Filippo Passerini, credits vendor partnerships with helping save the company $900 million in operating costs over a few years because of partnering with the IT organization. The CIO of Hilton Worldwide, Robert Webb, anticipates a set of critical vendors to work together with IT to *imagine new technology or methods well beyond contractual terms with those providers.*[4]

The three skill areas of this domain are technology strategy/adaptability, organization agility, and strategic project capability.[12]

Technology Strategy/Adaptability Skills

Your IT organization requires a technology strategy/adaptability that enables the company to develop and enhance new products and services. To accomplish this, you and your technology teams need a strong understanding of the available and emerging technology in the marketplace and develop a technology strategy that will enable IT to leverage these technologies into new and/or enhanced products and services.

Technology improves every day and how we use it will change our lives forever. Google Executive Chairman Eric Schmidt, in an interview by McKinsey's James Manyika, talks about how technologies disruption will impact our lives in the fields of biology, manufacturing, computer interaction, and man versus machine. Technological innovations in the field of medicine and biology are improving cancer patient outcomes. Printers are now manufacturing 3D materials, which used to be the subject of science fiction. Computer scientists are investigating new approaches to interacting with computers with a desired result of eliminating interfaces. Google Now captures behaviors and provides the user helpful information. The application captures what you do, like driving to the office. Therefore, when there is a traffic disruption, the application will provide you with an alternate route.[13]

Schmidt believes "the ultimate model is that the computer does what it does well, which is these complicated analytical needle-in-a-haystack problems, and has a perfect memory. And humans do what we do well, which is judgment and having fun, and thinking about things." The computer is making suggestions based upon your past behaviors.[13]

The challenge is to identify the technologies, which, as Schmidt states, will "have the greatest impact on economies, business models, and people." (ibid) Therefore, CIOs and their IT organization need to think outside the box to innovate different ways technologies can impact our lives. As a CIO, you need to ensure that your CTO has appropriate knowledge of how to use the newest technologies to enable business outcomes. The appropriate course of action is to first identify a business problem you are trying to solve and then determine if a technology could enable a solution. And if the answer is *yes*, which technology would be most appropriate for the organization. Most aligns with the infrastructure strategy and business needs of the company. Sometimes, the solution is just a process change and technology is not part of the solution. The challenge for any CIO is to make sure your IT organization does not fall into the trap of being a hammer looking for a nail. Sometimes, an IT organization is so enamored with technology, they will try to find ways to apply it, even if it does not solve a business problem.

Organization Agility Skills

Today's marketplace is very dynamic, placing new and demanding requirements on the IT organization. The only structure that enables the organization to respond to these ever-changing demands from the business is to develop organization agility skills, whereby your IT organization can quickly form teams to partner with the business to respond to new business opportunities. In today's competitive marketplace, speed is mandatory and the ability for IT to have personnel with multibusiness and technical skills is necessary.

SanDisk is the industry leader in flash memory cards for smartphones, computers, and cameras. SanDisk's focus had been on end customers. Now, they focus on large organizations to consume flash memory in terms of solid-state drives. The value of flash memory is that it is fast, highly dependable, and does not generate heat. Prior to Ravi Naik becoming CIO, in September 2009, the IT organization reflected the typical profile for a high-tech company. Hierarchical technical personnel focused on their jobs and implemented software solutions for SanDisk products and services. "IT personnel were good at what they do but the business was changing from manufacturing products for the consumer, through Sam Club, Best Buy, or Costco, to a company expanding its reach to OEM, smart phone, and tablet manufacturers."[14] Naik saw three major challenges that prevented the IT organization from responding adequately to the changing business needs of the company. The first was an internally-focused organization that did not partner with the business. The second problem was an organization that was multilayered, which hampered speed and efficiency. The third problem was IT leadership that lacked the business skills to support their technical skills.

To solve the first challenge of partnering with the business, Naik started with a meeting with the vice president of engineering. During the meeting, Naik said the following to the vice president to spark the conversation about improving the partnership between the two organizations:

> If you are going to start building drives for personal computers, we should start using them internally within the IT organizations. This will help the development process and improve time to market. I will treat your product development department as a true customer. This process will provide you feedback from our organization, your first customer, and prior to product launch. It will be a game changer.[14]

His idea sparked a new relationship with the product development organization. Both organizations worked together to develop new products and shortened the product development time dramatically. In fact, the partnership was so successful that the IT and engineering organization worked closely with one another and collaborated on product road maps. The success spread quickly throughout SanDisk. Business unit vice presidents began seeking out the help of the IT organization in solving their business challenges.

The second problem Naik dealt with was the multilayer inefficiency of the IT organization. His goal was to become lean. Naik believes that "multi-layer organizations are big and bureaucratic and need to become lean, where you can quickly and rapidly respond to business needs."[13] Naik wanted to change the structure, from layers of business relations directors, architects, systems architects, and developers to a two-layer organization: an IT manager and an execution organization. Naik explains why layered organizations have challenges:

> Most times, you lose your advantage in communications as you go from layer to layer. Most times when a relationship manager communicates to a process person, they interpret things in a slightly different manner, who then communicates to the project manager and then in the end the business doesn't get what it needs.[14]

Naik delayered his IT organization and developed a new role for an IT director for each of the four major business function. This person would have total responsibility for the relationship, own the business analysts, and have responsibility for the project team including all the developers and programmers. Following is an example.

Grace Liu is the director of finance and HR IT and reports to Ravi Naik, the CIO. Naik recruited Liu from the SandDisk finance organization. He wanted a multirole person who has business acumen as well as business knowledge. Naik wanted this person "to drive the relationship between IT and Finance," and Liu has the total responsibility for the relationship and IT projects that result from the relationship. Liu's role is to partner with the corporate services, which includes finance, HR, and legal.

How did the new relationship work? Liu cites an example:

> In the past, the Finance organization assigned a person to collect requirements, prioritize them, and then send me the listen. Now we facilitate the prioritization process. We work closely with Finance personnel to review the requests, provide our inputs, determine what makes sense, and prioritize the final list. I then work with my team to execute the projects.[15]

Naik meets regularly with the three IT directors who support the business. "We get together regularly at staff meetings, and meet offline as well, to share ideas and experiences." (ibid)

How has Naik's agile IT organization performed at SanDisk? "We have reduced the organization by one-third and we deliver twice as fast. It is a win-win for everyone. The business reduces time to market and IT personnel develop cross-functional skills, which improves their value to the business." (ibid)

Strategic Project Capability Skills

One of the greatest challenges for an IT organization is its ability to absorb strategic projects with current staff and budget constraints while still maintaining the nuts and bolts of the business. You can only accomplish this if you have visibility into the projects, whether they are enhancement of run and maintain projects, and can control execution with a set of robust processes and tools. Only then can you optimize performance and reap the rewards of reduced time and resources, which will free up funds for strategic investments. The graphic shown in the following depicts this strategy (Figure 10.5).

Developing competencies in your IT personnel that are responsible for run and maintain and enhancement projects is not an easy task. It is more than just following a few simple processes. It will require a change in behaviors of your personnel so they intuitively execute in a proactive way to reduce execution risk.

This is not the case for the Georgia Technology Organization (GTA), which manages IT for the State of Georgia. Calvin Rhodes is the CIO, and Tom Fruman is the director of enterprise governance

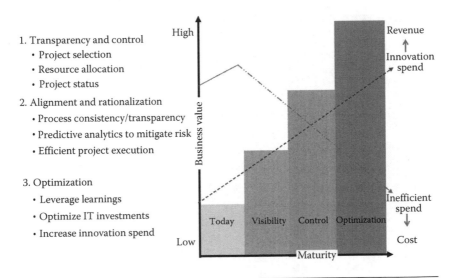

Figure 10.5   Transformation Path to Optimize Project Performance.

and planning. "We are the stewards of taxpayer dollars and need to manage project risk. If we execute well and improve our delivery time and associated costs we can process more projects from state agencies which benefit the citizens of Georgia."[16] Thomas Fruman who manages the governance processes for the state's IT organization, known as GTA, and reports to Rhodes believes that "project success is based upon applying a discipline of process and insight in the management of project portfolios."[17] This same principle applies to the support organizations that manage the run and maintain activities.

GTA implemented a "governance process, enabled by automated tools, which provided a governance layer of process discipline, best practices and predictive analytics to reduce risk and improve project success," says Fruman. (ibid) As a result, state agencies can process more projects through the IT pipeline benefiting the citizens of Georgia (see Chapter 5—How To Succeed At Project Governance— for more detail about GTA and how they manage project portfolios using an effective governance process).

Cross-Dimensional Competency Skills

A strategic CIO and his key personnel must have effective cross-dimensional competency and skills to lead an IT organization transitioning from a tactical to strategic focus. The skills associated with the cross-dimensional competency are vision, leadership, and communication. (Teaming is an implied skill that every employee should exhibit.) A strategic IT organization thinks, behaves, and interacts with business personnel in an entirely new way compared to a tactical IT organization. As we all know, behaviors are not easy to change. In fact, behaviors are one of the most difficult aspects of managing people. Most IT organizations develop using a tactical focus, whereas a strategic IT organization focuses on business outcomes. A tactical IT organization is technically oriented and performs tasks with a silo mentality. Personnel take direction from a few IT directors at the top of the organization who interface with the business when necessary. Most tactical IT organizations have DNA that drives reactive behaviors. They tend to respond to the directives from the business. On the other hand, a strategic IT organization has proactive DNA.

They tend to exhibit *sense and respond* behaviors based upon their business knowledge and constant interaction with business teams.

You cannot change a person's DNA but you can influence an individual's behavior through education and insight. People who smoke recognize the danger but continue for years until they rationalize that it is unhealthy. The same applies to individuals who eat compulsively. They know eating too much food is not healthy. However, they cannot stop this behavior until they finally realize that is not healthy. Changing personal behaviors is not an easy task. In the corporate environment, changing behaviors and culture is also not an easy task. It takes time. More importantly, the education process is composed of developing a vision, providing leadership, and communicating in a language that people can understand and internalize.

To solve business problems in today's highly interactive business environment, personnel from different organizations have to work together. IT personnel must have technical skills and interact effectively with other technology professionals. Technical people have a language all their own. When they interact with personnel from non-IT organizations, it is as if they do not speak the same language. They do not understand the context of the conversation. One of the biggest challenges today is to create cohesive communication skills that enable them to work together effectively in teams. How does a CIO help personnel understand the changing business environment and assess, analyze, and improve their cross-dimensional competency and skills?

- The first step is to convey a vision of how the IT organization needs to move up the strategic curve and collaborate with the business to create and enhance customer value and achieve corporate goals.
- The second step is to provide the leadership to key personnel, as well as the entire IT organization, that will guide them to implement the vision of transforming to a more strategic IT organization.
- The third step is to communicate the vision to key personnel, who lead and direct IT teams. Since this is an important competency in its own right, I devote the next chapter to this subject.

An excellent example of demonstrating cross-competency skills is Sanjib Sahoo, the CIO/CTO at tradeMONSTER Group®, an award-winning group including online resource providing stock market insight, options trade ideas, education to do-it-yourself investors, and a top-rated online brokerage tradeMONSTER.com.

Sanjib Sahoo: CIO/CTO, Building a Successful IT Team

Does your IT organization work well in teams? Are you hiring the right people? How do you prevent employee attrition? Do you have the right leadership style to drive employee success? Why is this important?

In today's complex business environment, IT organizations work more closely with the business than ever before. The pace of change is increasing at a rapid rate. As a result, IT personnel must respond to the demands of the business quicker than ever before. This is especially true for a business experiencing explosive growth. So how does a CIO of a start-up build a winning team of IT personnel who support and enable a business forecasted to double in size every few years?

Jon Najarian, Pete Najarian, and Dirk Mueller founded tradeMONSTER Group (earlier OptionMonster Holdings, Inc.) in 2006. As successful professional traders and respected investment experts, they realized people needed a *disciplined investment process to manage their money*.[18] With an aggressive business plan, the founders recognized that success required an innovative and strategic CIO who leveraged the skills of the IT organization to drive the explosive growth projected.

tradeMONSTER Group hired Sanjib Sahoo as CIO/CTO in 2006. With a successful track record in financial services through the use of his expertise in real-time trading systems and technology and architecture management, Sahoo was the perfect candidate. What made him stand out above all other candidates was Sahoo's approach to building an IT organization to achieve the projected success.

Sahoo designed and built trading/financial platforms for XpressTrade (now Charles Schwab), Citibank, Deutsche Bank, Desjardins Bank, and several other organizations. Engaged with technology for financial services businesses for over 14 years, Sahoo has a wide range of expertise in technology management, architecture and design, and project management and is an expert in real-time trading systems.

When speaking with Sahoo, you begin to realize his passion for building a team of IT leaders:

> The success of a CIO depends on his technology team. The way a CIO connects to the team is very important for the organizational operating system. Constant sharing of vision and an inclusive management style helps the team to understand the direction of the company and promotes low level decision making within the team, in turn promoting constant innovation and collaboration to build a culture of love, trust and respect across the organization.[19]

Sahoo created a vision for building a successful team, providing leadership to his organization to support their professional growth, and communicated his strategy for building a high-performing strategic IT organization. The results reflect his success. The employee attrition rate was less than 3% in the past 6 years ending in December 2012 and the performance uptime of tradeMONSTER applications *is currently at 99.99%.*[5] How has he accomplished this?

If you have the opportunity to meet Sahoo, as I did, it is easy to understand the underlying principles that drive his passion for building IT leaders. His four basic principles are as follows: (ibid)

1. Develop a culture of creativity that drives innovation and personal growth.
2. Build an organization of strong leaders.
3. Focus on quality over quantity.
4. Provide an environment to retain employees.

Using these basic principles, Sahoo developed the following framework as his model for building an IT organization of leaders. Sahoo presented his framework at a *2012 CIO Magazine Summit* in Chicago (Figure 10.6).[20]

Phase 1 creates the foundation. Phase 2 enables him to grow the organization. Phase 3 leverages the competencies and skills of IT personnel to optimize performance. An underlying set of enablers provides the governance necessary to build a successful

Creating leader-custom model

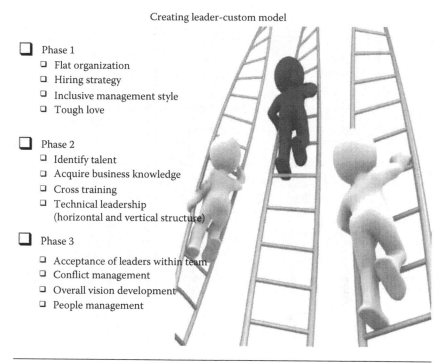

☐ Phase 1
  ☐ Flat organization
  ☐ Hiring strategy
  ☐ Inclusive management style
  ☐ Tough love

☐ Phase 2
  ☐ Identify talent
  ☐ Acquire business knowledge
  ☐ Cross training
  ☐ Technical leadership
    (horizontal and vertical structure)

☐ Phase 3
  ☐ Acceptance of leaders within team
  ☐ Conflict management
  ☐ Overall vision development
  ☐ People management

Figure 10.6   Leadership Model.

leadership-based team of IT professionals. One of the IT directors says it best:

> I feel my leadership skills and willingness to lead teams have grown here at tradeMONSTER. The way I have taken on more and more responsibilities with getting more and more involved with the team has given me confidence to take on more management tasks, which I was not sure was my forte before. This steady additional level of responsibility pushed me to make sure that my team performs at its best at all times. Today I feel more comfortable to take on more management tasks.[21] (tradeMONSTER Group IT Director)

Phase 1: Foundation Phase

The foundation phase focuses on developing a flat organization and hiring strategy, inclusive management style, and tough love.

Sahoo started with a flat organization to level the playing field. He used a well thought out hiring strategy to bring the right talent on board with a unique screening and interview process. Sahoo's inclusive management style utilized an open-door policy and coaching to build an effective team. He doesn't believe in silo management. New employees are coached and mentored:

> I want everyone to feel they are part of the team. (tradeMONSTER IT Director)[21]

Sahoo holds town hall meetings to update his team on company financials, goals, and upcoming corporate events. He also incorporated tough love to keep the team focused on the work needed to support the business. By sharing financials and what is happening in the business, his teams have a company and customer view with a strong connection to the business. One example of how he does this is by sharing the business benefits of the work performed by his teams. When a new application is launched, Sahoo shares the business objectives of the project. As business results are achieved, he shares them with the team. He wants the IT organization to *be part of the business*, and by sharing business outcomes, they don't feel like technology people, but part of the business team:

> Morale on our technology team has never been higher, and we are extremely excited about our products and the services that we provide. We have a culture of "whatever it takes" to meet many difficult challenges that we have overcome.[22] (tradeMONSTER Group IT Engineer)

Phase 2: Growth Phase

With a flat organization in place, Sahoo had clear visibility to identify talent within his organization. He could identify the skills exhibited by each person and the gaps that needed to be filled. He helped educate his organization with the business knowledge IT personnel needed so they could focus on the business outcomes required to achieve the ambitious growth goals. He then proceeded to cross-train his personnel to achieve a broad skill set within the IT organization, which had both the technical skill and business acumen to support the business.

Rather than promoting personnel into management roles, Sahoo looks for natural leaders. Sahoo started with a flat organization and then through performance and observation, he chose the ones that would naturally fit into leadership roles. Once he identified leaders, he rotates each into different assignments to accomplish three goals. The first is to experience different projects within the IT organization. The second objective is for each leader to have an opportunity to work with different teams. And finally, the third objective is to obtain a better understanding of the business by working on different projects.

> My experience at TM has taught me to ask many questions to lead the team to the desired outcome. Not only does it build better teamwork, but the solutions are more robust and the risks mitigated quicker. The team environment here and the vision of leadership from top has made me more comfortable as a leader and handle people much better in a challenging environment. (ibid) (tradeMONSTER Group IT Team Leader)

Phase 3: Optimization Phase

Building the right competencies and skills enabled Sahoo to identify the leaders he needed. Choosing the right leader is important, but gaining the acceptance of leaders within the team is critical. Through an open communication process and inclusive management style in Phase 2, the IT leaders earned the trust and respect of their team members. Managing teams is a challenge; every team faces conflicts at one time or another. How you manage conflict is a critical success factor for high-performing and well-motivated teams. Training IT personnel in conflict management enabled the teams to deal with issues and disagreements constructively. Sahoo also recognized that a key to successful IT organizations overall is vision development.

To help his IT organization remain focused on business goals, Sahoo incorporates varied communication techniques from one-on-one sessions to town hall meetings, which inform and educate his IT organization on the company vision. Providing IT personnel with 100% visibility of the company's strategies and performance enabled the IT organization to stay focused on the business needs and business outcomes required to maintain the rapid growth of tradeMONSTER. Group people management is the skill gap most prevalent in

IT organizations. IT personnel are trained in technology skills but not necessarily in people skills. They learn and practice the science of IT through education and work. The development of soft skills such as listening, communication, and cooperation is more of an art. So to help his leaders manage their teams more effectively, Sahoo provided coaching, mentoring, and people management training to build this skill area:

> The open and agile culture at tradeMONSTER has brought out a tough attitude in me with a no fear attitude to face critical issues. Working with great minds has increased my knowledge and confidence and my hard work has been acknowledged always and has helped me grow more and strong as a leader. (ibid) (tradeMONSTER Group IT Team Leader)

Enablers

Building an effective leadership-based team is no easy task, and Sahoo utilized a set of team-based enablers to aid him in his journey. At a *2012 CIO Magazine Perspectives Summit,* Sahoo identified the following enablers he used to build his leaders[23]:

- Nonpolitical open-door environment
- Open review process (supervisor, manager, peer reviews)
- Periodic 360-degree reviews for leaders
- Innovation committee and mapping to product plan
- Create passion and motivation within every level of the team
- Create communicational and inclusive management style

tradeMONSTER Group has grown rapidly. In 2008, it launched tradeMONSTER, an innovative brokerage featuring slick tools and trade executions, ranked #1 in 2012 by *Barron's* for technology and *best for options traders.* In 2013, tradeMONSTER was ranked among the top 2 online trading companies in North America competing with several big names like Charles Schwab, Ameritrade, and E-trade.

Sahoo was instrumental in making this happen. His success is a great example of how to build a leadership-based organization, which drives business success. He created a vision and utilized his leadership and communication skills to build a high-performing IT organization. His 3-phase approach is simple but effective and requires a lot of commitment and support from the executive leadership of the company.

The quality I admire most about Sanjib Sahoo is that he never speaks in the first person. He is always talking about *we* because he views himself as an integral part of the team and is not afraid to roll up his sleeves and work side by side with his team members:

> As technology leaders, we have a big responsibility of bringing in upcoming leaders not only for the interest of ourselves, but for the industry as a whole. This story highlights what we have been able to achieve with a different approach for creating leaders and different motivational approaches taken to retain talent in a high stress environment. Hope this approach helps all of you to get a new perspective![18]

Keep a lookout for Sanjib Sahoo. He was selected as the 2013 *CIO of the Year* award honoree by the Executives' Club of Chicago, the Association of IT Professionals, and the Society of Information Management.[14] He is the new wave of strategic CIO's who will lead IT organizations to create customer value, increase margin, and enhance shareholder wealth. I have a strong feeling you will be reading a lot more about Sahoo in the future.

Improving the Competencies and Skills of Your IT Organization

Understanding which competencies and skills are required for your IT organization to excel is only part of the solution. Another major component is helping your IT teams improve the competencies and skills. Many organizations try to do this themselves through in-house training. Another more successful approach is to seek assistance from professionals who have held leadership positions in IT, understand the skills sets required, and successfully transform IT teams to exhibit the needed competencies and skills that will make your IT organization succeed.

A number of professional organizations provide these services. One, which I am familiar with, is JCC Executive Partners, founded by John Chambers, a former CIO. Chambers walks the talk. The firm delivers IT business management analysis, guidance, and leadership for C-suite executives. One of their premier services is the Fast Track Enablement™ workshops customized to meet the needs of its clients. The workshop series, delivered in 1–2-day segments, delivers results quickly around the key competency and skill areas and includes both IT and business personnel. Through a robust methodology, the client teams use these new learned skills to identify their current state within a matter of hours, pinpoint the hard benefits to advance to the next maturity step, and, most importantly, determine how they can immediately institute the necessary changes to achieve significant business outcomes.[24]

Developing a cross-dimensional competency using vision, leadership, and communication skills is an art. You find that most seasoned executives who possess these skills attract attention as soon as they walk in the room. It is the way they walk, talk, and behave. These type leaders convey a vision that people grasp because of their leadership and communication skills. They speak in a language people understand and convey a vision that is easy to imagine. If you are a CIO who is seeking to transform the IT organization to be more business focused and strategic, hone your cross-dimensional competency and associated skills. The payoff will be tremendous.

Chapter Summary

In this chapter, I identified the four competencies and associated skills that a strategic IT organization must focus on to succeed at working with business teams to achieve successful business outcomes. Included in the discussion are examples of strategic CIOs and their teams, which excel in the competency and apply the associated skills effectively:

- Business knowledge (environment, opportunities, process centric)
- Market knowledge (product knowledge, industry insight, competitive landscape)
- Technology prowess (technology strategy/adaptability, organizational agility/strategic project capability)
- Cross dimension (vision, leadership, communications)

Business knowledge is an important competency for three important reasons. The first is that IT personnel need to understand how the business operates so they can intelligently communicate with business teams. The second is an understanding of the customer value provided as well as opportunities to provide improved customer value. The third is a process focus so IT personnel can identify the information intersects across the enterprise value chain, where value is created or can be created.

Market knowledge is an important competency since IT personnel cannot effectively improve customer value without a good understanding of the company products, the industry trends, and the competitive environment. CIOs recognize that to be successful, they need to have a good understanding of the market. It is almost more important that key IT personnel who interact with the business on a daily basis have the same skills. Otherwise, the IT teams that work with business units will not effectively contribute to any discussion involving business challenges, opportunities, and potential solutions.

Technology prowess is an important competency since technology is advancing at such a rapid pace. There are three major challenges CIOs face. The first is that not every new technology is an appropriate fit for your business. The right technology choice is the one that meets the needs of your business, not the one that is the latest and greatest. The second challenge is that business executives read about all the new technologies and want to know why the IT organization isn't implementing them. The third, and most dangerous, is that business unit executives are contacting software vendors and acquiring products and services avoiding the IT organization. This is dangerous because the acquired software by the business units can conflict with other enterprise-wide systems creating business issues. The key skills required by IT personnel are to develop a technology strategy that is flexible and can adapt to changing business conditions. Another key skill is to develop agility within the IT organization to quickly form teams to address business challenges and meet the demands of the business, which are changing at a quicker pace than ever before. The final skill is a strategic project capability that enables IT organizations to execute projects with speed and minimal risk and within schedule requirements. Doing so will enable the IT organization to process more projects through the pipeline and address the strategic project demands from the business.

Cross-dimensional competency is a critical component for a strategic IT organization. The CIO must convey a vision of how the IT organization operates and provides value to the business. Unless IT personnel can envision the future state in terms of strategies, projects, metrics, and business goals, as well as how it will benefit each person in their career paths, any change in IT strategy will fail.

Citations

1. Ravi Naik, CIO-SanDisk/Phil Weinzimer Telephone Interview, April 4, 2013.
2. McKesson Press Release, June 16, 2009; McKesson Announces New Group President of Technology Solutions Segment; http://www.mckesson.com/about-mckesson/newsroom/press-releases/2009/mckesson-announces-new-group-president-of-technology-solutions-segment/.
3. Rick Karlgaard-Publisher: *Forbes Magazine*, June 6, 2012, Interview with Randy Spratt-CIO/CTO-McKesson and Pat Blake-Executive Vice President and Group President of McKesson Technology Solutions; http://landing.newsinc.com/forbes/video.html?vcid=23820622&freewheel=91218&sitesection=forbes.
4. CIO of Pharmaceutical Company/Phil Weinzimer Interview, March 2013.
5. Harvey Nash/PA Consulting Group CIO Survey Reports IT Leaders Believe Innovation Critical to Retaining Market Share; Wayne, NJ, May 9, 2011; http://www.harveynash.com/usa/thehub/2011/05/harvey_nashpa_consulting_group.asp.
6. The Great Talent Hunt; *CIO Magazine*, May 1, 2003, p. 32.
7. Hary Lukens-CIO, LVHN/Phil Weinzimer Interview, July 26, 2012; August 13, 2012.
8. Rosa Sibilsky, Business Process Director, CSAA Insurance Group/Phil Weinzimer Telephone Interview, May 9, 2013.
9. Brian Beattie, CFO-Synopsys/Phil Weinzimer Telephone Interview, August 14, 2012.
10. Debra Martucci-Vice President and CIO-Synopsys/Phil Weinzimer Telephone Interview, August 8, 30, 2013.
11. Craftsman AssureLink™ Internet Connected DC Belt Drive Garage Door Opener with DieHard® Battery Backup. Craftsman Website; http://www.craftsman.com/craftsman-assurelink-8482-internet-connected-dc-chain-drive-garage/p-00930437000P?prdNo=2&blockNo=2&blockType=G2&sid=ISx20110429x00001&psid=64x174066&knshCrid=4025672&k_clickID=5b96dc90-7989-77e9-fabc-0000173d8734.
12. CIO Magazine; CIO's Forge Vendor Collectives to Extract Business Benefits: Kim S. Nash, *CIO Magazine*, November 28, 2011. http://www.cio.com/article/695280/CIOs_Forge_Vendor_Collectives_to_Extract_Business_Benefits.

13. http://www.mckinsey.com/insights/high_tech_telecoms_internet/disruptive_technologies Google Executive Chairman Eric Schmidt. This interview was conducted by James Manyika, a director in McKinsey's San Francisco office, in February 2013; Copyright © 2013 McKinsey & Company. All rights reserved.

14. Ravi Naik, CIO-SanDisk/Phil Weinzimer Telephone Interview, April 4, 5, 12, 2012.

15. Grace Liu -SanDisk Finance and Human Resources IT Director/Phil Weinzimer Telephone Interview, June 11, 2012.

16. Calvin Rhodes, CIO-State of Georgia/Phil Weinzimer Interview, February 4, 2013.

17. Thomas Fruman, Director of Enterprise Governance and Planning-GTA-State of Georgia/Phil Weinzimer Interview, January 23, 2012.

18. Sanjib Sahoo, CIO OptionMONSTER/Phil Weinzimer Interview, December 7, 2012.

19. Sanjib Sahoo, CIO OptionMONSTERMonster/Phil Weinzimer Interview, January 18, 2013.

20. Sanjib Sahoo, CIO OptionMONSTERMonster/Phil Weinzimer Interview, January 20, 2013; with permission.

21. OptionMONSTERMonster, IT Director/Phil Weinzimer Interview, January 30, 2013.

22. OptionMONSTERMonster, IT Team Leader, IT Group Leader/Phil Weinzimer Interview, February 7, 2013.

23. *Fort Mill Times*; Published: Monday, May 20, 2013/Updated: Monday, May 20, 2013 02:49 PM; http://www. fortmilltimes. com/2013/05/20/2703164/optionmMonster-holdings-sanjib.html.

24. John Chambers, Founder-JCC Executive Partners/Phil Weinzimer Interview, December 15, 2013/JCC Executive Partners Website; http:// jcc-exec-partners.com/.

How to Measure and Improve the Maturity of the Strategic IT Competencies and Skills of Your IT Organization

To measure is to know. If you cannot measure it, you cannot improve it.[1]

William Thompson (Lord Kelvin)

The previous chapter focuses on two main themes. The first is identifying the competencies and skills the chief information officer (CIO) and information technology (IT) organization must have in order to effectively collaborate in business teams to achieve business outcomes that improve customer value, revenue, and shareholder wealth. The second theme is how CIOs and their IT teams exhibited these competencies and skills in working on business teams. If you recognize the need to develop these competencies and skills in your IT organization, you need a process to assess the maturity of these competencies and skills. This chapter provides the process for you to do just that. Following are the objective, key messages, examples, and templates included in this chapter.

A. CHAPTER OBJECTIVE

1. Share a process for measuring the strategic IT competencies and associated skills using a *strategic maturity assessment*.

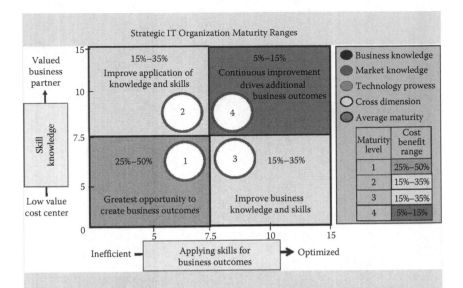

Strategic IT Organization Maturity Ranges

B. KEY POINTS

1. IT organizations need to exhibit four strategic competencies and associated skills if they want to effectively partner with business teams to improve business outcomes in the form of increased customer value, improved margins, and enhanced shareholder wealth.

2. What is common among strategic IT organizations is a varying level of knowledge across the four competencies—business, market, technology prowess, and cross dimensional. Knowledge by itself is important. What is more important is how this knowledge is applied using a set of skills to effect business outcomes.

3. A strategic CIO recognizes that to succeed in achieving business outcomes through collaborating with business leaders and teams is not a one-man process. It takes IT personnel using their skills and applying these skills in collaborative business and IT teams to identify issues, challenges, and solutions that enable business outcomes.

4. A strategic maturity assessment identifies how well IT personnel apply these skills and identifies the gaps in skill maturity that require improvement.

5. You can measure the strategic maturity of your IT organization by following a five-step process:

   a. Assess the level of knowledge and competency of your IT organization.

   b. Plot scores on a maturity index grid.

   c. Assess results to determine gaps.

   d. Develop a plan to improve scores.

   e. Implement a continuous improvement program to achieve positive momentum.

6. There are variations on how to use the strategic IT maturity assessment, from a quick gut check to a more detailed assessment across the IT organization and business:

   a. For items i through vii below: Figure 11.3 provides descriptions of competencies, skills, and the associated best-in-class practices. Table 11.1 is the Assessment Instrument.

   b. For item viii below: Figure 11.10 provides a template for you to use to capture examples of how your IT organization exhibits its skills.

      i. *Gut check assessment*: The CIO completes the assessment independently based upon his or her observations of IT organization. This provides the CIO with an initial point of reference baseline to determine if further assessments, at a more detailed level, are required.

      ii. *IT leadership assessment*: The CIO completes the assessment of IT leadership to determine their degree of maturity. This provides the CIO with a baseline data for identifying gaps and developing training programs with IT leadership.

      iii. *IT personnel assessment conducted by IT leaders as a team*: The IT leadership team performs an assessment, as a team, of the IT organization. This provides the IT leadership team with a perspective of the skill knowledge and application of knowledge for the IT organization, as a whole.

iv. *IT leadership conducts assessment of IT personnel in their organization*: This provides the IT leader, for their organization, a perspective of the skill knowledge and application of knowledge for his or her organization.

v. *Business vice president assessment of IT organization*: This assessment provides the CIO with a perception of how business unit leaders view the skill levels of the IT organization.

vi. *Business unit personnel assessment of IT organization*: This includes business personnel in the IT leadership assessment of their organization (number 3, above). This provides more of a 360-degree perspective on the skills of the IT organization.

vii. *Review results with IT personnel, business vice presidents, and business personnel*: Conduct meetings and town hall meetings to provide results to organization. This helps the entire company view IT in a proactive way as an organization that wants to work with the business to improve business outcomes.

viii. *Adding fields to provide specific examples*: When conducting assessments, you may want to add fields in the template to capture specific examples of where skill knowledge and/or applying skills is deficient or excels as a proof point for the numeric score.

C. EXAMPLES

1. Case example of measuring IT strategic maturity including templates and instructions

D. TEMPLATE EXAMPLES

1. IT Strategic Maturity Assessment—Template (Figures 11.2 and 11.3)
2. Strategic IT Maturity Ranges Framework (Figure 11.4)

3. Strategic IT Organization Maturity Assessment—6-Month Assessment Summary (Figure 11.5 and Table 11.1)

4. Strategic IT Organization Maturity Assessment—6-Month Assessment Scores Summary by Competency (Figure 11.6)

5. Strategic IT Organization Maturity Assessment—6-Month versus 2-Year Assessment Results (Figure 11.8)

6. Strategic IT Organization Maturity Assessment—6-Month versus 2-Year Assessment Results Table (Figure 11.7)

7. Examples of Additional Fields to Add to IT Strategic Maturity Assessment Template (Figure 11.9)

William Thomson was a Scottish mathematician and physicist, in the 1800s, who devoted his life to science. He developed concepts in the field of electromagnetics and submarine telegraphy. His most famous work was developing the Kelvin scale that measured absolute zero of temperature. He was bestowed the title of Baron Kelvin in 1892 as a reward for his lifelong work in science.[1] His life focused on measurement.

We have all heard the phrase "You cannot manage what you cannot measure." Well, it is true. We measure all the time. Whether it is how many yards we hit a golf ball, how much weight we can bench press, our cholesterol level, and, yes, even our stock investments. The goal is to improve. You cannot improve if you do not measure your progress. The same concept applies in business where we measure all the time. Sales targets are established and measured. We measure revenues and profits. We scrutinize productivity measurements constantly. We even use statistical process controls as a key to measuring whether activities are within acceptable parameters. For IT organizations, we measure downtime, uptime, mean time between failure, and a host of other metrics. When it comes to measuring the maturity of a strategic IT organization, you must look at how well the strategic competencies and associated skills, which we discussed in earlier chapters, are applied. This is the objective of this chapter. We will examine a process for measuring the strategic maturity of your IT organization's strategic competencies and skills.

How Can I Measure the Maturity of My IT Organization's Strategic Competency and Skills?

IT organizations need to exhibit four strategic competencies and associated skills if they want to effectively partner with business teams to improve business outcomes in the form of increased customer value, improved margins, and enhanced shareholder wealth.

What is common among strategic IT organizations is a varying level of knowledge across the three competencies—business, market, and technology prowess. Knowledge by itself is important. What is more important is how this knowledge is applied using a set of skills to effect business outcomes. In Chapter 10, we defined skills as a set of behaviors and knowledge or understanding of an activity or set of activities and competencies as the behaviors and knowledge used to demonstrate a set of skills. There is a metric that measures the level of knowledge and the degree to which IT personnel demonstrate the strategic competencies and skills. I identify this metric as the *IT Organization Competency and Skills Maturity Index.*

You can measure the strategic maturity of your IT organization by following a five-step process:

1. Assess the level of knowledge and competency of your IT organization.
2. Plot scores on a maturity index grid.
3. Assess results to determine gaps.
4. Develop a plan to improve scores.
5. Implement a continuous improvement program to achieve positive momentum.

Following is a detailed explanation and associated templates to use when measuring the strategic maturity of your IT organization. Following step 5, I include a section that provides alternative variations for using the maturity assessment to provide more detailed and accurate perceptions regarding the IT organization strategic maturity.

Assess the Level of Knowledge and Competency of Your IT Organization

Following are the four main strategic IT competencies and associated skills of a strategic IT organization identified in Chapter 10 (Figures 11.1 and 11.2).

Assessing the strategic maturity involves a two-step process:

1. The first step is to assess each of the skills with a score that reflects the degree to which the IT organization has skill knowledge and the degree to which the IT organization applies the skill in day-to-day activities (Figure 11.3).
2. The second step is to plot the results on a grid that reflects skill knowledge scores and applying skill scores (Figure 11.4).

Assess skill knowledge and application of knowledge for each of the three skills in each competency.

Following are the instructions for completing the assessment (Figure 11.3):

A. Score *skill knowledge* and *applying skills* for each skill in each of the four competencies
   a. Identify the skill knowledge (a) and the degree to which the IT organization applies the skill in their day-to-day activities (b) for each competency using a scale of 1–5 (1 for low and 5 for high):

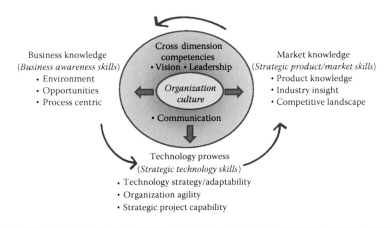

Figure 11.1   Strategic IT Organization Competencies and Skills Framework.

STRATEGIC COMPETENCY	ASSOCIATED SKILLS / BEST PRACTICE		CROSS COMPETENCY SKILLS
BUSINESS KNOWLEDGE Business Awareness Skills	1. Business Environment	IT Personnel Understand and Articulate the Enterprise Business Strategy, Objectives, Culture, and Internal Environment	**1. Vision** IT Vision that Aligns with Corporate, Business Units, and IT Organization
	2. Opportunities / Challenges	IT Organization Understands the Enterprise Business Opportunities to Enhance Customer Value, Revenue, Profitability as Well as Challenges that Impact Enterprise Growth.	
	3. Process Centric	IT Organization Understands How IT Services and Underlying Technologies Align and Enable Enterprise Business Processes that Create / Support Customer Value	**2. Leadership**
		MARKET	
MARKET KNOWLEDGE Strategic Product/Market Skills	1. Product Knowledge	Knowledge of How Customer Value is Derived from Enterprise Products / Services	CIO Guides the IT Organization in Developing the Skills / Competencies / Knowledge to Enhance and Develop the IT Services Aligned to Business Needs and Effectively Collaborates with Business Peers to Achieve Business Vision / Financial Objectives / Market Strategies
	2. Industry Knowledge	Understanding of Industry Landscape and Upcoming Trends and their Alignment to Enterprise Products and Services	
	3. Competitive Landscape	Insight into Competitive Environment and the Associated Customer Value Gaps and Opportunities	
		TECHNOLOGY	**3. Communication**
TECHNOLOGY PROWESS Strategic Technology Skills	1. Technology Strategy / Adaptability	Incorporates a Technology Strategy that Integrates Emerging and Existing Technologies into New and/or Enhanced Customer Value and Revenue Streams.	IT Personnel Effectively Communicate and Team with Business Personnel to Understand / Uncover Opportunities to Drive Revenue / Reduce Cost
	2. Organization Agility	Combined IT/Business Teams Rapidly Respond to Changing Business Needs Utilizing Enabling Technologies to Develop/Enhance Customer Products and Services	
	3. Strategic Project Capability	Increase Capacity to Implement Strategic Project by Reducing Run & Maintain / Enhancement Project Costs/Execution time and Improving IT Personnel Technology/Business Skills	

Figure 11.2 Strategic IT Competencies and Associated Skills-Best Practices.

COMPETENCIES AND ASSOCIATED SKILLS			
BUSINESS KNOWLEDGE			
SKILL	BEST PRACTICE	Score (1 = Low/5 = High)	
		Skill Knowledge (a)	Applying Skill (b)
Business environment	Best practice for Skill 1	(b1)	(b2)
Opportunity/challenges	Best practice for Skill 1	(b3)	(b4)
Process centric	Best practice for Skill 1	(b5)	(b6)
SUB TOTAL		(c1)	(c2)
MAXIMUM SCORE		15	15
COMPETENCY MATURITY % *(sub-total/maximum score)*		(d1)	(d2)

COMPETENCIES AND ASSOCIATED SKILLS			
MARKET KNOWLEDGE			
SKILL	BEST PRACTICE	Score (1 = Low/5 = High)	
		Skill Knowledge (a)	Applying Skill (b)
Product knowledge	Best practice for Skill 1	(b7)	(b8)
Industry knowledge	Best practice for Skill 1	(b9)	(b10)
Competitive landscape	Best practice for Skill 1	(b11)	(b12)
SUB TOTAL		(c3)	(c4)
MAXIMUM SCORE		15	15
COMPETENCY MATURITY % *(sub-total/maximum score)*		(d3)	(d4)

COMPETENCIES AND ASSOCIATED SKILLS			
TECHNOLOGY PROWESS			
SKILL	BEST PRACTICE	Score (1 = Low/5 = High)	
		Skill Knowledge (a)	Applying Skill (b)
Technology strategy/adaptability	Best practice for Skill 1	(b13)	(b14)
Organization agility	Best practice for Skill 1	(b15)	(b16)
Strategic project capability	Best practice for Skill 1	(b17)	(b18)
SUB TOTAL		(c5)	(c6)
MAXIMUM SCORE		15	15
COMPETENCY MATURITY % *(sub-total/maximum score)*		(d5)	(d6)

COMPETENCIES AND ASSOCIATED SKILLS			
CROSS-DIMENSION COMPETENCY			
SKILL	BEST PRACTICE	Score (1 = Low/5 = High)	
		Skill Knowledge (a)	Applying Skill (b)
Vision	Best practice for Skill 1	(b19)	(b20)
Leadership	Best practice for Skill 1	(b21)	(b22)
Communication	Best practice for Skill 1	(b23)	(b24)
SUB TOTAL		(c7)	(c8)
MAXIMUM SCORE		15	15
COMPETENCY MATURITY % *(sub-total/maximum score)*		(d7)	(d8)

COMPETENCIES AND ASSOCIATED SKILLS			
SUMMARY			
SKILL	BEST PRACTICE	Score (1 = Low/5 = High)	
		Skill Knowledge	Applying Skill
SUB TOTAL BUSINESS KNOWLEDGE		(c1)	(c2)
SUB TOTAL MARKET KNOWLEDGE		(c3)	(c4)
SUB TOTAL TECHNOLOGY PROWESS		(c5)	c6
SUB TOTAL CROSS COJMPETENCY SKILLS		(c7)	(c8)
TOTAL SCORE		(e1)	(e2)
AVERAGE MATURITY		(e1/4)	(e2/4)
MAXIMUM SCORE		60	60
MATURITY % *(TOTAL SCORE/MAXIMUM SCORE)*		(e1/60)	(e2/60)

Figure 11.3 IT Strategic Maturity Assessment: Template.

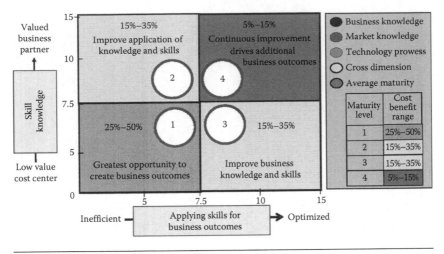

Figure 11.4 Strategic IT Maturity Ranges.

Business knowledge "skill knowledge" = b1, b3, b5
Business knowledge "applying skill" = b2, b4, b6
Market knowledge "skill knowledge" = b7, b9, b11
Market knowledge "applying skill" = b8, b10, b12
Technology prowess "skill knowledge" = b13, b15, b17
Technology prowess "applying skill" = b14, b16, b18
Cross competency "skill knowledge" = b19, b21, b23
Cross competency "applying skill" = b20, b22, b24

B. Total *skill knowledge* and *applying skill* scores for each competency:

    a. Total the scores for "skill knowledge" (c_1, c_3, c_5, c_7) and "applying skills" (c_2, c_4, c_6, c_8) for each competency (*business knowledge, market knowledge, technology prowess, cross-competency skills*)

C. Calculate the competency maturity percentage for each competency:

    a. Divide the total scores for skill knowledge for each competency by the total maximum score (15) to determine the maturity index ($c_1/15$, $c_3/15$, $c_5/15$, $c_7/15$).

    b. Divide the total scores for applying skills by the total maximum score (15) to determine the maturity index ($c_2/15$, $c_4/15$, $c_6/15$, $c_8/15$).

D. Calculate the average maturity numeric and the average maturity percentage for skill knowledge and applying skill for each competency:

a. Copy the subtotal scores for skill knowledge and apply knowledge from each competency into the summary table.

COMPETENCY	SKILL KNOWLEDGE	APPLYING SKILL
Subtotal business knowledge	c1	c2
Subtotal market knowledge	c3	c4
Subtotal technology prowess	c5	c6
Subtotal cross competency	c7	c8
b. Total scores and enter results in	e1	e2
c. Average maturity numeric index	e1/4	e2/4
d. Divide total scores by maximum score to calculate the total maturity percentage index	e1/60	e2/60

Plot the Results on a Grid That Reflects the Maturity of Skill Knowledge Scores and Applying Skill

The template records the *skill knowledge* and *applying knowledge* on a scale of 1–5 for the three skills in each competency. A maximum score of 5 for each of the three skills would result in a total score of 15 (5 times 3) for skill knowledge and a maximum score of 15 (5 times 3) for applying knowledge. You can plot the maturity scores across a vertical and horizontal axis for each of the four competencies. The following figure represents the maturity grid with no data plotted. The vertical axis represents the score for skill knowledge. The horizontal axis represents the score for applying knowledge (Figure 11.4).

Each of the four quadrants of the grid represents an area of potential improvement. Let us look at four possible scenarios. We will then explore a maturity assessment for a 1.5 billion dollar manufacturing company, which includes the scoring template, the grid results, and the areas for opportunities to improve the maturity score.

Scenario 1: Quadrant 1—greatest potential for improvement

- The greatest area for improvement is represented with a skill score that ranges from 0 to 7.5 and an applying knowledge score that ranges from of 0 to 7.5. The intersect of these two scores positions the maturity in the lower left-hand grid that represents the greatest potential for improvement in business outcome of 25%–50%.

Scenario 2: Quadrant 2—moderate opportunity for improvement (most probability of occurrence)

- A midrange score for skill knowledge that ranges from 7.5 to 15.0 and applying knowledge score that ranges from of 0 to 7.5 indicates that the skill knowledge is high but the application of these skills is low. Therefore, there is a midpoint range of potential opportunity for improvement of 15%–35%.

Scenario 3: Quadrant 3—moderate opportunity for improvement (least likely to occur)

- The inverse is also true. An organization can have a low range of skill knowledge, 0 to 7.5, but could apply those skills very well and attain a score of 7.5 to 15. This would also result in a midpoint range of potential opportunity for improvement of 15%–35%. This scenario, although mathematically possible, is rare. You usually do not find organizations providing significant business value by applying a low level of skill knowledge.

Scenario 4: Quadrant 4—continuous improvement

- The organization with the greatest maturity is one where they score 7.5–15.0 in skill knowledge and applying knowledge. This places their score in the upper right-hand quadrant. Continuous improvement programs can result in minor improvements of 5%–15%.

Now that we have discussed the scoring template and strategic maturity grid as a concept, let us examine a maturity assessment with completed data. In conducting interviews for this book, I found many CIOs who approached skills improvement using different techniques, although most followed a basic framework. It was difficult to find a good single example that approached skills improvement in all dimensions. Additionally, CIOs do not really want to share personnel or organization information when it comes to personnel skills improvement.

Following is an example of how to use the maturity assessment to improve the skills of your IT organization. One of the CIOs I interviewed represented the average of other companies who provided data. To maintain confidentiality, at the request of the CIO, I will use Able Manufacturing as the company name and Bill as the name of the CIO. Included is a maturity assessment at the 6-month point of Bill's role as CIO, as well as a maturity assessment at the 24-month period, to provide the reader a perspective on the improvements that CIOs achieved in improving skill knowledge and applying skills to achieve business outcomes.

Following is the maturity grid and the scoring template completed by Bill, the CIO of Able Manufacturing after 6 months in the CIO position. Take a few moments to review the grid and the scoring template. See if you can identify some implications based upon the positioning of the scores. Following the maturity grid and scoring template, we will examine the scores and associated implications (*the assessment we analyzed is the first six-month assessment; I include the 2012 assessment maturity grid in the section titled 5. Implement a Continuous Improvement Program*) (Figure 11.5).

The strategic maturity grid plots the scores for each of the four competencies. For each competency, the sum of the associated skill knowledge scores and the sum of the associated applying skill scores represent the intersection on the maturity grid (Table 11.1).

The scoring template contains the detailed data. (see Figure 11.6).

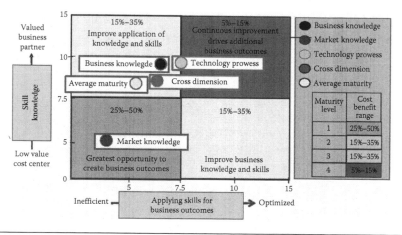

Figure 11.5 Strategic IT Organization Maturity Assessment—6-Month Assessment Summary.

Table 11.1 Strategic IT Organization Maturity Assessment: 6-Month Assessment Scores Summary by Competency

COMPETENCY	SKILL KNOWLEDGE	APPLYING SKILL
Numeric scores		
Business knowledge	9.5	6.0
Market knowledge	5.0	3.0
Technology prowess	9.5	7.5
Cross dimension	8.5	6.0
Total	32.5	22.5
Average maturity	8.1	5.6
Percentage scores		
Business knowledge	63%	40%
Market knowledge	33%	20%
Technology prowess	63%	50%
Cross dimension	54%	38%
Total	213%	148%
Average maturity	54%	37%

Assess Results to Determine Gaps

Assessing the results of the scoring is more than just analyzing the numbers. One needs to understand the culture of the business, as well as the culture of company personnel across all organizations, including IT. Let me begin with some observations based upon the scoring grid and follow up with additional information based upon my interviews with CIOs.

Observations Based upon the Scoring Template and Maturity Grid
There are some obvious observations and associated implications for Able Manufacturing, based upon the scoring completed by the CIO.
   Overall Summary

- *The IT organization needs to improve their knowledge skill scores and do a better job of applying that knowledge to achieve business outcomes.* The overall average maturity for skill knowledge is 8.1 out of 15, or 54%, and for applying skills is 5.6 out of 15 or 37%. This is substantiated by the CIO, who told me that IT personnel are fairly focused on the technology side of the house, which is supported by a 9.5 score for technology prowess skill knowledge.

COMPETENCIES AND ASSOCIATED SKILLS			
BUSINESS KNOWLEDGE			
		Score (1 = Low/5 = High)	
SKILL	BEST PRACTICE	Skill Knowledge (a)	Applying Skill (b)
Business environment	Understanding and ability to articulate the enterprise business strategy, objectives, culture, and internal environment	3.0	2.2
Opportunities/challenges	Understanding and ability to articulate the enterprise business opportunities that can enhance customer experience/value and enterprise revenue/profitability/ROI, and the challenges that impact enterprise growth	3.5	1.9
Process centric	Understanding and ability to articulate how IT services align and support enterprise process and innovate new processes as needed	3.0	1.9
SUB TOTAL BUSINESS KNOWLEDGE		9.5	6.0
MAXIMUM SCORE		15.0	15.0
MATURITY % (sub-total/maximum score)		63%	40%

COMPETENCIES AND ASSOCIATED SKILLS			
MARKET KNOWLEDGE			
		Score (1 =Low/5 = High)	
SKILL	BEST PRACTICE	Skill Knowledge (a)	Applying Skill (b)
Product knowledge	Knowledge of how customer value is derived from enterprise products and services	2.0	1.0
Industry knowledge	Knowledge of industry landscape and upcoming trends and their alignment to enterprise products and services	2.0	1.0
Competitive landscape	Awareness of competitive environment and the existing customer value gaps and associated opportunities to provide customers additional value in the form of new/enhanced products and services	1.0	1.0
SUB TOTAL MARKET KNOWLEDGE		5.0	3.0
MAXIMUM SCORE		15	15
MATURITY % (sub-total/maximum score)		33%	20%

COMPETENCIES AND ASSOCIATED SKILLS			
TECHNOLOGY PROWESS			
		Score (1 = Low/5 = High)	
SKILL	BEST PRACTICE	Skill Knowledge (a)	Applying Skill (b)
Technology strategy/ adaptability	Incorporates emerging and existing technologies into new and/or enhanced products/services that provide customer value that will drive additional revenue, reduce costs, and/or increase ROI	4.0	4.0
Organizational agility	Teams of IT/business personnel rapidly form based upon changing business needs leveraging enabling technologies to develop/enhance customer products and services	2.5	1.5
Strategic project capability	Capability to implement strategic projects by reducing costs of run and maintain activities and enhancement projects as well as improving IT personnel technology/ business skills to improve efficiencies	3.0	2.0
SUB TOTAL TECHNOLOGY PROWESS		9.5	7.5
MAXIMUM SCORE		15.0	15.0
MATURITY % (sub-total/maximum score)		63%	50%

Figure 11.6 Strategic IT Organization Maturity Assessment: 6-Month Assessment Scores by Competency. *(Continued)*

COMPETENCIES AND ASSOCIATED SKILLS			
CROSS-COMPETENCY SKILLS			
		Score (1 = Low/5 = High)	
SKILL	BEST PRACTICE	Skill Knowledge (a)	Applying Skill (b)
Vision	IT vision that aligns with corporate and all business units (including IT)	4.0	2.5
Leadership	CIO and key IT personnel guide the IT organization in developing the skills/competencies/knowledge to enhance and develop the IT services aligned to busines needs and the development and enhancement of products and services as well as effectively collaborates with business peers to achieve business vision/market strategies/financial objectives	2.5	2.0
Communication	IT personnel effectively communicate, collaborate, and team with business personnel to understand/uncover opportunities to drive revenue, reduce costs, and improve ROI	2.0	1.5
SUB TOTAL CROSS-COMPETENCY SKILLS		8.5	6.0
MAXIMUM SCORE		15	15
MATURITY % (sub-total/maximum score)		57%	40%

COMPETENCIES AND ASSOCIATED SKILLS			
SUMMARY			
		Score (1 = Low/5 = High)	
SKILL	BEST PRACTICE	Skill Knowledge	Applying Skill
SUB TOTAL BUSINESS KNOWLEDGE		9.5	6.0
SUB TOTAL MARKET KNOWLEDGE		5.0	3.0
SUB TOTAL TECHNOLOGY PROWESS		9.5	7.5
SUB TOTAL CROSS DIMENSION		8.5	6.0
TOTAL SCORE		32.5	22.5
AVERAGE MATURITY		8.1	5.6
MAXIMUM SCORE		60	60
MATURITY % (TOTAL SCORE/MAXIMUM SCORE)		54%	38%

Figure 11.6 (*Continued*) Strategic IT Organization Maturity Assessment: 6-Month Assessment Scores by Competency.

- *The IT organization needs to develop increased knowledge about the competitive market.* Business knowledge by the IT organization, in terms of how Able Manufacturing operates as a business, is fair (9.5 out of 15). However, that knowledge is only based upon their understanding of how the business processes operate, not based upon how customer value is created, the competitive value gaps, and industry trends. As the CIO told me, "*Implementing my business training program to help IT personnel become smarter when it comes to customer value, will help IT personnel to be proactive with our business units in helping them achieve significant business outcomes.*"[1]
- *The IT organization does not apply the business knowledge skills well but does apply technology prowess skills fairly well.* Overall,

the IT organization exhibits skills in business knowledge and technology prowess but does not know how to apply them to improve business outcomes. One of the reasons for this score is that historically, the IT organization focused on technology and took direction from a few IT leaders. This is acceptable if the CIO desires this type of culture. However, in the long run, it is important to develop business skills within the IT organization so multiple IT teams can work with business teams to address their challenges and collaboratively participate in formulating solutions.

- *The IT organization needs to develop organization agility and strategic project capability skills as well as applying those skills effectively.* Technology prowess did not score as well as one would think for an IT organization, whose main skill is technology. The IT organization skill knowledge for technology prowess is 9.5 out of 15. The IT organization applying skill for technology prowess is 7.5 out of 15. Remember, there are three skills that comprise the technology prowess competency. The first is technology strategy/adaptability. The CIO scored the IT organization 4 out of 5 for both skill knowledge and applying knowledge. However, for the second skill, organization agility, the CIO scored only 2.5 for skill knowledge and applying skill. Organization agility provides the IT organization flexibility in moving resources to meet the needs of the business. This has more to do with IT personnel having a variety of skills that can be drawn upon based upon the changing demands of the business. The third skill set is strategic project capability. The CIO scored skill knowledge 2 and applying skill 2. This is very poor. This skill enables the IT organization to efficiently execute projects without excessive overruns, rework, quality issues, or scope creep. Most projects have failure rates of between 25% and 35%. IT organizations that have a strategic project capability perform better than average. As a result, the IT organization can process more projects through the pipeline, providing greater value to the business.
- *The IT organization needs to develop cross-dimension skills in both knowledge and application if they are going to work effectively with business teams.* The CIO scored 4.0 out of 5 for skill knowledge

in the vision skill. He did this because he has started holding town hall and small group meetings to educate the IT organization of the vision for IT. The CIO also scored 4.0 for applying the vision skill because he is beginning to see IT leaders and IT personnel referring to the IT vision during team meetings. However, skill knowledge and applying skill for leadership and communication still need a marked improvement. The CIO scored the IT organization 2.5 and 1.5, respectively, for skill knowledge and applying skill for leadership. The CIO scored 2.0 for both skill knowledge and applying knowledge for communication. The IT organization is deeply rooted in technology skills and the CIO is just beginning to educate and train his leadership team in developing leadership and communication skills. This accounts for the low scores for leadership and communication.

Develop a Plan to Improve Scores

It is difficult to draw an accurate conclusion from just looking at the numbers on the scoring template or maturity grid. You need to understand the IT organization, its existing culture, and the capabilities of the CIO to truly get a handle on the implications of the scoring.

Following is some background information that provides additional perspective regarding the IT organization at Able Manufacturing:

- Able Manufacturing is headquartered in the midwest region of the United States and started manufacturing operations in the 1920s.
- The company has grown dramatically in the past 12 years.
- The previous leader of the IT organization had been employed by Able Manufacturing for the past 30 years.
- The average tenure of IT organization personnel is 17 years, with very little turnover.
- I asked the CIO to complete two assessments: the first based upon his first 6 months on the job (Figures 11.5 and 11.6) and a second assessment based on the organization performance in the year 2012 (Figures 11.7 and 11.8).

COMPETENCIES AND ASSOCIATED SKILLS MATURITY ASSESSMENT								
SUMMARY								
	SKILL KNOWLEDGE				APPLYING KNOWLEDGE			
COMPETENCY	6 months	24 months	Delta	% Delta	6 months	24 months	Delta	% Delta
Business knowledge	9.5	11.0	1.5	15.8%	6.0	8.0	2.0	33.3%
Market knowledge	5.0	7.5	2.5	50.0%	3.0	7.0	4.0	133.3%
Technology prowess	9.5	13.0	3.5	36.8%	7.5	9.5	2.0	26.7%
Cross dimensional	8.5	10.0	1.5	17.6%	6.0	10.0	4.0	66.7%
Total score	32.5	41.5	9	27.7%	22.5	34.5	12.0	53.3%
Average maturity	8.1	10.4	2.3	28.4%	5.6	8.6	2.3	53.6%

Figure 11.7 Strategic IT Organization Maturity Assessment: 6-Month versus 2-Year Assessment Results Table.

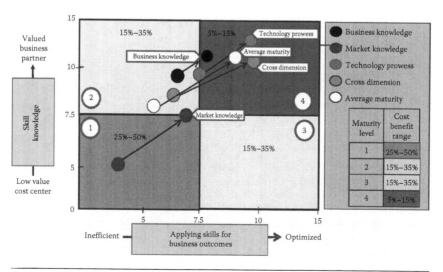

Figure 11.8 Strategic IT Organization Maturity Assessment—6-Month Versus 2-Year Assessment Results.

With the previous background information, you can better understand the reasons the CIO scored each competency with mediocre scores. The assessment analyzed earlier in the chapter is based upon the CIO's assessment of the IT organization 6 months into his new job. For example, the CIO gave high marks for knowing the business, a score of 4.0 for both skill knowledge and applying knowledge, because the average tenure of IT personnel is 17 years. These people know how the company operates. What they do not know is the competitive landscape and an understanding of customer value. Another example is the low scoring for cross-dimension skills. The IT director, who held the leadership role prior to the new CIO, held tight reigns over his organization. It was rare when IT personnel sat in meetings with business teams. The IT director was tactically focused. He provided instructions to the IT organization. The result was a very mechanical responsive IT organization that performed as instructed.

Able Manufacturing hired the CIO to provide the company a strategic perspective on how IT could leverage the competitive position of the company and work with business unit vice presidents to develop technology solutions that would fuel the future growth of the company. The job was a challenge. The CIO recognized that the role at Able would not be a cakewalk. However, he was up for the challenge. Following is a summary of the key components of the plan the CIO developed to improve the strategic maturity of the IT organization:

1. Communicate a vision to the IT organization: Schedule a set of meetings with IT leadership and IT organization town hall meetings to communicate a vision of how leveraging IT can enable the growth of Able Manufacturing and share a roadmap of how the IT organization would accomplish that objective.

2. Understand the business: Meet with business unit vice presidents and industry subject matter experts to understand the business and competitive environment.

3. Identify company challenges and opportunities: Meet with business unit vice presidents to gain a better understanding of the business processes that drive the company and identify areas of opportunity where IT could potentially improve the effectiveness and efficiency of those processes.

4. Develop an IT strategy and roadmap to support business needs: The CIO would codevelop with business unit vice presidents an IT strategy and roadmap based upon meetings with business leaders. The objective is to develop a business-aligned IT strategy supported by the business and implemented by joint business and IT teams.

5. Educate key IT personnel in business: Help the IT leadership team understand basic business concepts and company vision, strategy, and corporate initiatives. The objective is to begin a process of educating IT personnel in basic business skills to help them improve their ability to work with business teams.

6. Focus on basics services: Share with IT personnel perceptions of service performance by business vice presidents and business unit teams. The objective was to develop a plan to improve these services and use this as an initial opportunity for IT teams to work with business teams in a collaborative manner. Focusing on basic services is an easy entry point to help IT personnel. Improving the delivery of basic services is a subject IT personnel can speak to easily.

7. Gradual indoctrination of IT personnel with business teams: Work with business units to develop projects, which improve business outcomes and achieve corporate objectives. The objective is to gradually introduce IT personnel into business discussions. An IT leader would always be present during these meetings to help move the discussion in the right direction.

8. Mentoring and coaching of key IT leaders: Provide mentoring and coaching to IT leaders and IT personnel to help educate and improve the business and teaming skills needed to effectively work with business teams.

Implement a Continuous Improvement Program to Achieve Positive Momentum

How effective was the CIO's plan? It was very effective. As I mentioned earlier, the CIO completed two maturity assessments: the first based upon his first 6 months on the job and the second based on the maturity of the IT organization at the end of 2012. Figure 11.7 shows the numeric scores for skills knowledge and their application for each competency for 6 months and 24 months as well as the numeric and percentage delta between the two periods. Figure 11.8 is a graphical representation of the numbers. Figure 11.7 is a maturity assessment grid that reflects the scores for each of the two assessments. Review the chart and then let us examine the improvements and some of the outcomes achieved.

It is obvious just by looking at the grid that scores for skill knowledge and applying knowledge moved both vertically (improvements in skill knowledge) and horizontally (improvements in applying skills to business outcomes). How much did they improve? Following is a table that compares skill knowledge and applying skills for each competency category for the 6- and 24-month assessment.

As you examine the table, you notice that the scores improved fairly well:

- On a percentage basis, average maturity for skill knowledge improved almost 30%. However, the application of skill knowledge to produce business outcomes improved by almost 55%. I would say this is a very good improvement. Each of the competency scores increased as well (Figure 11.7).

Take a second look at the grid and look at the applying knowledge improvements. This is where the payoff is. In my interviews with the CIO, he explained his program of building a foundation for growing the skills of IT personnel and some of the business outcomes achieved by the IT organization.[2]

Building a foundation for growth

1. The CIO devoted a lot of time to educate the IT leaders and personnel in understanding basic business concepts, concepts of customer value, and the competitive market. His objective was to help IT personnel think how Able Manufacturing provides value to its customers and value chain partners, instead of writing lines of computer code. He hired a few key IT leaders who had both IT and business experience to build up his leadership team. He did not replace any of the IT leadership team, except for two individuals who decided to retire.

2. The CIO reorganized. He assigned each of the IT leaders to a business unit. They would be responsible for working with the business unit to understand their challenges and coordinate any IT activity required to support the business unit.

3. The CIO started a *walk in the shoes of the user* program. He started with the IT leadership team, which were the six directors reporting to him. He accompanied the six key IT leaders on a series of interactive meetings with each of the business unit vice presidents. The objective was to introduce the IT leadership team to the business unit heads and vice versa. He then followed with a series of events where each team leader spent 3 days in the business unit to understand how the business processes function, from a user perspective. To ensure stickiness to this process, he asked each IT leader to write up observations based upon their 3-day experience and identify potential ways IT could improve the business processes. He then asked each IT leader to work with their respective IT teams to share their experiences.

4. The CIO sponsored a once a month *brown-bag lunch* for each IT leader and the leadership team of the business unit they align to. This helped build a relationship and discuss business issues in a more informal atmosphere.

5. The CIO also brought in an outside consultant to help his leadership team improve their management and communication techniques. He also ran this program for selected IT personnel who would interact with the business on a regular basis.

6. One of the key components to building a foundation for growth was to help the IT leadership team think like business people. The CIO instituted a process for reviewing the IT plans for each IT leader. At each meeting, the IT leader would have to answer the following four questions:
   a. What was the monthly financial performance of the business unit you are supporting?
   b. What are their business challenges and how can IT support their needs?

   c. What is the status of the major projects for each business unit and what is the business outcome desired and associated metrics?

   d. How has the IT organization helped the business unit achieve business outcomes, in terms of specific outcomes and associated metrics?

Achieving business outcomes

1. The IT infrastructure to support Able Manufacturing was a dinosaur: architecture platforms not built for growth and homegrown applications patched and wired together, a financial management system that needed dozens of analysts to churn data and a manufacturing and logistics system that was archaic. To keep these information systems up and running, numerous personnel were required for support, maintenance, and implementing enhancements. It was a mess.

2. The CIO met with business unit leaders and together, they codeveloped a 3-year plan with business unit vice presidents to implement an Enterprise Resource Planning (ERP) system. The board approved the plan.

3. The company purchased an ERP system that included the following modules:
   a. Financial
   b. Manufacturing
   c. Logistics
   d. Sales
   e. Material management
   f. Human resources

4. The 30 month implementation accomplished the following major results:
   a. Monthly financial closing cycle reduced from 15 to 3 days
   b. Reduction of financial analysts required preparing closing and analytics data (there were employee reassignments, resignations, and reduction in force programs implemented; the goal was to retain employees, where possible)
   c. Logistic cycle times reduced by 30%
   d. Inventory reduction of 15% due to better planning
   e. Improved customer satisfaction scores (+25%)

f. Sales improvement (20%) due to improved visibility of sales opportunities and improved process for tracking prospects and associated data

The CIO at Able Manufacturing is an example of a strategic CIO who thinks business. He succeeded by reskilling IT personnel, focusing on business results, and collaborating with business unit leaders.

Now let us look at the four quadrants of the grid and provide you with some tips on how to move your IT organization's skill knowledge and application of that knowledge to achieve improved business performance (Figure 11.9).

Quadrant 1: If your IT organization scores fall in this quadrant, you have a tremendous opportunity for improvement:

- Scores in this quadrant usually reflect a very tactically oriented IT organization. Sometimes, this is required for organizations that do not have the correct skills in place.
- It is also representative of an IT organization where the CIO and leadership team have a very tightly controlled communication chain with the business.
- If you want to improve the skills of your IT organization to improve business outcomes, you could achieve an improvement of 25%–50%. These improvement percentages

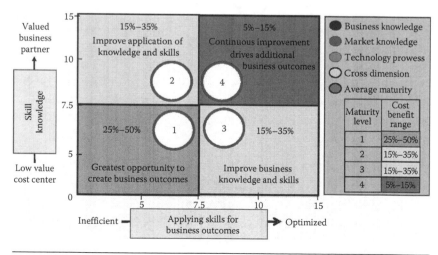

Figure 11.9 Strategic IT Organization Maturity Assessment Improvement Ranges.

apply to process improvement initiatives and apply to skills improvement programs.

Look at some of the plan components the CIO from Able Manufacturing implement for possible ideas on developing a skills improvement plan for your IT organization.

Quadrant 2: Scores in this quadrant reflect an organization that has skill knowledge but does not apply this knowledge to achieving business outcomes:

- Scores in this quadrant are reflective of an organization with high-degree skill knowledge but a lower level of applying skills for business outcomes.
- This is an example of an IT organization that finds it difficult to utilize the domain skills to translate the activities that drive business outcomes.
- The implication for this type of IT organization is that the knowledge and skills training need to be reevaluated. Discuss the training outcomes with the groups of IT teams that scored high in applying skills for business outcomes to identify any training gaps.
- Develop a training plan to help IT personnel improve their knowledge about the company's challenges and opportunities. Sponsor brown-bag lunch programs and include personnel from the business to add reality into the conversations. Look at some of the elements of the development plan from the Able Manufacturing example, in this chapter, to help develop some ideas.

Quadrant 3: Scores in this quadrant represent an IT organization that achieves business outcomes but has low skill knowledge in the four competencies. You might ask yourself, how can this be? Well, the answer is simple:

- This is representative of a highly structured IT organization with a tight governance model and led by a business savvy team that provides specific direction to IT personnel.
- The downside to this scenario is that IT personnel don't have an opportunity to grow professionally.

- You might want to rethink your strategy and develop a training program to help build skill knowledge of your IT organization. It will help you and your leadership team in the long run, as well as help your IT personnel improve their professional skills.

Quadrant 4: Scores in this quadrant indicate a strategic CIO and IT leadership team that have successfully improved the skill knowledge and application of that knowledge to achieve business outcomes. Continuous improvement programs will help improve scores:

- Look for opportunities to identify additional opportunity areas through a continuous improvement process.
- Initiate a process of monthly meetings that include IT personnel and business personnel to discuss business challenges and potential opportunities to drive business value through leveraging IT (i.e., process improvement, data mining, and application enhancement).
- Schedule monthly meetings for you, your IT leaders, and business unit vice-presidents and staff. This is a good opportunity to have strategic discussions to identify opportunities to improve business value throughout the value chain.

Alternative Variations for Using the IT Strategic Competencies and Skills Maturity Assessment (Figure 11.3)

There are variations on how to use the strategic IT competency and skill maturity assessment, from a quick gut check to a more detailed assessment across the IT organization and business. Following are some suggestions ordered in degree of complexity:

1. Gut check assessment: CIO completes the assessment independently based upon his or her observations of the IT organization. This provides the CIO with an initial point of reference to determine if further assessments, at a more detailed level, are required.
2. IT leadership assessment: CIO completes the assessment of IT leadership to determine their degree of maturity. This provides CIO with a baseline of data for identifying gaps and developing training programs with IT leadership.

3. IT personnel assessment conducted by IT leaders as a team: The IT leadership team performs an assessment, as a team, of the IT organization. This provides the IT leadership team with a perspective of the skill knowledge and application of knowledge for the IT organization, as a whole.

4. IT leadership conducts assessment of IT personnel in their organization: This provides the IT leader, for their organization, a perspective of the skill knowledge and application of knowledge for his or her organization.

5. Business vice president assessment of IT organization: This assessment provides the CIO with a perception of how business unit leaders view the skill levels of the IT organization.

6. Business unit personnel assessment of IT organization: This includes business personnel in the IT leadership assessment of their organization (Figure 11.3). This provides more of a 360-degree perspective on the skills of the IT organization.

7. Review results with IT personnel, business vice presidents, and business personnel: Conduct meetings and town hall meetings to provide results to the organization. This helps the entire company view IT in a proactive way as an organization that wants to work with the business to improve business outcomes.

8. Adding fields to provide specific examples: When conducting assessments, you may want to add fields in the template to capture specific examples of where skill knowledge and/or applying skills are deficient or excel as a proof point for the numeric score. Following is an example (Figure 11.10).

9. Review results with respondents: Reviewing results with respondents provides an opportunity to add clarity and capture specific examples to support respondent numeric scores. Some ideas follow (Note: Comments below are for reviewing results with IT personnel. If Business Unite Personnel complete the assessment, then you should review with them as well.):

    a. Meet with each respondent to ensure that their answers were in line with their thinking.

    b. Identify specific examples. Have each respondent provide examples, both positive and negative, that reflect the scores.

EXAMPLES OF HOW IT ORGANIZATION APPLIES BEST PRACTICE (Provide a short description of how your IT organization applies these best practices based upon your scoring)	
BUSINESS KNOWLEDGE	
Business environment	
Opportunities/challenges	
Process centric	
MARKET KNOWELDGE	
Product knowledge	
Industry knowledge	
Competitive landscape	
TECHNOLOGY PROWESS	
Technology strategy/ adaptability	
Organizational agility	
Strategic project capability	
CROSS DIMENSION	
Vision	
Leadership	
Communication	

Figure 11.10   Examples of Additional Fields to Add to IT Strategic Maturity Assessment Template.

   c. Review examples () with IT personnel.

   d. Meet with the IT organization to inform them of the assessment results and inform them the IT will schedule follow-up meetings to review assessment specifics.

   e. Review training and modify as necessary.

   f. Work with business partners to ensure that messaging to IT personnel is adequate. Include business personnel in training workshops so IT personnel can begin forming business relationships and improve their communication techniques.

10. Review results with respondents: Review results of examples provided using Figure 11.10 with business unit and IT personnel individually and in groups. This provides an opportunity to add clarity and capture specific examples, and identify any gaps, potential areas for improvement, and lessons learned.

Chapter Summary

A strategic CIO recognizes that to succeed in achieving business outcomes through collaborating with business leaders and teams is not a one-man process. It takes IT personnel using their skills and applying these skills in a collaborative business and IT teams to identify issues, challenges, and solutions that enable business outcomes. The objective of this chapter is to help you understand the important skills needed and how to measure those skills through a strategic maturity assessment.

Take a moment to reread this and the previous chapters of the book. The people component of a successful strategic IT organization is the most difficult to improve. It takes time, skill, and patience. Assess the competencies and skills maturity of your IT organization and develop a plan to improve their skill knowledge as well as how they apply these skills to achieve business outcomes. Review the techniques used by CIOs to improve the skills and application of skills in their IT organizations. They could apply to your IT organization.

The general rule of thumb is that people want to do a good job. However, sometimes they need help to develop the necessary skills to accomplish this. A strategic CIO understands this and works hard to build the skills of IT personnel and works collaboratively with the business, using IT and business teams to achieve remarkable results. Try it. You will not be disappointed.

Citations

1. Zapos Productions intradimensional (ZPi); http://zapatopi.net/kelvin/quotes/; Lord Kelvin Quotations; Measurement section.
2. Interview with Able Manufacturing CIO/Phil Weinzimer February 15, 2013.

12

SECTION OVERVIEW

Implement Initiatives to Improve Margin (Sales/Cost)

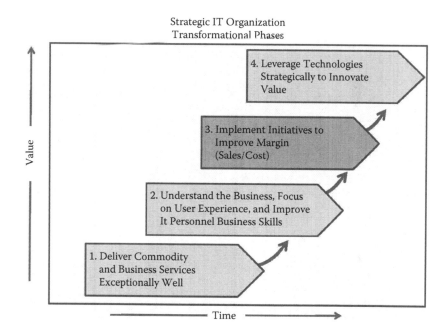

Strategic IT Organization
Transformational Phases

4. Leverage Technologies Strategically to Innovate Value

3. Implement Initiatives to Improve Margin (Sales/Cost)

2. Understand the Business, Focus on User Experience, and Improve It Personnel Business Skills

1. Deliver Commodity and Business Services Exceptionally Well

Value

Time

With a solid foundation of delivering services exceptionally well and personnel that understand, communicate, and demonstrate business competencies and skills, the information technology (IT) organization is positioned to collaborate in business teams that focus on initiatives to drive margin in the form of increased revenues or reduced costs. There is a reason a profit and loss statement and balance sheet are recognized measures of a company's potential worth. This is a basic principle of business. The logical path then is to focus on initiatives that improve the company's revenue, reduce cost, or improve the balance sheet.

If you as a Chief Information Officer (CIO) want to be recognized as a strategic contributor to the business, you need to work with C-Suite executives to evaluate market opportunities that will improve the competitive position of their company. To do so requires the trust from the business that is established by delivering services exceptionally well and showing that your IT personnel can demonstrate business competencies and skills, the first two phases of Strategic IT Organization Transformation Phases. How do CIOs successfully focus on initiatives to drive margin? This section of the book demonstrates how five (5) CIOs focused on initiatives to drive margin for their respective company.

With an improved delivery of basic services (Phase 1) coupled with a business-focused IT team (Phase 2), IT organizations are poised to focus on Phase 3 and collaborate with business teams to focus on initiatives that drive margin, both in improved revenue and reduced costs. Included in Chapter 13—How Strategic CIOs Focus on Initiatives to Improve Margin are success stories from five strategic CIOs. Following are the key questions this chapter will answer:

1. Why is it *important to focus on initiatives that improve margin* (increase revenue/reduce costs)?
2. What are the *success stories of CIOs who focus on initiatives that improve margin*?
   a. How did *Tom Grooms, CIO at Valspar, successfully work* with business units to improve processes, reduce IT support costs, and drive initiatives that enabled Valspar to move forward with *an aggressive growth strategy*?
   b. How did *Randy Spratt, Chief Technology Officer (CTO) and CIO at McKesson*, the multinational health-care services and IT company, successfully harness a company-wide team to develop a unified architecture, which improved *customer service and improved sales*?
   c. How did *Clif Triplett, while CIO at Baker Hughes*, drive the development of a product life cycle management system

that *reduced development time for products and services resulting in improved customer service and reduced IT costs?*

d. How did *Anne Wilms, while CIO at Rohm and Hass,* drive a number of strategic initiatives that increased revenue through an improved pricing system, reduced IT costs, optimized inventory investment savings millions of dollars, as well as a host of other initiatives?

e. How did Steve Heilenman, CIO at CAI Inc., implement a visibility, control, and optimization strategy to *reduce IT spend by 50%* through reduced legacy support costs and improved project management governance, *while at the same time develop a testing solution the company sells to external customers?*

13

How Strategic CIOs Focus on Initiatives to Improve Margin

21st-century CIOs have a dual responsibility: driving down costs and creating new business value. Managing this seeming dichotomy is the domain of top business executives, and CIOs everywhere are learning to step it up.[1]

Randy Spratt
Executive Vice President and CIO/CTO at McKesson

In the previous chapters, we focused on the first two transformational phases: *deliver commodity and business services exceptionally well* and *understand the business, focus on user experience, and improve IT personnel business skill*. As a chief information officer (CIO), if you succeed at implementing the first two phases, you and your information technology (IT) organization are positioned to truly collaborate with the business and focus on initiatives that drive margin and leverage technology strategically to innovate value.

Following are the objective, key messages, and examples used in this chapter:

A. CHAPTER OBJECTIVE

1. Share examples of strategic CIOs whose journey took them through the first two phases of the IT Strategic Transformation Phases and implemented initiatives that focused on improving margin (phase 3).
2. This chapter will be especially helpful for those of you who are still in phase one or two of your transformation

journey and interested in leveraging examples from CIOs who have succeeded at stage three.

B. KEY POINTS

1. Strategic CIOs follow a simple but effective process for transforming their IT organization and implement initiatives that drive margin in the form of increased revenues and/or reduced costs.

C. EXAMPLES

In this chapter, we highlight six strategic CIOs who focus on initiatives that drive margin, through improving revenue and/or reducing costs. Each of these CIOs has broad and deep experience in business and IT at the executive level. Further, each applies these skills in a strategic and focused manner.

1. *Tom Grooms, CIO at Valspar*, joined the chemical coating company after a long career in IT at Medtronic—the medical device company. Although Valspar is in a totally different industry, Grooms took a strategic approach to professionalize the IT organization by working with the business units to improve processes, reduce IT support costs, and drive initiatives that enabled Valspar to move forward with an aggressive growth strategy.

2. *Randy Spratt, chief technology officer (CTO) and CIO at McKesson*, the multinational health-care services and IT company, is an example of an executive who is both left- and right-brain dominant. He thinks strategically but is just as comfortable at the tactical level designing company-wide architecture. Customers had difficulty integrating McKesson products, due to incompatible architecture, until Spratt harnessed a company-wide team to develop a unified architecture, which improved customer service and improved sales.

3. *Clif Triplett, while CIO at Baker Hughes*, took on some rather large projects. Baker Hughes is an oil industry services company. Triplett turned the IT organization into a world-class organization, developed a common data platform to optimize customer information, and developed a product life cycle management system that reduced development time for products and services. Improved customer service, reduced IT costs, and a transformed IT organization make Triplett a true example of a strategic CIO.

4. *Anne Wilms, former CIO at Rohm and Hass*, embarked on a number of strategic initiatives that increased revenue through an improved pricing system, reduced IT costs, optimized inventory investment savings millions of dollars, and a host of other initiatives.

5. *Steve Heilenman, CIO at CAI*, focused on improving the value of the IT organization while driving down the cost of IT. He succeeded. Over a 5-year period, Heilenman reduced IT costs by about 25% while supporting a business that grew by 50%. The net metric of IT costs as a percentage of revenue is 2%; one-half of the best in class percentage for IT service companies.

6. *Helen Cousins*, former CIO at Lincoln Trust, revitalized and reengineered the major document processes by leveraging technology. This positioned the company for a spin-off of some of its business units and enabled the company to focus on a core competency for future growth.

The objective of this chapter is to provide you with some examples of strategic CIOs whose journeys took them through the first two phases and the initiatives implemented that drove business success. This chapter will be especially helpful for those of you who are still in phase one or two of your transformation journey or ready to embark on phase 3, and are interested in understanding how to leverage examples from CIOs who have succeeded at phase three of the transformation journey.

Strategic IT Organization
Transformation Phases

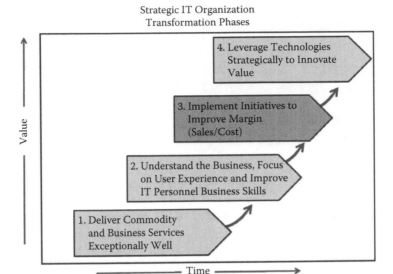

The first example is Tom Grooms, CIO at Valspar, who came from the medical device industry to take on the CIO role. He focused on initiatives to improve process so the company could successfully embark on a growth strategy and reduce inefficient IT spend so his organization could focus on value-added initiatives that would improve margin.

The second example is Randy Spratt, CTO, CIO, and executive vice president at McKesson, the multinational health-care services and IT company dedicated to helping health-care organization achieve better clinical, financial, and operational health. Spratt focused on initiatives to improve the integration of acquired businesses and developed a technology strategy across McKesson's different divisions to provide improved service to its customers.

The third example is Clif Triplett. While CIO at Baker Hughes, the oil industry services company that provides a variety of products and services to improve oil and gas field exploration, he developed and executed an IT strategy involving several initiatives across multiple divisions that were used to operating independently, an almost insurmountable task. The objectives were to create a world-class IT organization, develop a common data platform to optimize customer information, and improve customer service through the development of a product life cycle management system that would dramatically reduce development time of products and services.

The fourth example is Anne Wilms, former CIO at Rohm and Hass, the global company that pioneered technologies and solutions products for the specialty materials industry. Dow Chemical acquired Rohm and Hass as a wholly owned subsidiary in 1999. Wilms focused on numerous company-wide initiatives to improve margin. She implemented an Enterprise Resource Planning (ERP) system, led the reengineering of major processes, improved the product profit margins through an automated pricing system, and other initiatives that drove revenue and reduced costs.

The fifth example is Steve Heilenman, CIO at CAI, where he accomplished two major initiatives. The first was to reduce IT costs by about 25% while supporting a business that grew by 50%. The second initiative was to turn an internal development project to reduce development time into a market product that generates revenue for the company.

The sixth example is Helen Cousins, former CIO at Lincoln Trust, who revitalized and reinvented a major document management process positioning the company for a profitable spin-off.

Tom Grooms, CIO at Valspar

Tom Grooms is CIO at Valspar, the global coatings company. Prior to his appointment as CIO in June 2012, Grooms spent 17 years in the IT organization at Medtronic, a global company with 46,000 employees in over 140 countries. Medtronic develops and manufactures innovative medical device technologies and therapies such as cardiac, vascular, diabetes, and restorative therapy devices and products to treat chronic diseases worldwide. Grooms worked his way up the IT ladder from programmer to project manager to director. His roles took on more responsibilities within IT as well as business responsibilities, which included leading a business unit in Asia. The combination of his business and IT expertise is exactly what Valspar was looking for in a CIO.

Valspar operates globally in over 25 countries with 9500 employees and provides coatings to a variety of industries in the form of paints, rigid packaging coatings, automotive refinish, specialty coatings, and a host of other coating products. Consumers are familiar with Valspar's home paint products, sold in Lowe's and other home product stores. What consumers may not know about Valspar is they manufacture specialty paint. Did you ever wonder why older John Deere Tractor, with its branded green color, or a Caterpillar tractor, with its branded yellow color, never fades? The colors are always vibrant. Well, that is because Valspar manufactures the specialty paint for the two companies that is guaranteed not to fade or rust.

The opportunity at Valspar was enticing to Grooms. Executive management had an aggressive growth plan but realized that IT was an obstacle to achieving their growth strategy. Unfortunately, Valspar had an internally focused IT organization that developed solutions for the various business units without questioning the need or checking to see if similar solutions developed previously for other business units could be leveraged. The result was a set of IT solutions that were unique to each business unit. The company needed to leverage IT to enable business growth through IT, and this was not going to happen with the current IT organization. Company executives decided they needed to transform the IT organization, and it needed a leader who was technologically savvy with a good understanding of business. The IT organization needed to be an equal player with other business units and collectively work together to fuel the growth engine that would drive the company in future years. They needed a strong leader, experienced in IT and business that could implement the transformation strategy.

When Grooms joined Valspar, his first task was to understand how Valspar operated as a business. Remember, his prior 17 years was with Medtronic, a completely different business. Grooms met with each business unit and asked a series of questions focused on how they conduct their day-to-day activities. The dialogue was refreshing to the business unit leaders. "They were not used to IT approaching them to see how the information technology organization could help them succeed." The business unit executives developed a new appreciation for the IT organization. Grooms learned that many of the business units were pleased with IT because they always responded to the needs of the business. What the business executives didn't realize is that many of the solutions developed for the business units were unique to the business units, even though there were similar solutions developed for other business units. IT was suboptimizing. They did not check with other business units to see how they addressed a similar problem. The IT organization never checked to see if previous IT projects addressed a similar issue. "As a result, the IT organization developed solutions that were unique for one business unit but never leveraged across all business units."[2]

Grooms' first order of business was to develop an IT strategy and present it to the board. The strategy was simple but realistic. Valspar IT needed to run the business but also focus on how to grow the business. The basic blocking and tackling for running the Valspar business needed improvement. Grooms' focus in this area was to improve the *connectivity* with the business by meeting with business unit leaders to understand their needs. To improve the running of the business, Grooms would improve the *reliability and efficiency* of the basic services provided to the business. To grow the business, Grooms needed to *leverage IT across the business units*. His strategy was to develop capabilities that would serve the needs of multiple business units versus developing unique solutions for each business unit, unless they were necessary. By optimizing IT resources and improving efficiencies, Grooms could then focus on improving the *competitiveness* of the business by leveraging IT to enable the business to expand markets, improve and develop new products, and provide increased value to its customers (Figure 13.1).

Grooms conducted a series of town hall meetings with the IT organization as well as meetings with his key staff. He needed to reorient their focus from internal to external. He helped them understand how the business was hindered by an internally focused IT organization. They needed to begin partnering and working with

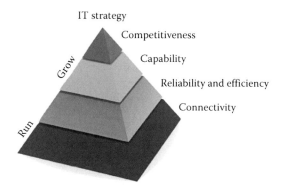

Figure 13.1 Valspar IT Strategy.

business units to leverage solutions and work together to find new ways to leverage IT. Over a short period, the organization started to show results. Basic services improved, business unit scores for IT improved, and Grooms was building a trust-based relationship with business executives.

Grooms' management style is pragmatic. He approaches problems scientifically and ensures that solutions align to his strategic plan. Following are three good examples of how Grooms focused on initiatives to improve margin.

Example 1

To stop the development of unique solutions, Grooms developed a review process for IT requests. He needed to stop the bleeding of developing unique solutions for business units as well as responding to every request from the business. Grooms initiated a process to screen all business requests for services, which scored the request according to financial assessment, business need, and probability of success (Figure 13.2). The IT organization was very tactical and reactive to business needs. Grooms explains the need for the process. "To be strategic, we needed to develop a process to vet each request to ensure that it aligned with the growth strategy and would add value to Valspar."[3]

Financial	Score: 10	Score: 5	Score: 0	Weight	Score
Projected ROI	30%	20%	<20%	15%	
Immediacy of Benefits	6 months	> 6 months	> 1 year	15%	
Required Investment	< $100,000	< $250,000	> $250,000	15%	
Business Need	**Score: 10**	**Score: 5**	**Score: 0**	**Weight**	**Score**
Strategic Relevance	Makes the Strategy	Contributes to the Strategy	Marginal Contribution	15%	
Relative Competitive Performance	Urgent Competitive Needs	Competitive Issues Emerging	Few Competitive Issues	10%	
Impending Market Changes	Major Changes Imminent	Major Changes in 2 years	Major changes in distant future	10%	
Probability of Success	**Score: 10**	**Score: 5**	**Score: 0**	**Weight**	**Score**
Strength of Sponsorship	Very Strong – top 1 or 2	Strong – a top 5	Weak – one of many	5%	
Amount of Change Required to Existing Processes	Minimal Change	Streamlines	Fundamental Redesign	5%	
Manageability of Initiative Scope	Involves 1-3 Departments	Involves > 3 Departments	Involves External Parties	5%	
Change Readiness of Affected Parties	Actively Supported	Understand and Accept	Uncertain or Resistant	5%	
TOTAL					

Figure 13.2   Business Case Builder.

The vetting process worked well. An example of this is a request the IT organization received from Valspar's Pittsburgh facility. The customer service organization had a specific need to improve the status of customer orders. Previously, IT would approve this request and develop a custom solution; however, with the new vetting process, the IT team chartered to assess incoming requests scheduled a meeting with the Pittsburgh customer services team to review their requirements. The IT team and Pittsburgh business team analyzed the requirements, in detail, as well as the business problem they were trying to solve. The requirement was to improve the order management process. They wanted to provide customers with visibility of the manufacturing timeline and delivery date. The IT team investigated similar requests and solutions developed for other business units that addressed customer service issues. Sure enough, the IT team found a similar solution developed for a Valspar plant in Garwin, Iowa. Grooms was not surprised (Figure 13.2):

> The IT team and the Garwin Customer Service Team demonstrated the solution to the Pittsburgh Customer Service team. The solution met 80 percent of Pittsburgh's requirements. We convinced the Pittsburgh team to use the same solution. In addition, we socialized the solution with the Customer Service teams at all the Valspar plants. Amazingly, the Garwin team received many calls and emails regarding the solution and wanted to use the solution for their customer service needs. (ibid)

This was a win–win solution for three reasons. First, the business units incorporated a consistent process for the customer inquiry of orders versus separate unique processes previously utilized. Second, the IT organization focused on more value-based initiatives instead of developing one-off solutions. Third, the consistency of process forced business units to collaborate more frequently and resulted in continuous improvement of processes.[4]

Example 2

Another initiative that improved margin was the reduction of application maintenance costs, which can be significant. Valspar acquired a basic Oracle ERP system a number of years earlier. Grooms analyzed support calls and found that

> Oracle support calls totaled about 100 calls a year. Response times were slow and in most cases, Valspar personnel figured out the

solution prior to a response from Oracle. The support cost contract totaled $3 million, or $30,000 for every call; a very large number. I worked with the sourcing group, and we found a services company that could handle our Oracle support for an annual cost of $300,000, a 90 percent reduction in support cost. Now, we get better service for a fraction of the cost.[5]

Example 3

Valspar has an aggressive growth strategy. One component of this strategy is growth through acquisition. One of the due diligence activities in an acquisition plan is analysis of the IT integration component. This is an estimate for integrating the information systems of the acquired company into the Valspar operating model. Normally, an assessment is conducted as part of a due diligence activity.

Valspar business units operated independently. Grooms discovered this when a business unit was well on the path of acquiring a business and estimated the IT integration costs without any input from Grooms' organization. In one acquisition, the Valspar business unit made a huge error and didn't realize that the acquired business was composed of five different businesses, running on five different platforms. None of the email systems connected. Neither did the phone systems. Accounting systems were different for each of the businesses. The list grew bigger by the day. Subsequent to this acquisition, Grooms instituted a process, sanctioned by executive management, making the CIO an integral team member for any acquisition and involved from the early discussions throughout the entire process. Now, Grooms' organization is part of the due diligence team.

Grooms transformed the IT organization that now proactively works with business teams and focuses on initiatives that drive growth in terms of revenue and margin. He approached the transformation in a pragmatic way. He coaches and mentors his staff to be more business focused, collaborative with business teams, and focused on user experiences. All new requests for IT services now include investment justifications. As a result, there is a true alignment of IT projects to business strategy and goals. Grooms summarized his transformation as follows:

We are changing the dynamic of the business model. We take a request, foster conversations with business teams, develop working relationships, understand the business unit processes and associated activities, and leverage existing solutions across the entire company. We've saved lots of money, standardized many of the processes across Valspar, and have become more strategic in enabling the business to grow through leveraging information technology. (ibid)

Randy Spratt, Chief Technology Officer, CIO, and Executive Vice President at McKesson

In today's complex global environment, IT finds its way into almost every product and service. Additionally, IT enables business processes across the entire value chain. With the proliferation and accelerated development of new technologies, almost every company has a CTO to scan the market and understand new technologies. With this knowledge, CTOs need to determine how to apply those technologies to create business value and leverage technology across the enterprise. It is a very technical and complex position. It is rare when you find an individual who understands the complexities of today's technologies but also excels at the executive role of leading the IT organization as the CIO. McKesson management wanted an executive who was strategic, intuitive, and creative as well as logical and business focused. Randy Spratt is such an individual.

Spratt is the CTO, CIO, and executive vice president at McKesson, the $122 billion health-care services and IT company. With 43,500 employees spread globally across two core business segments—Distribution Solutions and Technology Solutions—McKesson has more than a dozen business units that provide products and services to customers. Every one of these businesses utilizes technology heavily to provide a competitive edge.[6] Combining the CTO and CIO role makes perfect sense, especially when there is an executive with the technical and business experience such as Spratt.

Spratt's role as CIO focuses on leading all technology initiatives at McKesson. As CTO, Spratt guides the overall technology direction for the company, specifically focusing on health-care technology products. He also provides oversight of company-wide application development processes. Spratt not only has an excellent technical background but also an impressive business background. With 18 years of experience at McKesson, Spratt knows how the company operates on a day-to-day level. He had the opportunity to put on his business hat in what was known as McKesson Provider Technologies (MPT), the company's medical software and services division based in Alpharetta, Georgia. He was responsible for all processes and held the title of chief process officer. In addition, Spratt managed the Business Development, Information Technology, and Strategic Planning offices, as well as MPT's Technology Services business. His experience prior to McKesson was at Advanced Laboratory Systems (ALS), where he held a variety of positions with increasing responsibility, leading to the role of chief operations officer (COO).[6,7]

Spratt has accomplished a lot at McKesson to improve the way IT enables business success. Following are two examples of initiatives that improved customer satisfaction and reduced costs. The first example is how McKesson improved the speed of integrating IT systems of acquired companies. The second example is how developing compatible technology platforms improves customer satisfaction and reduces technology development costs.

Increasing the Speed of Integrating Acquired Businesses

One of McKesson's strategies is growth through acquisition. Those of you who have experienced the integration of an acquired company's IT systems know it is a memorable experience, often laden with surprises. Spratt learned this at McKesson after he became CIO. He explains one example:

> I was involved in a complicated acquisition in which we divided the acquired company into several businesses. There was no integration manager, so the CEO asked me to fill the role. We ultimately needed four separate integration projects for each new business. The team performed well but could have increased the integration timeline had we been able to leverage organizational learning.[8]

With a focus on improving processes, Spratt decided to tackle the integration challenge. When he first told the CEO about his experience leading the integration project, he said "…we need to improve this process. The faster we integrate, the sooner we will derive the economic benefit." (ibid) The CEO approved Spratt's request to form a new department named the Business Integration Office (BIO), which became responsible for *kick-starting* the integration of acquisitions into the McKesson business model. The team's charter was to contact previous integration teams and capture lessons learned and keep this fresh with each new acquisition. The team documented the information into a *process playbook*, defining the specific processes, work activities, and artifacts used by all McKesson departments for integrating actions. The result was a 75% improvement in integration kick-off time from an average of 12–3 weeks. The benefit of a speedier integration process enables McKesson to derive greater cost and reduction and revenue enhancement.

Aligning Technology Strategy across McKesson's Product Groups

McKesson sells approximately 40 technology products to hospitals. Many of the hospitals could own multiple products. These products are developed across McKesson's various business units—many of which utilize different technology platforms and lack compatibility with one another. For example, a hospital using McKesson's pharmacy system and McKesson's medication and supply dispensing and inventory management system might have difficulty integrating the two systems since they are built on different technology platforms.

Spratt recognized an opportunity. He organized the *Technology Advisory Board*, which is a group comprised of the company's top technology leaders and development managers from each of McKesson's business units. The goal was to align business strategies and leverage common technology platforms. This strategy improved customer satisfaction and reduced the cost of technology development for the company, a true win–win scenario that any CIO would want.

Clif Triplett, CIO at Baker Hughes (2008–2013)

As CIOs gain access to the C-level executive table discussing market opportunities and developing strategy, the ability to lead as well as execute at a tactical level becomes critical. Generally, C-level executives spend much of their time developing strategy and leading their organizations in the execution of strategy. When it comes to the role of the CIO, the need to lead as well as ensure superb execution is paramount. Sure, CIOs generally have good technical skills. After all, they spend most of their careers in the IT organization. However, developing executive leadership skills is one of the main challenges for CIOs. As you scan the marketplace, more and more CIOs are learning how to become good leaders to supplement their technology expertise. Sometimes, you find a CIO who has natural leadership ability and technical expertise. When this happens, the CIO becomes an integral member of the C-level suite developing strategy and leads the IT organization to leverage IT as a driver for successful growth. Clif Triplett is a prime example.

Clif Triplett earned his engineering degree at the United States Military Academy at West Point. He leveraged his engineering degree with additional training in computer science and telecommunications. Triplett learned about discipline and order in the military, while at the same time learning about leadership and the responsibilities associated with commanding troops. He leveraged his leadership and technical skills in Washington, DC, at the Department of Defense in the Command, Control, Communications, and Information Joint Program Management Office, where he was responsible for architecture and software quality assurance for the Department of Defense's Joint Operations Planning and Execution Systems.[9]

With a rewarding military career, Triplett ventured into private industry with experience in a variety of IT leadership positions at Allied Signal and Energy Services leading up to executive positions at General Motors and Motorola. At General Motors, Triplett was responsible for all IT systems operations as well as the associated processes. At Motorola, Triplett leveraged his technical and leadership skills to become the corporate vice president of Global Services. This background poised Triplett for the CIO role at Baker Hughes, the $20 billion leader in supplying oil field services, products, technology, and systems to the worldwide oil and natural gas industry.

Baker Hughes hired Triplett as CIO in 2008.[10] His charter was to establish an IT direction and develop a world-class IT team. Triplett had a huge challenge. At the time, Baker Hughes was composed of multiple divisions in over 80 countries with 60,000 employees that service customers in the oil and gas industry; Baker Hughes was very decentralized. As you can imagine, each division had their own unique needs for IT. As a result, IT systems were diverse and misaligned, and the associated processes to support the developed systems were immature and inefficient. Triplett had to figure out how to take a tangled web of systems and processes and transform the IT organization into an aligned and efficient IT organization.

I'm sure you've heard the idiomatic phrase, *can't see the forest for the trees*. The phrase is very relevant in business. If the head of an organization focuses too much attention to detail without understanding what is important at the strategic level, the organization can flounder in inefficiency and disjointed activities, which can lead to chaos. This is what occurred when Triplett arrived at Baker Hughes. He relied on his military training in precision and accuracy coupled with his leadership skills to develop a set of key initiatives, embedded in an IT strategy that would leverage Baker Hughes for future growth. Following is how Triplett accomplished this goal.

From Chaos to Order

To implement a growth strategy for Baker Hughes, Triplett needed to develop an IT strategy that aligned with the business and could leverage IT to grow the business. His goal was to develop a set of strategic initiatives to accomplish this. His approach consisted of the following three-step process:

1. Listen to the needs of senior management.
2. Assess the skills of the IT organization.
3. Improve IT and business processes by focusing on user experiences.

Listen to the Needs of Senior Management   Triplett honed his listening skills in the military and exercised them regularly in his role as a CIO. To build trust, he met with all the business unit executives to listen to their needs. "I heard some common themes. One of the major ones was a lack of trust in the IT organization in their ability to deliver as well as the lack of providing information needed to conduct business." During the meetings, he asked each executive, "What is the information you need?" As a result, Triplett developed a set of 12 initiatives that "focused on business capabilities and challenges" based upon the needs of the business executives. He called these initiatives *Baker's Dozen*. Triplett quickly focused on improving the delivery of basic services so that he could improve outages. The business quickly saw the improvements and started to build a layer of trust with Triplett. His organization also picked up some quick wins as a result of some information challenges the business executives identified during the initial meetings with Triplett.[11]

Assess the Skills and Competencies of IT Personnel and the IT Assets   Triplett met with all his senior staff as well as key IT personnel to assess their skills and competencies. His conclusion was that the organization was composed of personnel who had many skills, but no real mastery is specific competencies. "For example, we had desktop skills but no real strategy, communication, or architecture skills." Triplett brought in about 20 people in key positions to mentor and coach his IT organization in basic business, communication, and strategy skills. "When we retooled the skills and competencies of our IT organization, we could then focus on working with business teams."

When Triplett evaluated his assets, he uncovered that approximately 80% of his organization was focused on support activities (run the business) and only about 20% were focused on strategic initiatives (grow the business). To reverse the focus, Triplett identified the core competencies needed and outsourced the remaining support activities to vendors. Triplett also assigned business analysts to each business unit, who would engage with the business unit on a regular basis. This helped develop a good working relationship between business units and IT personnel. It took about 2 years of hard work to reorganize IT, re-skill personnel, and begin engaging with the business units on a regular basis. With the basic foundation in place, improvement of the basic delivery of services, and a retrained and reorganized department, Triplett could move to working on initiatives that would improve margin and grow the business. (ibid)

Improve IT and Business Processes by Focusing on User Experiences
Attaining Quick Wins   Triplett assigned account managers to each operating division to work with the business unit vice president and staff to create a shared IT strategy, road map, and plan based on a

process model created by Triplett. He worked with the business units to improve processes. Triplett's teams helped the business understand that quality, cycle, and cost are three main metrics whose scores needed to improve. The teams tackled each of these areas one at a time and developed a set of 20 process improvement projects that favorably impacted these metrics. The IT members of the team drove the process[12]:

> The IT Account Managers drove the process and educated the business personnel on how information systems can leverage improvements in division performance. To educate business personnel on best practices, we took them on field trips to other companies. We also instituted an employee exchange program so personnel could exchange experiences. On some occasions, we hired an expert for our process teams. (ibid)

One of the processes Triplett needed to strengthen was supply chain. To accomplish this, he hired an expert in the field from an aerospace company. This person helped the supply chain team improve their knowledge in areas such as change management, communication, and strategy. Probably, the most important skill he taught the IT team was how to engage with the business on a regular basis using a common language that focused on *business speak* versus *technology speak*.

One by one, each of the major processes achieved improvement, and business unit performance increased dramatically. Triplett was still concerned about the product development process. This was his major process initiative.

Major Strategic Transformation Initiative   Until 2009, eight independent and decentralized divisions comprised Baker Hughes, each developing a set of products and services for their individual customers. Oil and gas companies purchased products and services from different Baker Hughes divisions. The problem was that Baker Hughes was not viewed as a company that provided products and services to enable customers to drill, evaluate, complete, and produce energy. Customers saw Baker Hughes as comprised of separate divisions with different brands. Baker Hughes was not attracting new customers and increasing their footprint in an existing customer base.

Customers, on the other hand, had challenges dealing with Baker Hughes. Following are three examples as explained by Holger Stibbe, chief engineer in the Enterprise Engineering Office at Baker Hughes.[13]

1. Planning a Drilling Project

   Customers who were planning to drill a well would have to contact seven different Baker Hughes divisions. "The customer would call one group to get the well plan and directional drilling drone, then another to develop sensors to drill, and still another to plan the post-drilling evaluation. It was very frustrating for the customer. Our competition has one contact point; we had eight different contact points." Each division had homegrown systems used to document drawings, computations, and test reports needed to develop products and services. None of these systems communicated with each other. "If we want to be a complete service provider, we have to leverage the information across all divisions. We need to figure out how to reuse information from one division to another to provide better value to our customers."[13]

2. Inefficient Inventory Control Processes

   In addition to development, there were inefficiencies in inventory control. An *o-ring*, commonly referred to as a gasket, connects oil well pipes during the drilling process. Each of the eight divisions stored inventory to service their customers:

   > Each division would stock a specific o-ring, but identify it using a different number. Well, guess what. There might be 300 hundred o-rings, of a certain dimension stocked across the eight divisions under different part numbers, when it would be prudent to store approximately 75. Overstocking inventory is expensive. In this case 225, o-rings costing 100 dollars each results in $2250 in inventory cost that is unnecessary. Multiply this example by hundreds and you begin to see the investment in inventory that is wasted. (ibid)

3. Managing Customer Data

   Another major area of inefficiency was data management. "Customer data stored by one division may be different from the data stored in another division selling to the same customer. What makes matters worse is that the customer has to contact each division when ordering parts." (ibid) You begin to see the business issue faced by Baker Hughes. The suboptimization of data and processes inhibits the growth of a company. Customers today want unique user experiences and one-stop shopping.

Triplett recognized that Baker Hughes needed to find a solution that would remedy the frustration customers experienced as well as the unnecessary inventory investment of duplicate parts stored as separate unique part numbers. Triplett decided that "we needed to manage our intellectual property, manage our supply chain, and make it easier to integrate the suite of Baker Hughes products and services into one single Product Development Lifecycle Management system (PLM). We were looking for a vendor who wanted to become a strategic partner with us and move quickly. We found one who had the technical skills and was looking to move into this market."[14]

Triplett's solution was to develop a multi-tiered strategic initiative for a solution usable for product development as well as product exccution in the drilling of oil and gas wells for customers.

Triplett first tackled the product development challenge. He developed a strategy and socialized it across the different Baker Hughes divisions and executive management. "We had to educate, share the vision, show them the benefits, and develop a roadmap." (ibid) They worked with the vendor to develop the tool and even paid for mentors to come in and work with the various implementation teams on how to use the tool and how to manage change in the organization. "I didn't want this to be an IT thing. It needed to be driven by executive management and the business divisions." The project completely transformed how Baker Hughes managed their products and services. "We started small with a few quick wins and expanded the use of the tool over time." (ibid)

The first year of the implementation focused on working with the supplier to developing the solutions. The second year consisted of piloting the solution and launching it in one division. In future years, they will expand the solution across all divisions. Triplett said, "The vendor never saw a customer move as fast as us." (ibid)

Baker knew from experience that for this initiative to be successful, it had to be driven by the business. Engineering was excited about the strategy and assigned an engineering person to PLM Champion. Engineering became very proactive in working with the business units during the development and deployment of the solution. They brought together subject matter experts from all the divisions to work on common processes and design solutions for the PLM.

The new PLM system is being implemented in stages. When complete, it could be used to simulate an entire drilling process. The process, which is almost totally academic and mechanical, can become a virtual model. Pat McGinley, director of IT Engineering at Baker Hughes, describes the benefit. "In the old days, we would try something and if didn't work, we would make modifications. It was very inefficient. Every time you have an idea, you have to cut metal and see how it performs. The drilling process could take up to 5 years. With a simulation tool, we can virtually develop a scenario in days. The savings will be huge!"[15]

Baker Hughes reaped huge benefits from this strategic initiative. Not only is it easier for customers to work with Baker Hughes, but it also helped in other ways. Triplett brought together engineers from different divisions to share ideas, experiences, and challenges. "It helped drive a common process of how the divisions work with customers...it used to be a threat to the business to come up with the answer and ask IT to deliver. Now, IT is a partner in the development of solutions. We walk the walk."[16]

Baker Hughes achieved increased sales and reduced costs resulting from the PLM strategic initiative. Triplett developed the strategy. Successful execution required a partnership with the business. Triplett's leadership style and focus on execution are skills that every strategic CIO requires. For Triplett, the journey was like following a road map. Computerworld wrote an article about Clif Triplett, 1 year after he became CIO at Baker Hughes, describing his management style:

> Triplett sets the bar high, says Jim Heaton (senior director of architecture and compliance at Houston-based Baker Hughes). Triplett sets the bar high, but he also leads by example. "He'll turn things around himself and follow the advice he's giving faithfully." He calls Triplett a "Renaissance man" because he is as comfortable discussing technical

details with the chief software architect of any major technology vendor as he is discussing intricate business issues with the CEO. "There aren't many like him," says Heaton.[17]

The Baker Hughes IT organization has been recognized as a leader among manufacturing IT teams, green IT, and as one of the top 100 places to work in IT. CIO magazine also recognized Triplett as a top CIO100 winner in 2011 and 2012, and the Enterprise CIO Forum awarded Triplett the Transformation CIO Award in 2012.

Postscript: Clif Triplett resigned from Baker Hughes in January 2013 to join SteelPoint Partners, LLP in Houston, Texas, as managing partner, where he assists clients in the oil and gas industry in leveraging the benefits of IT.

Anne Wilms, Executive Vice President, CIO, and Director of Human Resources, Rohm and Hass

Anne Wilms has worked most of her career in IT organizations. Her executive positions in IT organizations at Wisconsin Power and Light, Oracle Corporation, and Sonat, Inc. provided her with a foundation of technical and business skills she leveraged when Rohm and Hass hired her as CIO in 1999.

During her 10-year career at Rohm and Hass, Wilms focused on numerous initiatives to improve margin. Her focus on improving people skills, process excellence, and technology innovation helped Rohm and Hass position itself as a $10 billion global leader in pioneering developing technologies and solutions for the specialty materials industry. Its products include advanced materials and chemistries used in electronics, coatings, packaging, building and construction, water, clean energy, and a host of other industries. In fact, Rohm and Hass was so successful, Dow Corning assessed the company as a prime acquisition as part of their growth strategy. In 1999, Rohm and Hass became a wholly owned subsidiary of Dow Corning.

Prior to the acquisition by Dow Chemical, Rohm and Hass was comprised of 144 manufacturing sites with 11 different business lines, all operating independently. IT inefficiencies resulting from decentralized operating divisions were evident. When an organization with decentralized divisions develops their own platforms, the result is incompatible architectures across the entire enterprise. When divisions acquire different Project Portfolio Management (PPM) solutions to manage the portfolio of projects, the enterprise does not have visibility across all the project portfolios. Furthermore, when divisions procure their own solutions, there could be multiple vendor applications performing similar activities, resulting in increased maintenance costs.

Each of these inefficiencies results in unnecessary costs. When added together, costs could add up to millions of dollars. The net effect of these inefficiencies was that the IT organization was spending more money and resources on running the business instead of growing the business.

Wilms saw this as an opportunity to transform the IT organization to become more strategic, focus on growing the business, and work with the business units to leverage IT for strategic advantage.

During her 13 years at Rohm and Hass, Wilms embarked on a structured plan to transform the IT organization. Following are some of her initiatives that focused on improving margin.

Improve the Topline

IT organizations continually struggle with internal cost reduction initiatives; however, when the IT organization can affect revenue in a favorable way, heads turn. Wilms figured it out. She realized that raw material costs in producing Rohm and Hass products fluctuated frequently. "When oil and natural gas fluctuate in erratic ways, you have to be able to instantaneously include these changes in prices quickly. Pricing changes to customer contracts was a manual process. The group responsible for this activity would review each customer contract and then change the product pricing manually based upon changes to raw material costs."[18]

Wilms thought about the problem and came up with a solution. She organized a small IT team and challenged them to develop an automated solution to help the sales organization. If she could accomplish this, profit margins would increase, improving top-line performance:

> The team built a model to demonstrate how pricing changes could be incorporated quickly and, when compared to the manual process, would

improve margins by 1–4%. With a core set of requirements defined, they then scoured the market and found an automated solution. Our team met with the Sales executive team to demonstrate the solution. They loved the concept and volunteered to work with us to write the rules. (ibid)

The solution included 72 variables for developing product pricing, from a reactive to a proactive process. "Now salespeople can meet with customers and tell them what impact changes in raw material costs will have on prices in real-time." The pricing solution made the process more quantitative, improved customer satisfaction, and turned the sales relationship into a strategic partnership. Wilms told the IT team, "the solution removed the emotion from the buying decision and sales relationship by providing the salespeople the ammunition to have a business discussion." (ibid)

Wilms' initiative to automate the pricing process improved margin, which translated directly to top-line growth. For the coating business, "we were able to generate a 2% increase in margin. This is just one example of how information technology can improve margin." (ibid)

Instill Creativity in Organizations

Wilms has an affinity for organizing personnel to achieve goals they did not think were possible. Management recognized this competency and awarded Wilms with the title of director in Human Resources in addition to her role as the CIO. One of the programs Wilms implemented was hiring recent college graduates into roles where they could think *out of the box*. One of the advantages of hiring recent college graduates is they aren't tainted with bad habits. One often observes new hires, directly out of college, asking many questions, wondering why activities aren't performed differently, and suggesting alternative ways to accomplish work. Wilms observes, "Recent graduates aren't constrained by how to work and add refreshing new ideas." (ibid) Not only did Wilms hire recent college graduates and encourage them to be vocal about their observations, but she also encouraged divisions to solicit ideas through *crowd-sourcing*, a concept wherein companies solicit ideas from the marketplace for solutions to problems. Wilms explains the concept:

Procter and Gamble wanted to put an image on Pringle potato chips. They posted the problem all over the world to solicit ideas. An Italian baker had figured out how to solve the problem and recommended a solution to Proctor and Gamble. A second example is an Australian mining company that makes available all their intellectual property as a way to solicit improvements to its mining process. Crowd-sourcing is a wonderful idea and I encouraged using the concept within Rohm and Hass. (ibid)

Leverage Business Intelligence

One of the areas that Wilms targeted as an initiative to improve margin was business intelligence. Business intelligence is turning into a proactive discipline. IT used to be performed analyzing historical data to determine business performance. Competitive intelligence—understanding market trends, customer satisfaction, and competitive positioning—was also important and on her target list, but she needed to quickly help business executives understand their own divisional performance using real-time data versus historical data. "I was convinced that providing business unit executives more visibility into their division's performance would help in decision-making that would positively help the business."[19]

Wilms met with business unit executives to identify the "five important metrics you need to know about your business unit, which would enable you to take action to improve business performance." (ibid) Keeping the list down to five was not easy. Many business unit executives identified about a dozen metrics. However, Wilms wanted to keep the list to five. Some of the metrics were similar to other business units, but some had unique metrics specific to their business. The IT organization developed an automated solution that provided real-time data on the key metrics. "Even our CEO could get visibility into all the business unit metrics on his Blackberry."

Improve Business Processes

Improving business processes was a major goal for Wilms. She understood that acquisition was a key growth strategy for Rohm and Hass. The bad news was that divisions performed major processes differently across the company. There were many Band-Aid-type solutions available; however, the best solution was a multiphase approach that identified key processes that would improve business performance. Financial closing, acquisition integration, and vendor consolidation are three good examples.

The financial closing process is a perfect example of an existing process that needed improvement. Many corporate decisions depend on the availability of current financial performance data. The sooner financial data are available, the quicker the business executives can react to the data and make the necessary business decisions to grow the company. At the time, the financial closing process took 20 days. Wilms set a target of closing the financial books in less than 5 days, an 80% improvement. "The team, consisting of IT, finance, and business unit personnel, exceeded the goal. We were able to close the books in two days, a 90 percent reduction."[20]

The acquisition process was critical for Rohm and Hass. As part of their growth initiative, it was imperative to reap the benefits of the integration as quickly as possible. Acquisitions occurred all around the globe, and business units used different integration processes. Wilms knew that "business units have grown through acquisition versus organic growth, and improving the integration process was critical."[21] The IT/business team developed an acquisition playbook that all integration teams used. The benefit not only was a smoother and speedier integration process but also provided seamless insight by corporate management into the status of all acquisitions. Reporting using a common process enabled corporate management to view the status of all acquisitions.

Wilms also targeted inventory levels as a critical area that required improvement. "We spent $3 billion on oil, gas, and other bulk purchases. We also spent $2 billion on office supplies, computers, and other indirect purchases."[21] In addition, Rohm and Hass spent hundreds of millions of dollars on chemicals and other products with shelf life expiration dates. Controlling inventory levels is a process that is critical to controlling inventory costs. "The key to optimizing this type of spend is to develop relationships with a few critical vendors. We implemented a vendor consolidation program and improved the quality of products, inventory levels, and procurement costs." (ibid)

During her tenure as the executive vice president, CIO, and director of Human Resources, Wilms focused on initiatives to improve margin. Some of her major accomplishments are as follows:

a. Implemented a corporate-wide ERP system
b. Reengineered major business processes to shorten cycle times
c. Reduced inventory levels
d. Improved vendor relationships and product quality
e. Increased product profit margins using an automated pricing calculator solution
f. Generated innovative ideas based on collaboration with recent college hires encouraged to ask questions and challenge current thinking

Rohm and Hass benefited substantially from Wilms' leadership and technology expertise. Wilms semiretired after she resigned from Rohm and Hass and now provides consulting services on the subject of IT. She is also the chair of the advisory board of NPower PA, the Red Cross, SE Pennsylvania, and a member of the Villanova University CIO Advisory Council.

Steve Heilenman, CIO at Computer Aid, Inc. (CAI)

Listen up CIOs: are you interested in driving down day-to-day costs so you can free up funds to invest in innovation without adding to your IT budget? If you are, then there is an IT spend optimization strategy you can employ that makes you a hero to your C-level peers. How do CIOs optimize IT spend to invest in innovation? In today's competitive environment, management focuses on innovating value for their customers. The IT organization is an integral part of the team. Most IT organizations spend, on average, 70%–80% on running the day-to-day operations, which leaves only 20%–30% to grow the business through innovation. As business executives exploit the marketplace to identify new and sustainable value for its customers, the management tasks the IT organization with developing, implementing, and supporting new and enhanced business solutions. The budget challenge faced by IT organizations today is how to meet increasing demand from the business—for projects that drive topline and bottom-line growth, while at the same time reducing the day-to-day operations spend, which comprises most of the IT spend.

Most IT organizations do not have a good handle on their costs. Sure, they have a budget and spend monies on infrastructure, applications, support, and projects. Some even recognize that their day-to-day costs are too high. But most of their focus is on running the business and dealing with the challenges and issues of execution. CIOs need to step back and figure out how to reduce inefficiencies and increase innovation spend without any budget growth. This is the only way they will meet the demands of the business and succeed at being a strategic business partner. They can succeed by implementing the following three-phase strategy:

a. Gain *visibility* of IT spend. Develop cost categories and capture and analyze your costs in each category.

b. Implement *control* in the form of new tools, techniques, and processes to reduce inefficient spend.

c. *Optimize* IT investments to continuously reduce inefficiencies and increase spend on innovation that grows the top and bottom line (Figure 13.3).

An example of a strategic CIO who successfully implemented an IT spend optimization strategy is Steve Heilenman, CIO at CAI Inc.,

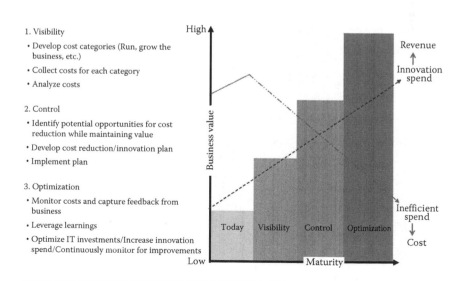

Figure 13.3 IT Spend Optimization Strategy.

a 460 million dollar plus global IT services firm headquartered in Pennsylvania, with offices and staff throughout the United States, Canada, Europe, and the Asia Pacific region.

Heilenman is an experienced IT executive. He graduated with honors from Widener University, with a BS in Information Systems. Heilenman's 25-year career at Electronic Data Systems (EDS), Price Waterhouse, and Vanguard Investment Company provides him with a solid IT background. Heilenman also spends a lot of time helping his peers grow their skills. He has served as President of Philadelphia Society of Information Management (SIM) board and currently is on the SIM Board. He is a member of the Greater Philadelphia Senior Executive Group (GPSEG), a former CIO roundtable subgroup chairman, a member of SIM's Advance Practices Council (APC), and a finalist for SIM Philadelphia's 2011 and 2012 CIO Leadership Awards. Heilenman also wrote the first chapter of a new book, *Driving Business Value With Innovative Technology Strategies*, as part of the *Inside The Mind Series* published by Thomson Reuters in July 2014.

More importantly, Heilenman has a solid business perspective. "It's all about understanding the business and helping the business grow."[22] Heilenman is in good company. Adriana Karaboutis, CIO at Dell, says "to be an effective CIO you need to understand how the business operates and the financial structure of the business."[23] So, when Heilenman decided he wanted to understand the financial structure of CAI, he scheduled a series of *lunch-and-learn* meetings with the CFO.

Heilenman executed all three transformation phases—visibility, cost, and optimization. During the period 2008–2013, his IT team accomplished the following:

a. Reduced IT spend by almost 25% almost while corporate revenue increased by approximately 50%.
b. Day-to-day operations cost reduced by 20% as a percentage of sales while spend on growing the business increased by 20%, as a percentage of sales.
c. Ended 2013 with a total corporate IT cost at 1.95% of revenue.

These are quite impressive results. How did he do it? Let's find out.

Visibility

When Heilenman was promoted to the CIO role at CAI, he knew the first order of business was to find out what IT was spending. What he found was the following:

- IT spend was 4.5% of revenue/average IT spend of revenue for IT service firms was 4.7%.
- Day-to-day-operations costs were 51% of IT spend.
- Growing the business spend was 49% of spend.

As CIO, Heilenman is part of the CAI executive management committee. The company was on an aggressive growth strategy to double its business in 3–4 years. IT was a big part of the plan. His initial instincts told him that IT spend was too high, even though spend, as a percentage of sales, was in line with that of other IT service firms. "I had to figure out a way to do more with less."[22] Heilenman's next step was to dig into the components of IT spend and analyze the data to identify what he could do to better control expenditures. He identified the following five cost reduction areas where productivity could be improved:

1. Development platform is outdated and inefficient.
2. Development methodology used by teams is inefficient and too costly.
3. There is no metric to measure business functions on development projects.
4. Testing is inefficient and costly.
5. IT organization needs to work more effectively as a team.

Control

Heilenman developed a program for each of these five areas with the goal of improving productivity and driving down cost, while at the same time enabling the CAI growth strategy.

Development Platform is Outdated and Inefficient The IT organization used the Rational tool suite. "The tool was difficult to use, especially when working offsite. Also, the tool suite was not easy to learn, consisted of complicated tools that weren't intuitive, and required 2 full-time equivalents to administer the tool." The development teams were very frustrated with the product for all the reasons previously mentioned.

Heilenman and his team investigated other tools and, using a methodical process, chose Microsoft Team Foundation Server (TSF). "The IT teams loved it. It significantly simplified the development platform and process, leveraged existing tools and knowledge." (ibid) The financials also made a lot of sense. The 3-year cost ownership was a fraction of the Rational tool suite cost.

How did it actually help in reducing IT costs. Heilenman estimates that productivity improvement using TSF was 30%–40%. Licensing and support costs were reduced by over $150,000 per year.

Development Methodology Used by Teams Is Inefficient and Too Costly Heilenman attended a number of development meetings for different projects. The teams used the Waterfall methodology for all development projects. The Waterfall methodology includes a set of specific phases with appropriate checkpoints and deliverables at each phase. Problems and issues were identified at each meeting and, as is always the case, the user was always changing the requirements (not an uncommon practice since users don't always really know what they want). As a result, timelines were extended. Projects were completed but timelines were extended and cost rose accordingly:

> We implemented an Agile Development methodology within the IT organization. Agile methodologies are all about iterations of work involving business and IT teams who work together, to define and refine the requirements to solve the business problem, and develop proof of concepts and prototypes quickly. (ibid)
>
> Heilenman is a real proponent of Agile development because
>
> these short sprints work well because they identify defects earlier in the cycle, highlight whether the project is off course, and allow us to provide more value to the business in shorter durations. This minimizes risk, improves quality and reduces rework. (ibid)

There Is No Metric to Measure Business Functions on Development Projects Determining the business value of a development project is always a challenge. The value is in the business functionality designed into a solution. So, measuring the amount of business functionality is a good starting point.

The IT team was not using a function point as a metric to measure their development efficiency. "We analyzed the function points of past projects and calculated that, on average, it took 38 hours to produce a function point. We instituted function point analysis as part of the performance metrics he used to for the IT organization. Through analysis, learning, and continuous improvement, his team was able to reduce the average function point by 50 percent to 19 hours. This is considered world-class performance." (ibid)

Testing Is Inefficient and Costly

One of the major initiatives undertaken by the IT organization was a new solution that required a lot of testing. A variety of testing tools used by the IT organization were extremely expensive and not as efficient as the IT team wanted. The team built their own automated testing tool using shareware. The results were astounding. (ibid)

a. On a major development project, 96% of testing was accomplished using automated test scripts. Testing process was integrated into the development process. Without automation, over 800 hours of manual testing over a 6-week period was required. With the new automation tool, only 70 hours of automated testing over a 2-week period was required.

b. Automated testing, on another major internal project, reduced a 1000 hour test to 9 hours.

Additionally, automation added nothing to the development time, and defects found in the test phase were drastically reduced since the developer had the ability to run the test automation scripts and fix defects prior to sending to testers.

Heilenman realized that the test automation tool was a solution that other companies would want. He turned the internal tool into a product offering for other IT organizations. Heilenman's team developed a product website (http://www.testinseconds.com/) and created a marketing brochure (Figure 13.4). The CAI IT department, thus, had their first product marketed to external customers. At the time of this writing, CAI has their first client, a retail department store

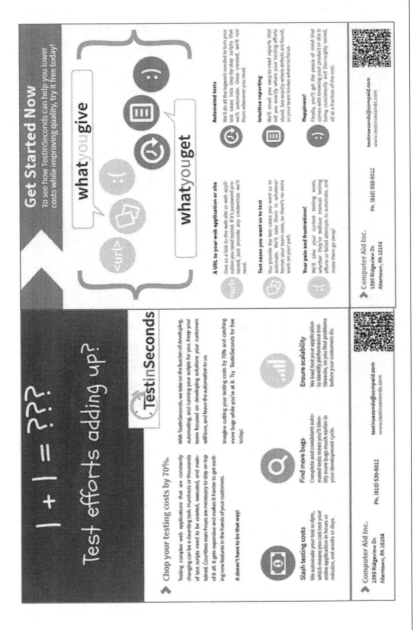

Figure 13.4 CAI TestInSeconds™ Test Automation Tool Brochure. (From MIS Quarterly Executive, APC Forum: Software Test Automation at Computer Aid, Inc, Volume 11, Number 2; June 2012, University of Minnesota, Minneapolis, MN, Copyright 2012.)

chain, and a number of proposals outstanding. This product not only dramatically reduced testing time within CAI resulting in cost savings but also enabled the CAI IT organization to become a revenue producer. The MIS Quarterly Executive publication highlighted an article on the testing tool developed by Heilenman's team.[24]

The tool and process, which took only a month to develop and implement, significantly reduced the testing cycle and dramatically improved the testing consistency. Defects are now found much earlier in the development process. Developers are able to execute the same automated test scripts and fix/repair defects before getting to the test team. As a result, they have experienced a 300% reduction of defects found in the testing phase (Figure 13.4). The tool has been so successful that Heilenman decided to develop a self-service web-based version that has taken off in the market. *The web-based self-service solution was built in two months and within three months of release to the market we have had over 200 customers use our product. I am really excited about this and very proud of our development team.*

IT Organization Needs to Work More Effectively as a Team   Every good leader recognizes a well-functioning team that drives success. Heilenman had a good team working for him, but he sensed that the teaming among the individuals did not harness the energy and leverage the thought leadership that he had seen in other IT organizations. He embarked on an organization-building program that comprised of a number of key team-building activities:

a. Information sharing program: IT and business topics are identified by IT personnel. Training programs are conducted via recorded webinars and available to all IT personnel, as well as business personnel, through intranet site (one idea Heilenman has is *to make this available to other companies*— another revenue-producing product developed by IT).

b. Innovation Fridays: Forum for IT personnel to get together and brainstorm about any subject or idea they desired. The automated testing tool idea, previously discussed, resulted from an improvement idea at one of these sessions.

c. CAI IDEAS program: A program where anyone at CAI can submit an improvement or innovation idea. The *ideas* are then reviewed and assigned to various businesses and IT leaders for additional review and implementation consideration. At the time of this writing, the CAI IDEAS program received 220 ideas, of which 100 have been approved and 25 implemented. The numbers continue to rise as more suggestions are submitted, researched, and implemented. Some ideas that have been successfully implemented include

   i. Ideas presented by Tom Swider and Kevin Sweeny suggested a CAI Organization Process Assets Repository to help CAI conform to industry standards

   ii. The CAI Info Share program allows CAI to leverage the vast knowledge of all of our associates and provide a model with which to help educate our peers

   iii. A CAI/Microsoft Webcast Boot Camp to strengthen current developer skills and provide a solid foundation for interns to build upon

   iv. An emergency notification system suggestion, an electronic signature idea, email signature concept, and many more

d. Dotnet development factory: Training program for developers using the Microsoft Development Platform. This helps up skill new and existing employees very quickly. (Heilenman is also thinking about *how we can develop this as an offering to other IT organizations and generate revenue for the IT organization.*)

e. Monthly meeting with business divisions: To help build better relationships with the business, the IT organization meets with business divisions on a monthly basis to solicit feedback on IT performance as well as report to the business on the major IT activities and their business value.

f. IT scorecard dashboard: To help communicate the business value of IT, Heilenman's team developed an IT business dashboard that graphically displays metrics that business people can understand: this dashboard is reviewed by the company's exec team each month. There are monthly metrics and also trending for each key category.

g. Financial updates to IT personnel: (1) IT cost as percentage of business revenue, (2) day-to-day operating costs and growing the business costs as a percentage of total IT costs, and (3) productivity and efficiency data.

h. Development: (1) estimates versus actual, (2) defects, (3) support tickets, and (4) employee retention.

i. Support: (1) divisional support by hours and dollars and (2) percentage of uptime by quarter.

j. Customer satisfaction: convenience, interaction, responsiveness, satisfaction, and value.

k. R&D highlights.

l. Function point performance and efficiency.

Heilenman is proud of his IT team. One of the programs he is most pleased with is the mentoring program. Heilenman is part of the Advanced Practice Council (APC) of the Society for Information Management (SIM). One of the programs instituted is a mentoring program where APC members (all CIOs) mentor high-potential personnel from other organizations whose CIOs are part of the APC. One of Heilenman direct reports was mentored by the CIO from Constellation Brands. Joe Bruhin, the CIO, said that mentoring Matt Peters, from Heilenman's IT organization, has been beneficial to both Matt and himself. "In addressing some of Matt's challenges, I am not just pulling from my experience base and sharing relevant stories, but I am also sharing what I would do differently today— and frankly it is highlighting my growth over the years."[25]

Heilenman mentors senior IT leaders from both Pepsi and Howard Hughes Medical Institute and feels the same way as Bruhin. The mentoring process was highlighted in the July 30, 2013, issue of *CIO Magazine* article CIOs and IT Staff Learn From Unusual Mentoring Program.

Heilenman started a formal internship program to acquire and train top talent. Internship programs provide an opportunity for the company to vet a potential employee during the internship process. "It reduced the risk of a wrong hire," says Heilenman. The goal is "that every intern will be hired for positions within CAI when he/she graduates." Full-time employees coach interns, and CAI gets to know them over the course of a year to ensure they are a good fit for the company. Unlike other internship programs, CAI looks for *the best of the best*: high-aptitude students with good analytic and social skills. A peer coach is assigned to each intern. The peer coach is responsible for their work. Over time, the intern works independently with less *over-the-shoulder supervision* and more mentoring. The SIM was so impressed with the program and its results that they commissioned a white paper/case study on the program.[26]

Optimization

CAI has improved services revenue by almost 50% in the past 3 years. Their focus is on helping clients in four major areas: (1) reduce legacy support costs by 30%, (2) improve project management governance and drive down costs by 40%, (3) through their IT Governance Management Suite, and (4) thought leadership of IT best practices. Heilenman's IT organization walks the talk. His team supported the revenue growth of 50% while at the same time reducing IT costs by 25%. When you look at IT costs as a percentage of revenue the results are impressive. IT costs are 2% of revenue, a drop from 4.7% in 2008 ago, where 4% is a recognized global best in class metric. These metrics are pretty impressive (Figure 13.5).

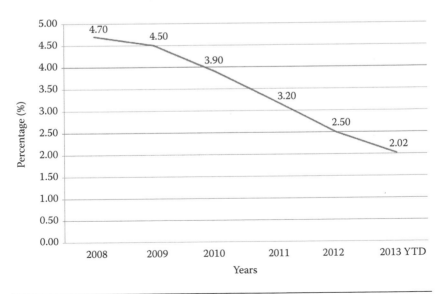

Figure 13.5   Percentage of IT Costs to Revenue from 2008 to 2013.

Heilenman is pleased with the results. But he's not sitting on his laurels. "There are always improvements to be made."[22] He and his team continue to figure out ways to improve development time, reduce rework, and improve employee performance. Heilenman is leveraging his knowledge and sharing it with his peers. He recently wrote the first chapter for *Driving Business Value with Innovative Technology Strategies: IT Leaders on Strategies for Differentiating a Company and Increasing Profit* (*Inside the Minds*), published by Thomson Reuters/ Aspatore 2014. Heilenman and his team continue to figure out ways to drive costs out of IT. He says it best:

> Through cost reduction, prioritization, productivity, and efficiency improvements we continue to look for new and innovative ways to improve our performance and support the needs of the business. There's no better success story than driving down IT costs and at the same time enable a dramatic growth in revenue. (ibid)

Helen Cousins, Former CIO for Lincoln Trust Company (Retired November 2013)

As the executive vice president and CIO for Lincoln Trust Company, Helen Cousins was a driving force that reengineered Lincoln Trust into an analytical organization by focusing on enterprise initiatives to improve margin. Cousins and her team leveraged technology coupled with a business process reengineering focus encompassing business intelligence and workflow management across the entire organization.

Lincoln Trust provides trust and custodial services. Included in these services is an open architecture 401k platform that includes over 24,000 mutual funds. The differentiator for Lincoln Trust is its transparency-based service model. Simply stated, 401k plans incur expenses that are often difficult for plan holders to understand. Lincoln Trust provides a *personalized expense ratio* for each plan participant, so fees are visible at a detailed category level. This helps 401k plan participants properly evaluate plan fees, which over time can dramatically impact net returns.

When Cousins joined Lincoln Trust in 2006, she observed a huge opportunity to improve business performance, impact the bottom line, and increase customer satisfaction, which would drive future growth. Cousins' success at transforming Lincoln Trust is an example of how a strategic CIO looks beyond the tactical technology that supports the business to an enterprise strategy that leverages technology and process innovation to enable business success.

Helen Cousins: Background

Helen Cousins arrived at Lincoln Trust in 2006 from Dex Media, where she was the senior vice president and CIO. Cousins led the enterprise implementation of a new technology platform. As part of the executive team, Cousins participated in what was, at the time, the second largest leverage buyout in US history, an IPO and subsequent sale of the company. Her previous roles were at Cendant, where she was responsible for orchestrating one of the largest outsourcing deals with a major technology firm as well as leading the IT due diligence and integration for several major acquisitions, which increased revenue by $15B. She has held several other executive positions managing global organizations, spending her first 25 years on Wall Street with top Fortune 100/500 firms. She has won various awards and recognitions for her accomplishments. Helen graduated summa cum laude with a BS in accounting and economics from Fordham University and an MBA from Pace University, both located in New York.

The Challenge/Opportunity

We have all heard the idiomatic expression; *you can't see the forest for the trees*. Simply stated, this means that focusing too much on detail will divert you from the bigger picture. Cousins learned this early in her career, and she is careful not to let details derail the bigger picture. When Cousins took on the CIO role at Lincoln Trust, she made it a high priority to understand the business so IT could properly respond to the needs of the business units. Her meetings with business unit leaders also included a tour of the offices. What she saw was a paper factory. Customer documents received via postal service, email, and faxes were processed manually. "There were upwards of 100,000 plus customer documents received each month with instructions regarding their IRA's.[27] What was more evident were the metal file cabinets filled with paper. "The problem with paper is filing and retrieval. It takes time. Customers contacted us multiple times to check status of inquiries. Our ability to respond to customers was poor." (ibid)

During 2009, Fiserv was divesting a large part of the business. The remaining portion of the business, which became Lincoln Trust Co., would still be burdened with 95% of the paperwork. Cousins saw an opportunity to help Lincoln Trust overcome the paper deluge. She knew that by leveraging technology, business process improvement, and improving the skills of personnel, Lincoln Trust could reinvent itself and become a premier provider of services to its clients.

Building the Trust of the Business

Cousins is smart enough to know that to be an effective business partner with business unit executives requires a foundation of trust, which needed to be improved between the business units and the IT organization. Previous attempts, prior to joining Lincoln Trust, at working with business to improve processes failed. As Cousins explains it, "the relationship was so toxic that a business unit executive said, she would fire all of it if it were under her control." (ibid)

Cousins realized that trust is earned and not granted. She realized it would take time to build the trust necessary for her IT teams to work with the business. Her approach was simple but effective. Cousins met with the head of business operations and discussed the need to resolve the paper-handling problem if Lincoln Trust was to achieve the business results needed subsequent to the divestiture. Cousins has always believed that business results is the main goal and that "IT and, in particular, the CIO need to clearly understand that they have a shared responsibility with the rest of the executive team to run a company and focus on business results, not just the technology side of the equation." (ibid) Cousins presented the business operations executive with a road map of how they could work together to resolve the paper logjam by leveraging technology and process improvement. It worked. The business operations executive and Cousins codeveloped a plan to begin small, gain success, and leverage the improvements across the company.

Driving a Shared Initiative to Improve Operational Efficiency

Cousins learned from experience that the best approach for any enterprise-wide initiative is "to start out simple and build incrementally on the solutions to get continuous improvement." (ibid) A common shared process for handling paper electronically was rolled out across the enterprise. The executive team agreed that no customization would be included in the initial rollout. This kept things simple and uniform across the enterprise. The initial project discontinued paper documents and focused on delivering imaged documents in a business process workflow. The goal was to be *paperless*. In less than a year, 100,000 documents per month were routed electronically through the process.

The partnering of IT and operations proved successful. Business executives across the company watched the progress and slowly started to recognize the value the IT organization brought to the business.

Focusing on Creating New Value for the Business

After the initial success, it was time to look at additional features that would help the business teams process electronic documents. It became apparent that a sophisticated business process management solution suite was needed. To do so required buy-in from the executive suite. With the initial success, Cousins was able to share a vision that process improvement coupled with the right technology could further improve not only the electronic flow of paper but also other key strategic business processes at Lincoln Trust.

Over time, more and more processes were streamlined. The handling of legal documents and associated correspondence is one example. Cousins explains the streamlined process leveraged with technology as follows:

> We implemented a Cloud-based legal document solution that turned the lengthy and complex experience of completing multiple legal documents into a "white glove" experience for new clients and their financial advisors. The sales team would hold one online meeting bring the client and advisor together with pre-filled online documents and coach them through the electronic signature process. Immediately after the client

had electronically signed the documents, systems integration with the electronics document software vendor imports and attached the document into the workflow process where the new business specialists are notified of its arrival. At the same time the signed PDF documents are imported into the imaging system. (ibid)

Prior to the improvements, the plan conversion processes associated with the handling of legal documents were cumbersome on both the customer and the company. Because of the improved process and enabling technology, personnel could handle many more plan conversions without adding staff. What used to take hours for a plan conversion now took minutes. The management could view status in real time versus the excel spreadsheets used previously. Another important improvement was the automated checklist function that provided personnel with alerts if an activity in the process was not completed properly. As Cousins describes this, "the ability to integrate straight through processing throughout the entire process saved a tremendous amount of time and greatly reduced financial risk and errors." (ibid)

Cousins also knew that integrating the customer into the process was extremely important. One of the areas that integrated the customer into the process was customer errors in completing forms. As errors are discovered during the review process, emails are automatically sent to the customer for correction. This provides full transparency to the customer by seamlessly integrating them into the process. Other features enabled customers to interact with Lincoln Trust via the web.

Cousins helped change the business model at Lincoln Trust. The benefits of marrying technology with process improvement changed the face of the company, improved customer service, and drove growth. Annual savings amounted to approximately $5 million per year, productivity increased 40%, and customer satisfaction increased proven by a 90% drop in customer complaints. Lincoln Trust's main competency is providing custodial services for 401k plans. In order to provide value to its customers, it has to manage the processes associated with document management superbly. Cousins was able to see the silver lining and drove the Lincoln Trust executive team to see the value in leveraging technology coupled with process improvement as an innovative solution that provided the company strategic competitive advantage.

Helen Cousins is currently the president of CIO Executive Advisors. In addition to strategic consulting assignments, she is looking at ways to encourage young women into math and science fields and currently mentoring and coaching the next generation of IT leaders.

Chapter Summary

In this chapter, we highlighted six strategic CIOs who focus on initiatives that drive margin by improving revenue and/or reducing costs. Each of these CIOs has broad and deep experience in business and IT at the executive level. Further, each applies these skills in a strategic and focused manner.

Tom Grooms, CIO at Valspar, joined the chemical coating company after a long career in IT at Medtronic, the medical device company. Although Valspar is in a totally different industry, Grooms took a strategic approach to professionalize the IT organization by working with the business units to improve processes, reduce IT support costs, and drive initiatives that enabled Valspar to move forward with an aggressive growth strategy.

Randy Spratt, CTO and CIO at McKesson—the multinational health-care services and IT company—is an example of an executive who is both left- and right-brain dominant. He thinks strategically but is just as comfortable at the tactical level designing company-wide architecture. Customers had difficulty integrating McKesson products due to incompatible architecture until Spratt harnessed a company-wide team to develop a unified architecture, which improved customer service and sales.

Clif Triplett, while CIO at the oil industry services company Baker Hughes, took on some rather large projects. He turned the IT organization into a world-class organization, developed a common data platform to optimize customer information, and developed a product life cycle management system that reduced development time for products and services. Improved customer service, reduced IT costs, and a transformed IT organization make Triplett a true example of a strategic CIO.

Ann Wilms, CIO at Rohm and Hass prior to its merger with Dow Chemical, embarked on a number of strategic initiatives that drove revenue through an improved pricing system, reduced IT costs, optimized inventory investment that resulted in millions of dollars in savings, and led a host of other initiatives.

Steve Heilenman, CIO at CAI, focused on improving the value of the IT organization while driving down the cost of IT. He succeeded. Over a 5-year period, Heilenman reduced IT costs by about 25% while supporting a business that grew by 50%. The net metric of IT costs as a percentage of revenue is 2%, one-half of the best in class percentage for IT service companies.

Helen Cousins, former CIO at Lincoln Trust, revitalized and reengineered the major document processes by leveraging technology. She positioned the company for a spin-off of some of its business units and focused on a core competency for future growth.

What do these six strategic CIOs have in common? They followed a simple but effective process for transforming their IT organizations to become strategic and implemented initiatives that drove margin in the form of increased revenues and/or reduced costs.

To be able to implement these initiatives, each of these strategic CIOs focused first on improving basic services and understanding the business. Doing so enabled each to develop and leverage business relationships with their C-level peers to partner and identify solutions to grow the business. Sometimes, these solutions were simply improving business processes. Sometimes, these initiatives involved IT. Regardless of the initiative, these CIOs have one focus: to work as a team with their C-level peers to achieve business outcomes. For those of you trying to find the magic bullet, my advice is to work with your business partners and focus on achieving business outcomes. If you do this, you are well on your way to becoming a strategic CIO.

Citations

1. Book Jacket Quote by Randy McKesson from the book: *On Top of the Cloud How CIOs Leverage New Technologies to Drive Change and Build Value across the Enterprise* by Hunter Muller; Copyright Hunter Muller 2012, Published by John Wiley & Sons, Hoboken, NJ. http://www.amazon.com/On-Top-Cloud-Technologies-Enterprise/dp/1118065824.
2. Tom Grooms, CIO-Valspar/Phil Weinzimer Interview, January 18, 2013.
3. Tom Grooms, CIO-Valspar/Phil Weinzimer Interview, February 27, 2013.
4. Tom Grooms, CIO-Valspar/Phil Weinzimer Interview, April 25, 2013.

5. Tom Grooms, CIO-Valspar/Phil Weinzimer Interview, June 7, 2013.

6. McKesson Website; Key Facts Page; Our Businesses/Technology Solutions, http://www.mckesson.com/about-mckesson/key-facts/, July 31, 2013.

7. Randy Spratt Biography on McKesson Website: http://www.mckesson.com/about-mckesson/our-company/executive-officers/randall-n-spratt/.

8. Randy Spratt, CTO, CIO-McKesson/Phil Weinzimer Interview, December 12, 2013.

9. Clif Triplett, CIO-Baker Hughes/Phil Weinzimer Interview, October 10, 2012.

10. Clif Triplett resigned from Baker Hughes in January 2013 to leverage his experience and take on a new challenge. He is Managing Partner at SteelPointe Partners, LLP in Huston Texas where he focuses on Information Technology and Services.

11. Clif Triplett, CIO-Baker Hughes/Phil Weinzimer Interview, November 5, 2012.

12. Clif Triplett, CIO-Baker Hughes/Phil Weinzimer Interview, November 7, 2012.

13. Holger Stibbe-Chief Engineer, Baker Hughes/Phil Weinzimer Interview, November 5, 2013.

14. Clif Triplett, CIO-Baker Hughes/Phil Weinzimer Interview, November 15, 2012.

15. Pat McGinely-IT Director, Baker Hughes/Phil Weinzimer Interview, November 13, 2013.

16. Clif Triplett, CIO-Baker Hughes/Phil Weinzimer Interview, November 15, 2012.

17. Premier 100 IT Leader Profile: Clif Triplett; Robert L. Mitchell; December 7, 2009; Computerworld; http://www.computerworld.com/s/article/343792/Clif_Triplett_CIO_Baker_Hughes, Robert Mitchell, December 7, 2009.

18. Ann Wilms, Former CIO, Rohm and Hass/Phil Weinzimer Interview, June 19, 2012.

19. Ann Wilms, Former CIO, Rohm and Hass/Phil Weinzimer Interview, June 26, 2012.

20. Ann Wilms, Former CIO, Rohm and Hass/Phil Weinzimer Interview, July 10, 2012.

21. Ann Wilms, Former CIO, Rohm and Hass/Phil Weinzimer Interview, July 24, 2012.

22. Steve Heilenman-CIO, CAI Inc/Phil Weinzimer Interview, May 28, 2013 and June 4, 2013.

23. Adriana Karaboutis, CIO-Dell/Phil Weinzimer Interview, January 25, 2013.

24. MIS Quarterly Executive; APC Forum: Software Test Automation at Computer Aid, Inc; Volume 11, Volume 2; June 2012; University of Minnesota, Minneapolis, MN, Copyright 2012.

25. A New Approach to Internships at ComputerAid; Heather Smith-Queen's University School of Business. Advanced Management Council, Society for Information Management; Copyright 2013.

26. CIOs and IT Staff Learn from Unusual Mentoring Program: A pilot program from the Society for Information Management shows the value of taking on a protege from outside your own organization. http://www.cio.com/article/736829/CIOs_and_IT_Staff_Learn_From_Unusual_Mentoring_Program.

27. Helen Cousins-Senior Vice President and CIO-Lincoln Trust/Phil Weinzimer Interview, July 2, 2013.

SECTION OVERVIEW

Leverage Technologies Strategically to Innovate Value

Strategic CIOs have a business focus and work with C-suite executives to improve the competitive position of the company through leveraging technologies strategically to innovate value. There are three predecessor stages that information technology (IT) organizations need to complete before the C-suite and business units will allow them to work on strategic initiatives that change the course of the company.

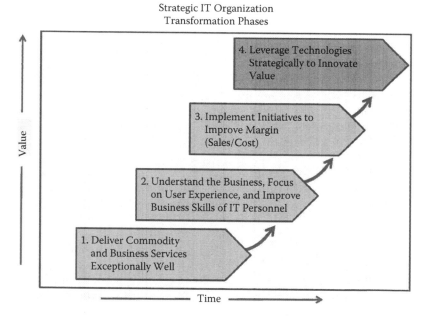

Strategic IT Organization
Transformation Phases

What are these stages? First, CIOs and the IT organization have to build credibility by delivering services exceptionally well. Second, the CIO and key IT personnel have to develop a well-founded understanding of the business, industry, and the competitive environment, along with a set of business-oriented competencies and skills. Third, the CIO and IT personnel have to successfully work in business teams to focus and implement initiatives that drive margin and/or reduce cost. These are not easy steps. It took Rob Carter a number of years to build the trust of the business. If you are a CIO, you understand the challenge. If you are not, have a talk with your CIO to find out how he or she built the trust from the business. The real fun part, from the CIOs I have spoken with, is working on the really cool stuff that dramatically changes the business model, results in new products, develops new processes to service customers, or expands into new markets. This is what this section of the book addresses.

Section Overview

The section starts with a chapter that explores the significance of leveraging technology strategically and examples of where information and associated technologies seamlessly weave into our daily lives. With this foundation, we highlight eight CIOs, in subsequent chapters, who have successfully leveraged technologies strategically to innovate value.

Following is a summary for each of the chapters in this section.

Chapter 15, Why Leveraging Technologies Strategically to Innovate Value Is a Game Changer, provides an overview of how technology leveraged strategically, provides innovative value, and is a game changer when it comes to creating customer value.

- What is the significance of leveraging technology strategically and examples of where information and associated technologies seamlessly weave into our daily lives?

Chapter 16, How FedEx Leverages Technology Strategically to Innovate Value, is devoted entirely to FedEx and Rob Carter, who leads the IT organization and is a member of FedEx's executive team. Carter and his IT organization have dramatically changed the way business units use IT, and he and his team have been instrumental in molding a more information-rich business model to enable business units to more effectively work together but still maintain this independent structure.

- How did Rob Carter and his IT organization have dramatically change the way business units use IT?
- How did the IT organization provide a more information-rich business model to enable business units to more effectively work together but still maintain this independent structure?
- What are some examples of how business personnel use information to improve operational performance?

Chapter 17, How Procter & Gamble Leverages Technology Strategically to Innovate Value, focuses on Procter and Gamble (P&G) and Filippo Passerini—group president of Global Business Services and CIO. Passerini and his team digitized the information infrastructure eliminating the complexities caused by separate information databases, which disrupts the analysis and decision-making process. His implementation of decision cockpits and business sphere conference rooms enable business teams make well-informed business decisions.

- How did Passerini and his team digitize the information infrastructure eliminating the complexities caused by separate information databases, which disrupts the analysis and decision-making process?
- How do workstation decision cockpits and business sphere conference rooms enable business teams to make well-informed business decisions?

Chapter 18, How Five CIOs from Different Industries Improved Their Companies by Leveraging Technology Strategically to Innovate Value, focuses on five CIOs and how they exploited technology to innovate value.

- How did Dave Finnegan, CIO at Build a Bear, leverage technology to change the business model?
- How did Gary Wimberly, CIO at Express Scripts, leverage technology where information about patient care is used to improve health outcomes.

- How did Harry Lukens, CIO at Lehigh Valley Health Network, leverage technologies to save lives for patients in critical care units.
- How did Stephen Pickett, CIO at Penske, help business units leverage information to improve their competitive positions?
- How did Perry Rotella, CIO at Verisk, leverage his knowledge of predictive analytics to lead a new business unit into an expanding market?

15

WHY LEVERAGING TECHNOLOGY STRATEGICALLY TO INNOVATE VALUE IS A GAME CHANGER

Value comes from seeing what customers need and delivering it.[1]

James McQuivey
Forrester Research

Strategic IT Organization
Transformation Phases

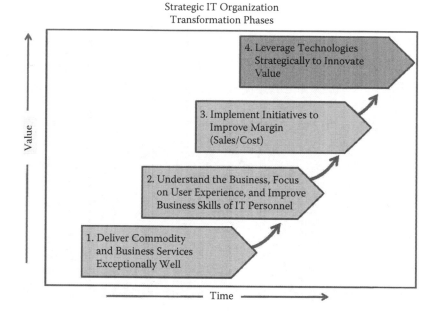

This chapter introduces the fourth phase of transforming into a strategic IT organization—leveraging technologies strategically to innovate value. The chapter begins with the results of two global surveys that identifies the importance of including technology as a key subject in today's executive boardroom discussions and then provides current examples of how technology is used to expand the value network as well as create new value. The chapter concludes with an overview of the following three chapters, which are examples of how CIOs are leveraging technologies to innovate value.

Following is a brief overview of the chapter objective, key messages, and examples included.

A. CHAPTER OBJECTIVE

1. Provide you with examples of strategic CIOs have navigated through all four of the strategic IT transformation phases and leverage technology strategically to innovate value.
2. Provide insights to those of you who are still on a transformation journey but want to understand the strategic value of leveraging technology in innovative ways.

B. KEY POINTS

1. Leveraging technology to innovate value is a recognized global trend exploited by world-class companies.
2. A recent McKinsey global survey of over 1000 chief executive officers (CEOs), chief information officers (CIOs), and other C-level executives supports this trend.

   ...companies are using digital technology more and more to engage with customers and reach them through new channels... and companies are making digital marketing and customer engagement a high strategic priority.[2]

3. An MIT Sloan study of 1600 executives on how they are using digital technologies found that companies must "adopt new technologies effectively or face competitive obsolescence."[3] Leveraging technology is a strategic imperative for every boardroom to embrace or else executives will watch their competitors race ahead in record time.
4. The role of technology in products, services, and processes has never been more important than it is right now. We are

the cusp of the *Internet of Everything* (IoE). People will connect in ways we are just beginning to experience:

a. Wearable technologies enable us to use Google Glass as if it were a laptop computer. Except it is voice activated.

b. Data will be processed more intelligently than ever before. Instead of just capturing data that accessed for further analysis, predictive analytics will incorporate sophisticated algorithms that evaluate data and help us make faster and more intelligent decisions.

c. Processes as we know them today will expand to incorporate human behavior. Proactively engaging shoppers is a reality today.

d. The 2014 Mercedes-Benz S-Class uses 60 onboard computers to control almost every aspect of the vehicle. Mercedes dubs this *intelligent drive*.

e. 3D printing is changing our lives.

f. Wearable devices are improving our health care.

g. *Smart* contact lenses help diabetics control their sugar level.

h. Digital toothbrushes help improve dental health.

i. The list is growing every day.

C. EXAMPLES

1. CIO examples of applying technology to innovate value include the following:

- A group of executives meets to analyze marketing trends.
- A father wants to ship a package to his son at college.
- A young child pleads with her mom to take her to a store to build a stuffed animal.
- An elderly man is having difficulty adhering to the doctor's instructions for taking medication.
- A patient in a hospital or at home care, who is concerned about their health outcome.

Leveraging Technology to Create Innovative Value Needs to Be a Core Competency for Every Major Corporation

The role of the CIO in today's global marketplace is very challenging as executives recognize the value of IT in their products, services, and processes. CIOs in major companies around the world engage with the C-level executives to leverage technologies for strategic advantage. A recent McKinsey global survey of over 1000 CEO, CIO, and other C-level executives supports this trend.

> …companies are using digital technology more and more to engage with customers and reach them through new channels… and companies are making digital marketing and customer engagement a high strategic priority.[2]

An MIT Sloan study of 1600 executives on how they are using digital technologies found that companies must "adopt new technologies effectively or face competitive obsolescence."[3] Leveraging technology is a strategic imperative for every boardroom to embrace or else executives will watch their competitors race ahead in record time.

Exploiting the Internet

The role of technology in products, services, and processes has never been more important than it is right now. We are the cusp of the Internet of Everything (IoE). David Evans is chief futurist at Cisco. He talks about IoE and how we are entering an era where everything we do will be accomplished by connections to the Internet. The Cisco website describes it as follows[4]:

> It's bringing together people, process, data, and things to make networked connections more valuable and relevant. The IoE turns information into actions that create new capabilities, richer experiences, and unprecedented economic opportunity for businesses, individuals, and countries.[5]

People will connect in ways we are just beginning to experience. Wearable technologies enable us to use Google Glass as if it were a laptop computer. Except it is voice activated. Think of your local electricity or telephone repair technician climbing up a pole to connect or repair wires. He experiences a problem. Wearing glasses that incorporate Google Glass, the technician accesses the help desk, views wiring diagrams, and makes the necessary connection without having to climb down the pole and call the home office.

Data will be processed more intelligently than ever before. Instead of just capturing data that accessed for further analysis, predictive analytics will incorporate sophisticated algorithms that evaluate data and help us make faster and more intelligent decisions. P&G translates data into actionable decisions that help the company compete more effectively. The ability to store data onto smaller chips is a reality today. The devices are getting smaller and smaller. Tiny processors, the size of a grain of sand, store more information than your computer did a few years ago. Today, you can ingest a large pill into your digestive tract that is a video camera. Think of the possible medical applications. Sensors applied to your skin will read your blood sugar in real time. Devices, the size of a grain of sand, will analyze blood vessels, diseased organs, and brain function. The possibilities are endless.

Processes as we know them today will expand to incorporate human behavior. Proactively engaging shoppers is a reality today. A smartphone application called Swirl uses in-store sensors to track shoppers' locations to send them personalized offers and recommendations. Hilmi Ozguc, CEO of Swirl Networks, headquartered in Boston, talks about retailers who want to communicate with their customers: "Retailers want to give consumers something that's value-added and does what an expert salesperson might do. For example, 'Here's a special offer because we know you've been looking at handbags.'"[6]

The possibilities of how technology will be used to create value are endless. Just look around you. The IoE is actually happening now.

The 2014 Mercedes-Benz S-Class uses 60 onboard computers to control almost every aspect of the vehicle. Mercedes dubs this *intelligent drive*. It is amazing. Computers control the ride so you do not even feel a bump in the road. Stereo cameras, integrated into the windshield, look for shadows and contrast in the road ahead and automatically adjust the air suspension to compensate for the bump in the road. If you are on a long drive and start to lose focus on the road ahead and your car drifts into an adjacent lane, the *active lane departure* feature automatically applies the front brakes asymmetrically to gently nudge the car back into the driving lane. Rear sensors can anticipate the threat of a pending impact and begins a series of automatic functions that close the windows, tighten the seat belts, lock the brakes, and activate strobe lights to alert the driver in back of you. The list goes on and on. The car has *situational awareness*. It knows where it is at all times and automatically adjusts the controls, using technology, to keep you safe and alert other drivers of any potential hazard. Oh, and by the way, it also has a very nice 4.6 liter V8 engine![7]

Everyone knows what a copy machine does. It makes copies of documents. In the early days, copy machines were just mechanical devices. Today, these complex mechanical and computer-integrated machines connect to your company network to manage your printing and copying needs. These machines are complex computers, and managing their use is not a core competency for manufacturing and service companies. Xerox, a longtime manufacturer and service provider of document management services, now focuses on Managed Print Services (MPS), where Xerox consultants work with clients to help them gain visibility of printing needs and reduce costs, improve productivity, and prevent document security breaches.

Next, we move into a whole new world of printing. It is not just printing documents. It is printing physical objects. Called additive printing, new emerging companies like Stratasys Ltd. and 3D Systems Corp are providing new capabilities in the art of printing. Doctors are using 3D printers as a life-saving tool to prepare for sophisticated operations. Surgeons in Japan were preparing for a complex operation. A young child would receive one of their parent's liver. "The challenge was how to fit the organ into the child's smaller cavity. They created a replica of the donor's liver built by machine that resembles an office printer. The model helped the doctor figure out where to carve it, leading to a successful transplant."[8] Three-dimensional printers are used to make physical models of toys, artificial limbs, and other objects. This new technology is changing the way parts are designed and manufactured. This new technology is changing our lives.

Every doctor and nurse knows the importance of washing one's hands during the day. Doing so is the best way to prevent the spread of germs and infections. SwipeSense is the Evanston, Illinois, company that has come to the rescue of hospitals with a portable wearable device that, through a wireless network, tracks, analyzes, and incentivizes hand hygiene. The device has the size of a computer mouse and worn on the garments of nurses and technicians. The device "wirelessly collects, and analyses, the who, how often, where and when of hand washing." General Electric's GE Healthcare also has an automated system that tracks hand washing. It is estimated that 100,000 deaths occur annually due to improper hand hygiene. These companies are using technology to create new products that innovate value.[9]

Technology Trends That Innovate Value

Technology advances impact our lives in ways we would never have imagined. Walter Mossberg is an American journalist who writes a technology blog on AllThingsD. He also was the principal technology columnist for *The Wall Street Journal* since 1991. His last column for *The Wall Street Journal* was Wednesdays, December 18, 2013. In the article, Mossberg wrote about the top tech products of the last 22 years. A number of products changed the way we work, shop, and communicate. Following are a few that Mossberg identified and their significance.[10]

Netscape Navigator (1994)	First successful consumer web browser
Windows 95 (1995)	Cemented the graphical user interface and mouse as the way to operate a computer
The PalmPilot (1997)	First successful handheld personal digital assistant adopted by consumer
Google Search (1998)	Propelled the entire web with a fast and effective search engine
The iPod (2001)	The first handheld mainstream digital player that could hold 1000 songs
Facebook (2004)	Revolutionized the use of social media using the web
Twitter (2006)	A global instant messaging system using 140 character limit that has changed the digital communication experience
The iPhone (2007)	The first multitouch user interface smartphone that combined the iPod, Internet, and phone
Android (2008)	Google created a dominant smartphone platform with a large selection of applications as the cost-competitive solution to Apple's iPhone
The iPad (2010)	The first tablet to hit the market and begin to replace the laptop as the main computing device as other companies developed competitive tablet devices

Another interesting technology trend is in educating the boardroom on the value of technology. Every major company has an employee orientation program that includes training in the major applications employees will use in their jobs. The board of directors and C-suite executives do not get a pass at technology training anymore. Companies are beginning to invest heavily in training senior executives of social media technology so they can understand how technology trends can improve business results.

For the 18 months ending in December 2013, "senior staffers from companies including American Express Co, NYSE Euronext, and PepsiCo Inc have gone to the Manhattan classrooms of General Assembly, which offers courses in coding and product design, to learn how to analyze data and think like a tech entrepreneur." The Citigroup Inc., Latin American unit used 15 University of Miami students to mentor senior executives.[11]

The training is designed to help executives keep pace with the changing times. This was evident at FCBHEALTH when new ideas from junior staffers weren't getting any traction. Senior executives just didn't *understand the tech-heavy proposals*. Training boardroom members to understand the value of technology is a sound investment in helping the company leverage technology strategically to innovate value.

Health care is where leveraging technology strategically will pay off handsomely, not only in improved health outcomes but also in reduced costs. Besides all the health-care companies entering the market to provide health-care services that improve health outcomes leveraging technology, there are new digital health-care products being introduced in the market. Google has developed "the first contact lens, aimed at diabetics. It takes a glucose level reading every second from the tears that wash over your eye when you blink, and transmits that data wirelessly" to any device.[12] Another example is the *Kolibree toothbrush*, developed by Smart. The device is a digital toothbrush. You brush your teeth, and all the brushing data are captured, stored, and transmitted wirelessly to any device. The accompanying application on your device records all your brushing data. "It works just like a regular toothbrush. The only difference is that all the data are stored on your phone so you can see how you're brushing. Sensors record the length of time you brush, which quadrants in your mouth you are brushing, and the direction of your brushing pattern."[13]

Technology is enabling health-care providers and citizens improve patient outcomes and reduce costs. Following are five technology trends that are dramatically changing the course of health care[14]:

1. Virtual care: Doctors monitor vital signs of critical care patients from *remote command centers* (see Lehigh Valley Health Network example in Chapter 18).
2. Medical detectives: Patients using crowd sourcing to post their symptoms online seeking diagnostic solutions.
3. Doctor on demand: Physicians extend their reach with virtual consults with other doctors seeking specialists' opinions not readily available in their office, hospital, or immediate geographic area.
4. High-tech charts: Hospitals are beginning to use tablets at patient's bedside to text nurse as well as check charts and lab results.
5. Health-care math: Consumers can check health-care pricing between hospitals to calculate their out of pocket costs.

Technology has been a blessing for consumers. Now they can browse the web and shop for any item that they could otherwise purchase in a store. The 2013 holiday season kicked off with a bang for e-retailers with double-digit increase in online orders from the previous season. That's the good news. The bad news is that "as much as a third of all Internet sales get returned." To minimize returns, retailers are trying to help customers make better purchasing decisions based upon their buying history. The process is simple. Retailers access customer buying patterns, using business analytics, including article purchased, size, and color. When the customer accesses the store website and orders, for example, two different sizes of a shirt, one is small and the other is medium, a pop-up window appears reminding the customer, "Are you sure you want to order the small? The last five times you ordered both sizes, only kept the medium." Retailers are also rewarding customer with fewer returns, more discount coupons than customers who are frequent Internet shopping will only continue to increase in the future, and e-retailers have to use the power of technology to help customers buy products they like and minimize returns. If they can succeed at this, it is a win/win for both the customer and the retailer.[15]

Leverage Technology Strategically to Innovate Value—Five Scenarios

There are numerous ways technology is used strategically to innovate value. Following are five scenarios:

1. A group of executives meets to analyze marketing trends.
2. A father wants to ship a package to his son at college.
3. A young child pleads with his/her mom to take her to a store to build a stuffed animal.
4. An elderly man is having difficulty adhering to the doctor's instructions for taking medication.
5. A patient in a hospital or at home care, who is concerned about their health outcome.

Each of these scenarios represents opportunities to leverage technology strategically to innovate value. In the following three chapters, you will learn about five CIOs who are exploiting technology in innovative ways.

Chapter Summaries

Chapter 16 provides examples of how Rob Carter, executive vice president of Information Services and CIO at FedEx, created a more effective and efficient business model. He and his team are totally redesigning the infrastructure for business units to compete collectively, manage collaboratively, and operate independently. In addition, Carter and his team leverage technologies to provide superior service to its customers in new and innovative ways.

Chapter 17 focuses on Filippo Passerini, president of Global Business Services and CIO at P&G. Passerini and his business-focused team digitized data at P&G, so business teams accessing a single source of truth make well-informed business decisions using predictive analytics and sophisticated graphic displays that present data in meaningful ways.

Chapter 18 highlights five CIOs. Dave Finnigan, CIO at Build-A-Bear Workshop, drove the transformation of a physical stuffed animal experience into a digital theme park. A customer now can extend the in-store experience across the entire stuffed animal process, where customers explore, learn, and use their imagination to play games and interact with avatars. Stephen Pickett, CIO at Penske, leverages technology successes from each business across the entire Penske enterprise, which consists of numerous businesses competing in different industries. Gary Wimberly, CIO at Express Scripts, has reinvented the drug prescription fulfillment process to where the dispensing of drugs is secondary to technology-enabled services that improve health outcomes of subscribers. Perry Rotella, CIO at Verisk Analytics, leads the IT organization but focuses his energies as group executive at Supply Chain Risk Analytics to leverage technology to grow the business. Harry Lukens, CIO at Lehigh Valley Health Network, leverages technology to improve health-care outcomes. His *wild idea team* developed the concept of a remote ICU that monitors critical care patients during the low-staffed evening shift. Technology integrates health records and uses video and audio to communicate with patients' nurses and technicians providing bedside care. It is more efficient and saves lives.

We are definitely beginning to experience the Internet of Everything (IoE). The examples in the following chapters are just some of the ways strategic CIOs leverage technologies strategically to innovate value.

Citations

1. *Digital Disruption: Unleashing the Next Wave of Innovation*; James McQuivey, Forester Research, Amazon Publishing, Las Vegas, NV, 2013, p. 3.
2. Bullish on Digital: McKinsey Global Survey Results; McKinsey & Company: Insights and Publications; August 2013; by: Brad Brown, Johnson Sikes, and Paul Willmott; http://www.mckinsey.com/insights/business_technology/bullish_on_digital_mckinsey_global_survey_results?cid = other-eml-ttn-mip-mck-oth-1310.
3. Embracing Digital Technology: A New Strategic Imperative; by: Michael Fitzgerald, Nina Kruschwitz, Didier Bonnet and Michael Welchmit; Sloan Management Review; Digital Transformation Report, October 2013; http://sloanreview.mit.edu/projects/embracing-digital-technology/?utm_source=WhatCounts+Publicaster+Edition&utm_medium=email&utm_campaign=DT+Report+Oct+8+2013&utm_content=Embracing+Digital+Technology%3a+A+New+Strategic+Imperative.
4. David Evans, Chief Futurist-Cisco/Phil Weinzimer Interview, September 13, 24 2013.

5. Cisco Website: What We Do/Internet of Everything; http://www.cisco. com/web/about/ac79/innov/IoE.html#content.

6. Smartphone Apps Guide Shoppers to In-Store Deals: Natasha Baker; Reuters; *The Morning Call*, July 7, 2013.

7. Mercedes S550: A Technological Tour de Force: Dan Neil; *The Wall Street Journal*; September 7, 2013.

8. 3-D Printing, Under the Knife: Surgeons Practice with Replicas of Patients' Organs before Surgery: Juro Osawa; *The Wall Street Journal*; April 9, 2013.

9. SwipeSense: Forget to Wash?: Startup's Wearable Device Seeks to Improve Hand Hygiene Among Hospital Staff: Tom Corrigan; *The Wall Street Journal*; October 8, 2013.

10. Top Products in Two Decades of Tech Reviews: Walt Mossberg on the Products That Changed the Digital Industry: Walt Mossberg; *The Wall Street Journal*; December 17, 2013; Citing http://online.wsj.com/news/ articles/SB10001424052702304858104579264313155801216.

11. Bosses Learn Not to Be So #Clueless: C-Suite Executives Take Pricey Courses, Learn to Use Social Media: Melissa Korn; *The Wall Street Journal*; December 17, 2013; http://online.wsj.com/news/articles/SB100 01424052702304173704579264482617957734.

12. Google's Smart Contact Lenses for Diabetics: Another Step Towards the Google-Powered Cyborg; Sebastian Anthony; January 17, 2014; http:// www.extremetech.com/extreme/174979-the-next-step-in-googles-cyborg-plans-smart-contact-lenses-for-those-with-diabetes.

13. Smart' Toothbrush Grades Your Brushing Habits; Brandon Griggs, January 9, 2014; http://www.cnn.com/2014/01/09/tech/innovation/ smart-toothbrush-kolibree/index.html.

14. 5 High-Tech Fixes for Patients: Laura Landrow; *The Wall Street Journal*; December 23, 2013; http://online.wsj.com/news/articles/SB1000142405 2702303773704579270450565101982.

15. Rampant Returns Plague E-Retailers: Sellers Suggest Sizes and Redirect Discounts to Break Bad Habits: Shelly Banjo; *The Wall Street Journal*; December 22, 2013 http://online.wsj.com/news/articles/SB1000142405 2702304773104579270260683155216.

16

HOW FEDEX LEVERAGES TECHNOLOGY STRATEGICALLY TO INNOVATE VALUE

"The information about the package is as important as the package itself"[1]

Fred Smith
Founder and CEO of FedEx

FedEx is an innovative company. Leveraging technology to innovate value is at the core of the company DNA. At a time when the mass production era was winding down and the phrase consumerization of technology was not even a sparkle in anyone's thoughts, Fred Smith had a vision of using airplanes to deliver packages in 24 hours. Today, this 46 billion dollar company is revered for its innovative ideas.

OVERVIEW

This chapter describes the evolution of FedEx and its use of technology to innovate value. The chapter is structured as follows:

- Brief history of FedEx
- How Rob Carter, CIO, transformed IT, through a four-stage transformation model, into a strategic organization leveraging technology innovatively
- How Ken Spangler, senior vice president of IT responsible for FedEx Freight and FedEx Ground, leads the IT group and his innovative use of technology that transforms how freight moves through the delivery handling process
- How David Zanca, former senior vice president of Customer Access Solutions, leverages technology to provide a superior service experience to FedEx customers

- How Doug Bonebrake, former IT manager of FedEx Services, uses innovation, in its simplest form, to dramatically improve the quality of IT-developed applications
- What you should remember from this chapter: Summary and key learnings

Brief History of FedEx

Imagine sitting in the offices of Charles Lewis Lea, Jr., executive vice president at New Court Securities Corporation in 1971, a private investment bank in New York, and listening in on a phone call with another investment banker who talked about "an intriguing opportunity in Memphis." The discussion focused on a "28 year old, ex-marine captain, a Vietnam veteran with a silver Star, a Yale graduate, who had started with his own money a small-package airline with great potential." (ibid) The 28-year old was Fred Smith, founder of Federal Express, who at the time needed investment capital to expand his business. Smith developed the concept of a consistent and reliable service while attending Yale. He came up with the name Federal Express based upon his desire to get a contract transporting checks and other documents for the Federal Reserve System. Smith wasn't awarded the Federal Reserve contract, but as a result of a follow-up meeting with Lea, and a series of research studies, Smith received his funding. On Tuesday, April 17, 1973, a small fleet of 14 aircraft delivered 186 packages to 25 cities within the United States. Getting to that point was no small feat. Today, the daily number of packages is in the millions, and the aircraft fleet is now comprised of 650 planes flying out to 375 airports around the world.[2]

Ever since that day in 1973, Federal Express started delivering packages overnight, and that continues today with FedEx team members delivering exceptional customer service. Fred Smith always believed that the company had to develop a unique relationship with its employees if it were to become and remain a leader in the express cargo transportation industry. Smith was "determined to make employees an integral part of the decision-making process, due to his belief that when people are placed first they will provide the highest possible service, and profits will follow."[3] This is the foundation of what FedEx calls the People–Service–Profit (PSP) philosophy and was the foundation of the business.

Building upon the PSP philosophy, FedEx incorporates the mantra, the Purple Promise, a seven-word phrase—"I will make every FedEx experience outstanding"—that embodies the core values of the PSP philosophy. Every team member knows the Purple Promise and practices its principles in every process that affects a customer interaction: these are the cornerstones of the FedEx culture. However, to deliver on that promise requires technology to leverage information about the package and provide tangible services customers use to make every interaction with FedEx an experience second to none.

When Fred Smith founded Federal Express, now FedEx, he embraced technology, even in the early days. FedEx did not just improve an existing service. It created an entirely new product and electronic network to pick up, transport, and deliver packages and information about every shipment at every point in the FedEx physical network. Sure, a local transportation company can move a couple of hundred shipments with a fleet of trucks, drivers, and a couple of computers. However, to move 10 million packages a day requires great people, sophisticated technology, and a culture of innovation that creates customer value.

Today, FedEx is the $46 billion company that moves more than 10 million shipments per day across 220 countries and territories. This figure includes the entire FedEx enterprise. On the ground, FedEx Ground Systems has 33 ground hubs, and over 500 pickup/delivery terminals: FedEx Freight has 370 service centers. The entire ground fleet between FedEx Express, FedEx Ground and FedEx Freight includes over 100,000 motorized vehicles. The FedEx network includes 37,500 FedEx drop boxes, and more than 1,800 FedEx Office locations. In the air, FedEx Express has approximately 650 aircrafts that fly in and out of 375 worldwide airports. This physical network can deliver packages to any address in the United States and to countries and territories around the world that represent 99% of the world's GDP. Just imagine what it takes for FedEx Express, FedEx Freight, and FedEx Ground to manage the data associated with picking up, sorting, moving, and delivering over 10 million shipments every day using these assets. It's a mammoth data management challenge.[4]

Built on a vision by Fred Smith when he was in his 20s, FedEx has become a powerhouse among giants. The company has leveraged information and technology throughout its history, which propelled

FedEx to become one of the most information-centric companies in the world today. IT is the foundation that efficiently drives the movement of packages from pickup to delivery and provides an unparalleled level of superior customer service. This is the underpinning that drives the company's focus on empowering the solutions that matter. Over the years, FedEx has received awards for reliability, quality, best places to work, and community-minded companies. The list of awards is long. In 2014, *FORTUNE* magazine named FedEx as number 8 on its World's *Most Admired Companies* list and number one in the delivery industry. (ibid)

How FedEx Transformed IT into a Strategic Organization
Leveraging Technology Innovatively: Four-Prong Approach

When Fred Smith says that the "information about the package is as important as the package itself," he means what he says, commonly referred to as walk the talk. The eight-member FedEx Strategic Management Committee guides the direction of the company and is the pinnacle of the management chain. Sitting at the table along with Fred Smith, CEO, is Rob Carter, CIO for FedEx Corporation. The other members are the corporate executives responsible for finance, legal, marketing and communications as well as the presidents of FedEx Express, FedEx Ground and FedEx Freight. Carter is involved in working with these top executives, as an equal, in setting the strategic direction of the company and has been instrumental in operationalizing Smith's vision of leveraging information strategically for competitive advantage.

To better understand how FedEx has risen to the top of the ladder and uses technology strategically to innovate value, you need to know more about Rob Carter.

Carter attended at University of Florida receiving a bachelor's and a master's degree in computer and information science. In his 30-plus years of work experience, Carter leveraged his education and business experience innovating value. He joined GTE Corporation in 1980 and, during his 13 years at GTE, held various IT positions leading up to the director of Systems Development. In 1993, Carter joined FedEx as vice president of Corporate Systems Development. In 1998, he became chief technology officer (CTO) in 2000 and then promoted to CIO in

2001.[5] Carter sits on the eight-person FedEx Strategic Management Committee, which plans and executes the corporation's strategic business activities.[6] FedEx Chief Fred Smith truly understands the value of IT. Smith always believed that digital technology would change the logistics business. Carter has received numerous awards, including recognition from InformationWeek, CIO magazine, and other organizations, and sits on various boards, including Saks.[7]

If you ever have the opportunity to meet Rob Carter, you will find him to be humble yet thought provoking. Do not be fooled by his soft-spoken style. He truly understands how to leverage IT to drive value for FedEx. "Fred Smith always believed that leveraging information was of strategic importance and a critical key to the success of the company. And this philosophy is embedded into the culture of our team members and is in the DNA of the company," says Carter.[8] In my interview with Carter, he praises the previous CIO and his team for building the foundation of leveraging technology to grow the business as well as Fred Smith's vision of valuing information as part of the secret sauce:

> Fred Smith saw the world as information centric. There is the physical world in FedEx that includes people, trucks, pallets, and airplanes. Then there is the digital world. Fred Smith understood the value of information. He saw the value of connecting the physical world with the digital world. (ibid)

Multiprong Information Strategy

Carter talks about a two phase. The first addressed process improvement and the second focused on enabling customers to access shipping information strategy that Fred Smith envisioned as a cornerstone for growing the business.

Improving Process by Leveraging Information

In the period 1975–1980, FedEx experienced hypergrowth. Although Carter started his career at FedEx in 1993, he describes the challenge FedEx experienced from growing quickly. "There was no way to provide a level of services without a systematic and transactional based quality control system." (ibid) For example, package tracking systems enabled FedEx to manage the quality of our operations in a way that leads to continuous improvement. FedEx needed to measure every activity so FedEx could improve the service to customers. Smith has a strong belief that 100% customer service is a tangible goal, and he instills this into the FedEx culture.

Smith recognized that measuring the critical points in the package handling process was the key to achieve dramatic growth. Smith viewed performance from the customer perspective as critical to the success of FedEx. As the story is told, Smith asked his management team to identify the key activities FedEx could do wrong that customers would view as critical to receiving excellent customer service. This was the beginning of what FedEx called the Service Quality Index (SQI). This evolved over the years to represent 71 critical points in the package handling process, measured in real time, and reported daily to management. These critical points are weighted to reflect their relative importance to providing excellent customer service. In fact, the 12 most important SQI measurements represent 51% of the total weighting factor.

The SQI is designed to improve customer service. This is not just a *check the box* exercise. Managers receive summary reports and daily updates on these measures, which they share with their work teams. Employees and managers dissect problems and improve processes based upon the SQI measurement system. Sharing this information with team members enables each person to see how their work affects the customer, and as a result, the company, and improves performance. The National Institute of Science awarded the Malcolm Baldrige Award in 1990 to FedEx for their SQI process.[9]

Over the years, FedEx improved the SQI process. As a result, customer satisfaction improved. Carter describes the success of SQI as follows: "SQI provides a view of key areas that are most important to our customers. SQI provides visibility from the local FedEx station all the way up to the weekly executive meetings and enables us to continuously improve our processes."[10]

Enabling Customer Access

The second piece of Smith's strategy was to enable customers to access information. In 1994, FedEx created its fedex.com,

which allowed customers to track shipments online. Carter says, "...
this was the first transactional website that existed on the internet and
FedEx received a Smithsonian Award for it. We got a lot of attention
because of this."[8]

Over the years, FedEx has improved the type of information customers have access to. In the early days, FedEx utilized technology to
enable drivers to enter shipment status information from their vans.
Customers could track shipments by entering the tracking number on
fedex.com. This was innovative at the time. Since then, technology
has enabled FedEx to take innovation far beyond tracking a package. Today, customers can interact with FedEx via the Internet for
any aspect of their shipment or account. They can pay bills, update
account information, schedule a pickup, reroute a shipment to a different address, and much more. It is almost as if the customer is watching the package movement, via streaming technology, from the time
of pickup to time of delivery. FedEx also developed SenseAware[SM], a
service that provides sensors in the packaging containers of high-value
materials that capture pertinent logistical data via telemetry signals,
providing location, air temperature, humidity, exposure to light, and
other data critical to the safety of many sensitive packages. This is
discussed in more detail later in this chapter.

Improving business processes first, and then providing customer
access to shipping information, was smart business. But these competencies needed continuous improvement through an innovative use
of technology.

Leveraging Technologies Strategically to Innovate Value

When Carter took on the role as CIO, he knew that to leverage technology strategically required building trust-based relationship with
his fellow FedEx executives. To do this required a lot of hard work
by dedicated IT professionals as the IT organization moved through
the Strategic IT Organization Transformation Phases. First, service
delivery to the business needed improvement. Second, IT teams had to
focus on user experiences when working with the business to improve
both internal and external processes across the value chain. Third,
Carter and the IT teams focused on driving initiative that improved
both sales and optimized cost.

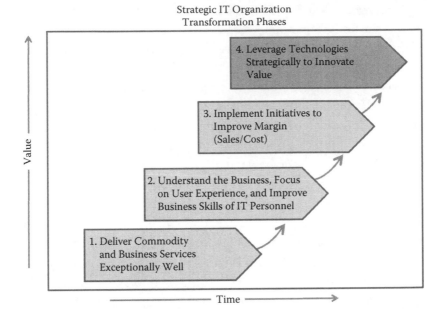

Strategic IT Organization
Transformation Phases

Until Carter accomplished these three phases, he could not embark on phase four leveraging technology strategically to innovate value. This was not an easy process. It takes time. David Zanca, retired senior vice president of Customer Access Solutions, talks about Carter's first few years building the foundation:

> The first few years were about establishing that valued, trusted relationship. Without that trust, you couldn't walk in and make a technology transformation pitch. The CIO cannot attack complexity without a high degree of business support and that support comes from years of cultivating it. To make technical overhauls, you have to have that credibility. Rob focused on being a trusted business partner, surveyed the business, provided transparency into IT, concentrated on high value items, and even ran part of the business during those first six years. Then he focused on the technical transformation.[11]

Carter built upon Fred Smith's two-prong strategy in continuing to leverage technology to improve processes and provide customers access to shipping information. He also incorporated the FedEx Purple Promise culture of providing excellent customer service, internally and externally, as a stepping stone to leveraging technology strategy to innovate value.

Fred Smith's Two-Prong Information Strategy

- The first prong improves internal processes by leveraging information.
- The second prong allows customers access to information about shipments.

Rob Carter's Technology Strategy to Innovate Value

- The third prong is one Carter is passionate about. It addresses leveraging technologies strategically to innovate value. This includes the building of an efficient infrastructure based upon newer technologies and leveraging other technologies to create value.

Culture—FedEx Purple Promise

- The fourth prong is the culture of the FedEx organization, which embodies the goal of great people making every FedEx experience outstanding and delivering complete customer satisfaction.

I call this *the Four-Prong Strategy, which is depicted in* Figure 16.1.

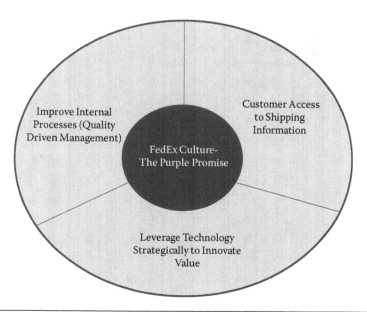

Figure 16.1 The Four-Prong Strategy.

Carter leverages technology to achieve business value in two ways:

1. The first was to totally revamp the information infrastructure from a decentralized maze of applications, servers, and customer interfaces that, when depicted graphically, resemble a complex maze.
2. The second approach Carter implemented was leveraging technology advances to improve process efficiency. Let's explore each of these initiatives separately.

Infrastructure Improvements

There is an expression, "with much success comes great responsibility." The source of this quote is often debated but the implication is daunting. Around 2008, at the start of the recession, Carter saw a major problem. He recognized that operating the IT infrastructure, as it then existed, was not sustainable. The infrastructure to manage information for the four main FedEx businesses (FedEx Express, FedEx Ground, FedEx Freight, FedEx Office) was very complex. Each business operated independently and required information to manage their business services. Complicating the requirement was the need to make information available in certain departments across the enterprise across all the business units, and the infrastructure to manage these businesses was very complex. Each of these businesses had an expectation of information that cuts across many different processes across the FedEx business units. At the CIO100 conference in 2012, Carter depicted this complexity in Figure 16.2.

Carter mapped out the entire FedEx infrastructure and found that there were 3,200 applications, 12,000 servers, and 18,000 process intersections. These intersections, commonly referred to as customer interfaces, represent where people, information flow, communication process, and applicable policies and procedures impact customer and company activities. Carter could not let this morass or systems continue, and he needed to do something about it. He mapped out the complex infrastructure, which he calls *an ugly picture* and made a clear point of explaining, "this complexity is not sustainable." He socialized his message and *ugly picture* with all the business unit leaders.

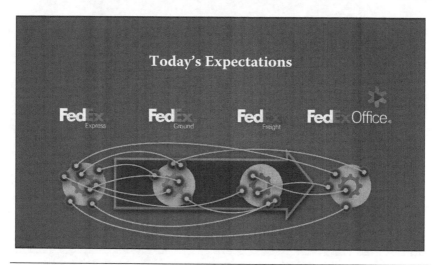

Figure 16.2 Business Expectations.

Carter scheduled a meeting with Fred Smith and told him, "we can't let this continue." After looking at Carter's ugly picture, Smith got on board and the business leaders agreed to Carter's vision. "FedEx went on to completely revamp its IT strategy and infrastructure and created a centralized IT services group that acts almost like a Platform as a Service (PaaS) provider to the various businesses and business units inside the company."[12]

Figure 16.2 depicts a set of FedEx competencies required, for each of the business, that Carter defines as the *customer corridor*. This is the pathway for a set of business processes (corridors), which are efficiently supported and enabled by a management infrastructure. The management infrastructure provides all the information required for each of the businesses to manage their *customer corridors*. (ibid) "Do not think the industry didn't see this as a superb business strategy." InformationWeek named Carter *Technology Chief of the Year* three times prior to 2012, and *Fast Company* ranked him #18 on its list of the *100 Most Creative People in Business* in 2010 (Figure 16.3).

In my opinion, a true test of leveraging technology strategically to innovate value is when a company uses technology to improve competitive advantage and/or creating a new business model. Carter has done both. FedEx created a new business model where each of the main business units operates independently while at the same

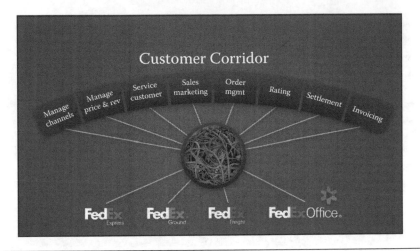

Figure 16.3   The Customer Corridor.

time competing collectively in the marketplace by managing collaboratively with the other business units using real-time data. FedEx communicates this model using the following phrase: *compete collectively, manage collaboratively, and operate independently.* These six words describe how each of the FedEx business units works together to successfully compete in the marketplace and together grows the FedEx business.[13]

Leveraging New Technologies

Over the years, FedEx has leveraged technologies to innovate value. Following are a few examples: [15]

- Using EDI technology in the 1980s enabled FedEx to communicate with other companies in their logistic network.
- In 1994, FedEx leveraged the Internet to allow customers to track shipments.
- Interactive video instructions (IVIs) enabled FedEx employees to complete training courses at their own pace based on the demands of their work schedules.
- Monitored customer transactions to identify potential gaps in achieving 100% customer satisfaction (was package damaged? was billing correct? etc.). SQI is an example of one process used to achieve this.

- Integrated wireless solutions and Bluetooth technologies to track packages.
- Handheld computers and digital pens to document shipment status throughout the delivery process.
- Radio-frequency identification (RFID) has been in use since 1999, tracking certain high-value packages during the delivery process.
- Velcro Wristband RFID transponders to allow drivers *to open* or *to unlock* vehicle doors without using keys. Next time you see a FedEx driver delivering packages, you'll notice that his hands are busy handling packages. It's very inefficient to stop, put down the packages, and find the vehicle keys to open the same cargo door.
- Six-sided sensors and sortation technology to scan packages moving at 400 feet per minute.

FedEx has adapted innovations in technology to their package handling and customer interaction processes. As new technologies are developed, FedEx figures out a way to leverage them. One of the areas that Carter is investigating is the use of analytics using computer memory to improve package delivery. Some might consider managing data elements associated with millions of packages handled each day by FedEx as a data management nightmare. FedEx does this every day. One of the challenges is analyzing data for shipments that might be in jeopardy of not meeting delivery commitments. For example, a package is in transit from New York to California, via FedEx Ground. A Midwest storm suddenly erupts and will affect roadways in a few hours. The quicker weather patterns and truck routes are analyzed, the sooner logistic changes can be made. Michael Vizard, in an online article on how Rob Carter sees analytics driving change, states, "analyzing this type of data in computer memory versus storage devices strewn across any number of databases kept in disk storage systems too slow to support advanced, real-time applications." Carter talks about the "line between memory and storage is blurring," and technology advances are improving data analysis in memory that transportation companies will benefit handsomely. The real beneficiary will be the customer, who will receive improved customer service.[14]

FedEx Culture: Creating Superior Customer Experiences

FedEx understands the concept of creating a superior user experience. This is the mantra that leading companies strive to achieve today. It is all about developing a culture focused on customer experiences. FedEx has taken the concept to another level.

FedEx team members have a culture of providing superior customer service. It is embedded in their behaviors. It is the result of a culture steeped in training, processes, and programs, which evokes a customer-focused behavior. These processes include the PSP culture; the SQI; discussed earlier in this chapter; as well as a quality-driven management (QDM) process, and a number of programs that reward employees for exemplary performance.

People-Service-Profit

One of the key components of the FedEx culture is the Purple Promise, which says, "I will make every FedEx experience outstanding." This is a company-wide mantra known to every FedEx team member.

Predating the Purple Promise, FedEx was founded on the operating philosophy of People-Service-Profit, or PSP. FedEx relentlessly focuses on hiring great people and empowering them to provide excellent service to customers that in turn leads to increased sales and associated profits, which is reinvested in people, services, and growth for shareholders. As a result, the Purple Promise is embedded in the behavior of every FedEx team member. They just know how to do the right thing and are empowered to do it. Following is an example:[15]

> Learning that a package containing a wedding ring had missed a flight from Paris to Stockholm for a ceremony the next day, FedEx Express customer care agent Eddie Bradbury quickly arranged for it to be sent on a commercial Air France flight. The following morning, ramp coordinator Mats Barrefors personally delivered the ring to the church, arriving with five minutes to spare.

QDM

QDM is a collection of principles and techniques to help groups and departments across the FedEx enterprise accomplish continuous as well as breakthrough improvements. This is not a new concept. But applying technology improves the process. Using the results of the SQI, discussed earlier in this chapter, FedEx team members focus on continuously improving business processes. According to Carter, SQI points, which reflect the number of absolute failures of the service quality across the 71 metrics, *keep reducing.*[9] This is remarkable considering the number of packages processes increase each year. It is a true testament to the QDM process at FedEx. According to Carter, "we use SQI and Quality Driven Management relentlessly to improve customer satisfaction. Sure, we miss a few from time to time, but we use this as an opportunity to analyze what is wrong and improve the process. You can put up posters and hold town meetings, but if you don't have a culture and supporting processes, you will never get the results you aim for."[12]

QDM Cup

The QDM Cup is an award given to quality action teams that demonstrate excellence in improving SQI metrics and making other improvements in the company. It does not take a complicated solution to solve a big problem. Sometimes, it is the simple and obvious ideas that can solve big problems. An example of this occurred in the Northwest Auburn FedEx Ground facility, where a three-member FedEx team solved a huge problem for FedEx with an innovative but simple solution.

FedEx Ground personnel work very hard to deliver packages on time. Sometimes, there are problems with the delivery information provided by the shipper. Names are incorrect, addresses are wrong, and people move and do not leave forwarding addresses. These packages end up in the Quality Assurance or "QA" department. At the time, it took approximately 7 days to deliver packages that were more than 2 days late from the estimated delivery date. Sandy Chritcher of the Northwest Auburn FedEx Ground team wanted to do something about it. She and her team wanted to reduce the 7 to 1 day late due to address errors.

Chritcher and her team met to brainstorm an approach to the problem. They decided to pilot a four-step process across a couple of locations:

- Step 1: Identify the packages in the QA area that were more than 2 days late.
- Step 2: Identify the various categories of packages that were more than 2 days late.
- Step 3: Develop a communication plan to work with FedEx Ground personnel to resolve address issues and delivery packages.
- Step 4: Track results and improve the process.

Step 1: Identify the packages in the QA area that were more than 2 days late

Sandy and the team brainstormed and thought about painting the shelves fire engine red to evoke the perception of *hot flames*. "The team wanted the perception to be that we had to keep the intensity up on the research to get these package to our customers," says Chritcher in the *I am FedEx* video that summarizes the team project.[16] The team named their project *The Red Shelf Project* (Figure 16.4)

Step 2: Identify the various categories of packages that were more than 2 days late

One of the tools that quality action teams are trained to use is the Pareto analysis, sometimes referred to as the 80/20 rule. The process identifies the major causes of a problem. The theory is that 20% of the situations cause 80% of the problems. So the team decided to use the Pareto analysis to identify the major causes of package delays beyond the 2-day-late SQI metric. Figure 16.5 reflects the categories and the associated percentages. You will note that *no scan* represented almost 50% of the packages delayed more than 2 days

Figure 16.4   Red Shelves.

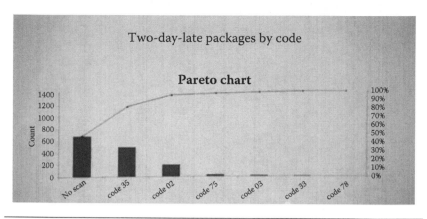

Figure 16.5 Two-Day-Late Packages by Code.

beyond the on-time metric. The analysis also identified two other areas that when added to the *no scan* category represented more than 80% of the packages that were delayed by more than 2 days. With the top three problems identified, the team moved into action in the pilot project to start expediting packages on *the red shelf* to the proper shipment address.

Step 3: Develop a communication plan to work with FedEx Ground personnel to resolve address issues and delivery packages

The team documented package information for those packages associated with the top three categories and worked with field personnel to expedite the delivery of the packages (Figure 16.6).

Step 4: Track results and improve the process (ibid)

The team tracked the progress of the pilot project. The pilot project improved the delivery times for over–2-day-late packages (Figure 16.7).

Figure 16.6 Communication Plan.

Figure 16.7 Tracking Progress.

The team recommended the process to management who directed that *the red shelf* process becomes a standard process across the entire FedEx Ground network.

At the annual QDM Cup award ceremony where the *red shelf* team was awarded the Gold QDM Cup, Fred Smith said, "...a can of red paint eliminated 47 percent of the over 2 day late ground packages. That's pretty extraordinary." (ibid)

Rob Carter would be the first to say that the FedEx culture is what makes the company successful. However, Carter's business and technical knowledge coupled with a strategic view is a factor in the success of FedEx and why he sits on the eight-person Strategic Management Committee and works with his peers to effectively guide the company. His focus on delivering business value lies in his belief that "the most important critical success factor for effectively delivering business value through technology is when the business and IT are pulling together in the same direction solving problems, delivering solutions, and creating capabilities. All I have to do is get out of the way and watch good things happen."[10]

Ken Spangler, Senior Vice President of IT Responsible For FedEx Freight and FedEx Ground, Innovates IT to Transform How Freight Moves through the Delivery Handling Process

Ken Spangler is the senior vice president of IT supporting FedEx Ground and FedEx Freight. This includes responsibility for FedEx Ground, FedEx Home Delivery, and FedEx SmartPost services.

With a degree in information sciences and mathematics from the University of Pittsburgh, Spangler's first job was as a systems programmer for Roadway Package Systems, which was purchased by FedEx in 1998 and rebranded as FedEx Ground. In 2000, he was fortunate to work on automated package sorting systems that moved small packages. With his background in software development, he was always the person called upon when equipment failed in the field. "With business growing at 40 percent per year we were stretching technology to its limits." Working in the field enabled Spangler to learn about the business quickly, and he applied these learnings as he moved up the management ladder. Spangler has developed a reputation in the industry as a leader of applying advanced technology in large, high-transaction IT systems. Rob Carter, Spangler's boss at FedEx Services, has high praises for Spangler. "He applies technology in innovative ways to provide value for our customers."[8]

High-Speed, Real-Time Rotation Technology

The market differentiator for FedEx Ground is real-time, high-speed systems that manage millions of packages a day and billions of information transactions. All of the FedEx Ground hubs are fully automated. Each package is touched by human hands only twice during the hub sortation process: once when the package arrives at the sorting facility and is physically moved from the truck to the belt, and for the second and final time when it is loaded onto the delivery truck. In between, inside the hub, technology does all the work. "At peak Christmas holiday season we are managing over 9.7 billion transactions in a single day", says Spangler when he talks about the complexities of the business.

Technology drives the business for all the services at FedEx Ground. "To serve the needs of our customers we utilize high speed sortation equipment that receive instructions at 450 milliseconds, on-road technologies that enable real-time access for all logistic operations, and driver hand-held mobile computers that maintain real-time status of every single package handled by FedEx Ground personnel."[17]

How does FedEx Ground move millions of packages a day, which need to be delivered to any address within the United States and

Canada? It is all about the data. Data management is a complex problem. The only way to optimize the process is to leverage technology in an innovative way. Following are the five basic steps used in the process, which the customer can track in real time:[18]

1. Data collection starts when the shipper enters appropriate information into the FedEx shipping systems located in the shipper's location either on the physical form or on the online form.
2. When the driver picks up the package, the appropriate data (dimensions, shipping location, etc.) are entered into the FedEx information systems by the driver via scanning technology.
3. Automated sortation systems at each of the FedEx hubs and satellite operations use these data to optimize the movement of packages across the FedEx Ground network.
4. The FedEx information system plots the logistical route for the package based upon the destination, distance traveled, and any special instructions provided by the customer.
5. At FedEx Freight, shipments are assigned to a specific route or area and loaded onto trucks to optimize the most efficient delivery sequence. Upon delivery to the customer, the shipment data are scanned into the system to confirm delivery.

FedEx goes a step further to ensure that any errors in the process are immediately alerted. "Package handlers wear scanning devices on their finger or wrist and an audible signal alerts them to an error, whether it is moving the package to an incorrect sorting line or loading a package into an incorrect van." (ibid)

Superior Customer Service

Technology alone does not make FedEx Ground a leader in the market. It is also the customer service provided to its customers. Customer interaction points throughout the entire process are important to us. "We want the customer to interact and track the movement of packages from the time the pick-up is ordered to the time it is delivered." (ibid)

The customer can track each point in the delivery process, in real-time. This process has dramatically improved package processing time. In addition, performance measured by FedEx Quality Index has improved significantly. From a competitive standpoint, we have become a better company every year. (ibid)

The customer is connected electronically throughout the entire process:

1. The customer chooses the service and provides information to start the package handling process.
2. During the package handling, the customer can track the status of the package. The package movements are captured through scans at the FedEx hub facilities and by the drivers between the hubs and the delivery location.
3. The customer can track, in real time, the status of a shipment, even if it rerouted due to weather conditions. For example, if a shipment needs to move to Hartford, Connecticut, and weather conditions interfere with the preplanned route, FedEx Ground will reroute the shipment to another distribution center.

As Spangler says, "Because of our automated package sortation capability, we can dynamically change the routing of shipments in real time, even during peak season. We even plan any rerouting, resource scheduling, or timing changes that impact the shipment; as long as the package is not out for final delivery This is the secret sauce. We have a totally integrated network."[17]

Spangler loves his job. "It's all about understanding the business and providing value to our customers. When we provide real value, customers use our services, we generate revenue that we can reinvest to improve the way we manage packages. Every quarter I hold a town-hall meeting. We spend 70% of the time addressing business issues. We can't be great people if we are not great business people. It's who we are." (ibid)

FedEx as well as the IT industry recognize Spangler's accomplishments. He is the recipient of FedEx's prestigious Five-Star Award and 2010 recipient of the Computerworld's Premier 100 IT Leaders Award and, in 2011, recognized by the Pittsburgh Technology Council as CIO of the year.

David Zanca, Former Senior Vice President of Customer
access Solutions at FedEx Services, Leverages Technology to
Provide a Superior Customer Experience to Customers

David Zanca is the former senior vice president of Customer Access Solutions at FedEx Services. He retired from FedEx in December 2013. He reported directly to Rob Carter. His organization developed and delivers the customer-facing systems that provide services to FedEx customers across all the business units. Zanca is all about providing a world-class customer experience for all the customer-facing systems used by FedEx customers. What he and his team have accomplished is a great example of leveraging technology strategically to innovate value.

Zanca earned a bachelor's degree from Duke and an MBA from Emory University. Prior to joining FedEx, Zanca worked at Anderson Consulting for 12 years. At FedEx, Zanca held a variety of senior IT positions. At FedEx Freight, he was the senior vice president of IT, leading IT strategy operations, applications, and infrastructure. He also served as FedEx's first CIO. Zanca rounds out his business skills with certifications as a certified public accountant, general information assurance–information security officer, certified data processing professional, and a certified production and inventory control specialist.[19]

Zanca understands the business environment, the competitive landscape, and consumer behavior. "Today, it is all about providing unique customer experiences that drive value, and that experience with FedEx should be whenever and wherever the customer wants to engage, and with whichever device or channel they chose to use." The unique customer experience is the end game. Technology is the enabler, and Zanca understands this very well. Zanca calls this change in consumer behavior, *connectedness.*

Zanca provides an example. "I remember early in my career when I wanted to ship an express package, I had to walk to the shipping department and hand them the package and tell the shipping supervisor to ship it via Federal Express." Zanca calls this the *destination model.* He further explains, "Today, we don't want to be a destination, we want the customer to integrate and connect with us on whichever channel they choose."[11] This also applies to FedEx business processes.

When you analyze the FedEx business, you find that today, almost every part of the delivery process is automated using technology. Zanca says,

> Almost every piece of our business is instrumented: it has some degree of intelligence and automation on it. Our planes are all intelligent and we always know where they are. The trucks, the couriers, the knowledge workers, the hubs-almost everything has technology embedded in it and tells us where it is or what its state is. Without the connectivity, we would not get the information about the package that we and our customers value so much. (ibid)

FedEx realized this strategy was key to their success and spent a number of years rearchitecting the core customer-facing systems and software to connect with customers via FedEx Services or via fedex.com. High-volume customers can deploy FedEx tools within their infrastructure and integrate with enterprise resource planning (ERP) systems, order-processing systems, and warehouse management systems. As a consumer, you can access FedEx via the web from your home computer, laptop, tablet, or smartphone. FedEx applications can be deployed for any customer on any channel. Zanca says, "This was critical to our strategy. Our customer accesses the same core services whether he or she is a high-volume customer or individual shipping a package from their home."[19]

Zanca tries to be one step ahead of customer demands. The consumerization of technology creates an ever-increasing degree of customer expectations. Zanca says, "a big part of my job is to build and deploy solutions to enable the customer to engage with FedEx, on their term...." (ibid)

He believes that customers today are expecting more and more from companies. He cites the *law of rising consumer expectations*. For example, people with iPhone just love the FaceTime feature. "I use it when speaking to my daughter and her kids. It's terrific. There is nothing better than connecting visually with a person. It creates an emotional connection, which is much stronger than just an audio connection." Zanca uses the example of a customer who calls FedEx customer service with a question about a package. The customer has an iPhone and wants to show the customer service agent the package via FaceTime. The customer uses this feature all the time to speak to friends and family. Why shouldn't the customer be able to use it when talking with a FedEx customer service agent? A picture is worth a thousand words. Zanca believes his mission is to help FedEx team members understand customer expectations and to think in terms of the customer. "It's not only about writing code. It's about providing a level of service the customer is expecting, and where possible, exceeding those expectations." (ibid)

Zanca and his team provide customers with an array of services that enable them to communicate whenever and wherever they are and use whichever platform they chose. These services include FedEx iPhone applications, the My FedEx website, application plug-ins, and a suite of web services. One of the latest innovations is a living example of anticipating and meeting customer expectations. Consider this scenario:

> Sarah, the owner of a high-end art gallery in London, calls her local shipping company. Sarah informs the customer service agent that she has a valuable painting that must be delivered to a customer in New York City by a specific date. She also defines the need for the painting to be temperature, humidity, and light controlled within a specific set of parameters that she can set. In addition, she wants to know, every 15 minutes, where the shipment is in the delivery process. She also wants visibility, via an electronic dashboard, accessible on a computer, laptop, tablet, or smartphone of all the parameters and status. If any of the parameters approach or exceed the limits, which she designates, an electronic alert, e-mail, and phone call are initiated to whatever location she designates. Further, Sarah tells the shipping company that when any alert is initiated, the shipping company should intercept the shipment and make the necessary adjustments to temperature, light, and humidity, to keep the parameters within customer accepted range.

Does this sound like a scene from a science fiction novel? Well, it is not. SenseAware[SM] is a service offered by FedEx to customers who have high-value or critical shipments. This service provides customers with visibility and near real-time access to a package's vital statistics, such as location, temperature, light, humidity, and barometric pressure. The service consists of two components. The first is the device, which includes a set of sensors packaged into a single unit and placed

Figure 16.8   FedEx SenseAware^SM.

inside the package. The second component is the set of services, which make the information actionable and available to the customer. The device is unique. The software, and *connectedness* to FedEx and customer systems makes this a perfect example of leveraging technology strategically to innovate value (Figure 16.8).

Think about drug companies shipping valuable drugs for testing and hospitals shipping tissue samples or organs for transplants. What about this scenario? A personalized drug treatment has been engineered for a patient and is being shipped from the United Kingdom to the patient in the United States. The drug, critical to the patient's treatment, must be temperature controlled. As the shipment crosses from the United Kingdom to the United States, US Customs authorities note that due to the unique nature of the drug, additional documentation is needed to clear the package. When the package arrives in the United States, the shipment is temporarily *caged* or held by Customs. The unforeseen delay in processing allows time for the shipment coolant to lose efficacy and the package is trending toward its upper temperature boundary. Because the shipment has a SenseAware^SM device inside, it sends an alert, and the FedEx proactive alert personnel take action. They contact Customs, provide specific location information regarding the package, and arrange a supervised intervention where FedEx personnel open the package, refresh the coolant, and reseal the package. The package now has sufficient coolant for the time awaiting clearance and for the remainder of its journey.

This is a very real scenario that combines the uniqueness or value of the contents of the shipment, with sometimes unpredictable events, and the need to intercede to protect the integrity of the shipment as well as the ultimate customer, a mixture of people, process, and technology to deliver value to the customer.

Zanca is proud of this service and the story behind is just as fascinating. "For years customers said our tracking system is wonderful but it did not tell them the condition of the shipment throughout the delivery process. There was clearly a need and we needed to be proactive and figure out a way to meet our customer expectations."[11]

Zanca was part of a team that met with a group of customers for 18 months defining the service and product, how customers would use it, the information needed from it, etc. Zanca tells how "this was a collaborative effort between FedEx and a group of customers. We had to define the requirements, build a solution, including the web site, and test it with the customers before we could launch SenseAware[SM] to our customer." (ibid)

What's even more interesting about the service is how SenseAware[SM] can be ideal for customers to improve their reliability and quality, for example, customers who test packaging for items such as wine, drugs, or other temperature-, humidity-, or light-sensitive products to ensure the quality of their products. With SenseAware[SM], they have access to data points that they did not have before. Where does Zanca see this capability in the future?

> With advances in technology and costs decreasing, it should not be too far in the future that this service becomes economically viable for a broader customer base. More importantly, companies are integrating technology and software in their products and services at a rapid pace. We are all becoming technology and software companies. It is critical that business executives need to be technology savvy and understand the power that "connectedness" provides in delivering a unique and superb customer experience. (ibid)

How Doug Bonebrake, IT Manager at FedEx Services,
Uses Innovation, in Its Simplest Form, to Dramatically
Improve Quality of IT-Developed Applications

FedEx is a company with a very interesting culture. People just want to do the right thing. It is not about winning awards, it is about helping the company deliver excellent service to external and internal customers. This is a major focus for Doug Bonebrake, an IT manager who works with colleagues on a variety of initiatives to improve the quality and speed of IT projects executed for FedEx Freight business units.

FedEx Freight is the FedEx transportation company that provides less-than-truckload (LTL) service within, and in between, the United States, Canada, Mexico, Puerto Rico, and the US Virgin Islands. Every customer has a different shipping requirement. Some require fast transit delivery of time-sensitive freight (FedEx Freight® Priority), while others need reliable and cost-effective delivery of their shipments and can trade time for savings (FedEx Freight® Economy). Varieties of services are available for customers depending on need. For example, customers can chose *time-definite shipping options* when a shipment has to arrive on a certain date. FedEx Freight Advance Notice® notifies customers of shipment status prior to delivery. IT enables these services. Those familiar with the world of IT organizations know that demand for improvements and/or development of new services places enormous pressures to deliver on time and with superior quality.[20]

FedEx Freight was born out of a number of acquisitions. In 1998, FedEx acquired Viking Freight, a provider of freight services to the western United States. Three years later, in 2001, FedEx acquired American Freightways, which provided freight services to 40 contiguous states in the U.S., including the eastern part of the country. Finally, in 2006, FedEx acquired Florida-based Watkins Motor Lines, a leading provider of long-haul LTL services. There were a number of challenges for IT personnel from these acquired companies when they integrated into the FedEx process-centric environment. In small companies, everyone wears a different hat and things get done. In a process-centric organization, personnel need to follow a set of policies and guidelines developed to deliver quality and speed for a large company environment. (ibid)

Bonebrake's background was a perfect fit for FedEx. Bonebrake received his first IT education when the US Army sent him to software and systems engineering school in 1986 to prepare him for his secondary specialty of systems automation. His first assignment as a systems automation officer was as the network security officer for the United States Army Information Systems Command–Pentagon

(USAISC-P). He was subsequently selected to serve as the chief of the USAISC-P Security Office. His responsibilities included the physical and systems security of the army broadband network and seven mainframe data centers. He was also responsible for the distributed systems supporting the army staff and information systems, which the army was designated as executive agent for the Department of Defense (DOD), such as the DOD Post Office, the Pentagon Automated Message Center, and interfaces with the White House Communications Agency.

In 1999, Bonebrake retired from his position as the chief operations officer for the U.S. Army Military Police School and Training Center and transitioned his skills to the business world. He worked initially as a management consultant to a telecommunications company before turning his interests to program and project management supporting software development companies or IT organizations, which ranged from small to mega enterprises. In 2003, Bonebrake was recruited by FedEx Freight to help build their software development QA team, as this was relatively early on in Viking/American Freightways integration process.

In 2004, as Bonebrake guided QA support to FedEx Freight projects, he observed that a significant number of defects were being uncovered by QA testing, which were rooted in requirements ambiguity. In analyzing the issues, he noted, "either business personnel, project leads or programmer analysts were attempting to write requirements specifications, without the benefit of business analysis training. This resulted in requirements, which were ambiguous or incomplete. The result was rework by development teams to ensure software solutions met business needs before solutions were released to production."[21] Defects and the rework to correct them translate to additional resources and time, which add cost to the project. The real issue is that the extended timeline, to allow for the rework, delays the potential benefit of the project. The QA team was catching the defects prior to production release, but the challenge was, "how can we discover and remove defects earlier in the project life cycle?" (ibid) Bonebrake wanted to minimize defects discovered late in the project life cycle to avoid the extraordinary efforts IT personnel would go through to ensure projects were delivered on time. Executive management was also discussing these same questions.

After the organization assessed the quality improvement opportunity, Bonebrake was selected to build a Business Systems Analysis Group from scratch for FedEx Freight. As Bonebrake describes it, "Testing is our last line of defense to prevent defects from escaping into production, but it is a very costly project stage to detect defects rooted in the early analysis of the project. It means that as a result of incomplete or ambiguous requirements, we worked to deliver the wrong solution, then, we had to do the same work over to get to the right solution. Additionally, while development teams are doing rework, they are falling behind on other opportunities to generate business value. By investing in removing requirements ambiguity and gaps early in the life cycle, we are removing defect sources at much less costly stages of the project and we are removing a major driver of project rework. The result is project teams which deliver quality solutions at a much lower cost." (ibid)

Bonebrake describes how the group works with project teams:

> Identify the business process and associated business rules which may be enabled with a technical solution, document the business need in the form of business requirements, then, work with project teams to specify the system requirements which define what the solution must do to satisfy the business need and deliver business value. (ibid)

The objective is for Bonebrake's team to become involved from the very beginning of the project, usually at the initial kickoff stage, all the way through the project life cycle. "They develop a variety of requirements work products to make sure that the behavior of the systems requirements satisfies the business needs." The group uses a third-party tool to simulate user interfaces. The tool creates realistic simulations of web, desktop, and mobile applications that stakeholders can actually use and test—all before writing a single line of code. "Using this process really helps the user confirm their requirements as well as speed up the requirements definition process." (ibid)

As the Business Systems Analysis Group continues to work with project teams to mature requirements development and management capabilities, rework rates continue to decline. Bonebrake often points out that "Requirements analysis is a team sport, therefore, it requires the focus of the entire project team to ensure requirements quality." He also notes that, "Process improvement is also a team sport. While one person might have an innovative idea, it only results in value when teams work together to assess it, understand the potential, optimize it and apply it." (ibid)

Bonebrake points out that, "Our quality advances did not come from one bold stroke, but through encouraging a culture of continuous process improvement and quality management. The result is less wasted effort which means more efficient and economical focus upon the timely delivery of business value." (ibid)

It is evident that FedEx has a unique culture. Bonebrake says it very well. "We have a great culture within FedEx. It empowers individual contributors and management to work together with a constant desire to deliver on the Purple Promise which is to make every FedEx experience outstanding." (ibid) (Author's note: I interviewed Bonebrake in September 2013. He retired from FedEx in December 2013.)

Chapter Summary

- Fred Smith's vision to become a leading package delivery company focusing on exceptional customer service leveraging IT is the result of exceptional employees who practice the Purple Promise credo and the company's relentless desire to leverage technology strategically to innovate value.

Rob Carter has assembled an outstanding team of business-focused technology professionals.

Ken Spangler, senior vice president of IT responsible for FedEx Ground and FedEx Freight IT systems, *loves business first, and technology second* and has leveraged his skills and knowledge in sortation technology into services that customers can rely on. Carter built the technology capability around the culture of FedEx, leveraging the goal of providing every customer a superior experience. In today's fast-paced globally competitive environment, technology is at the heart of innovating creative value.

Dave Zanca, former senior vice president of Customer Access Solutions at FedEx Services, was always relentless about *being the voice of the customer* and translates their needs in superior products and services, like SenseAware[SM]. Doug Bonebrake, IT manager within FedEx Services, just knows that speed and quality are of utmost

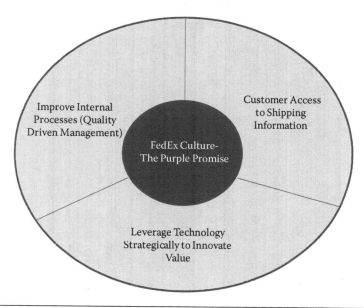

Figure 16.9   The Four-Prong Strategy.

importance for technology solutions executed by the FedEx IT organization, which I illustrate in Figure 16.9.

- The graphic at the beginning of the chapter, and repeated in the following, identifies the four-prong strategy used by FedEx to achieve success.
- Improve internal processes (QDM).
- Provide customer access to shipping information.
- Leverage technology strategically to innovate value.
- Ingrained FedEx culture of the Purple Promise.

Together, these four strategic components provide FedEx with the energy to create superior customer service enabled by IT. The results have been amazing as FedEx continues to expand services that are focused on customer's need and enhancing value.

Key Points

1. Successful companies leverage technology strategically to innovate value.
2. A core culture for providing superior customer service drives innovation.

3. A good leader hires smart people who
   - Share a vision of leveraging technology to drive business value
   - Continue to push the envelope to find new ways to leverage technology
   - Maintain a clear focus for driving business value first and technology second

Citations

1. *Changing How the World Does Business*; Roger J. Frock; Copyright 2006; Berrett-Koehler Publishers, San Francisco, CA.
2. 10 Things You Didn't Know About Fred Smith/US News and World Report/By Jennifer L. O'Shea, July 24, 2008; http://www.usnews.com/news/campaign-2008/articles/2008/07/24/10-things-you-didnt-know-about-fred-smith.
3. FedEx Express Website/FedEx Attributes Success to People-first Philosophy; http://www.fedex.com/pk/about/overview/philosophy.html.
4. FedEx Website/About FedEx/Company Info/FedEx Innovation; http://about.van.fedex.com/fedex-innovation.
5. FedEx website About FedEx/Company Info/Robert B. Carter; http://about.van.fedex.com/executive_bios/robert_b_carter.   Bloomberg Business Week, and http://investing.businessweek.com/research/stocks/people/person.asp?personId=223306&ticker=FDX.
6. FedEx Website: About FedEx/Company Info/Robert B. Carter; http://about.van.fedex.com/executive_bios/robert_b_carter.
7. Forbes; http://www.forbes.com/profile/robert-carter/; Rob Carter has been honored with numerous professional awards including being named a member of *FORTUNE* magazine's C-Suite Dream Team Starting Line-up at CIO (2011); #18 on *Fast Company* magazine's 100 Most Creative People in Business (2010); InformationWeek Chief of the Year Award (2000, 2001, 2005); and InfoWorld Chief Technology Officer of the Year (2000). He is a seven-time recipient of CIO magazine's 100 Award and was a charter inductee into the publications CIO Hall of Fame.
8. Rob Carter, Executive Vice President, Information Services & Chief Information Officer at FedEx Corporation/Phil Weinzimer Interview, January 29, 2013.
9. NIST: Baldridge Performance Excellence Program/NIST/Home/Baldridge/Federal Express Corporation. http://www.baldrige.nist.gov/FederalExpress_90.htm.
10. Rob Carter, Executive Vice President, Information Services & Chief Information Officer at FedEx Corporation/Phil Weinzimer Interview, March 6, 2013.

11. Dave Zanca, Senior Vice President, Customer Access Solutions, FedEx Corporate Services/Phil Weinzimer Interview, September 6, 2013.
12. Fedex CIO: Use your ugly pictures to get stuff done; http://www.techre public.com/blog/hiner/fedex-cio-use-your-ugly-pictures-to-get-stuff-done/9511; By Jason Hiner; October 19, 2011, 7:17 AM PDT.
13. The Four Horsemen of Dominant Design; Robert B. Carter; Executive Vice President, Information Services, Chief Information Officer, FedEx Corporation; http://www.hmgstrategy.com/assets/imx/PDF/RBC-SIM_Memphis_Strategy_Series-HMG.pdf; slide 17.
14. FedEx CIO Sees Analytics Driving a World of Enterprise Change by Michael Vizard; October 4, 2012; http://slashdot.org/topic/cloud/fedex-cio-sees-analytics-driving-a-world-of-enterprise-change/.
15. FedEx Web Site/pdf file download, *I've seen the power of Purple.* http://www.fedex.com/purplepromise/docs//en/fedex_pp_booklet_purple-power.pdf.
16. I am FedEx; https://www.iamfedex.com/Our-Stories/Approved-Stories/QDM-Honors.aspx.
17. Ken Spangler, CIO FedEx Ground/Phil Weinzimer Interview, Tuesday July 16, 2013.
18. FedEx Ground meets rising customer expectations by shortening its package processing time; IBM article: http://www-01.ibm.com/software/success/cssdb.nsf/CS/JSTS-6ZJP8D?OpenDocument&Site=powersyste ms&cty=en_us/Published on March 26, 2007; IBM.
19. FedEx Website/Blog/David Zanca: http://blog.van.fedex.com/users/david-zanca; David Zanca, Sr. Vice President, Customer access Solutions, FedEx Corporate Services/Phil Weinzimer/Interview, September 6, 2013.
20. FedEx Website/About FedEx/Company Info/History/History of FedEx Operating Companies; http://about.van.fedex.com/fedex-opco-history.
21. Doug Bonebrake, IT Manager, FedEx Freight/Phil Weinzimer Interview, September 3, 2013.

17

How Procter & Gamble Leverages Technology Strategically to Innovate Value

What we stand for is to transform the way business is done... and to drive business value through innovation.[1]

Filippo Passerini
Group President of Global Business Services and CIO

Procter & Gamble (P&G) is an excellent example of a company that creates value by leveraging technology. Innovation is deeply rooted in its culture and is at the core of its success. Today, consumer tastes and perception of value change quickly. Company size is irrelevant in today's digital market, and companies continue to develop strategies to stay ahead of the competition. P&G, the global powerhouse, is reinventing itself to stay ahead of the competition. It leverages technology in innovative ways to be a significant and unique provider of consumer products. P&G is changing the way it runs the business, and leading the charge is Filippo Passerini, group president of Global Business Services (GBS) and CIO.

Following are the chapter objectives, key messages, and examples used:

A. CHAPTER OBJECTIVE

This chapter focuses on how P&G leverages technology strategically to innovate value. Filippo Passerini, president of GBS and CIO, is a business-focused executive who understands the P&G business and how to leverage technology to create new business models. The chapter focuses on four key areas: history of P&G, business value of P&Gs Business Services Group, information strategies employed by the CIO and his team to innovate value, and a use-case example of how P&G leverages technology for innovative value.

B. KEY MESSAGES

1. The primary objective of the CIO is to create business value for the enterprise.
2. IT should be used to help business leaders make well-informed decisions.
3. Present data meaningfully to help business leaders focus on analyzing root causes of business challenges.

C. EXAMPLES

1. P&G history and today's competitive environment
2. Passerini's background and how the Business Services Group helps management make well-informed decisions
3. An innovative *what, why, how* business model and *digitize, visualize, and simulate* data strategy to manage, display, and model data

P&G is an excellent example of a company that creates value by leveraging technology. To help you understand how Passerini and his organization leverage technologies to provide business value, this chapter includes information about

- P&G history and today's competitive environment
- Passerini's background and how the Business Services Group helps management make well-informed decisions
- An innovative *what, why, how* business model and *digitize, visualize, and simulate* data strategy to manage, display, and model data
- Use-case scenario of Passerini's initiatives that demonstrates how an innovative CIO is changing the way P&G runs its business

P&G History

William Procter and James Gamble signed a partnership agreement on October 31, 1837 in Cincinnati, Ohio, with just $7000 in assets. They had a strong bond to build a successful business that sold soap and candles. Not only were they partners but also brothers-in-law. William married Olivia Norris, and James married Elizabeth Norris, daughters of a successful local candle maker. William and James never imagined their partnership would grow into what is now an $84 billion dollar business with almost 5 billion consumers in 70 countries.

Four major milestones catapulted P&G to success prior to the twentieth century. The first milestone was the demand for soap and candles that launched the business. The second milestone occurred in 1859 when P&G revenues reached $1 million. The third milestone was the rising demand for soap and candles by the Union army, which further drove sales upward. The fourth milestone was in 1879 when James Norris Gamble, son of James Gamble, invented Ivory soap.[2]

During the early years, P&G recognized that innovation was an important concept to apply to its business. P&G was one of the first companies to embark on the concept of applying innovation in its business model. In 1887, William Cooper Procter, grandson of the founder, started a profit-sharing program to reward workers and recognize their contributions to the company's success. Just before the turn of the century, P&G added a variety of soap choices to its portfolio. Ivory Flakes for washing clothes and dishes, Chipso soap that consumers could use in washing machines, and Crisco all-vegetable shortening that consumers raved over were part of the 30 soap products that helped fuel P&G's growth. P&G's research teams studied consumer needs and pioneered the concept of market research as an important element in the continued growth of the company. Continuing the use of innovative concepts, P&G expanded its advertising from print media to radio. The company also began providing product samples as a means of introducing new brands to the market, as well as promotional premiums as an incentive for consumers to try new products. In 1946, P&G introduced Tide, which fueled international growth. P&G research labs applied pulp-making technology to develop toilet tissue and paper towels. Another product developed through the research labs was disposable diapers, giving birth to Pampers. Innovation in both market research and technology fueled the growth of P&G. In future years, P&G continued to grow as it added consumer products that today line the shelves of every grocery store.[2]

P&G Business Environment and Challenges

Almost everyone is familiar with P&G. However, you might be surprised at how big and complex the company actually is. Of the 7 billion people in the world, almost 5 billion people in 70 countries are consumers of P&G products. Can you imagine how many times a day a cash register rings up a sale of a P&G product? To satisfy the demand for the many brands manufactured by P&G requires operations in 70 countries around the world. These brands include Charmin, Bounty, Gillette, Cascade, and a host of others that are household names. There are 25 billion dollar brands; Charmin is one of those. This mammoth organization generated more than 84 billion dollars of sales in fiscal year 2012–2013. Imagine what it takes to keep the engine for this company churning out products each and every day, let alone the complex supply chain required to maintain stock levels for customers. The rewards of success can also come with challenges that threaten to impede growth. As P&G developed into the global giant we know today, it faced the typical challenges of growing companies.

Small companies and start-ups, by nature, have an organizational structure that breeds speed and agility, and a communication structure that enables activities to be completed efficiently. Personnel take on multiple roles to *get the job done*. When I worked at start-up ITM Software as managing principal professional services, I wore many hats. I worked with marketing, sharing ideas and customer input in developing product improvements. I participated in client meetings with the sales executives. I implemented and managed consultant teams, in the United States and Europe, implementing solutions. I would even run out and get lunch for the group when I was at the home office. Other team members wore numerous hats, as well. We were a small group in the early years, and when any of us needed help, we would send an e-mail and call each other on the phone, and we made things happen quickly.

However, as companies grow, they add new manufacturing facilities and expand their supply chains. They develop structure, processes, and a governance model to ensure consistency across the business. Job descriptions define roles in detail. Hierarchical organization charts identify the formal *command and control* structure personnel should abide by. Information systems expand exponentially as massive amounts of information are required to manage the business. Reporting needs proliferate, individual databases are created, and the IT organization develops unique applications to satisfy the increasing information demands of different departments. This was the scenario experienced by P&G as its operations expanded to 70 countries providing consumer products to 5 billion consumers.

Information overload and data accuracy are two of the greatest impediments to a company's continued successful growth in a complex marketplace where speed and agility are requirements. Gone are old market drivers. Companies in the 1950s–1980s could simply manufacture products and *push* demand in the marketplace by filling shelves with products. Then, in the 1990s, everyone was abuzz about providing customer access via the Internet, as well as providing superior customer service, and *pull* demand from the marketplace. Now, we are in an entirely different market. Size does not matter anymore. We have evolved from *push* to *pull* to *personalized*. Today, consumers' behaviors are different. They demand more, want to be in control, and want to be treated as individuals. No longer can companies dictate what the consumer wants. Nimble start-ups that learn to quickly respond to changing market needs can become a competitive threat to large, established companies. The consumer is now driving the train. As a result, large companies need to develop business models that include the processes and enabling tools that capture, measure, and anticipate consumer needs. Large companies still need the processes, controls, and governance models to maintain their global reach but also have the speed and agility of a start-up. Jack Welch describes the dilemma GE faced in the early 1990s.[3]

> At the beginning of the decade, we saw two challenges ahead of us, one external, and one internal. Externally, we faced a world economy that would be characterized by slower growth, with stronger global competitors going after a smaller piece of the pie. Internally our challenge was even

bigger. We had to find a way to combine the power, resources, and reach of a large company with the hunger, agility, spirit, and fire of a small one.

Around 2005–2006, P&G recognized that it needed to figure out how to move with the speed and agility of a small company. This is where P&G's innovation roots kick in. From its early days using research labs to develop products, providing employee incentives and creating new advertising techniques, P&G was good at staying one step ahead of its competitors. It values its employees and provides the opportunity for every employee to learn, engage, develop, and apply their skills to help the company grow and prosper. Filippo Passerini, group president of GBS and CIO, has benefited from this culture. He recognizes the changes in today's market and skillfully articulates the challenge.

> In today's highly competitive marketplace, companies have to change the game. They have to be 'relevant and distinctive.' The worst position is to be viewed as a commodity. Being a commodity is all about cost not about value. It's not about running faster. It's about changing the way we ran.[4]

Filippo Passerini, Group President of Global Business Services and CIO

Passerini is helping change the way P&G thinks about and conducts business. Changing the game is about staying relevant, being distinctive and connecting to customers to understand their needs and, more importantly, *anticipate* their needs, even before they are able to articulate them. He is doing this by leveraging technology in innovative ways. Passerini believes that CIOs are not just about technology, but they are about creating new business models and new markets that help their companies grow and prosper. He learned early in his career that first, success is about business results and value creation and, second, how technology can play a role in the winning formula. To Passerini, technology is just an enabler, a tool to draw upon when needed. He thinks strategically about the business and relies on developing business models that can reshape and drive competitive advantage. Also important to Passerini is the realization that it takes a group of talented people to get things done. He is a respected leader, mentor, and coach to his leadership team. He is consistent, results oriented, and strategically focused. When Passerini speaks, people listen and magic happens.

When you meet Passerini, you are immediately struck by his charm and thick Italian accent. As he speaks, the words become clearer, the message is very strategic, and you think you are listening to a CEO, business unit executive, or chief strategy officer. Passerini is not your typical CIO. With a doctorate in statistics and operations research from the University of Rome, Passerini has an impressive 30-year career at P&G. He held a variety of positions of increasing responsibility in the IT organization in Italy, Turkey, and the United Kingdom, leading up to the director level in 1994, where he was the director of Management Systems at P&G Latin America. Three years later, he was named the vice president of Management Systems at P&G North America.

As his reputation for getting things done resonated across the company, Passerini moved to the business side during 1999–2002 where he was the vice president of IT for the Global Beauty Care and Global Health Care business units and subsequently the vice president of Marketing Operations Team and corporate marketing leader, Western Europe and Greece. His business experience was invaluable. In 2003, he moved back to IT as the GBS officer. In that role, he managed a $4.2 billion strategic sourcing agreement, executed in 11 months, which at the time was considered one of the largest IT deals ever accomplished.

His big break came in 2004 when he was promoted to CIO in addition to his GBS responsibilities. He brought together the IT organization and the shared services organization that is responsible for all back-office functions, including facilities, people management, finance, strategic sourcing, and procurement. In 2008, executive management awarded Passerini the title of the president of GBS (later changed to group president) and CIO. Passerini's reputation traveled well beyond P&G, however, and in 2012, the Institute for Business Innovation, Haas School of Business, University of California, Berkeley, awarded Passerini the Fisher-Hopper Prize for Lifetime Achievement in CIO Leadership.[5]

Leveraging Technologies Strategically to Innovate Value

Passerini is a strong believer in leveraging IT strategically to innovate value. Doing so is not possible unless the IT organization achieves success in the first three phases of the transformation model.

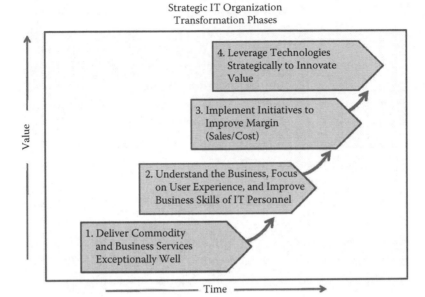

Strategic IT Organization
Transformation Phases

To transform into a strategic IT organization, Passerini implemented the following strategies:

Phase 1/2: Reorganize business services and IT into a solutions provider that delivers and measures service delivery, realign roles to be business focused and drive business value, and run the new organization as a business.

Phase 3: GBS launch of a number of initiatives to improve service levels and reduce costs.

Phase 4: Utilize an innovative approach to deliver a single source of data truth across P&G to eliminate disparate islands of data that create organization disruption and decision-making delays. Create a new business model to improve decision making, through *digitization, visualization, and simulation* technology.

A more in-depth view of these strategies provides a clearer understanding of how Passerini and his team leverage technologies strategically to innovate value.

Phase 1/2: Reorganize business services and IT into a solutions provider that delivers and measures service delivery, realign roles to be business focused and drive business value, and run the new organization as a business.

Passerini is a strong believer in *driving business value by focusing on business first and technology second*. To execute against this belief, Passerini needed to change the perception of IT from a technology provider to a business solutions enabler. This is exactly what Passerini did in 2003, combining the shared services organization with the IT organization to become GBS. Passerini wanted to combine the two groups because he saw *more value together than alone*. The merger of the two organizations changed the way P&G valued IT and shared services. The three main objectives were as follows: (ibid)

1. Change the perception of IT as a technology provider to a solutions provider: Naming an organization information technology evokes technology as the primary goal. To resolve this misperception, Passerini renamed the group Information Decision Solutions (IDS). The focus is on delivering information that helps the business make decisions by providing value-added solutions. Role responsibilities in IDS changed. IDS leaders focused on transforming P&G by connecting business needs with potential IT enablers. Changing the name and role responsibilities sent a clear message to the business (Figure 17.1).

2. Run GBS as a business: Passerini believed that he needed to run GBS as a business. He prices GBS competitively to those available in the open market. Additionally, he instituted profit and loss responsibility within GBS and

Figure 17.1 P&G Business Units.

generated P&G statements for each business service function. GBS implemented P&G business practices and policies and operated as equal to any other P&G business. This alone reshaped how GBS viewed its role and transformed its interactions with the business. Passerini's team became more than just mere technology providers; they became valued business partners.

Passerini organized the unit around a broad range of business and employee services. There is no mention of IT. Passerini created a huge cultural shift in P&G by not only positioning GBS as a business but also delivering business value.

3. GBS as a solutions provider: Passerini is a believer in not adopting technology for technology's sake. He believes technology investments need to drive business value through solutions that improve productivity and efficiency. This philosophy further helped GBS establish itself as an equal business solutions provider along with every other P&G business unit.

Phase 3: To accomplish phase three of the transformation model, GBS launch of a number of initiatives to improve service levels and drive business value while also reducing cost.

In the 10 years since leading GBS, Passerini has initiated a number of strategic initiatives that have significantly reduced costs for the business. A segment of these initiatives involved forming strategic supplier partnerships that changed the way P&G worked with vendors. The goal was to "develop a unique collaborative partnership model that results in a win-win for both P&G and our partners."[5] The strategic relationships differed from the traditional model. "We work to 'grow the pie' together and co-invent new business-building capabilities, creating joint value creation." (ibid) Following are three great examples. (ibid)

In 2003, P&G partnered with three major service providers to outsource nonstrategic services (HP for IT services and later accounts payable, Jones Lang LaSalle for facilities management, and IBM for nonstrategic elements of employee service infrastructure). The $4.2 billion dollar service contract was deemed, at the time, one of the largest undertaken by any company. Since then, additional vendor partnerships have been implemented and provide value for the vendor as well as P&G. This joint value creation model is a prime example of leveraging strategic partnerships to innovate value.

In 2007, GBS collaborated with Cisco to implement TelePresence studios in top P&G sites around the globe in 9 months. Since that time, P&G has continued to add these studios, which enable face-to-face communication and improve collaboration and decision making. Reduced travel costs are also a result, for those meetings that would have traditionally required travel. Cisco acknowledges that P&G has developed the most innovative use of TelePresence technology they have experienced.

In 2008, GBS established a partnership with Xerox to leverage its Managed Print Services. Xerox has a strong competency in this area, and together, the teams have been able to significantly reduce printing costs as well as paper consumption and energy costs.

Aside from these strategic initiatives, GBS played a key role in integrating newly acquired businesses into P&G. In 2005, P&G acquired Gillette, and executives looked to GBS to integrate Gillette's IT systems into the P&G model. At the time, the integration was one of the largest in history. Gillette had operations in 69 countries, with 148,000 customers served by 115 distribution centers. The number of integration projects exceeded 1000 and involved disparate order management, shipping, and billing systems along with the core financial and business reporting systems. This integration was the largest P&G had undertaken, and when it was complete, industry experts considered it best in class. To top it off, the integration was finished ahead of schedule and below budget.

Phase 4: Utilize an innovative approach to deliver a single source of data across P&G to eliminate disparate islands of data that create organization disruption and delays in decision making. Create a new business model to improve decision making, through digitization, visualization, and simulation.

During 2007–2008, Passerini and the executive team recognized a shift in the market. The executive team routinely looks at megatrends in the world to understand what impact they will have on the business. Innovation cycles were dramatically reducing in a number of industries. Also evident were the emergence of the consumerization of technology, rising expectations by consumers of product varieties, and competitive pressures in certain markets. All these trends impact P&G, and data were at the heart of these changes. The ability to quickly evaluate and analyze data became increasingly important. As the head of GBS, Passerini was acutely aware that the variety of information management systems across the company sometimes slowed business decisions. It was difficult for groups to make decisions when no one could agree on the accuracy of numbers.

Passerini met with Robert McDonald (at the time COO of P&G) to discuss the issue. Passerini and McDonald envisioned a digitization strategy that would provide data in real time, to all employees who needed it, regardless of location. Passerini calls this *information democracy*. The objective was to have consistent data, which management throughout P&G could use to plan, strategize, and make the necessary business decisions to create customer value. McKinsey & Company believed this digitization strategy would result in "creating one of the world's most technologically-enabled companies."[6] Passerini's leadership was critical to its success. McDonald said, "IT is the key enabling function in delivering this strategy...and I hold Filippo accountable for implementing this all-important strategy." (ibid) In short, Passerini was tasked with transforming the way P&G does business.[6]

Passerini is an avid chess player. Strategy and modeling chess move scenarios are all part of the game. He uses his chess techniques in business as well. To frame the challenge, Passerini developed a simple model around three questions to address the information challenge.

The model, shown in Figure 17.2, is simple. In any business meeting, you want to answer three questions.

1. What is happening?
   This answer needs to be fact based, not opinion. Everyone should agree on one source of truth for the data. For example, a group of managers meets to review issues pertaining to out-of-stock challenges for one of their major products. They need to review supply chain data along with market share trends from global markets to understand the impact of delivery

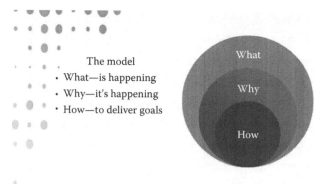

The model
- What—is happening
- Why—it's happening
- How—to deliver goals

Figure 17.2 Passerini's *What, Why, How* Model.

issues. They need real-time data for each of these areas. They cannot make the necessary business decisions if different data sets exist and people argue over data accuracy. Eliminating the debate on data accuracy enables the group to move quickly into the analysis phase.

2. Why is it happening?

When looking at data, you need to understand the trends. This is where analytics comes into play. A pragmatic analysis of real-time data enables business teams to uncover the dynamics about events. In P&G's case, an example would be market trends. Why are sales in one region surpassing sales of the same product in another region? Why are sales of a product in a particular country falling? Business teams need to understand why events are happening, and data analytics is a great technique to use in objectively analyzing data. This is where an intimate knowledge of the business along with market trends provides value in analyzing the issue.

3. How to deliver the goals?

Once you understand why events occur, you need to identify the actions to take to achieve the goal. Using the examples earlier, business teams would want to identify the actions to improve market share deterioration.

By using this model, Passerini and his GBS team could begin developing the strategies, which would provide the framework to answer these three questions.

The first step was to develop one source of truth for data. The second step was utilizing the data around a three-step strategy of digitize, visualize, and simulate.

Step 1: Single source of truth

P&G utilized SAP in a number of global locations but recognized the need to standardize on the SAP platform. To accomplish this, P&G entered into a strategic partnership with SAP to expand the SAP ERP applications across the corporation. This expanded use of SAP "would improve the P&G core operations and also step-change innovation in business services and enhance the efficiency of our core business operations."[7]

Step 2: Digitize, visualize, and simulate

These three simple words are changing the way P&G runs the business. Digitizing the data would provide everyone data in real time. Visualizing data though graphics and charts would improve the ability of personnel to understand the significance of the numbers they previously read on computer screens and computer reports. Simulating would enable P&G to dramatically reduce cycle times in key business processes such as innovating new products to market.

To gain buy-in from the executive team, Passerini developed a prototype he called a *decision cockpit*. It emulated a decision support application that used forward-looking projections rather than historical reporting, with 3, 6, and 12-month projected trend lines for market share, cost of goods, and margins. Previously, executive teams analyzed reports with historical data and then debated subjectively the implications of the data. Passerini's strategy was to provide future trends with analytics and metrics, using visual graphs and charts that would enable them to easily understand the data in business terms. It worked. The executives could look at product performance from a global view and, then with one click, drill down to view country- and regional-level performances. They could also hone in on brands and products for each of the geographic categories. But this was only a prototype, and while some of the data were available in real time, a lot of manual work was required to make it operable. However, the richness of the graphics and ability to drill down to details and project trends helped the executives see what was possible. By the time the meeting was over, Passerini had the green light to proceed.[8]

Digitize Strategy

Passerini's vision of *information democracy* centers on the belief that P&G decision makers should all have the same information and in real time. Debating data accuracy creates wasted energy. Employees around the world make decisions every day, and Passerini wanted to make sure they had the right information, in real time. "By having access to the right data at the right time, we can make informed decisions and address the needs of our customers and consumers."[9] His vision was to capture data from all available sources and provide the relevant information, via decision cockpits, to all employees at their workstations.

Decision Cockpits

Employees have access to a decision cockpit configured on their computers. Data can be configured based on the individual's needs and provide a display of real-time information and alerts relevant to the individual's responsibility. Passerini says, "we now have the ability to see trends and get alerts...this way, we can manage by exception and eliminate all the redundant information that slows down the decision-making process."[6] The ability to manage by exception eliminates the need to look at all the data. Only the data that are relevant need to be looked at, greatly improving the decision-making process. Figure 17.3 shows two reports. The one on the left is the report previously used by personnel. The graphic on the right is the decision cockpit that graphically displays the data in meaningful business terms. Clearly, the decision cockpit enables speedier decisions.

According to Passerini, "the use of Decision Cockpits has transformed all our standard business reporting into a visual, one-stop shop illustration of the business status and trends." Graphs and control charts, which provide drill-down capability, provide the user with alerts to manage by exception. The user can analyze data in real time. "We call this tool Decision Cockpits, because they have enabled us to make better, faster decisions."[9]

Passerini is passionate about the value of decision cockpits.

In the past, there was no one-stop shop for all information, but today, with Decision Cockpits, all the data that had been collected through

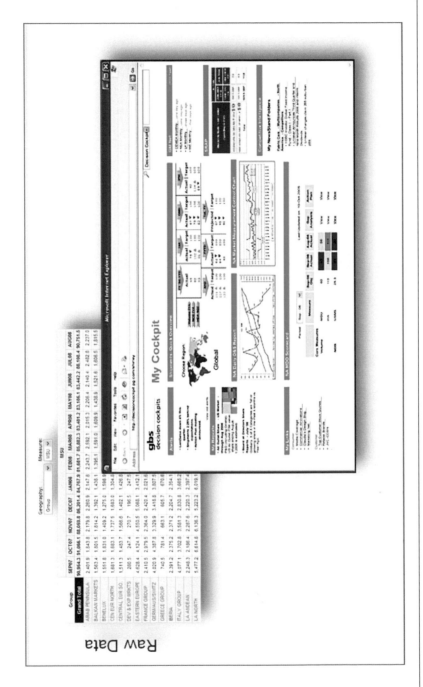

Figure 17.3 Decision Cockpit.

emails, letters, phone calls and reports resides in this system. This has dramatically reduced the cost and complexity associated with creating reports and the duplication of data.[7]

Visualize Strategy

Portraying data visually is nothing new. It has been used for hundreds of years to portray geographic maps and ocean currents. The ancient Egyptians used hieroglyphics to portray a story. Today, the art of visualization has evolved into a competency in medicine, engineering, and business, aided by advances in IT. Interactive data visualization techniques provide greater insights than rows and columns of data on an excel spreadsheet.

GBS embedded visualization as a technique for P&G management teams to analyze data to make faster business decisions as well as improve innovation-to-market cycle times. The team created conference rooms, called *business spheres*, to help teams evaluate data more meaningfully and bring to life pertinent data into visual representations that highlight key exceptions and business drivers. Analytic models, combined with this immersive business sphere environment, help business leaders focus on what really matters. To improve cycle times, Passerini uses visualization techniques and analytic models to help P&G teams integrate feedback on market, packaging, product, and media quickly into the production and marketing process.

Business Spheres

The second component was to provide a conference room version of the decision cockpit. He called these meeting rooms *business spheres*, where groups of P&G personnel at all levels within the company could efficiently evaluate data to address business challenges.

When teams gather in a conference room to discuss a business issue, the first part of the meeting usually focuses on identifying the problem they are trying to solve. Data are usually presented as part of this discussion. Passerini wanted to bring the concept of the decision cockpit into the conference room. He created spherical-shaped conference rooms, called *business spheres*, across the company. Executives, managers, and business teams meet in these rooms using large graphical displays to show data. These conference rooms combine video with sales, market share, financials, advertising, supply chain data, and other information required by attendees to make well-informed business decisions efficiently.

Laurie Heltsley, a 23-year veteran at P&G and currently director of Innovation and Strategic Projects, was involved in the business sphere project.

> We converted rear-view business reporting into large format visualization of business data. This innovation allowed our executive and leadership teams to immerse themselves in relevant data, instead of looking at paper reports, and make necessary, immediate business decisions (Figure 17.4).[10]

P&G is a global company, with subject matter experts around the world at different facilities. A partnership with Cisco enabled a videoconferencing capability at all P&G locations. When executives, managers, or teams gather in a business sphere conference room, team members from different P&G locations can join the meeting using their iPhone, iPad, or any smartphone device. Personnel can even join using a personal computer using WebEx or any of the videoconferencing services. Passerini is a strong believer that better decisions are the result of people meeting in a face-to-face environment.[11]

There are two critical components to the success of using business sphere, besides one source of data truth. These are consistent models for addressing different types of business challenges and business

Figure 17.4   Business Sphere Conference Rooms.

analysts who attend meetings to provide the insight and business knowledge in analyzing the data.

P&G rotates personnel between brands to learn about different parts of the company and apply learnings across the organization. When it comes to data analysis, P&G uses business sufficiency models that identify the specific type of information used when working on problem types. When a team evaluates a supply chain challenge, the model identifies which variables to use. P&G has developed a set of *business sufficiency models* for each core competency of the business. This process provides consistency for analyzing data as well as a basis for continuously improving the models.[4]

The second critical component of the business sphere concept is the business analyst. The digitization strategy brings all the relevant data into the discussion, displayed elegantly on large graphical screens. The challenge is to understand the data and its implications. This is where the business analyst comes into play. In the *what, why, how* business model, previously discussed, the *why* is the area where business value is created, according to Passerini. This is the area where an intimate knowledge of the business, along with a working knowledge of business analytics, is beneficial. It adds the critical insight decision makers need to make the well-informed business decision. At every business sphere meeting, a business analyst or analysts participate, either in person or via videoconferencing. These business analysts know how to slice and dice the data to make the information relevant to the business discussion.

Passerini believes this business analysis skill is critical in analyzing the data to be meaningful for decision makers. Let's look at an example. A group of managers meets to review market trends in South America for their top-selling P&G brands. Graphical displays provide relevant data color coded to represent specific trends. However, what do these data imply? Meeting attendees may have a different view and interpretation of the data. What is missing is the subject matter expert. This is where the business analyst provides insights to the group using IT skills along with data modeling and simulation skills. The business analyst interprets the data, drills down into relevant data segments, and explains to the group the relevance of the data. The group can then make better decisions more quickly.

GBS has business analysts throughout P&G who have analytic, IT, and business skills. They bridge the gap between IT and the business and form a partnership that creates business value for P&G. Industry experts and innovation organizations have acclaimed *business sphere* as a true innovation in leveraging technology to create business value. P&G was the Silver Winner in the "Innovative Services: Collaboration/Knowledge Management" category for the 2013 Edison Awards Competition.[12]

Simulate Strategy

The ability to convert physical objects into digital formats is an innovative use of technology. Architects have been using computer-aided technology to design buildings for many years. The technology is now used by the automotive industry to design cars, airplane manufacturers to design aircraft, and product companies to design intricate manufacturing components. It is a remarkable technology. P&G recognizes its value and partners with the College of Engineering and Applied Sciences at the University of Cincinnati to use simulation in the development, marketing, and packaging of P&G products.[13]

P&G uses simulation technology to develop new products and test changes to the manufacturing process. Another use of simulation technology is the creation of a digital shelf that enables consumer groups to evaluate P&G and competitive products. Let us explore each of these uses in more detail.

Develop New Products and Manufacturing Process Improvements

Simulation technology has helped P&G solve a host of product challenges. Laura Michalske is the section head for One Health Modeling & Simulation. Her 24-year career provides her with intimate knowledge of the P&G business, and she helps the company apply simulation techniques to drive business value. P&G manufactures high volumes of product. Michalske says that P&G produces about 7 billion individual products for every 1 billion dollars in sales. With almost 80 billion dollars in sales, that's a lot of product rolling off P&G manufacturing lines. P&G manufactures 1 billion diapers in a few days, says Michalske. Whether it is designing an improved diaper or other new or improved products, P&G uses modeling and simulation techniques to improve innovation to market.[14]

Prior to using simulation modeling, the company physically created a prototype of the production line, called a *racetrack*, to test new products and packaging changes. Changes in speed and parts to improve the conveyor process were accomplished manually. "If there was a problem with the test run, such as the bottles tipping over on the line, the packaging and/or racetrack would need to be redesigned and reproduced for more testing. They basically had to start from square one." Today, thanks in large part to Research & Develop and Product Supply, P&G is using simulation and modeling, which improve the manufacturing process in addition to reducing the time it takes to implement changes. A great example of this is packaging. Previously, any changes to packaging required physical activities to prototype the package. This process would take 6–7 weeks. With simulation and modeling, the process takes a few hours. Changes can be made instantaneously and avoid the physical efforts previously required. From designing a bottle, changing package design, determining the best process for mixing liquid detergents, or how to stack products without damage, simulation modeling improves time to market, a strategic goal of P&G. (ibid)

Shelf Product Strategies

Another area where Passerini and his team add value is in product marketing. In the past, P&G would build replicas of store shelves and stock them with P&G and competitor products. Consumer focus groups would comment on the products, packaging, labeling, location, and other elements that impact buying decisions. When focus group customers would say, "The package should be on a lower shelf," P&G personnel would physically move the items. If the packaging was not vibrant or informative enough, P&G would create new physical packaging and then invite the focus group back to view the changes. This was expensive and time consuming.

Enter the world of computer simulation. Now multiple projectors simultaneously display store shelving digitally. Consumer groups can interact with these digital store shelves. If someone suggests moving an item, a P&G team member can digitally move the item, similar to

Figure 17.5   The Virtual Shelf.

using a mouse cursor to move a graphic on a slide. If a focus group member does not like the packaging color, a P&G team member can change the package color on the fly. According to Passerini, P&G can calculate revenue impact possibilities based upon changes consumer focus group members recommend. All interactive graphics visually mimic a real physical shelf in a store. Passerini and his team, in partnership with R&D and others, have used virtualization and work flow reality to mimic the physical shelf. This use of technology has accelerated P&G innovation to market process dramatically (Figure 17.5).

Use-Case Scenario of Leveraging Technology Strategy to Innovate Value

The use of business sphere and data analytics helps P&G executives and managers improve decision making. Passerini provided a detailed example of the model and framework at the InformationWeek 500 event in September 2012, in a keynote interview with InformationWeek Editor Chris Murphy. Passerini, the InformationWeek 2010 CIO of the Year, shared how executives, reviewing business performance, examine the drivers impacting market share of products around the world.[9a] Before I share the example, let us look at a meeting scenario without the benefit of a business sphere.

Picture a group of executives or managers sitting around a conference table reviewing global market trend performance of key P&G products. Previously, executives would hand out Excel™ reports or PowerPoint™ slides prepared by a board of analysts, who worked feverishly into the night preparing for the meeting. The data could be as much as a few days, weeks, or even a month old. Next, meeting attendees would debate why the data trends occur. It is opinion with maybe some fact, but still everyone often has a different view as to why. The group discusses options and, after much discussion, agrees that further analysis is required. The group schedules a follow-up meeting for the following week since the analysts have to rechurn and analyze additional data.

Now let us look at a similar meeting using a business sphere. Groups of executives meet in a conference room with large digital screens. The objective of the meeting is for business executives reviewing business performance to examine the drivers impacting market share of products around the world. Attending the meeting are the presidents of each of the business units as well as business analysts who are intimately knowledgeable in the business and the data the group is reviewing. The lead analyst starts the meeting by sharing the following objectives and approach to attain the objective.

During the meeting, the business analyst displays a series of dashboard reports on the screens that surround the room. The data are real time and are presented in the context of the business discussion: It is extremely important for P&G to understand market share of its key products and the drivers that impact market share. The business analysts in the meeting provide the insight and market intelligence behind the numbers to help attendees understand the impact each data point has on market share. The analysts have intimate knowledge of the P&G business and the competitive market.

The business analyst then tells the group that they need to understand the P&G regions and product categories contributing to market share. With a click of the mouse, the business analyst displays a new chart, which adds data to the previous chart. P&G and other companies are listed in the middle of the chart. The business analyst clicks on P&G, and the P&G regions are displayed along with a vertical bar that represents the degree of impact each region has on market share.

The next question the group wants to answer is *why market share is changing*.

To better understand market driver changes, the business analyst displays another dashboard that shows all the regions of the world. Each region is color coded in various shades of green and red. Using this type of imagery with colors that change in tone is often referred to as a heat map. It is a great visualization technique and helps the leaders identify the regions contributing the greatest to market share and their contribution to share growth.

One of the attendees wants to understand what is happening in the United States. The business analyst clicks on the United States to provide more insight on the market share drivers in the United States.

The business analyst notes to the group the various commercial initiatives, media spend, and in-store fundamentals. Each area impacts market share. Understanding what is happening by area and why it is happening is important in determining what actions to take.

After about 30 minutes, the business analysts have presented all the data and answered questions from the attendees. The next portion of the meeting is for the attendees to focus on the actions they need to take to shore up any deterioration in market share. The data reviewed by the attendees are real time and informative. The business analyst provides the necessary insight for the attendees regarding the implication for the data and helps the group understand not only *what* is happening to market share but also *why* market share is changing. The business sphere helps the group make well-informed business decisions.

New Challenge: Running Business in Real Time

P&G always wants to be a relevant and significant leader in the marketplace. To do so, it needs to stay ahead of the competition. One way to accomplish this is to focus on competencies that help to predict consumer behaviors. In the past, historical data were the key to analyzing business. Today, it is about predicting what will happen so P&G can develop the appropriate strategies. Tom Davenport, in his book *Competing on Analytics: The New Science of Winning*, addresses the subject of how data-driven analytics is used to develop competitive strategies and includes P&G as one of the leading companies leading the charge.

Business analytics is a core competency of P&G. In the late 1960s, P&G used analytics to address supply chain challenges. Over the years, the skill set improved and P&G invests heavily to ensure that this competency is leading edge. An MIT Sloan study in 2010 shows the ranking of investments in how companies use data and how they anticipate using data 24 months in the future. As you can see in Figure 17.6, historical trend analysis and standardized reporting, ranked one and two, move to the bottom of the list. Data visualization and simulation and scenario development move to the top of the list. Other categories, such as applying analytics to business processes, simulation, and modeling, move up in ranking.

This study confirms that P&G was absolutely on the right track by digitizing, visualizing, and simulating data in ways that help the business make well-informed decisions.

Passerini's thinking is heavily influenced by three factors. The first is his education in statistics and focus on precisely measuring business

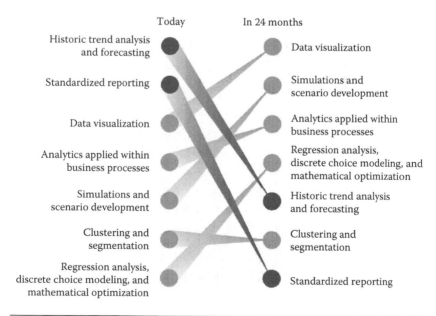

Figure 17.6 What Matters is Changing. (From Analytics: The New Path to Value, MIT Sloan Management Review, Research Report, Fall 2010, October 2010, http://sloanreview.mit.edu/reports/analytics-the-new-path-to-value/.)

value. Second is his relentless passion to help P&G business leaders make well-informed business decisions. The third is his strong belief in *outside-in* thinking. He listens and learns.

Passerini and his GBS organization lead the charge in developing partnerships with universities, academics, thought leaders, and companies to listen, learn, and apply new thinking inside of P&G.

Business Value Provided to P&G by Filippo Passerini

Since 2003, Passerini has brought new insights into how IT can be applied to create new business models and value for P&G. For Passerini, it is never about the technology, but it is about the business. Technology is an enabler. He never speaks about Cloud, million instructions per second (MIPS), or consolidation of data centers. Every word is business speak. His *what, why, how* model and the *digitize, visualize, simulate* strategy (both discussed in this chapter) are six words that have changed the course of how P&G runs the business.

To put this in tangible terms, think about the heat map visual discussed in the use-case scenario. It is not just a pretty picture of boxes and different shades of red and green. This technique is one of many P&G uses to visually display data in meaningful terms. The objective is to provide a simple, but elegant, method to hone in on a business issue. Guy Peri, a P&G GBS executive, talks about the business value of using visual analytics.

> Historically, we used to celebrate businesses or initiatives being "green" or spend time on businesses/initiatives that were red— when in comparison to the broader portfolio, those businesses/initiatives were relatively immaterial to the overall performance. With visual analytics, we are able to quickly focus business decision makers on the businesses issues that are material.[16]

Another measure of an executive's value is the business relationships developed with C-level peers. Melanie Healey is group president at P&G North America. She applauds Passerini for his contribution to the business.

> He (Passerini) has brought the business angle to the table. It's about growing the business and becoming more productive. It's been

transformational for the company. He's (Passerini) brought new technologies to collaborate better, placed IT leaders in the business and is an active partner in working with us to grow the business.[17]

Chapter Summary

This chapter focused on how P&G leverages technology strategically to innovate value. Filippo Passerini, president of GBS and CIO, is a business-focused executive who understands the P&G business and how to leverage technology to create new business models. The chapter focused on the following four key areas that provide the background and strategies employed by P&G to leverage the value of IT:

1. P&G history and today's competitive environment and challenges.
2. Filippo Passerini's career background and how the Business Services Group helps management make well-informed decisions.
3. An innovative—*what, why, how*—business model and *digitize, visualize, and simulate data strategy* to manage, display, and model data.
4. Use-case scenario toward the end of the chapter ties Passerini's initiatives into a great example of how an innovative CIO is changing the way P&G runs its business.

The key lessons learned from this chapter are as follows:

1. The primary objective of the CIO is to create business value for the enterprise.
2. IT should be used to help business leaders make well-informed decisions.
3. A single source of truth available in real time is an absolute imperative.
4. Present data meaningfully to help business leaders focus on analyzing root causes of business challenges.
5. Leverage outside-in thinking.
6. Passerini knows that good people are the magic ingredient, and his team members value his leadership and coaching. His first priority is to focus on creating business value

by leveraging technology to create new business models. Industry peers and thought leaders respect his contribution as an innovative business executive who leverages technology for strategic value. Passerini is consistent, results oriented, and strategically focused. When Passerini speaks, people listen and magic happens.

Citations

1. Filippo Passerini, Group President-Global Business Services, and CIO/ Phil Weinzimer Interview, December 5, 2012.
2. P&G Heritage and Archive Center; http://www.pg.com/Heritage; and P&G Heritage and Archive Center-Origin Story; http://www.pg.com/ Heritage/origin-story.php.
3. Lynda M. Applegate, Time for the Big Small Company. Mastering Information Management Series. *Financial Times*, March 1, 1999.
4. Filippo Passerini, Group President-Global Business Services, and CIO/ Phil Weinzimer Interview, February 1, 2013.
5. P&G Candidate Submission for Fisher-Hopper Prize for Lifetime Achievement in CIO Leadership, July 20, 2012 provided by P&G Public Relations.
6. How Procter & Gamble CEO Bob McDonald has placed digital technology, and CIO Filippo Passerini, at the heart of the business; Global Intelligence for the CIO; www.I-CIO.com; issue 13; April–June 2012; pp. 22–26; http://www.fujitsu.com/downloads/ABOUT/icio/I_Global_ Intelligence_for_the_CIO_-_Issue_-13.pdf.
7. P&G Ramps Up Standardization on SAP's ERP, Supply Chain and Finance Apps; Computerworld/UK; Leo King, Thursday October 30, 2008 http://www.cio.com/article/2432635/enterprise-software/p-g-ramps-up-standardization-on-sap-s-erp--supply-chain-and-finance-apps.html.
8. P&G's CIO Details Business-Savvy Predictive Decision Cockpit, Doug Henschen, informationweek.com September 11, 2012; http://www.informationweek.com/global-cio/interviews/pgs-cio-details-business-savvy-predictiv/240007069.
9. Why P&G CIO Is Quadrupling Analytics Expertise; *Information Week*; Chris Murphy, February 16, 2012.
9a. Keynote Interview of Filippo Passerini-P&G with Chris Murphy at the Information Week 500 Conference; September 10, 2012; St. Regis Monarch Beach in Dana Point, CA; http://www.informationweek.com/ iw500/2013/postconf.
10. Laurie Heltsley-Director Innovations & Strategic Programs/Phil Weinzimer Interview, August 23, 2013.

11. Data Wrangling: How Procter & Gamble Maximizes Business Analytics; Brian P. Watson | Posted January 30, 2012; http://www.cioinsight.com/c/a/Business-Intelligence/Data-Wrangling-How-PG-Maximizes-Business-Analytics-782673/.
12. P&G's Business Sphere Earns Silver in 2013 Edison Awards Competition; P&G Corporate Newsroom; Wednesday, May 1, 2013; http://news.pg.com/blog/2013-edison-awards/pgs-business-sphere-earns-silver-2013-edison-awards-competition.
13. Together at last: P&G, UC forging closer alliances to spark innovation; Cincinnati Business Courier; Dan Monk; November 6, 2012; http://www.bizjournals.com/cincinnati/print-edition/2012/11/16/together-at-last-pg-uc-forging.html?page=all.
14. Procter & Gamble Highlights its Digitization Strategy Plans to become the first company to totally digitize its business via modeling, simulation and PLM. Desktop Engineering; Jamie J. Gooch, In New Products, News, Simulate Published May 27, 2011; http://www.deskeng.com/articles/aabbcm.htm.
15. Analytics: The New Path to Value; MIT Sloan Management Review; Research Report; Fall 2010; http://sloanreview.mit.edu/reports/analytics-the-new-path-to-value/.
16. How P&G Presents Data to Decision-Makers; Tom Davenport; HBR Blog Network; April 4, 2013; http://blogs.hbr.org/2013/04/how-p-and-g-presents-data/.
17. Visionary Leaders: How Procter & Gamble Learned To Love YouTube: Forbes interview: Rich Karlgaard-Forbes Staff with Melanie Healey, Group President of North America and Filippo Passerini, Group President of Global Business Services and CIO; May 9, 2012; http://capitalisthistory.com/2012/05/07/procter-and-gamble-learned-to-love-youtube/.

18

How Five CIOs from Different Industries Leverage Technology Strategically to Innovate Value

Kids brains are wired differently than those of previous generations. They live in a world centered on technology.

Dave Finnegan
Chief Information Officer, Bear—Build-A-Bear

We have created sophisticated business intelligence to find the golden nuggets from each of our business, and leverage them across the Penske enterprise.

Stephen Pickett
Senior Vice President of Information Technology
and CIO of Penske Corporation

We help patients improve drug adherence through a set of services enabled by technology, which reduces costs and improves health outcomes.

Gary Wimberly
Senior Vice President and CIO of Express Scripts

We provide insurance companies options to analyze various driving characteristics (driving location, driving style, safety score on how you drive, how your brake, speed, angle of your turns, etc.), and develop rate plans that correlate vehicle and driver characteristics versus zip code or credit score. It's a new way to rate policies.

Perry Rotella
Group Executive at Supply Chain Risk Analytics and
Senior Vice President and CIO at Verisk Analytics

We leverage technology to make doctors' and patients' lives easier.

Harry Lukens
Senior Vice President and CIO of Lehigh Valley Health Network

In the previous two chapters, we learned how Procter & Gamble and FedEx are leveraging technology strategically to innovate value. These two global giants are recognized around the world for their competitive strengths and using technology in innovative ways. Other companies also leverage technology for strategic advantage. This chapter highlights five such companies and their CIOs.

Following is a summary of the chapter objective and key messages:

A. CHAPTER OBJECTIVE:
To share experiences by five CIOs who leverage technology strategically to innovate value.

B. KEY POINTS
1. Understand and anticipate customer needs (Build-A-Bear).
2. Look beyond initial competencies to create new business model (Express Scripts).
3. Leverage the best from each operating division and integrate across the entire enterprise (Penske).
4. Create a true unique differentiator for competitive advantage by leveraging technology (Verisk).
5. Listen and learn about the needs of the business, build a strong team, leverage technology strategically (Lehigh Valley Health Network [LVHN]).

C. EXAMPLES

1. Chief information and interactive officer, Build-A-Bear Workshop
2. Perry Rotella, group executive of Supply Chain Risk Analytics and senior vice president and CIO, Verisk Analytics
3. Gary Wimberly, senior vice president and CIO, Express Script
4. Stephen Pickett, senior vice president of Information Technology and CIO, Penske Corporation
5. Harry Lukens, senior vice president and CIO, Lehigh Valley Health Network

Dave Finnegan is Chief Information Officer at Build-A-Bear Workshop. He is leading the charge in transforming the physical experience of building a stuffed animal into an interactive digital experience. Perry Rotella, CIO of Verisk, leverages his insurance and risk experience in improving business services but also leading a new business unit as part of the company's growth plan. Gary Wimberly, CIO of Express Scripts, is creating a new business model where dispensing medications is secondary to providing subscriber services, leveraged by technology, which improves drug adherence and reduces health-care costs. Stephen Pickett, CIO—Penske Corporation, demonstrates that speed and agility can succeed in a conglomerate composed of different businesses that operate independently but still need leadership in how to leverage technology strategically. Harry Lukens, CIO of LVHN, leverages technology that not only improves health outcomes but also saves lives.

These five CIOs represent a cadre of forward thinking innovative executives who leverage technology strategically to create customer value, improve margins, and enhance shareholder wealth. Their stories are interesting and great examples to learn from.

Dave Finnegan, Chief Information and Interactive Officer, Build-A-Bear Workshop®

Today, companies leverage technology in innovative ways. One of these companies is Build-A-Bear Workshop. A leader in interactive retail, the company has transformed their stores by enhancing the interactive entertainment experience with newly designed digital elements. The story will inspire any entrepreneur to keep on plugging away at fulfilling dreams.

A Great Idea Is Born

On a sunny Saturday in 1996, Maxine Clark and her best friend, Katie, who was 10 years old at the time, were on their way to a toy store to shop for Beanie Babies. At the time, the Beanie Baby was a must-have toy for every child. Ty Warner, the manufacturer, could not maintain the demand. Parents waited for hours in lines outside stores for the chance to grab the limited supply of Beanie Babies. Parents pushed and shoved others as they raced to the shelves to grab the precious Beanie Baby for their beloved child.

When Maxine Clark and Katie arrived at the store, they could not find a single Beanie Baby that Katie did not already have. Katie picked one of the small toys up, turned to Maxine, and said, "These are so easy, we could make them." Katie meant that they could start a craft project, but Maxine heard a bigger idea. A year later, the first Build-A-Bear Workshop store opened in 1997 in the Saint Louis Galleria in Saint Louis, Missouri. Today, Build-A-Bear Workshop has 400 stores in 16 different countries, sold more than 120 million bears since it opened the first store, and has total revenues of over $380 million annually.[1]

The original business model was simple. The customer experience is interactive. Kids, mostly accompanied by adults, choose a bear or other animal to stuff, dress, and chose a personality and a name. When completed, the store associate packs the stuffed animal in a *Cub Condo* carrying case and provides a printed birth certificate for the stuffed animal.

The interactive process of making a stuffed animal has been transformed into a magical digital experience. Customers can *preshop* for their favorite stuffed animal on the company website using interactive digital menus prior to their visit. When in the store, they can personalize and customize their new furry friend with a combination of digital and real experiences designed to make their visit magical. When customers take their bears home, they can create interactive experience on the company's virtual world website bearville.com where they can bring their stuffed animal *to life*. In addition, they can visit buildabear.com to shop for stuffed animal accessories or schedule a birthday party at a local Build-A-Bear Workshop store.

The story of the evolution from a brick and mortar store to a cross-channel retailer is fascinating. Let me take you through the journey as explained by one of the cuddliest CIOs I know. He is Dave Finnegan. His title on the business card is "Chief Information and Interactive Bear."

Role of Technology in Building Brand: Dave Finnegan, CIO

Dave Finnegan joined Build-A-Bear Workshop in 1999 after a 1-year consulting assignment at the company. His information technology (IT) career started in the early 1990s working for Novell, then on to Interchange Technologies building fiber-optic networks and infrastructure for various clients. "One day in mid-1998, I was asked to talk to a company that had four retail stores that needed help with building a technology road map for the future. (ibid) The company was expanding and needed advice on what it would take to roll out stores, further develop their website, and implement an email system and a computer network to connect all stores together. When the seventh Build-A-Bear Workshop store was getting ready to open in Washington DC, Finnegan went to the store to put technology in place. He explains the experience.

> I remember going to the new store for the first time. I arrived at the local mall early in the morning. Because our store had not officially opened yet, the gate was pulled down over the store entrance. When I arrived, one of the store associates rolled up the gate to allow me to enter the store and then rolled it down until the 10 am store opening the next day. I remember we had just completed connecting the computers and all the systems were working, so I began helping the store employees unpack the stuffed animals and other merchandise. During the day, as we put products on the shelves, I noticed a group of children watching from outside the gate. As they watched us move merchandise throughout the store, their eyes widened as smiles formed on their faces. They couldn't wait to visit the store. I heard a few of the children ask their moms, 'When will the store open? I can't wait!' I saw the magic in their faces. They had never

seen a Build-A-Bear Workshop store before and they were so excited to come in to explore.

The next morning, when we cut the ribbon and officially opened up the store for the first time, the kids ran in, smiling and laughing, trailed by their moms, both eager to build their very own furry friend. At that moment, I knew there was something special about Build-A-Bear Workshop. I could see it in our guests' faces, I could see it in the shared experience these kids had with their moms. I could see it in the energy they had. It was magic. I had to be part of this team. (ibid)

Finnegan officially joined Build-A-Bear Workshop to lead the technology team in December 1999. It was about the time that the Internet was becoming a part of daily life, used to communicate, play, socialize, learn, shop, and browse information. It was fast becoming a natural extension of a child's life as a seamless blend between digital and real interactions. Over the years, *digital play* for kids has continued to develop. Finnegan explains the transformation as follows:

When we first started Build-A-Bear Workshop in 1997, if you asked a child what they wanted for their birthday, kids would say very traditional play items. Things like, Barbie or Bratz dolls for girls. Boys would ask for things like GI Joe or a board games. Today, sixteen years later, when you ask a child what they want for their birthday, their answer: iPhone, iPad, Tablet, Cell phone, Interactive Game Boy, Mario, Xbox, Playstation, video games. Many things on their wish list are either digital or digitally connected. This is the most digitally connected generation in the history of our planet. In fact, some studies support the notion that the wiring inside a child's brains may be different from the prior generation because of their instant understanding of technology, immediate access to information to solve problems and develop solutions. I've seen two-year old toddlers, who haven't yet developed language skills who can easily navigate an iPad. It's a totally different world. They get it naturally. An understanding of technology is part of this generations DNA. And for brands that matter to kids, it has to be part of our DNA, too. (ibid)

The Changing Marketplace

The Build-A-Bear Workshop executive team recognized this emerging digital play pattern for kids. In the spring of 2010, they decided that although kids love the existing interactive experience, they needed to develop a digitally enhanced store experience. "We often said, it's not about the technology, it's about the experience so this was not an exercise to simply 'sprinkle technology' into our stores. It was about building meaningful experiences that were a blend of high touch retail with high tech. We had a vision for what the experience could be and we wanted to do this quickly." Finnegan said added, "We wanted to accomplish this using the agility and flexibility of a startup. I organized a meeting with the digital team to start thinking about defining the experience we want for our customers. We developed an interesting process we called 'smile mapping.'" (ibid) Finnegan took the digital team to the Build-A-Bear Workshop store in the Mall of America in Minneapolis, Minnesota. The objective was to create a *smile map*. He wanted to identify the points in the Build-A-Bear Workshop store experience where guests had an *emotional connection* with the brand. Each digital team member was equipped with a clipboard and a map of the store. They just stepped back and watched. Every time a child smiled during the bear-making process, the team member would place a smiley face sticker next to the activity. By the day's end, each member of the team had a map filled with stickers showing where guests were smiling and having fun in the store. The team met that evening to answer two questions based on the smile map.

1. In the place where we see the most smiles, can we *enhance* those experiences with digital to increase the magic in our store?
2. In the place where we see the fewest smiles on the map, are there any digital experiences we could *add* that would increase the magic in our store?

The team brainstormed for a few hours, nibbling on pizza, and distilled down the original vision to 10 ideas. "Our initial vision was taking shape and was tightly connected with our guest experience," Finnegan said. Finnegan thought the session was interesting and was excited to take the next step. "When you talk about innovation, it's often difficult to really understand the concept unless you can actually experience it."

Finnegan had a plan. He wanted to build a prototype of the Build-A-Bear Workshop newly imagined store so the team could actually experience each element and see its potential. The downside of building a new prototype store is that it can be costly and take time. They came up with an idea that helped propel the innovation forward and for a fraction of the cost. "We decided to create a short five minute video that would show the 'store of the future' to management and create that 'aha' moment where they could emotionally connect to the ideas by actually processing the idea visually." (ibid)

So instead of spending months and months building a prototype store, they spent the next several weeks producing a 5-minute video.

> The video was not simply showing the technology ideas; it was capturing the emotional connection of our brand for kids who were building a bear and interacting with the new digital experiences inside our store. We used green screen technology in the store to place the digital experiences in the store and then in post-production we added the digital animation. The value was we showed the technology in the context of the store. How guests would interact with it, how it would make an emotional connection and how it would fit into the flow of our existing store. We showed how it would enhance the Build-A-Bear Workshop magic. (ibid)

Using what they learned from the video, they narrowed down the 10 ideas to the top five and rapidly began the prototyping process. The team went to the local hardware store and bought materials to create the physical framework that would prototype each store fixture. They placed the digital interactive screens running prototype software into the *mock* fixtures. Then the team set up the entire store in a meeting room that served as their temporary model store at corporate headquarters. Rapidly prototyping these mock fixtures allowed the team to get proper dimensions and flow before they built the final fixtures. It was time to share these prototypes to their guests to ensure they were on track and to help evolve the ideas to the next level (Figure 18.1).

The strategic planning and guest experience team at Build-A-Bear Workshop created a *Cub Advisory Board*, which includes 15–20 children ranging in age from 5 to 11 years old. "Every two weeks a group of Cub Advisors visited the newly imagined store at corporate headquarters and interacted with the ideas the team

Figure 18.1   Cub Advisory Board.

were creating." Finnegan said of the process, "The kids were great. We outfitted each Cub Advisor with a white lab coat and a little security badge that said 'VIB Very Important Bear.' They loved it. We knew we had something magical. When lab door opened, the kids looked in for the first time and gasped. A number of them said 'wow!', and ran in. It was like a holiday morning moment."[2]

An Innovative Idea Is Commercialized

In September of 2012, Build-A-Bear Workshop opened its first newly imagined store in St. Louis at West County Center. Six stores converted in 2012, and the company expects to operate approximately 30 locations in this new store format by the end of 2013.

Build-A-Bear Workshop considers itself a leader in *interactive entertainment retailing*.[4] The half entertainment and half theme park store added digitally enabled interactions. It is fascinating to watch. At the time of this writing, there are five major digital interactive stations that guests use to make their stuffed animals.

Figure 18.2   Build-A-Bear Workshop Interactive Storefront.

When guests enter a Build-A-Bear Workshop store, an *interactive storefront* enables them to view the latest product offerings and play games using an interactive touch screen that uses Microsoft Kinect (Figure 18.2).

As they make their stuffed animal, the *Love Me* station enables guests to add special personality attributes (brave, silly, and smart), displayed as emoticons on an interactive table, to their furry friend's red satin heart (Figure 18.3).

As guests progress along the stuffed animal making process, they can add high-quality sounds to stuffed animals at the *Hear Me* station. The guest uses an interactive touch screen to select popular songs, or they can chose from an assortment of sounds, to add to their stuffed animal. The guest can also personalize the sound using his or her own voice recorded onto a chip (Figure 18.4).

The heart is added during a magical *heart ceremony* at the Stuff Me station where a guest stuffs his or her own bear with the assistance of a bear builder. One of the cutest workstations is the *Fluff Me* station where guests interact with a digital bathtub (Figure 18.5).

When the stuffed animal is complete, the guest moves to the *Name Me* stations, where guests can peek into their furry friend to see all of

(a)   (b)

Figure 18.3   Build-A-Bear Workshop—(a) Love Me Station and (b) Girl Playing at Love Me Station.

Figure 18.4   Build-A-Bear Workshop—Hear Me Station.

Figure 18.5   Build-A-Bear Workshop—Fluff Me Station.

Figure 18.6   Build-A-Bear Workshop—*You've Earned Friendship* Station.

the cool things inside and generate a one-of-a-kind birth certificate (Figure 18.6).[3]

Another innovative use of technology is monitoring guest interactions at each digital workstation. As a guest moves through each experience in the store, the store customizes the next experience based on what the guest has already shared. The result is a highly personalized experience that connects with each guest.

Extending the In-Store Experience through Imagination

Whether it's a guest who browses the latest collection of furry friends online or mobile, or the personalized in-store experience, or their apps and online virtual world bearville.com, Build-A-Bear Workshop executives are very careful to ensure that their brand is marketed properly and leveraged across their customer base. The objective is to provide an imaginative, fun, and personalized brand experience. We all know that children have wonderful imaginations and love to explore and create. It is fun.

What makes Build-A-Bear Workshop unique is that the process of making the stuffed animal is more of a game than a physical activity. It is as if the guest is going to an amusement park and wanting to experience all the cool rides. The experience is the value. The stuffed animal is the reward. The interesting part about the newly imagined store is that the experience is *Apple simple*. The technology is intuitive. The guests do not have to figure out how it works. It just does.

The Age of Mobile

Every adult who is over the age of 50 with children remember how kids always played with a toy phone. Well, today, it is not a toy phone anymore. Many kids today have a smartphone. The age of mobility is upon us, and business people recognize that this is an area of market opportunity. Build-A-Bear Workshop is no exception. In July 2013, Build-A-Bear Workshop launched a Bear Valley application for iPhone, iPad, and iPod touch. If your child has access to a mobile device, he or she can make his or her own furry friends as he or she visits and explores Bear Valley and engages in lots of fun activities. Your child can take their bears shopping, enjoy a day at the spa, visit Paw Print Park, and enjoy slides, swings, and a merry-go-round. There is even an outdoor theater where bears perform music and fashion shows. If your child is into farming, he can grow crops, milk cows, and gather eggs. Young guests can visit Bearemy's Bakery and prepare delicious cakes and cookies.[4]

Value of Leveraging Technology Strategically

For Finnegan, the key to succeeding with the newly imagined store concept was to stay focused on the ultimate goal, that is, to deliver a magical guest experience. Finnegan wanted to make sure that the team did not fall into the trap commonly referred to a *hammer looking for a nail*. Some organizations find some really cool technology (hammer) and look for a place to apply it, regardless of the desired outcome (nail). This was not the case for Build-A-Bear Workshop. The objective was to identify the desired guest experience and then find the appropriate technology. Finnegan said, "We would literally walk through the experience from the guests' perspective and change the prototype based upon what we learned from putting it in front of our teams and guest." (ibid)

Finnegan is an innovator first, a businessperson second, and a technologist third. He has helped take the concept of a physical in-store experience and transform it into an interactive digital theme park where children can explore and learn by making a stuffed animal and extending the experience on the web or smartphone. And this approach is paying off. This newly imagined store concept is driving a double-digit same store growth, and millions of guests each year interact with Build-A-Bear Workshop digitally. Build-A-Bear Workshop is a great example of a company who knows how to successfully leverage technology to innovate value.

Example

My 6-year-old granddaughter, Madeline, is very fond of Build-A-Bear. She has six of their stuffed animals. When I completed writing this chapter segment on Build-A-Bear workshop, I thought it would be appropriate to take my granddaughter to Build-A-Bear. On a brisk Monday morning, 2 days before Christmas, my wife, Lynn, and I picked up my daughter Danielle and her two children, Madeline (6 years old) and Maxwell (10 years old), and Max's friend, Tyler (10 years old), for a trip to the local Build-A-Bear Workshop at the Lehigh Valley Mall in Allentown, Pennsylvania.

I wanted this experience to be very special for the kids so I called the store a week earlier and spoke to Tara, the store manager, to advise her of our forthcoming trip. When we arrived, the two store assistant managers, Camille and Karen, greeted us warmly. For the next 2 hours, Camille and Karen helped each of the kids through the exciting animal stuffing experience.

The next 2 hours were filled with fun, laughter, and joy as the kids experienced the animal stuffing process. Madeline chose a doll, named her Rapunzel, and dressed her as a princess. Maxwell chose Frosty the Snowman, named him Frosty, and dressed him as baseball player, complete with glove, bat, and ball. Tyler, Maxwell's friend, chose Monkey, named him T-Chicken, and also dressed him with a bat, glove, and ball. Maxwell and Tyler are best friends and avid baseball players, so the wardrobe they chose for their stuffed animals was very appropriate.

When the kids completed dressing their stuffed animals, I captured the experience in the following photo. Karen and Camille, the assistant managers, are in the back row. In the front row are Tyler with T-Chicken, Madeline with Rapunzel, and Maxwell with Frosty. Needless to say, when we left the store, all three children were smiling and prancing as we walked through the mall (Figure 18.7).

Figure 18.7   Build-A-Bear Workshop Visit.

Perry Rotella, Group Executive of Supply Chain Risk Analytics
and Senior Vice President and CIO, Verisk Analytics

Companies have been analyzing data for many years in their quest of predicting future outcomes. In the 1970s, when I was materials manager for a pharmaceutical company, my team of inventory analysts projected inventory replenishment based upon historical data. To determine the amount of stainless steel tubing we would purchase for products using this material, we would look at the previous year demand for the finished products, the past 3 months data, and then projected the future 6-month need. Today, it is not about historical data, it's about predicting future buying behavior based on analysis of customer habits, market dynamics, and competitive markets. The other day, I was browsing the Redbox website to look for a movie our family could watch in the evening. During the 2 minutes I was viewing the possible choices, I received a phone call from a client asking me to open up the e-mail he just sent so we could discuss the contents. When I opened my e-mail, I saw the client's e-mail but also saw an incoming e-mail notification from Redbox. The tag line on the email read, "Ready to check out? Come back and reserve it before someone else gets it!" In a matter of 2 minutes, Redbox knew I was looking for movies but had not made a selection yet. So they sent me an e-mail reminder.

Data analytics has progressed dramatically in use to help business make improve decisions. The gaming industry uses data analytics to determine customer satisfaction. Caesars Palace does not want customers walking out the door of their casinos thinking about the bad experience. Caesars monitors all the gaming machines, and if it see a person loosing and the individual has a history of visiting the casino, they want to "…intercept them before they go, saying, 'Here is a free meal at the buffet; maybe when you come back things will be better.'—In such cases, the likelihood that they return is 40% (as opposed to 20%)."[5]

Today, a new profession of data scientists is emerging, and companies are hiring these professionals to help mine data that computers and software applications use to reduce risk, predict customer behavior, and develop scenarios to improve customer experiences. One of the industries that use data analytics pervasively is the insurance industry. Companies in this industry provide insurance for a variety of events: life insurance, health insurance, auto insurance, property insurance, etc. These companies want to minimize risk by understanding the probability of catastrophic events and use the data to price its products and services. In a free economic society, when there is a need, someone comes up with a product or service to fill the need. In this case, Verisk Analytics is such a company.

Verisk Background

Verisk Analytics is a $1.5 billion provider of information about risk to professionals in insurance, health care, mortgage, government, and risk management. Headquartered in Jersey City, New Jersey, with approximately 7000 employees, Verisk uses advanced technologies to collect and analyze billions of records and draws on vast industry expertise and unique proprietary data sets to provide predictive analytics and decision support solutions in fraud prevention, actuarial science, insurance coverage, fire protection, catastrophe and weather risk, data management, and many other fields. In the United States and around the world, Verisk Analytics helps customers protect people, property, and financial assets.[6]

Verisk was created in the 1970s by the Property and Casualty industry as a data utility setup to manage state regulatory reporting for insurance companies across the United States. Insurance companies used Verisk to submit state-required insurance filings about their insurance products. Verisk grew to develop a standard set of loss costs, forms, and policy language that could be used by all insurance companies. As part of their data collection, from each insurance company, Verisk was able to establish a robust database of information on claims, losses, costs, etc. Over time, Verisk created a set of benchmark product offerings using this data and sell it to insurance companies. This information was valuable to insurance companies in developing rate filings for their products. These product offerings drove the growth of Verisk.

The company expanded its decision analytics capability to offer its products and services to a number of different industries to help risk-bearing businesses understand and manage their risk. These include property/casualty insurance, financial services, health care, government, and human resources. Verisk's offerings can be categorized into two major reporting segments—risk assessment and decision analytics. The risk assessment business serves customers in the property/casualty industry by helping to define, measure, and manage risk. The decision analytics business serves customers in a variety of industries with tools that help them make informed decisions about managing their assets and the associate risk in predicting future losses, selecting and pricing risk, detecting and preventing fraud, and quantifying losses that have already happened.

In 2009, Verisk management realized that as an information-rich company, it needed a CIO who was business focused and knew the insurance industry and how decision analytics can be used to manage risk. Verisk management found their ideal candidate.

Perry Rotella, A Business-Focused CIO

Perry Rotella graduated from the University of Pennsylvania and began his career at American Management Systems, a full service management consulting company based in Arlington, Virginia, where he worked in AMS's Telecom and Health Care practice. He moved to New Jersey to join AMS's Insurance Technology Group and soon after was appointed Chief Technology Officer (CTO). American International Group, Inc. (AIG) came knocking on the door to offer Rotella an opportunity in the corporate technology office managing emerging technologies. Within a year, Rotella was promoted to global CTO, which quickly led to his role as CIO of their property and casualty business. In 2006, Rotella moved on to join Moody's as their first corporate CIO. Moody's provides unique tools and best practices for providing credit ratings and research and risk analysis and measuring and managing risk through expertise and experiences in credit analysis, economic research, and financial risk management.[7]

At Moody's, Rotella leveraged his experience to grow his competency in risk analytics. Rotella developed a reputation in the industry and as a savvy IT executive that is business focused and understands how to leverage technology into products and services for addressing potential risk scenarios. In 2009, Verisk came knocking and offered Rotella the CIO role.

One of the top items on Rotella's to-do list when he took on the CIO role was to assess the value of the IT organization.

He concluded that business units didn't truly understand the business value of IT services, especially when the allocation method for distributing IT costs to the business units was a complex black box with little transparency. One of his first orders of business was to develop a service portfolio, assess the value for each service, begin a program to improve service delivery, and implement a service costing system solution from Apptio to measure the cost of each service and provide transparency to communicate the value of services to the business. (See Chapter 6, Improving the Business Value of IT Services, where measuring service delivery is discussed in great detail.) In parallel with this activity, Rotella realized that IT personnel involved in service delivery needed to change their way of thinking. They need to recognize that they are managing a technology business rather than just managing hardware and the technical aspects of the service. During a meeting with IT personnel involved in each of the services, Rotella said the following:

> I want you to think differently. You are managing a business; a set of services that help the business conduct their daily activities that provide value to customers. To the storage team, you are not managing storage technology, you are responsible for a storage business. Your customers have different needs and will pay different rates depending on those needs. Some systems require high speed tier 1 storage with hot backups while others can survive on lower cost solutions with 2 day recovery times in the case of a disaster. I want you to think in terms of the actual services you provide, the cost of the services, the different service options and how business units are using these services to support their customers. There is a cost of the hardware, software, people, physical space, etc. These are all the components of providing various services to the business. If you think of yourselves as managing a business, you'll be more focused on the value it provides your customer. (ibid)

Leveraging the Credibility and Trust of the Business to Improve Margin

Over time, the delivery of services improved, which helped build credibility for Rotella and his IT team. With a foundation of improved service delivery underway, Rotella turned to his next initiative to help the business improve margin. His strategy was simple. He looked at the infrastructure costs and realizing that by consolidating the data centers, the company could derive significant savings that would improve operating profit, which is an important metric for a publicly traded company. Rotella needed to convince the business unit heads that instead of having data centers physically located near each of the business units, it would be more economical to consolidate them into one central data center. Rotella was concerned about selling this to the business unit leaders. "No one likes to lose control and have the supporting infrastructure that runs their business move from down the hall to some other location. So I needed to develop a communication strategy that would result in the business unit leaders to adopt a move to a centralized infrastructure." (ibid) Rotella put on his thinking cap and came up with a simple but effective strategy. He needed to communicate the cost savings in business terms that would be compelling and outweigh the business unit leaders' concerns about losing the physical control of the infrastructure. The way he did it was simple. He presented his case to the business leaders highlighting the following key facts (actual numbers have been omitted to maintain confidentiality):

- Two centralized data centers would result in "x" dollars of additional cash flow to the business.
- The resultant cash flow savings would improve margin by "y" percent.
- The improved net profits would result in an increased EPS of "z."
- The increased EPS could drive the stock price to a range of "a–b" dollars *based on historical trading multiples.*
- To achieve the same increase in margin and share price would require each of the business unit leaders to increase sales by "x" percent.

Rotella's closing message sold the plan. "He told his colleagues that the increase in share price would benefit each of them. The risk for successfully consolidating data centers was low. However, if each of the business units had to increase sales and margin, the risk would be greater." To seal the deal, Rotella had to successfully implement a pilot to show the business unit leaders that he could achieve the cost savings. Once he did that, the business leaders were on board, and

Rotella's plan was implemented. Two years into the data center consolidation effort, Rotella's team had achieved the goals identified in the original business case.

Leveraging Technologies to Develop New Business Model

Rotella had the trust and confidence in the business. As part of Verisk's continued expansion, management recognized that the competency in risk assessment and decision analytics not only supported the various vertical markets they service but could also support horizontal processes across all industries. One of these areas is supply chain. Companies all around the globe are expanding their supplier and distributor networks as well as forming strategic relationships that form a stronger bond and trust between suppliers and the companies they serve. Manufacturing and distribution companies have a supply chain. The movement of raw materials and semifinished as well as finished goods across various locations represents risk for manufacturers, retailers, transportation companies, and others. Verisk's competency in measuring risk and using decision analytics to assist companies in understanding the potential risks across their supply chain presents a business opportunity to expand their offerings.

Verisk started a supply chain offering to help companies to manage supply chain risk and compliance. To accelerate the growth of the business, management turned to Rotella, in June 2013, to lead the business unit, in addition to his role as CIO. Growing a new business line takes a lot of focus and effort, and Rotella realized that he needed to devote a lot of effort to the supply chain business while still maintaining the level of performance and service provided by the IT organization. Rotella was fortunate to have a high-performing IT leadership team.

> Two of my IT executives, Eric and Mike, were well positioned to take on more leadership responsibility for the several hundred IT personnel. I reorganized IT into two distinct areas, each headed by one of the two executives I promoted into IT leadership roles. Eric managed the day-to-day technology operations. Mike managed the strategic part of IT in indentifying emerging technologies and potential areas where those technologies can leverage business growth. The reorganization enabled me to spend 80 percent of my time on the supply chain business and 20 percent on IT strategy." (ibid)

Rotella is a good fit for leading the supply chain business unit. Rotella understands the Verisk business model and potential opportunity. "Our Heritage is in property and casualty. We have selectively moved into new markets leveraging our risk and analytics competencies. We understand where risk could occur across different industries." (ibid) Verisk has grown both organically and through acquisition. They acquired and assimilated several companies to build a healthcare analytics business combining clinical and analytical expertise with advanced technology to help payers, employers, and providers solve complex problems with measurable results. Verisk also acquired financial services companies that assist banks, credit card companies, and mortgage companies manage risk. In 2012, Verisk entered the supply chain service space because it leverages their core competencies. The risks associated with supply chain have grown enormously. With just in time inventory strategies, companies expose themselves to enormous risk when there is any disruption to inventory replenishment. Companies are also shedding manufacturing processes to vendors so they can focus on their core business. As a result, their vendor partnerships and supply chains are growing. Rotella describes it as follows. "There has been a huge push in the last 10–15 years to optimize the supply chain. Disruptions to the supply chain have tremendous impacts to the business. In today's environment, you cannot have a perfectly optimized supply chain. At Verisk, we address this using an adjusted supply chain optimization model. When you have a storm bearing down on the port of Hong Kong, your perfect supply chain is now your perfect storm." (ibid) The Verisk supply chain solutions help clients manage risk across their supply chain through the following three solution offerings:

- *Chemical, regulatory, and compliance services*: Verisk's 3E Company is a global provider of services that help you comply with government-mandated environmental health and safety (EH&S) requirements for hazardous chemicals and other products.
- *Retail and crime analytics*: Verisk provides point of sale leakage solutions for retailers as well as a national database and information-sharing system designed to prevent cargo theft and increase recovery.

- *Verisk climate* provides software, data, and analytics for enterprise climate risk management. The organization's solutions help corporations improve resilience and profitability while enhancing service to their customers.

Verisk has grown their supply chain business through acquisition and cross-selling. Verisk acquired an EH&S company in 2010 to help clients manage supply chain risk due to potential noncompliance of government and industry regulations. In 2012, Verisk acquired a company that focuses on loss prevention for retailers. Cross-leveraging competencies occur through leveraging disaster-forecasting models that apply not only to insurance companies but also to manufacturing companies. Rotella leadership is paying off. The business is growing. "We've established a beachhead and we want to continue growing the business," *says Rotella*. (ibid) When asked why the executive leadership and the board chose Rotella to lead the supply chain business unit, he said, " I believe I've demonstrated that IT is a business and my leadership has helped improve the value of IT to the business." (ibid) When asked about how he helps clients understand the need to address potential risk, Rotella quotes Mike Tyson. "Everyone has a plan until you get punched in the face!" (ibid) Rotella says, it always gets a laugh, but more importantly, it gets people thinking about addressing the potential risk in a proactive manner.

Gary Wimberly, Senior Vice President and CIO, Express Scripts

Gary Wimberly's career plan included the following critical success factors. Study hard, learn from working for companies in different industries, and develop a set of technical and business skills to become a leader within a large organization where one could leverage technology innovation to affect positive change on a large scale and improve lives. He succeeded. Wimberly is the senior vice president and CIO for Express Scripts, the nation's largest pharmacy benefit management corporation, serving 100 million Americans. He is responsible for overall IT. Under his leadership, IT and business teams develop innovative solutions to make the use of prescription medications safer and more affordable and to help improve the health outcomes of patients who subscribe to Express Scripts services through their employer, union, or health plan provider. Express Scripts transformed from a pharmacy fulfillment service into a preventative health-care provider, when a group of health-care advocates began applying the rigors of scientific research to the pharmacy benefit. It offers a variety of services to improve drug adherence, optimize drug expenses, and prevent potential adverse drug interaction, by leveraging technologies in innovative ways.

Express Scripts Overview

Express Scripts is one of the largest pharmacy benefit management organizations in the United States. It has grown from its initial offering in 1992 into a $93 billion company in 2012, through strategic acquisitions, including Wellpoint's NextRx subsidiaries in 2010 and Medco Health Solutions, Inc., in 2012. During this growth period, Express Scripts faced two major challenges. The first was to support the expanded customer base resulting from the acquisitions and maintain operational efficiency of the IT infrastructure. The second was the changing business landscape. Health-care providers recognized they needed to move from a fulfillment model, provider of health services (medical, nursing, prescription refills, etc.), to a model that would affect health outcomes as well as reduce health-care costs. Each challenge required IT organizations to work hand in hand with business unit teams and collaborate on potential solutions. This is where Gary and his business-focused IT team rose up to the challenge and enabled Express Scripts to overcome each challenge and become a leading supplier of pharmacy benefit services to more than a 100 million Americans.

Gary Wimberly, a Strategic Thinker and Business Focused CIO

Gary Wimberly graduated as part of the first computer science class at the University of Missouri 1983. Wimberly knew to succeed in the business world required diverse business experiences that could broaden his skill set and provide opportunities to lead. Through college and his first years as a postgraduate student, Wimberly worked for a small grocery chain developing systems to manage inventory, back office, accounting, and sales. This experience taught him accountability, responsibility, and the importance of quality. "Working in a small company is hard work. You wear many hats, but the business experience is invaluable."[8] In 1985, he moved to an IBM business partner, Geophysical Survey Systems, Inc. (GSSI), where he focused on managing accounts and implementing Enterprise Resource Planning (ERP) systems. At GSSI, he could leverage and apply his earlier experiences to larger businesses. From 1987 to 1995, Wimberly oversaw corporate information systems for Bairnco, a multinational company with subsidiaries operating in two business segments: engineered materials and components and replacement products and services. During his time at GSSI and Bairnco, Wimberly honed his interpersonal skills, spending time with clients, understanding and learning the market needs, and developing an executive presence. In 1995, Wimberly joined E&Y (Ernst and Young), at the time, one of the big five consulting firms, where, as part of their consumer package goods vertical, he focused on implementing Oracle solutions for a number of large clients. When E&Y first contacted him, Wimberly described it as "a case of preparedness meeting opportunity." (ibid) It was the right time in his career to move to a fast-paced organization and put his skills to the test. His experiences at E&Y and at his next assignment—director of logistics systems at Tyco/Mallinckrodt from 1999 to 2004—taught him speed, agility, and integration: how to deliver high quality in a fast-paced environment. In 2004, opportunity knocked with an offer from Express Scripts. They were looking for an executive to lead the supply chain systems group. It was a perfect fit for Wimberly. During the following few years, Wimberly expanded his role with responsibility for corporate systems, payroll, data warehouse, patient systems, and home delivery applications. In 2007, Wimberly was appointed CIO.

Rising Up to the Challenge

Any CIO who has experienced an expanded customer base resulting from acquisitions, while at the same time ensuring that there are no disruptions to the base operating systems that support business needs, will tell you it is a challenge. This challenge is further compounded when the IT organization is also involved in leveraging technology in innovative ways to create new value-based solutions for the customer base. The latter requires a lot of brainpower and the talent and skills of business-focused IT personnel. Wimberly describes this challenge.

> We need to do the traditional technical jobs that IT departments have done for years—the so-called "keeping the lights on." In this category of work, we are expected to reduce costs to operate base functions each year. Frankly, it's a constant struggle to do more for the same budget or less. The bigger challenge and opportunity is that we are increasingly a part of the innovation puzzle at Express Scripts. So much of what we do, from an innovation perspective, has IT at its core, whether it is with our virtual pharmacy or data analytics teams.[9]

Wimberly's solution was to develop strategic partnerships with key vendors, who had a strong competency in operational support. These strategy-enabled, business-focused IT teams develop innovative solutions to improve health outcomes and reduce health-care costs for its customers.

Affecting Health Outcomes and Health-Care Costs

Wimberly focuses on identifying opportunities to leverage technology strategically. One area is to improve health outcomes and reduce health-care costs. One of the major challenges we face as a society is the growing cost of health care. Express Scripts estimates that there is "more than $400 billion in pharmacy-related waste every year due to poor health decisions."[10] These poor health decisions come in three general areas:

1. *Drug choices*: People unknowingly choose more expensive medications, not realizing that they may be less effective.
2. *Pharmacy choices*: Physicians who are constantly trying to see as many patients as possible may sometimes fail to catch potential drug interactions based upon patient medicine treatment history.
3. *Health choices*: Patients sometimes fail to take prescribed medicines, which impacts their health and creates medical issues.

To address this major problem, Express Scripts utilizes Health Decision Science™ as an approach to identify the reasons people

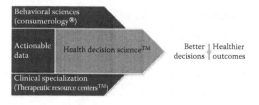

Figure 18.8 Health Decision Science. (ibid)

make medical decisions and embrace behaviors that negatively impact their health with the ultimate effect of increasing health-care costs (Figure 18.8).

1. *Behavioral science*: Through the advanced application of the behavioral sciences to health care, Express Scripts seeks to understand who is most at risk for making a bad health decision and why, so the company can implement a customized intervention.

   For example: The Express Scripts *ScreenRx®* solution is the industry's first medication adherence solution that predicts when a patient will not take his or her medication as prescribed and proactively provides tailored interventions to increase a patient's adherence with their therapy. The United States wasted $317.4 billion last year treating unnecessary medical complications that could have been avoided if patients had taken their medications as prescribed, that is, more money than the country spent treating diabetes, heart disease, and cancer combined. The ScreenRx predictive modeling tool considers more than 400 known variables to identify who is most likely to stop taking their medications with up to 98% accuracy.

2. *Actionable data*: Serving more than 100 million Americans, Express Scripts manages an unprecedented amount of data—15 petabytes and counting. A petabyte is a term used to measure the quantity of data. One petabyte of data is the equivalent of 60,000 movies. For those of you who enjoy listening to music, a petabyte of MP3 coded songs would take 2000 years to play. A petabye is a lot of data. The company processes more than 1.4 billion prescriptions

a year and warehouses more than 100 million life years of integrated medical and pharmacy claims. How does Express Scripts use this data? Every time a prescription is entered into the Express Scripts network, sophisticated IT solutions check for 3200 drug rules, including potential drug interactions, overdosing, and therapy duplication. At the same time, the systems check 2203 medical rules to identify if any patient drugs in their profile taken together could create potential life-threatening situations (also referred to as potential contraindications). These comparisons occur every 22 milliseconds, a thousandth of 1 second.[4]

3. *Clinical specialization*: Express Scripts has 15 Therapeutic Resource Centers[SM] (TRCs). Each TRC pharmacy is dedicated to one of 15 different therapeutic specialties, such as cancer, diabetes, and heart disease. The TRCs are staffed by more than 1500 specialist pharmacists and nurses focused on helping patients with needs in their specialty, and their doctors make better health decisions for safer, more effective, and more affordable treatment. Specialist pharmacists' condition-specific training and experience provide them with a deep understanding of treatment of disease in their specialty; quickly identify obscure, yet critical, concerns; and empower them to address important questions to physicians that otherwise may not have been asked. An example of the unique value these TRCs provide is when during a call with a patient, an Express Scripts pulmonary specialist pharmacist was reviewing the patient's pharmacy claims and discovered that the patient was not refilling her controller medication—a therapy asthma patients need to use daily to prevent the onset of asthma symptoms—as often as she should. The pharmacists asked her why and learned that the patient misunderstood that her controller medication prevented asthma attacks and that she needs to take it every day (not just when she was experiencing asthma symptoms). The pharmacist explained the importance of using this medication every day and the possible side effects of nonadherence. The patient confirmed her understanding and was thankful for the information. She agreed to take

A.P., a 64-year-old woman with a recent blood clot, was prescribed *Prempro®*, a combined estrogen-progestin hormone-replacement therapy.

Medical history	Potential risk	Program action	Patient outcome
Taking Prempro for menopausal symptoms Has had deep vein thrombosis or blood clots	Serious cardiovascular events including heart attack and stroke	RationalMed identified the risk Alert was sent to the prescriber	Prempro was discontinued

The prescriber responded by expressing gratitude for the RationalMed safety alert:

I believe these were "Lifesaving" to my patients. Thx

("I believe these were "Lifesaving" to my patients. Thanks.")
-Nurse

Figure 18.9   RationalMed Intervention Case Study.

the medications as prescribed, and the specialist pharmacist followed up with the patient to monitor the correct use of the medications.

As a result of applying Health Decision Science to its customer base, Express Scripts can predict potential negative health outcomes. The data resulting from this science become actionable and provide the following proactive solutions that improve health outcomes and reduce health-care costs.

RationalMed®: This Express Scripts solution helps prevent costly hospitalizations by providing timely alerts to physicians about potential safety risks due to adverse drug events, coordination of care issues, and omission of essential care. RationalMed integrates data from medical claims, pharmacy claims, and lab data to generate these alerts (Figure 18.9).

> A physician prescribed estrogen hormone replacement therapy for a 64-year old patient, unaware that another doctor was treating her for a blood clot. Since estrogens can increase the risk of stroke and heart attack in patients with blood clots, RationalMed alerted the physician. He quickly changed the patient's therapy and later sent a thank-you note that called the alert "lifesaving."[11]

Express*Alliance*®: Patients with chronic and complex conditions often have multiple players on their care team—pharmacists, physicians, case managers, caregivers, nurses, and more. With so many people involved, the chances of an error or omission of care due to miscommunication are significant. With Express*Alliance*, Express Scripts data resources give every member of a patient's health-care team real-time access to the patient's health-care information. Case managers for a heart failure patient, for example, are able to view the patient's prescription history, as well as potential gaps in care, such as nonadherence or the omission of critical drug therapy. This allows case managers to address potential issues before they lead to hospital readmission. Payers and health-care professionals can focus on one patient at a time through a detailed patient profile, including claims history, eligibility, and clinical and savings opportunities or review cases across their population to allow nurses and case managers to prioritize patients based on their condition or risk. Express*Alliance* also offers doctors and nurses the ability to collaborate on a case through an online exchange of treatment notes.

ExpressPAth®: Another example of using data to coordinate care is in the management of specialty medications, which are commonly injected or infused drugs that treat complex and rare conditions, such as HIV and MS. They are incredibly expensive, with some therapies costing hundreds of thousands of dollars. Research estimates these drugs will make up 40% of all drug spend by 2018. Fifty-three percent of specialty drug spent is billed under the pharmacy benefit where programs, like those traditionally operated by Express Scripts, help guarantee appropriate use, improved safety, and reduced costs. The remaining 47% is covered by major medical insurance where, until now, there is limited/no visibility or effective tools to manage costs. The result is an estimated $8 billion of unnecessary spending each year from lack of medication adherence, overutilization, and other inefficiencies.

Wimberly and a cross-functional team developed an industry-first solution called ExpressPAth™, which manages 100% of a client's drug costs regardless of whether the medications are covered under the patient's pharmacy or medical insurance plan. The ExpressPAth innovative platform draws upon terabytes of data and clinical results collected over the past two decades and connects the data with a real-time, user-friendly portal available to physicians and other prescribers via mobile devices or desktops.

Express Scripts' clients receive an average savings of 10%–15% on specialty drug spend in the medical benefit with ExpressPAth. For example, in 2012, ExpressPAth saved one small health plan client more than $350,000 in specialty drugs costs billed under the medical benefit. ExpressPAth saved another client $6,563 when it identified the correct dose of a drug claim for $10,400 under medical benefit system and repriced claim for the proper amount of $3,837.[12]

Using Predictive Analytics to Combat Fraud and Abuse

Prescription drug abuse is deadlier than cocaine and heroin combined. Each year, the United States loses between 3% and 10% of every health-care dollar spent—as much as $224 billion last year[13]—to fraudulent prescriptions. More importantly, prescription drug overdoses kill more than 15,000 people[14] and result in 1.2 million[15] emergency room visits each year.[16]

Wimberly's advanced analytics team focused on developing a predictive model to address this very serious problem. Leveraging its vast data capabilities, Express Scripts looks at more than 290 predictive indicators of fraud to identify potential cases of abuse. Because many prescription narcotics have limits on how much can be dispensed to a patient, the company looks at the data to find the ways people work around the system, such as the number of doctors visited or the distance traveled to the physician or pharmacy.

When it identifies patterns of abuse, the company's fraud, waste, and abuse team collaborates with a network of public and private organizations to assist the abuser and works with the appropriate authorities to bring criminal charges to phantom pharmacies, pill mills, etc. In 1 year alone, this process enabled Express Scripts to save the health-care system an estimated $500 million.[16]

Innovating Value with Technology

Wimberly is very concerned about health-care costs in this country. "Patients who don't adhere to medication directions cost $317 billion a year in the United States in healthcare costs (see infographic). Of all the cardiovascular patients who undergo surgery, 20 percent are readmitted because they don't take their medications as prescribed."[8]

He cites statistic after statistic on the impact to patient health outcomes and costs relating to the current model of patient care. Wimberly and the Express Scripts team are leveraging technology in innovative ways to improve health outcomes and reduce health-care costs. This is a win for the customer, a win for the company, and a win for our country.

Stephen Pickett, Senior Vice President, Information Technology, and CIO, Penske Corporation

Some companies grow organically where IT organizations support a base business that grows through developing great products and services, dynamic marketing, and product development techniques. IT organizations that support organic growth companies have the luxury of understanding the business and growing their business and technical skills to meet business needs. However, when a company grows organically as well as through acquisition, the IT organization needs to be business savvy, nimble, and responsive to different business needs across the various businesses.

An example of such a company is Penske Corporation, the 19 billion corporation headquartered in Bloomfield Hills, Michigan, with 39,000 people worldwide. Penske is a closely held, on-highway, diversified transportation services company, whose subsidiaries operate in a variety of industry segments, including retail automotive, truck leasing, transportation logistics, transportation component manufacturing, and professional motorsports. In addition, Penske also operates a venture capital business. Penske Corporation has nine major business groups and in total operates a total of 19 separate businesses (Figure 18.10).

In 1997, Penske executive management recognized the need for a strategic CIO who has a combination of deep technology knowledge and business savvy, and could also leverage technology across the different business segments that would drive business growth. Stephen Pickett was the ideal candidate to fill the role. Pickett graduated with a degree in computer science from Michigan State and later in his career an MBA in Advanced Management. His professional background is in transportation, a common theme across the various Penske business segments. Pickett has an impressive resume. His career started with American Motors where he rose to the position of manager of

Penske automotive

Penske Automotive Group is an international transportation services company, operating retail automotive dealerships, Hertz car rental franchises and commercial vehicle distribution. The company currently operates principally in the United States, Western Europe, Australia and New Zealand, employs approximately 17,000 people worldwide and is a member of the Fortune 500 and Russell 2000.

Penske truck rental

Penske Truck Rental operates one of the newest and most diverse truck rental fleets in North America. Our fleet of new, well-maintained rental trucks, 24/7 roadside assistance, easy reservations, and commitment to customer service ensure our customers enjoy high quality vehicles, service and peace of mind when renting trucks commercially or for a do-it-yourself household move.

Penske truck leasing

Penske Truck Leasing is a market-leading transportation services provider in North America that provides full-service leasing, contract maintenance, truck rentals for businesses and consumers, supply chain management and logistics solutions, and used truck and equipment sales. Penske Truck Leasing operates a fleet of more than 200,000 vehicles and serves its customers from more than 1,000 locations.

Penske logistics

Penske Logistics is an award-winning, industry thought leader known for its operational excellence in supply chain and logistics management. With operations and offices in North America, South America, Europe, and Asia, Penske provides a wide array of solutions including dedicated contract carriage, distribution center management, transportation management, lead logistics, and supply chain consulting to major shippers worldwide.

Penske motor group

Penske Motor Group owns and operates Toyota, Scion and Lexus automobile dealerships in California. Our flagship dealership, Longo Toyota in El Monte, California, is the world's largest dealership and the #1 Toyota retailer in the USA since 1967. Our mission is to deliver the highest quality automotive products, people, information and services that result in lifelong partnerships with our guests.

Figure 18.10 Penske Corporation Companies. (From Penske Corporation Website; Overview of Business Units; http://www.penske.com/about; Data supplied by Express Scripts Corporate Communications.) *(Continued)*

Penske racing

Penske Racing is one of the most successful teams in the history of professional sports. Competing in a variety of disciplines, cars owned and prepared by Penske Racing have produced 350 major race wins, 412 pole positions and 23 National Championships.

Truck-lite

Truck-Lite Co., LLC is headquartered in Falconer New York, with additional manufacturing facilities in Wellsboro, Coudersport, and McElhattan, Pennsylvania, as well as Birmingham and Harlow England, and other facilities around the world. Truck-Lite is a major producer of signal lighting, forward lighting, wiring harnesses, mirrors, turn signal switches, and safety accessories to the heavy-duty truck, trailer, and commercial vehicle industries.

DAVCO

Headquartered in Saline, Michigan. DAVCO is the North American leader in manufacturing of fuel-heater/water separators and filter systems for Class 8 heavy-duty trucks, medium trucks, marine and off-road applications, as well as the makers of industrial automatic oil replenishment systems, with regulators, slow flow meters, and fluid level switches. DAVCO products are designed for tough commercial applications including On and Off-Highway, Industrial, Gen Set, Construction, Military and Marine.

Ilmor

Ilmor Engineering is best known for its success in high performance engineering and motorsport – most notably, IndyCar, Formula One, NASCAR and P1 Powerboat. In addition to ongoing advancements in racing technologies, the company is also a leading marine engine and drive manufacturer, and provides engineering consultancy services to major automotive OEMs. The Ilmor family of companies employ over 150 employees worldwide at facilities in MLNC and the UK.

Figure 18.10 (Continued)   Penske Corporation Companies. (From Penske Corporation Website; Overview of Business Units; http://www.penske.com/about; Data supplied by Express Scripts Corporate Communications.)

Engineering Computing Center. He then moved to Volkswagen, as director of technology for North America, then Global Technology for the Volkswagen Group in Germany, and ultimately the leading IT position for North America.

As you can imagine, taking on the CIO role at a conglomerate has challenges. Each operating company has its own IT organization and focuses on the specific business needs of the business. The challenges for the corporate CIO is to leverage information and technology across the business companies, optimizing IT costs while improving business value, and support the IT needs of individual companies. It's a delicate balance that requires insight, focus, and perseverance. "When Penske hired me in 1997, they didn't have a true understanding of how IT could be leveraged across the business entities. They needed a strategy that would leverage IT to drive business growth," says Pickett.[18]

In his role, Pickett has integrated IT best practices across the different Penske companies. Global companies are at their best when they think global but also practice locally, the idea being not to lose sight of consumer needs at the local market but still maintain the value of the global brand. Penske companies operate independently and excel at providing services for the market they serve. But from a technology perspective, there are opportunities Pickett leveraged to optimize IT strategically to invoke value. Following are a few examples.

Proactive Envisioning of Business Needs

Pickett saw an opportunity in 2008 to be proactive in servicing the needs of Penske personnel. With the proliferation of computer devices flooding the market, Pickett realized that if he didn't get ahead of the curve by allowing personnel to use their own device of choice, it would be the same old story of business telling IT what they needed to conduct their day-to-day business activities. Instead of being reactive, Pickett chose a proactive strategy and enabled employee-owned devices to integrate with company networks. By the time bring your own device (BYOD) became a popular theme in IT circles, Pickett already had established this practice across the Penske companies.

This practice allowed us to jumpstart the smart device productivity opportunities without making a significant investment while the technology matured. The mobile device management software did not really mature until well into 2011, but we did not stall our innovation waiting for it.

Optimizing Vendor Services across Penske Companies

Each of the Penske companies manages their businesses and contracts with suppliers for services. This is true for IT services as well. Pickett recognized that IT services provided locally but contracted globally are the strategic course of action that optimizes IT investments while at the same time improving services. "The concern I had with recommending global IT contracts was that local IT management did not feel they were losing control of the service delivery. I wanted to make sure that services were delivered to meet the needs of the Penske company but at the same time provided corporate leverage over pricing and building a stronger supplier partnership." (ibid)

Pickett's approach was to start with one on the Penske companies, show the value of a global contract, and build buy-in from the other operating companies. The strategy worked. When we enter a new market, we go in with a complete array of cost reduction potential avoiding months of supplier negotiations, and the new entities immediately enjoy the breadth of expertise of the entire enterprise.

Improving Customer Service for Penske Customers

Maintaining an ever-improving brand is not an easy task, especially for a company like Penske, which has so many different companies operating in an entrepreneurial model. We have all experienced calling a customer service number, only to hear voice mail greetings and experiencing extended hold times. This happens all the time. How do you fix this? Well, there are a number of ways. One is to add customer service personnel to handle peak loads but remain idle during off times waiting for the phone to ring. This approach works, but it is expensive and drives up costs, reducing operating margins.

Another approach is to network all customer service personnel virtually into one seamless phone and customer service system. Pickett chose this strategy. "The advantage to this approach is when customer service representative in one location is busy handling calls, the system automatically transfers the call to another customer service center that is available. The initial implementation costs are high in terms of hardware, software, and training. But the payoff is improved customer satisfaction." (ibid) When a customer has a service question about the vehicle purchased a few months earlier and dials the local Penske dealership located in California, someone will always pick up the phone, even if the person answering the phone is from Phoenix. This is a win for the customer, a win for the dealership, and a win for Penske Corporation.

Pickett understands that today's competitive marketplace requires speed of response from the business, especially the IT organization. "The biggest challenges to CIOs today are keeping the energy level absolutely high, attention to detail, and integrity."[19] This is one of the reasons Pickett enjoys spending time with Penske Racing. He enjoys the sport. He also sees how people focus on speed and agility, a culture that needs to permeate every organization. "One of the roles I play is to take the racing culture and bring it into each of the companies. Some refer to it as a 24-7 pit stop. When a race car enters the pit area during a race, the team works feverishly to change tires, fix a bent bumper, etc. It's this vision of speed and quality that Pickett wanted to instill within the various Penske business entities. People need to understand precision, and quality. I'm more of a teacher. It's my job to take the company culture and instill it into the all parts of the enterprise." (ibid)

Pickett's latest interest is how to use data analytics to enhance each of the 41 brands across the Penske companies. His focus is "how to compare brands, determine which entity is operating most efficiently, find the golden nuggets, and transpose those to the others. My challenge is how to find the data and present it in a way to help management at each of the Penske companies make good decisions." (ibid)

Pickett is one of the strategic CIOs who loves his job and works with the Penske company IT organizations to leverage technologies strategically to innovate value. He focuses on speed and agility to help each of the Penske companies excel performance, just like Brad Keselowski of Penske Racing, who brought dreams to reality in 2012 by winning the first NASCAR Cup Championship.

Harry Lukens, Senior Vice President and CIO of Lehigh Valley Health Network

Harry Lukens graduated from St. Joseph's College with a BS in Economics and went on to earn a MS in Economics from Temple University. His entire career is in health care. At University of Pennsylvania Hospital, Lukens was the director of Systems & Financial Operations and then moved on to become the deputy associate executive director of Information Services and Finance Departments from 1979 to 1986. During the period 1986–1989, Lukens was the vice president for Professional Health Care Systems, where he developed the Systems' Support and Consulting Divisions. In 1989, Lukens formed the Lukens Group, as managing partner, providing health-care IT consulting services to hospital networks. Lukens joined LVHN in 1994. The hospital network, comprised of the Cedar Crest and Muhlenberg hospitals, has grown to a thousand-bed three Magnet-designated hospital located in Allentown Pennsylvania.

When I interviewed Lukens, he referred to the Roman god Janus, who was depicted with two faces on the same head. One looks backward and one forward. "The role of the CIO today is very different. You have to look forward and anticipate the needs of the business," says Lukens.[20] During his tenure, he has reinvented how the hospital network leverages IT. Lukens knows that the success of IT depends on the personnel succeeding at their jobs, and Lukens spends a lot time mentoring and coaching personnel. He transformed IT personnel and built a great leadership team that focuses on finding ways, using technology, to improve the health outcomes of patients. The IT leadership team and key IT personnel developed a sound understanding of the health industry and how LVHN operates on a day-to-day basis. These IT personnel integrat with physician, nursing, and technical teams to understand their needs and leverage technology to improve the delivery of health-care services. Lukens and his team have won numerous awards (Figure 18.11).

LEHIGH VALLEY HEALTH NETWORK

A SAMPLING OF OUR REPUTATION AND SUCCESSES

- 2006 & 2007 Hospitals & Health Network's Innovator Award
- 2007 CHIME's Transformational Leadership Award Presented by Newt Gingrich
- 2008 Healthcare Informatics Innovator Award
- 2010 Pennsylvania Outstanding Leadership in Technology - *awarded to Harry Lukens*
- 2010 Top 10 Breakaway Leaders – *awarded to Harry Lukens*
- 2011 CIO 100 Award – *awarded to Harry Lukens*
- 2012 Top 25 Healthcare CIOs - *awarded to Harry Lukens*
- 2012 & 2013 Computer World's 100 Best Places to Work in IT
- 2013 Healthcare IT News's Where to Work: BEST Hospital IT Departments *(ranked #2 in best super hospital IT departments)*

Figure 18.11   LVHN IT Awards—Successes.

Building a Foundation for Success

When he started, the hospital IT department did not have a good reputation, and turnover was about 15%. Today, the turnover in the 400 person IT team is about 2%, a true testament to the work environment and value IT personnel place on working at LVHN. Lukens built an effective team by listening to IT personnel and treating them with respect. Lukens focus is to enhance the delivery of health-care services and improve health-care outcomes by leveraging technology. First, he had to build a business-focused team.

> To help IT personnel understand how information technology adds value to health care, I started a 10 weeks education program that every IT person attends. I teach the program. In this workshop setting, they learn about the health care industry, the Lehigh Valley Health Network (LVHN) market environment, and the processes within our hospital network that enable doctors, nurses, and technicians to provide superior health care to our patients. The more IT personnel understand the business of health care, the better they will be at working with the hospital staff to develop solutions that improve health care outcomes. (ibid)

Lukens walks the talk. He is an energetic and vibrant executive who leads by example and mentors and coaches personnel to help them succeed. "When I worked at University of Pennsylvania, I coached an account manager to help him with improving his skills. Twenty years later, he sent me an email reminding me of how I helped him." (ibid)

To gain the trust of the LVHN doctors, nurses, and technicians, during the early years, Lukens and his IT team leaders toured the hospital corridors every Monday morning to learn how he and his IT team could help them provide better health care. Lukens remembers doctor using 3M sticky notes, while conducting rounds, to write instructions for nurses. When they finished their rounds, they would go to the nursing station, log in, and enter instructions into the system. "This led me to implement a wireless network at the hospital to improve communication and improve efficiency." (ibid) After we implemented the wireless network in the mid-1990s, physicians could access information from anywhere in the hospital.

Lukens is an avid reader and a great listener. He heard about a hospital in Minnesota that uses virtual reality games for burn patients. To minimize discomfort during treatment, patients play virtual reality games. One of these games is SnowWorld, where you throw snowballs at penguins. "The patient uses goggles and earphones and is involved with the penguins. It switches their consciousness to playing a game and not the treatment they are receiving." (ibid)

Lukens and his IT team also know how to leverage LVHN competencies to help smaller regional hospitals improve health outcomes for their patients. A number of regional hospitals connect their networks, using cloud technology, to LVHN. Here's an example. LVHN has a competency in fetal medicine. A local regional hospital doesn't. When a distressed patient goes to the regional hospital for care, the physician tele-connects with fetal specialists at LVHN to develop a treatment plan. The patient can obtain the same level of care at the local hospital without traveling long distances to LFHN hospital. LVHN radiology specialists read films from a local Pocono hospital when complex cases warrant specialist advice. At another regional hospital in Hazelton, PA, data on stroke patients are sent to LVHN neurologists for review. Leveraging medical competencies at LVHN expands specialty care provided to patients at regional hospitals. Health outcomes improve and costs optimized. This is a real win–win scenario.

Leveraging Technology to Innovate Value

Lukens always believes that people working together can develop innovative ideas in the proper setting. Lukens accomplished this. He organized a *Wild Ideas Team* comprised of doctors, nurses, technicians, and administrative personnel. Their task was simple. "Meet on a regular basis to analyze opportunities to improve hospital services. Then come to IT and present your ideas. We'll analyze them, flush out the details, and meet with you to discuss our findings." (ibid) Lukens provides the following example of an idea he had that he brought to the team.

> I have two Labrador retrievers. I read a few magazines that address animal health. I came across an article about a Veterinarians using portable ultra sound unit to provide readable images. I thought this was a cool idea. I met with the 'Wild Ideas Team' to present my idea. They discussed it and thought it had some merit. Instead of moving the patient to the lab for an ultrasound, why not use a portable device at the patients' bedside. Physicians who have to place IV lines in patients in the ICU need to make sure they find an appropriate vein. An inexpensive portable hand held device would allow the physician to look at an appropriate location to insert the IV without moving the patient. The device does not provide diagnostic quality as the regular ultrasound. It's not invasive. It's sufficient for finding an appropriate location for inserting an IV. The device was approved by the FDA and we starting using it at LVHN. (ibid)

One of the wildest ideas was coordinated by Lukens. The intensive care unit (ICU) at Lehigh Valley Hospital is fully staffed during the 7 am to 7 pm shift with physicians and nurses. LVHN admits approximately 70,000 overnight admissions a year, and 15%, or about 10,000, are admitted as critical care patients. Some of the physicians are interventionists. These are specially trained physicians certified in intensive care, pulmonary medicine, and internal medicine. These physician specialists are a rare breed. Lukens thought about the care provided during the night shift. "We need to find a way to provide the same level of care during the 7 pm to 7 am shift as exists during the 7 am to 7 pm shift. LVHN couldn't hire any. There had to be a way to get this done." (ibid) About the same time Lukens was thinking about this challenge, a few physicians approached him and suggested a way to have a centralized system that monitors ICU patients during the 7 pm to 7 am period. One of Lukens' most valuable skills is the ability to listen. Lukens gathered his *Wild Ideas* team and challenged them to come up with a solution. The result was what is affectionately known as *doc in a box*. An interventionist staffs this remote facility every evening from 7 pm to 7 am, along with three nurses. Together, they monitor each of the 140 critical care patients, by accessing patient records and viewing patients via a video, speaking to patients and nurses using audio. This specialist team can write prescriptions, order diagnostic procedures, and communicate with anyone in the hospital to provide care for any ICU patient at the same level of monitoring and care as during the 7 am to 7 pm shift. The story of *doc in the box* and how LVHN remote ICU is saving lives is a fascinating story.

LVHN leveraged information technology coupled with revised processes and teaming skills to drive down mortality rates and increase patient outcomes at their 140-bed ICUs. They developed an advanced ICU (A-ICU) capability, using telemedicine, which statistically saves 1 life for every 15 patients who requires ICU medical care. This amounts to over 1,800 lives saved over the course of a year.

Dr. Matthew McCambridge is chief of LVHN's Division of Critical Care Medicine. "We serve our community and strive to provide the best medical care we can offer. This is our greatest asset and we must do everything we can to ensure we succeed towards that goal."[21] The success of the A-ICU includes a great group of nurses, doctors, and technicians working and communicating as a team, a set of best-in-class processes that drive results, and a set of enabling technologies that provide real-time information. How did they do it? Read on to find out how ICU telemedicine started, the journey at LVHN, and three success factors that made it all possible.

In 2000, Harry Lukens, CIO at LVHN, and a team of physicians and nurses began looking at ways to improve intensive care outcomes. They heard about the concept of a telehealth approach used to improve health outcomes of ICU patients. At the time, there was only one telehealth ICU in the United States. After in-depth research and site visits in the Netherlands, LVHN acquired their first telehealth clinical information system from iMDsoft.

The LVHN A-ICU was implemented at a remote facility located 8 miles from the Lehigh Valley Cedar Crest Hospital—the largest of the network's hospitals. Affectionately known as the *doc in a box*, the A-ICU is a square room approximately 25 feet wide and 25 feet long. The facility includes four *computer pods*. Two rows of three computers provide real-time medical information. Three nurse manages each of the three pods while the fourth assists the A-ICU critical care physician. In addition, an administrator for the A-ICU handles ancillary communications and coordination activities. This team of six performs miracles each and every night.

Each nurse, experienced in critical ICU care, monitors approximately 35–45 patients—thus the three nurses can monitor the 140 intensive care beds at LVHN. At the center pod sits the intensivist, a critical care pulmonary physician who is specially trained and coordinates care for each ICU patient during the 7 pm to 7 am shift. The nurses and doctor practitioners rotate between the hospital ICU and the remote A-ICU on a regular basis. This enables them to effectively partner with hospital nurses, doctors, interns, and residents to provide the ultimate care for each of the ICU patients.

The nurses and doctor can display health care information on any screen and even adjust their working pod table up and down, electrically, to provide them with the most ergonomically oriented position. The six computer monitors provide the following information for the A-ICU team to provide medical care for each ICU patient (Table 18.1).

Table 18.1 LVHN Patient Information Types Accessible in A-ICU

PATIENT INFORMATION	INFORMATION DESCRIPTION
Patient's medical records	Blood pressure, heart rate, electrocardiogram, test results, bedside medication, etc.
Picture archiving and x-rays	X-rays and other medical picture records of patient
Audio visual monitoring system	Ability to visually examine patient symptoms such as dilated pupils, skin color, etc.
Medication administration record	Ability to view patient medicine history and order medicines electronically that will be administered within 60 minutes
Administrative information system	Listing of all ICU patients, their room numbers, doctors, etc.

How the A-ICU Provides Life-Saving Results: Three Success Factors

I had the opportunity to see firsthand how the LVHN A-ICU operates during two visits. The first visit was during the day when ICU care is administered at each of the hospitals. Four key players in A-ICU provided me an overview of the facility (Harry Lukens, CIO; Lorraine Valeriano, manager of A-ICU; Nancy O'Connor, IT director; Joe Tracy, vice president for Telehealth Services at LVHN). I learned about the history of the A-ICU, how it functions, and the enabling technology. To really understand how it functions, I was invited to see in action one evening.

I arrived at about 8 pm on evening for my 1 hour tour. Dr. Matthew McCambridge, the intensivist, was at the center pod listening to voice mail updates from each of the ICU lead pulmonary physicians. Dr. Matthew M. McCambridge, M.D., is the past president of LVHN Medical Staff and the assistant chief of medical critical care and the comedical director of LVHN's A-ICU (Figure 18.12).

Each of the nurses, Nancy Long, Rich Riccio, and Dara Patton, was monitoring his or her individual pods. Lorraine Valeriano, the A-ICU manager, greeted me and introduced me to Dr. McCambridge and the nurses (Figure 18.13).

Dr. McCambridge and the nurses described how they access various databases to displayed patient data on the monitors. They explained how the data can be displayed in different formats and

Figure 18.12　Dr. Matthew McCambridge.

Figure 18.13 A-ICU critical care nurse.

how they manage the care of 140 patients each and every night from 7 pm to 7 am.

To show me how the unit interacts with ICU patients, Dr. McCambridge explained how he can access a patient's medical history, current vital signs, and x-ray images for an ICU patient, all of the same information accessible at the bedside. He can connect to an ICU room via the two-way audio and video remote monitoring system to both see and talk to the patient. In turn, the patient can also visualize and communicate with the physician on a monitor screen in the ICU room. Dr. McCambridge explained to me that earlier in the evening, he was observing a patient and was able to answer some questions from the family members who were visiting the ICU patient. During the conversation, he reviewed some of the recent x-rays and noticed that a peripherally inserted central catheter (PICC) line was in need of repositioning for more efficient medication administration by the nurse. Dr. McCambridge immediately called the resident on duty to discuss the corrective action that needed to occur to reposition the line. The A-ICU nurse was also able to speak with the bedside nurse to update him or her on the situation.

Dr. McCambridge also explained to me that the resident also mentioned a distress situation with another patient. Dr. McCambridge immediately reviewed this patient's x-rays and discussed a course of action with the resident physician. These are two case examples of how critical care was administered in minutes instead of having to wait for multiple return phone calls or even until morning when the day-shift physicians made ICU rounds. Critical time was saved because of the A-ICU care provided to the patient.

To actually see how the A-ICU operates, real-time, is an eye opener. I asked Dr. McCambridge and the nurses why they work at the A-ICU as part of a rotating nursing assignment for critical care patients. For Dr. McCambridge, the answer was simple. "It's my passion to help people and critical care patients represent a population where urgent care administered 24 hours a day will save lives." (ibid)

The nurses, each with 20–35 years of critical care experience, had similar answers. (ibid)

Dara, with 34 years of critical care nursing experience, told me that "the AICU has proven to be very important in helping the newer RN's who are mostly on night shift with troubleshooting problems with their patients, and guiding them through difficult situations."

Richard, with 20 years critical care experience, finds that "one of the major values of the Advanced ICU nurses is that we act as a 'second layer of protection' for all patients, especially those whose caregivers are neophyte critical care nurses. We offer assistance to these nurses by helping them critically think when appropriate."

Nancy, with 25 years of critical care nursing experience, works at the A-ICU because "I feel I have an advantage to gain more knowledge by listening to the different cases, and challenges in caring for critical patients. I feel it personally is a 'win-win' deal for me. I can use this knowledge daily in my job, and help others when difficult situations arise through the experiences that I gained working in the A-ICU."

Lorraine, the A-ICU manager, a critical care nurse for 27 years certified as a neuroscience registered nurse, views the A-ICU as "... an extra layer of care in monitoring patients and an external resource for bedside clinicians."

The care these professionals provide to ICU patients requires passion, focus, and experience. They actually save lives incorporating three best practices that make the A-ICU successful.

*Three Best Practices That Make the A-ICU Successful: Great
Teamwork, Improved Processes, and Enabling Technologies*

Dr. McCambridge described to me what he considers the three critical success factors and some examples of each that led to the improved
mortality rates at the LVHN A-ICU. (ibid)

Great teamwork

    a. Great teams don't just happen. It's hard work and skill.

    b. The team of specially trained physicians, nurses, and tech-
nicians work together at the hospital ICU and rotate to the
A-ICU.

    c. Knowing your team members, their skills, and the experience
of working together builds a great critical care team focused
on improving patient outcomes.

    d. People communicate well with each other.

    e. Every team member knows their role, capabilities, and skill
levels.

    f. Every team member knows when to ask for help.

Improved process

    a. During the past 10 years, we've honed our A-ICU and hospi-
tal ICU processes.

    b. We enclosed each and every ICU room to maintain a sterile
environment.

    c. We set rigorous standards of experience for each critical care
nurse and intensivist that works in the A-ICU.

    d. We defined roles and skills required for each team member.

    e. We make sure that we rotate, on a regular basis, between the
hospital ICU and the A-ICU to make sure that we never lose
sight of our hands-on caring skills.

    f. The A-ICU intensivist is the primary care physician dur-
ing the 7 pm to 7 am shift and can write orders, prescribe
medications, and coordinate care with physician specialists as
required.

Enabling technologies

    a. Real-time medical information system that integrates key
data can be accessed by any team member.

b. Electronic ordering of medicines results in patients receiving their drugs within 60 minutes of the A-ICU intensivist writing the electronic order.

c. Automated alerts to A-ICU nurses when medical parameters are reached (temperature, blood pressure, heart rate, rhythm, etc.).

d. A-ICU intensivist, using computer applications, remote video monitoring, and communication equipment, can write orders, prescribe medications, and coordinate care with physician specialists as required during the overnight hours.

Saving a Life   On a cold February evening, a 17-year-old teenager, in the 11th grade, was rushed to the Lehigh Valley Hospital complaining of chest pains. Upon examination, the doctors admitted her to the Intensive Care Unit for observation where the remote A-ICU facility interventionist monitored her vital signs through the evening. The interventionist communicating with staff physicians, via a video-conferencing system, said, "I'd keep an eye on her while we determined the best treatment." The team of physicians uncovered a 4 in. blood clot extending into the heart. "Doing nothing wasn't an option. The clot could travel to her lung, which might be fatal," said the interventionist. Open-heart surgery had to be performed. The teenager made a full recovery and returned to her favorite sports of horseback riding and cheerleading. Reflecting on her care by the physician team led by the A-ICU interventionist, she said, "I'd like to be a midwife or surgeon, because the experience made me realize how precious life is."[22]

The doctors and nurses working as a team, practice critical care medicine using a stringent set of best practices enabled by technology. They save lives. We can all learn from health-care practitioners who apply these principles each day.

Harry Lukens has a passion for improving health-care outcomes. He has accomplished this at LVHN. He and his IT team are nationally recognized for their contribution in enabling improved patient care through leveraging technology to innovate real value, helping patients improve their health outcomes. At the same time, technology is helping to save lives. "We can make a difference, whether we're in a 50-bed hospital or a 10-hospital system. We can take technology and make doctors' and patients' lives easier."[23] One could not ask for a better scenario than this.

Chapter Summary

This chapter highlighted five CIOs who leverage technology strategically to innovate value.

Dave Finnegan led the initiative at Build-A-Bear Workshop to integrate technology into a new business model. The in-store physical experience is now a technology-based business model that enables a unique customer experience throughout the entire process of building a stuffed animal. Customers can browse the website to preplan the in-store experience. When customers arrive at the store, they use interactive workstations, at key points in the building process to choose a stuffing, add personality attributes, include sounds, and even take a bath with their stuffed animal. When they arrive home, the experience continues. Customers can play games with avatar versions of their stuffed animals, win points, and use their imagination to enhance their learning process. As this book went to press, Dave Finnegan took on a new role at Orvis, where he is the CIO\VP Technology and Interactive. Orvis, headquartered in Vermont, USA, is America's oldest mail order outfitter and longest continually-operating fly fishing business.

Perry Rotella has a lot of experience in the insurance industry and is helping Verisk expand their business into new markets by leveraging technology strategically. One of Rotella's first objectives was to improve the delivery of IT services by helping IT personnel change their thought process about services. He helped reshape their thinking from technologists to business people and that IT services are an important ingredient to the success of the business. Rotella also built credibility with business unit executives by communicating a plan to consolidate data centers based upon the positive impact it would have on the company's share price. As delivery of services improved and Rotella gained the trust of confidence of the business, Verisk expanded its insurance risk business to companies relying heavily on their supply chain. With a solid understanding of business processes, logistics, and risks associated with supply chain, Verisk management asked Rotella to lead the supply chain business as part of the company's growth strategy. Rotella is a perfect example of a strategic CIO who is well grounded in business process and strategy. Rotella is one of the up-and-coming CIOs recognized for their business acumen and not only for their technology prowess.

Gary Wimberly leads initiatives at Express Scripts to improve the outcomes of health care for patients who use prescribed drugs. Not only does Express Scripts prescribe drugs for customers, they also provide a host of services that proactively help manage health outcomes while at the same time reduce drug costs. Predictive analytics determines potential prescription adherence issues for different age groups. Special messaging, designed around patient age groups designed to induce adherence to drug instructions, reduces patient health incidents. Providing services for patients' health-care team to improve coordination of treatment improves patient outcomes. The core value provided to customers, which was once efficiently filling drug prescriptions, now focuses on improving their health outcomes attributed to medication adherence. Express Scripts has transformed the Pharmacy Benefits Management (PBM) business model by leveraging technology strategically to innovate new value.

Stephen Picket has a love for speed and racing cars, and he translates this into his role as CIO at Penske Corporation. A diversified company with different business units, this conglomerate needs a CIO who knows how to leverage success from one business unit to all other business units. And this is what Picket has done at Penske. He foresaw the need for personnel to use the device of their choice, years before the industry coined the phrase—bring your own device (BYOD). Although Penske business units operate as independent businesses, Pickett recognized a commonality of vendor services across the corporation. He implemented a vendor consolidation program slowly across the corporation. Business Unit Executives recognized that vendor consolidation across the corporation for key services didn't impact the independent business structure and actually helped improve the bottom line. Pickett also improved customer service at Penske by developing a capability where any customer service department, from any of the Penske businesses, would answer a customer call, even if the customer was calling a different business unit customer service office. Pickett is a strategic CIO who exhibits speed and agility in everything he does, a characteristic that helps Penske Corporation succeed in the marketplace.

Harry Lukens is helping improve health outcomes for patients at Lehigh Valley Health Network. He started by focusing on building a strong business-focused IT team. He roams the hallways listening to doctors, nurses, and technicians to understand their challenges and works together to leverage technology to improve patient care. He and his IT team leveraged medical competencies at LVHN across regional hospitals through the use of telemedicine, and other technologies, to improve health care for patients at remote hospitals. His *Wild Ideas Team* developed the idea of a remote ICU to monitor critical care patients during 7 pm to 7 am when staffing is minimal, providing them the same level of care received during day-shift hours. There is no greater gift than giving life, and Lukens and the LVHN team are saving lives each and every day by leveraging technology in innovative ways.

Key Points

1. Understand and anticipate customer needs (Build-A-Bear Workshop).
2. Look beyond initial competencies to create new business model (Express Scripts).
3. Leverage the best from each operating division and intergrate across the entire enterprise (Penske).
4. Create a true unique differentiator for competitive advantage (Verisk).
5. Listen and learn about the needs of the business, build a strong team, and leverage technology strategically (LVHN).

Citations

1. David Finnegan, CIO-Build A Bear/Phil Weinzimer Interview on August 30, 2013.
2. David Finnegan, CIO-Build A Bear/Phil Weinzimer Follow-Up Interview via Email November 7, 2013.

3. *Newly Imagined Build-A-Bear Workshop Store Coming Soon to Park Meadows.* Build A Bear Press Release; http://phx. corporate-ir.net/phoenix.zhtml?c=182478&p=irol-newsArticle_ print&ID=1848745&highlight= August 20, 2013/ *Build-A-Bear's New Retail Reality—A Look into Their Interactive Store-of-the-Future*; http://www.demandware.com/blog/2013/03/25/build-a-bears-new-retail-reality-a-look-into-their-interactive-store-of-the-future/March 25,2013CommerceBestPractices, In-StoreCommerce, Omni-Channel CommerceLeaveacomment.

4. http://finance.yahoo.com/news/build-bear-workshop-bear-valley-080000327.html. *The Build-A-Bear Workshop® Bear Valley™ App Brings the Teddy Bear to Life On iPhone*, iPad and iPod Touch Press Release: 505 Games—Monday, July 22, 2013 4:00 AM EDT.

5. A Brief History of Big Data Analytics, September 26, 2013 by Robert Handfield; http://iianalytics.com/2013/09/a-brief-history-of-big-data-analytics/ (International Institute of Data Analytics).

6. Perry Rotella, Group Executive, Supply Chain Risk Analytics, Senior Vice President and CIO- Verisk Analytics/Phil Weinzimer Interview, November 5, 2013.

7. Moody's Corporation/About Us Web Page; https://www.moodys.com/Pages/atc.aspx.

8. Gary Wimberly, CIO-Express Scripts/Phil Weinzimer Interview, September 10, 2013.

9. Turning Vendors into Trusted Strategic Partners, Peter High, Posted May 17, 2013; http://www.cioinsight.com/it-management/expert-voices/turning-vendors-into-trusted-strategic-partners/.

10. Express Scripts Website/Insights/Specialized Care: Health Decisions Science; http://lab.express-scripts.com/patient-behavior/health-decision-science/.

11. Gary Wimberly, Senior Vice President, CIO, Express Scripts/Phil Weinzimer interview, September 15, 2013.

12. Data supplied by Express Scripts Corporate Communications.

13. Data supplied by Express Scripts Corporate Communications.

14. Centers for Disease Control and Prevention Website/CDC Features CDC; http://www.cdc.gov/Features/VitalSigns/PainkillerOverdoses/.

15. Express Scripts Website/Insights/Drug Safety and Abuse/ INFOGRAPHIC: Prescription Drug Fraud, and Abuse; http://lab. express-scripts.com/pharmacy-waste/prescription-drug-fraud-and-abuse/.

16. Data supplied by Express Scripts Corporate Communications.

17. Penske Corporation Website Overview of Business Units; http://www. penske.com/about.

18. Stephen Picket, Senior Vice President, CIO—Penske Corporation/Phil Weinzimer Interview, October 17, 2013 and November 21, 2013.

19. Marianne Kolbasuk McGee, High 5: Stephen Pickett, CIO Of Penske, February 24, 2006; http://www.informationweek.com/high-5-stephen-pickett-cio-of-penske/d/d-id/1040847?.

20. Harry Lukens, Senior Vice President, CIO-Lehigh Valley Health Network/Phil Weinzimer Interviews, June 4, July 26, August 13, August 29, 2012.
21. Phil Weinzimer Tour of LVHN Remote ICU Facility, October 8, 2012.
22. High-Tech Healing; Lisa Collier Cool; Wall Street Journal; October 24–25, 2009, Page W6B; Special Advertising Section; Swedish Eurology Group, Seattle Washington http://swedishurology.com/files/high-tech-healing.pdf.
23. Harry Lukens Senior Vice President and CIO Lehigh Valley Hospital and Health Network. Allentown, PA. December 25, 2007 by Daphne Lawrence; http://www.healthcare-informatics.com/article/harry-lukens-senior-vice-president-and-cio-lehigh-valley-hospital-and-health-network-allento.

19

SECTION OVERVIEW

How to Measure the Strategic Maturity of Your IT Organization

Now that you have read how strategic CIOs deliver services exceptionally, learn about the business, focus on user experiences, and improve the business skills of their IT personnel, implement initiatives that improve margin, and leverage technology strategically to innovate value, I'm sure you are asking yourself the following five questions:

1. *How strategic is my IT organization?*
2. *Is there a process I can use to measure the strategic maturity of my IT organization?*
3. *How do I analyze the results?*
4. *What are the implications of the measurements?*
5. *What can I do to improve the maturity gap?*

Well, you are in luck. This chapter will help you answer these questions. The following is a summary of the chapter objective, key messages, and templates used.

A. CHAPTER OBJECTIVE

To define a process for measuring the strategic maturity of your IT organization.

B. KEY POINTS

1. Measuring the strategic maturity of your IT organization is a necessary step to determine how effectively you are leveraging information and technology for competitive advantage.

2. A set of best practices for each transformational phase will help you determine the degree to which your IT organization delivers business value and how efficiently it delivers value.

3. You need to measure each of the four transformation phases across two dimensions:
   a. Business value
   b. Efficiency of delivery

4. Measuring the business value and efficiency for each of the four strategic IT transformation phases will determine the strategic maturity of your IT organization.

5. Understanding the strategic maturity of your IT organization for each transformation phase is a basis for developing a plan to shore up gaps and improve the value IT provides the business and the efficiency of the delivery of value.

C. TEMPLATES USED

1. Strategic IT maturity assessment template (Figure 19.2)
2. IT organization maturity dimensions (Figure 19.3)

Strategic IT Organization Transformation Phases

The strategic IT organization transformation phases (Figure 19.1) represent the transformation path strategic CIOs follow to strategically leverage information and technology for competitive advantage. In each of the previous four sections of the book, strategic CIOs shared their insights, case examples, methodologies, and tools used in their transformation journey to excel in each of the four transformation phases.

To help you answer the five questions listed after the chapter opening paragraph, I have developed an assessment instrument you can use to assess the strategic maturity of your IT organization for each of these transformation phases. The instrument is easy to use and is an excellent beginning for you to determine the actions you need to embark on to improve the strategic maturity of your IT organization.

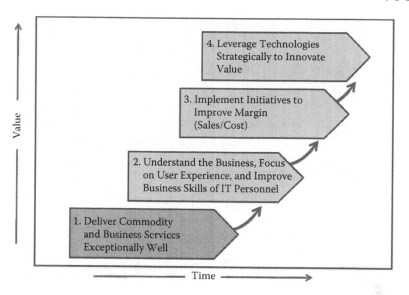

Figure 19.1   Strategic IT Organization Transformation Phases.

Measuring the Strategic Maturity of Your IT Organization

The process of measuring the strategic maturity of your IT organization is similar to the process used in Chapter 11, How to Measure and Improve the Maturity of the Strategic IT Competencies and Skills of Your IT Organization. The process includes an assessment instrument you can use to measure the maturity of the IT competencies and skills in your IT organization. The following is a quick refresher of the process because we will use a similar framework in measuring the strategic maturity of your IT organization. It may be beneficial to reread Chapter 11 if you desire.

Refresher on How to Measure and Improve the Maturity of the Strategic IT Competencies and Skills of Your IT Organization

- The instrument includes a set of best practices for the associated skills of each of the four competencies. For each best practice, you assign a numerical value, 1 to 5, to reflect how well your organization performs against each of the best practices across two dimensions.
- The first dimension is *skill knowledge*. How knowledgeable is your IT organization about the best practice associated with

the specific skill? Do they understand it? The second dimension measures the degree to which the IT organization is *applying the skill knowledge* in work activities to achieve business value.

- For each competency, you total the *skills* score for associated best practices and then divide the total score by the number of associated skills to calculate the average *skills* score. You apply the same process for the *applying the skill knowledge* dimension.
- Record the averages for each competency on a two-by-two grid, where the average *knowledge* score is reflected on the *y*-axis, and the average *applies* scores is reflected on the *x axis* (see Figures 11.4, 11.5, and 11.8 for examples).
- Analyze results to determine where scores reflect a gap (1 = lowest score and reflects the greatest gap, 15= best score that reflects no gap).
- Develop a plan to close gap and improve strategic IT competencies and skills.
- Continuously monitor to measure improvement and adjust plan accordingly.

Assess the Strategic Maturity of Your IT Organization

The assessment instrument to measure the strategic maturity for each of the IT transformation phases (Figure 19.2) utilizes a process similar in framework to the assessment in Chapter 11 that measures the strategic IT competencies and skills. The previous section in this chapter provides a summary of the process steps. There are, however, a few main differences in measuring the maturity of the strategic IT transformation phases. These are the following:

1. The assessment measures the four strategic IT transformation phases.
2. There are three best practice statements for each strategic transformation phase.
3. There two dimensions scored for each best practice statement, which are
   a. Business value derived by the business
   b. Efficiency of delivery

DELIVERING SERVICES EXCEPTIONALLY WELL			
		Score (1 = Low/8 = High)	
CATEGORY	BEST PRACTICE	Business Value (a)	Efficiency (b)
1. Business services	Regularly solicit business unit management to assess value of key business services (current value, trend, gaps, and opportunities). Develop/measure/communicate key metrics (business value and IT efficiency). Implement a business services continuous improvement process involving business unit/IT teams.		
2. Operational stability	IT organization uses reliable and repeatable processes to ensure operational stability. Operational stability: IT employs best practices from recognized authority (i.e., ITIL, COBIT). Operational security: successfully implementing security standards (i.e., SSAE 16, ISAE 3402, ISO 27001 and 27002).		
3. Project portfolio governance	Project governance process (all IT activities) is proactive, identifies key predictors for project success, and promotes teaming through an effective communication process.		
	Rounding	1	1
	Subtotal		
	Maximum score	25	25
	Maturity % (subtotal/maximum score)		

UNDERSTAND BUSINESS/FOCUS ON USER EXPERIENCES/IMPROVE BUSINESS SKILLS			
		Score (1 = Low/8 = High)	
CATEGORY	BEST PRACTICE	Business Value (a)	Efficiency (b)
1. Understand the business	Key IT personnel understand the business, key processes, customer value, and alignment to business services.		
2. User experiences	IT teams understand how customers use the company products and services. Key IT personnel team with business personnel to interact with customers, as well as strategic partners to better understand the value/gaps/opportunities of the company products and services.		

Figure 19.2 Strategic IT Maturity Assessment Template. *(Continued)*

3. Improve business skills of IT personnel	Regularly assess the maturity of your IT organization strategic competencies and skills to measure improvement, value, and gaps (understand industry landscape and upcoming trends and their alignment to enterprise products and services). Successfully implement a business skills learning program for IT personnel to improve their strategic IT competencies and skills.		
Rounding		1	1
Subtotal			
Maximum score		25	25
Maturity % (subtotal/maximum score)			

FOCUS ON INITIATIVES TO IMPROVE MARGIN (SALES/COST)			
		Score (1 = Low/8 = High)	
CATEGORY	BEST PRACTICE	Business Value (a)	Efficiency (b)
1. Margin opportunities	You and key IT personnel map business process value (sales/margin) to enabling business services and IT technical services.		
	Identify and successfully implement opportunities to improve process value through improving enabling business services or modifying performance metrics to reduce costs.		
2. Risk mitigation through improved decision making	Lower cost and improve margin by reducing decision-making risk using an enterprise-wide decision support system.		
3. Continuous improvement	Regularly measure/communicate with business teams to monitor performance and identify new opportunities.		
Rounding		1	1
Subtotal			
Maximum score		25	25
Maturity % (subtotal/maximum score)			

Figure 19.2 (*Continued*) Strategic IT Maturity Assessment Template. (*Continued*)

LEVERAGE TECHNOLOGY STRATEGICALLY TO INNOVATE VALUE			
		Score (1 = Low/8 = High)	
CATEGORY	BEST PRACTICE	Business Value (a)	Efficiency (b)
1. New/improved products and services	You and key IT personnel collaborate regularly with business teams to identify opportunities to create/enhance products and services.		
2. Technology strategy	You and key IT personnel are key influencers in developing an enterprise technology strategy that aligns and integrates to the overall business strategy and enables your company's current and future and products and services. Your CTO and IT teams understand how to leverage innovative technologies into new and improved products and services.		
3. Enabling value	The technology strategy is designed to improve customer value, increase margin, and enhance shareholder wealth.		
Rounding		1	1
Subtotal			
Maximum score		25	25
Maturity % (subtotal/maximum score)			

SUMMARY		
	Score (1 – Low/8 – High)	
CATEGORY	Business Value (a)	Efficiency (b)
Subtotal: Delivering services exceptionally well		
Subtotal: Understand business/focus on user experiences/improve business skills of IT personnel		
Subtotal: Focus on initiatives to improve margin		
Subtotal: Leverage technology strategically to innovate value		
Total score		
Average maturity		
Maximum score	100	100
Maturity % (total score/maximum score)		

Figure 19.2 (*Continued*)   Strategic IT Maturity Assessment Template.

4. The maximum score for how well your IT organization exhibits the best practice for each of the two dimensions is 8 (8 for business value derived by the business and 8 for the efficiency of delivery).

5. The maximum score, for the three best practices, for each dimension in each strategic transformation phase, is 25 (the maximum score of 8 for each best practice multiplied by 3 = 24, plus 1 as a rounding error to equal the total maximum score of 25 for the three best practices).

Take a few minutes to review the template by reading each of the best practices associated with each strategic IT transformation phase. These best practices were derived from the insights provided by the CIOs, business executives, and academic thought leaders I interviewed as part of my research for this book.

Scoring the Assessment

IT organizations that transform into a strategic enabler for business success traverse the four phases differently. Some IT organizations transform from phases one to two in a serial manner, and so forth. Others transform from phases one to two in parallel due to internal organization competencies and skills, trust-based relationships with business unit leaders, or a C-level suite initiative embraced by the entire organization. The sequence is important. The implementation can be serial or using overlapping parallel activities. The value of measuring the strategic maturity of your IT organization for each transformation phase is to determine the degree of maturity. You can identify the phase or phases moving in the right strategic direction or those that need improvement. Once you can determine the strategic maturity of your IT organization for each of the four phases, you can develop an effective transformational roadmap and continuous improvement process.

You can measure the maturity for each of the four strategic IT transformation competencies of your IT organization using a maturity grid composed of four categories (Figure 19.3). The maturity grid scores the assessment across the following two attributes:

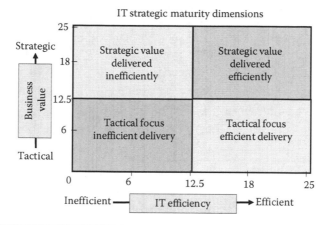

Figure 19.3 Four Strategic Maturity Dimensions of an IT Organization.

- Business value enabled by IT services, projects, and personnel
- The delivery efficiency of IT services, projects, and personnel in supporting business needs

Four Dimensions of the IT Strategic Maturity Grid

The four dimensions of the IT strategic maturity grid are as follows:

1. *Strategic value delivered efficiently (upper-right corner)*—This dimension reflects an IT organization that provides business value efficiently for the phase measured. The implications of a score in this region are as follows:
   a. The IT organization understands what the business needs and delivers it efficiently and the business derives measurable business value.
   b. The IT organization strategically aligns with the business.
   c. The IT organization needs to continuously measure its IT strategic maturity to ensure no deterioration in business value or delivery efficiency.
2. *Strategic value delivered inefficiently (upper-left corner)*—This dimension reflects an organization that provides business value inefficiently. The implications of a score in this region are as follows:

a. The IT organization strategically aligns with the business and understands what the business needs. However, IT personnel inefficiently deliver services and projects.

b. The IT organization needs to develop a plan to improve how it delivers value to the business. The gap is in efficiency of delivery, not in the business value.

c. The IT organization needs to continuously measure its IT strategic maturity to ensure improvements in the delivery of the business value.

3. *Tactical focus–efficient delivery (lower-right corner)*—This dimension reflects an organization that does not provide much business value, but efficiently delivers the associated projects and services. The implications of a score in this region are as follows:

a. The IT organization does not have a clear understanding of the business needs from the business units.

b. The IT organization has the capability to efficiently deliver the projects and services.

c. The IT organization needs to develop a plan that dramatically improves the alignment with business needs. IT leadership needs to meet with business leaders to understand their needs and codevelop the business services and associated projects that provide business value. There exists an apparent misalignment, which needs correction.

d. An active program needs to be in place for the business unit and IT leaders to meet on a regular basis to improve the business value and ensure that there is no degradation of service and project delivery efficiency.

4. *Tactical focus–inefficient delivery (lower-left corner)*—This dimension reflects an organization that has some serious alignment problems. This organization does not understand the needs of the business units; the IT organizations provide a low level of business value and inefficiently deliver services and projects. The implications of a score in this region are as follows:

a. The IT organization does not have a clear understanding of the business needs from the business units.

b. The IT organization does not have an efficient delivery model for services and associated projects.

c. The IT organization needs to develop a plan that dramatically improves the alignment with business needs. IT leadership needs to meet with business leaders to understand their needs and codevelop the business services and associated projects that provide business value. There is apparent misalignment that needs correction.

d. The IT organization needs to develop an efficiency improvement plan for the delivery of the services and associated projects by IT personnel.

e. An active program needs to be in place for the business unit and IT leaders to meet on a regular basis to improve the business value and ensure that there is no degradation of service and project delivery efficiency.

f. The IT organization needs to continuously measure the business value and efficiency of delivery for the services and projects.

Assessment Techniques

You can utilize different techniques using the assessment instrument to measure your IT organization's maturity for each phase of the strategic IT transformation. Use one or more of the following techniques you believe will provide the optimum measure of strategic maturity.

1. Perform a 360-degree assessment.
   a. Business unit leaders and their staff assess IT: This technique provides you with a business view of the strategic maturity of your IT organization.
   b. CIO and IT directors assess IT organization: This technique provides you with an IT view of the strategic maturity of your IT organization.
   c. IT directors assess their teams: This technique provides you with an IT director's view of the strategic maturity of their IT teams.
   d. IT teams self-assess: This technique provides you with an IT Team view of their strategic maturity.

2. Share the results with the business unit leaders, directors, and all IT teams in a workshop to discuss the implications. Use this as a learning experience. Share key points from the previous chapters of the case examples for each of the strategic IT transformation phases.

3. Develop an ongoing plan to reassess the strategic IT maturity for each of the phases and share the results with IT and the business units.

Chapter Summary

Measuring the strategic maturity of your IT organization for each of the four transformation phases is a first step on your journey to improve the business value derived by the business. The challenge now is to improve the strategic maturity of your IT organization. If you succeed, the advantages are numerous.

Your company will provide new and measurable value to customers. Market share will rise. Sales will increase. Operating margins will widen. Inside the company, IT personnel will partner opportunistically with business teams to identify and provide value in the form of new products, services, and enhanced business processes. On the personal side, IT personnel will develop new skills that will improve their performance and value.

As a strategic CIO, you will have a seat in the boardroom aside your C-suite colleagues. The CEO will recognize your value and your career will be on the rise. Remember what Bob Dylan said, "For the times they are a-changin." There is no better time to be a CIO and this is your opportunity to change the dynamics of your business enterprise by leveraging information and technology to achieve competitive advantage. Good luck comes to those who are well prepared. My wish is that this book provides you with the tools you will need to succeed.

20
FINAL THOUGHTS
An Executive Challenge

CHAPTER OBJECTIVE

The objective of this chapter is to conclude the book with a challenge to the executive suite. Strategic CIOs are now part of the executive team that drives business outcomes to improve customer value, increase revenue, and enhance shareholder wealth. Managing in the twenty-first century requires new thinking. The pace of change is so fast today that management delegates decision making throughout the organization, even those closest to the customer. Unfortunately, personnel don't have all the facts and, as a result, make decisions that create tremendous risks for the company (e.g., JP Morgan's *London Whale* scandal). The result is that decisions not made with all the correct facts, as well as the history of similar decisions and resultant risks, could negatively impact the company. A proactive *early warning* information system is required to coach and mentor decision makers throughout the organization to mitigate risks before they occur; in essence, *instrument the business* to avert risks through a set of early warning indicators, smoke alarms, and mitigating actions to prevent risks before they occur.

- Managing in the twenty-first century requires new approaches than used in the past. The dynamic and ever-changing business landscape requires companies to be agile, flexible, and aware of emerging issues that can quickly turn a profitable and competitively successful company into a potential disaster. Remember the 2012 JP Morgan's London Whale trading scandal that

> resulted in 6.2 billion dollar trading loss and 920 million
> billions in penalties. True, JP Morgan has a set of prod-
> ucts and services that provide significant revenues.
> • However, flaws in supporting processes that enable these
>   products and services did not provide early warning of a
>   potential trading issue. Herein lie the gap and the chal-
>   lenge for the executive suite.

The focus of this book is how strategic CIOs and their IT teams
are changing the business landscape. They accomplish this by collaborating with C-suite executives and business teams to leverage
information and technology for competitive advantage by developing
new products, services, and processes to achieve significant business
outcomes. I have provided you, the reader, with numerous examples
of how strategic CIOs transform their IT organization using a four-
phase transformation model. I sincerely hope that you apply the lessons, insights, and experiences shared by these strategic CIOs as you
begin the journey to transform your IT organization into a strategic
enabler of business success.

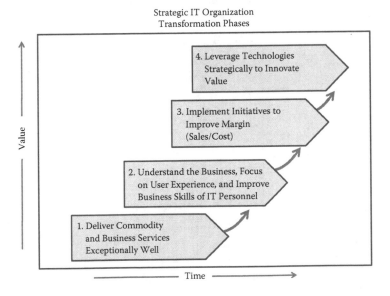

Business Challenge

There is, however, an important challenge the executive suite must address. Managing in the twenty-first century requires new approaches than used in the past. The dynamic and ever-changing global business landscape requires companies to be agile, flexible, and aware of emerging issues, from outside as well as within its business enterprise. Otherwise, unforeseen events can quickly turn a profitable and competitively successful company into a potential disaster. Remember the 2012 JP Morgan London Whale trading scandal that resulted in 6.2 billion dollar trading loss and 920 million in penalties.[1] True, JP Morgan has a set of products and services that provide significant revenues. However, flaws in governance and oversight processes did not provide early warning of a potential trading issue. Herein lie the gap and the challenge for the executive suite. This event led many executives in the C-suite to begin conversations regarding the flaws in key processes throughout their companies that often go awry. The *London Whale event* is an extreme example. However, each and every day, executives, managers, and personnel throughout your business enterprise make decisions, approve decisions, or are aware of decisions made by others. These decisions would be made differently if management and personnel had an *early warning system* to advise them of the potential pitfalls and associated risks based upon different decision scenarios.

Today's global business environment is more complex than ever before. This is due to the following three paradigm shifts in the competitive marketplace, each causing a governance chasm for the business enterprise:

- Expanding global marketplace requires constant vigilance to uncover competitive opportunities and threats.
- Consumerization of IT results in customers demanding new digital products and services that IT organizations need to develop quickly and cost-effectively.
- Changing organization models composed of virtual teams making complex business decisions replaces the traditional vertical and hierarchical structures.

Each of the three market changes listed has resulted in a new wave of information gathering by companies to better understand the competitive environment; pulse the needs, wants, and desires of its customers; and develop a more seamless communication process across the entire enterprise. The result is a broader and deeper enterprise structure overloaded with data. True, companies today focus externally to capture and mine much of this data, using social media and sophisticated analytical tools, to uncover customer behaviors and market trends. However, companies must also focus internally to mine process data to anticipate where process breaches could significantly affect company's revenues, costs, and potentially its survival. In effect, mitigate the risk of a potential disaster before it happens.

Take a look at all the major companies that have a global reach. Procter & Gamble, Johnson and Johnson, IBM, JP Morgan, Walmart, GM, Xerox, FedEx, and UPS are all familiar names to us and are just some examples of companies that have thousands of employees around the world making critical business decisions each and every day. The command and control structure of the past no longer works. Market dynamics require companies to make decisions and take actions faster than ever before. Customers demand it. As a result, organizational structures are more decentralized, and decision-making authority is delegated throughout the entire process, even to personnel closest to the customer.

A New Approach for Managing in the 21st Century

The dilemma facing executives is simple. In Chapter 17, *How Procter & Gamble Leverages Technology Strategically to Innovate Value*, we referenced a Jack Welch quote, which focused the subject from an external perspective, not from an internal control perspective. Read the same quote as follows, and relate it to the previous paragraphs that describe the dilemma faced by the executive suite today.

> At the beginning of the decade…we saw two challenges ahead of us, one external and one internal. Externally, we faced a world economy that would be characterized by slower growth, with stronger global competitors going after a smaller piece of the pie. Internally, our challenge was even bigger. <u>We had to find a way to combine the power,</u>

resources, and reach of a large company with the hunger, agility, spirit, and fire of a small one.[2]

I underlined the last sentence of the quote because this summarizes the challenge that the executive suite faces today. Following is a personal example. When I joined ITM Software in 2003, a new start-up, the founders and a cadre of 30 employees with a high energy level and entrepreneurial spirit worked hard and pushed the boundaries to grow the business. Everyone wore multiple hats and communication flowed freely and quickly. Everyone was aware of business decisions on product design, development, marketing, sales, customer service, etc. When a decision inadvertently resulted in a negative impact on the business, the team quickly banded together to correct the problem. At other times, when team members worked together to discuss a potential action and someone anticipated a potential problem, he or she spoke out and discussed the possible consequences, and the team agreed on an appropriate course of action. Such is the DNA of the small company. As companies grow, the management instill processes and structure to maintain a core of discipline and consistency in the execution of activities. Decision making is tightly controlled. However, information flows, which often traverse both vertically and horizontally, are often filtered as they traverse the management chain. There has to be a better way.

Here is a message to all CEOs, CIOs, and C-suite executives: take heed of the challenge and figure out how to develop and utilize an information system for managing in the twenty-first century that replicates the speed, agility, and spirit of a small company. Here's why? How would you answer the following questions?

- As your business has grown, have your processes and policies slowed down the communication of information across the business?
- Have you ever been surprised to find out after the fact that an incorrect decision negatively impacted your company's reputation, loss of market share, revenue, and share price due to a process not followed properly or, even worse, personnel inadvertently making a poor decision, even though everyone was telling you that everything is ok?

- Did you find out during the postmortem analysis that *someone always knew or* there were warning signs that could have prevented the problem if they were properly captured as data or appropriately communicated to the management team?
- Do you realize that the inability to monitor and govern appropriately could jeopardize the survival of your company?

If you answered yes to any of these previous questions, you need to figure out how to address the problem. This subject is explored by Lynda Applegate, the Sarofim-Rock professor of Business Administration at Harvard, in one of her many papers on the subject. In her paper, "Time for the Big Small Company,"[3] Applegate's main thesis is that, until recent times, information systems were not mature enough to handle the *volumes and complexity of information flows required* by complex organizational structures. However, advances in technology and information systems are now available to provide a digital governance layer across the entire business enterprise.

There are some examples of where this is happening in today's business environment. Procter & Gamble addresses part of the challenge with its *decision cockpit* and *business sphere* applications that help managers and teams make well-informed business decisions (see Chapter 17). Filippo Passerini and his IT/business teams digitized the company data and accomplished three major objectives. First, there is now one set of information, so there is no dispute about the accuracy of the data, which often plagues teams in accurately analyzing data. This enables 8000 employees to focus on data analysis versus data integrity when performing their job. Second, much of the non-value-added time resulting from capturing, organizing, and conducting some preliminary analysis is eliminated. Many managers will tell you that they spend 50%–80% of their time gathering, organizing, and interpreting data. Eliminating the *data accuracy confusion* provides managers the ability to spend a majority of their time on decision scenario analysis to make well-informed business decisions, which is a value-added activity. Third, data are analyzed extensively using business analytics and presented in various graphical formats for ease of interpretation. This strategic use of technology and information addresses the islands of information challenge that plagues many companies. The net result is managers and teams focus on reviewing analyzed data that result in personnel and teams making well-informed business decisions.[4]

The next evolution for effectively managing in the twenty-first century lies in the development of an information-based system that can predict and identify potential risk areas for the day-to-day decisions that, if made incorrectly, could negatively impact the company. The key to success will be monitoring key enterprise processes and identify potential risk areas.

Remember the Jack Welch quote, discussed earlier, where he addresses the challenge of combining *"...the power, resources, and reach of a large company with the hunger, agility, spirit, and fire of a small one."* One of my mentors is Tony Salvaggio, CEO of Computer Aid, Inc. (CAI). Salvaggio is a strategic thinker who has built a 500 million dollar world class IT professional services business with a global presence. Salvaggio describes CAI's value statement as follows:

> *"We are efficiency experts and we promise our clients a 20-30 percent productivity improvement coupled with increased operational visibility and control?*[5,6]

Salvaggio and I often meet to discuss business philosophy and global business challenges. During a recent meeting, we discussed Welch's quote and he articulated the implication as follows:

> *"Our challenge is to make sure that companies grow their business without devolving into anarchy and a total loss of control and increase in risks/mistakes, etc. The ultimate question is how do we leverage the energy of a valued workforce but not repeat the basic errors of the past over and over again?"*[6]

CAI is developing a suite of Software as a Service (SaaS) solutions named Advanced Management Insight (AMI). According to Salvaggio, *"CAI has been in the lead in creating a new management system that provides **visibility** of data, **control** of processes, and **optimization** of resource performance.*[6] Salvaggio founded CAI in the early 1980s and always believed that "process excellence is the road to success." Over its 30 plus years in business, CAI has developed methodologies, processes, and solutions, around their intellectual capital that focus on improving IT processes.[5,6]

Salvaggio says, *"The AMI solution incorporates advanced management principles supported by software that is easily adaptable to any management system."* When I asked Salvaggio to provide an example of where the AMI solution would be most effective, he said, *"In every company, managers oversee work teams that involve numerous activities that support business processes. There are hundreds of these work teams throughout a company, and in large companies, such as GE, Procter & Gamble, or FedEx, there are thousands."* CAI has identified these as *management cells.* (ibid)

One of the areas that Salvaggio spends a lot of time thinking about is the future evolution of management systems. He says, *"Management systems of tomorrow must focus on facilitating survival, optimization, and innovation."* An analogy to Salvaggio's thinking can be best described with a simple example of an airplane cockpit. Every plane has a cockpit with an intelligent pilot-assist performance-monitoring system while still being tightly interconnected with the FAA airline control systems. Salvaggio uses this analogy often in describing the AMI solution. At the heart of CAIs approach is to design an individual cockpit for each of the management cells in the corporation, logically link these, and tie them together in a knowledge network for the company.

CAI efforts are right on track. Today's business enterprise is composed of a very complex set of processes, just like airplane systems. These processes have to work in harmony to develop, sell, and deliver products and services for customers. I am sure your company focuses much effort on optimizing these processes. However, you may not be focusing enough energy on the need for a governance system that monitors these processes to avert risks that occur due to incorrect decisions made each and every day throughout the company and perhaps a major one that could even impact the very survival of your company.

An extension of the cockpit example is to look at the US Federal Aviation Authority National Airspace System (FAA–NAS). This organization is responsible for providing the safest and the most efficient aerospace system in the world. At any given time of day, approximately 5000 aircraft fly in the skies above the United States. In addition, on any single day, the FAA monitors approximately 85,000 flights.[7] Through an extensive network of systems, highly trained air traffic controllers stationed at airports and FAA facilities across the United States monitor all flights *to ensure that all traffic moves as smoothly as possible* and handle *constraints in the system, such as weather and runway closures.*[8] The air traffic controllers reroute aircraft based on early warning indicators. These include if planes are too close to each other, an adverse weather forecast, or if an aircraft needs to be rerouted due to an onboard medical emergency. Although each aircraft has their own onboard systems to monitor the plane's systems, the FAA's governance process ensures that all aircraft flying in the skies above the United States move safely through their filed flight patterns.

I would like to explore this analogy. Think of the airplane cockpit as one of your company's process cells where personnel from different parts of the organization perform a variety of process activities. Think about logistics, product development, projects, and vendor management as examples of processes that contain high degrees of risk. Major issues can occur if incorrect decisions are made or information about the process is not available to personnel performing process activities. Following are some examples

- Inadvertently routing of logistics carriers, vehicles, planes, trucks, or rail, without the knowledge of impending weather, traffic, or mechanical issues, can impact sales, cause product spoilage, and create havoc across the entire network for many companies because of the lack of an *early warning system.*
- Projects reflecting a *green* status may in fact be *yellow* or *red* due to team members being unaware of warning signals, resulting in project overruns, inefficient resource allocation, out of scope efforts, etc.
- A product development team makes a decision not realizing that the same decision previously implemented by another product development team resulted in untimely delays.
- One of your major strategic vendors, while providing similar services for another company, make decisions that negatively impact revenue and cash collection.

These events happen every day at many companies. Yet management has yet to figure out a way to proactively mitigate these negative outcomes. During my interviews for this book, many CIOs shared their experiences of being surprised at decisions made by personnel throughout the enterprise due to lack of an adequate governance process.

Managers at companies around the globe spend billions of dollars improving the effectiveness of business processes but not nearly enough to provide a governance *early warning system* to ensure that potential risk areas are identified and communicated and proactive actions taken to prevent negative outcomes.

Develop an Enterprise Early Warning Decision Support System to Reduce Enterprise Risk

My message to all CEOs, CIOs, and C-suite executives based upon the Executive Challenge is as follows:

1. Ensure the integrity of all enterprise data and eliminate disparate islands of information (see Chapter 17).
2. Continue initiatives to capture and mine customer data to learn about customer needs, wants, and desires, behaviors that impact buying behavior, and competitive intelligence.
3. Continue to optimize business processes to improve efficiencies and improve desired business outcomes.
4. Identify key processes and begin a program to capture key information about potential risk areas, key predictors, past negative outcomes, etc., for example, specific activities that resulted in risk as well as how you can identify the *predictors* of risk.
5. Investigate *early warning* applications available in the market that can analyze these data to predict potential risk areas and communicate alerts to include suggested mitigating actions.
6. Develop an enterprise-wide mentor program to capture, leverage, and incorporate decision learning as part of every company activity.

There is much more research and development required to explore this subject in more detail, perhaps the subject of my next book.

Citations

1. *Bloomberg News*: http://www.bloomberg.com/news/2013-09-19/jpmorgan-chase-agrees-to-pay-920-million-for-london-whale-loss.html. September 20, 2013.
2. Welch, J., Managing in the 90s, GE Report to Shareholders, 1988.
3. Applegate, L.M. Time for the Big Small Company. Mastering Information Management Series. *Financial Times*, March 1, 1999.

4. Note: See Chapter 17: How P & G Leverages Technology Strategically to Innovate Value for more information on Passerini, Digital cockpits, and Business Sphere Conference Rooms.
5. CAI website: http://www.compaid.com/.
6. Tony Salvaggio, CEO-CAI/Phil Weinzimer Interview, December 18, 2013.
7. FAA Website: http://www.faa.gov/nextgen/snapshots/nas/.
8. Citing: http://www.nycaviation.com/2011/04/faa-opens-new-air-traffic-control-system-command-center-in-virginia/#.Ut2f0BAo6Uk.

Afterword

Having spent 30+ years in the information technology (IT) industry from developing operating systems to full-scale enterprise applications; from founding and running start-ups, managing full blown enterprise IT departments as well as IT services providers; from mainframes, minicomputers, microcomputers, and PC to the world of ubiquitous cloud computing; as well as being a buyer and seller of IT products, services, and companies, I have seen a lot of change. But none of that approaches the dramatic changes and speed that is taking place as I write this. These changes are having a tremendous impact on the role of the chief information officer (CIO).

For the last 4 years, the innovation group at Dell has been researching the changes taking place in corporate IT. While the research identified the usual suspect about what is happening—bring your own device (BYOD), software as a service (SaaS), IT outsourcing (ITO), and the rest of the alphabet soup—it became clear that forces outside of IT were forcing changes upon IT: what IT is, how it is delivered, and how it is used, rather than just new technologies refreshing how IT was delivered as we have experienced in the past. The realization had us join forces with Forbes, HBR, and the Economist for a series of research projects, addressing over 800+ enterprises across the globe, not just on IT, but the business it supports and IT's relationship with senior management—roles, expectations, performance, and the future.

Via this research, I have studied these changes and the forces driving them, and written about them extensively, and I can tell you, first hand, that C-suite executives do not fully understand the power of leveraging information and technology to improve the competitive advantage for their company. This chasm provides the CIO with a perfect opportunity to lead the C-suite in leveraging information and technologies in innovative ways to create new value that drives revenue, creates satisfied customers, and enhances shareholder wealth. The operative question is: Are CIOs ready for this challenge?

There are two parts to answering this question—the first is how the CIO can gain the trust and respect of the C-suite as a contributor to the overall success of the enterprise, today and in the future. The second and the most pressing challenge for the CIO is how to reposition the IT organization from a techno-centric to a strategic enabler of business success. *The Strategic CIO* is a *how-to* formula for CIOs to follow if they want to achieve both of these goals.

The objective of an afterword is to provide you, the reader, with a summary of the book, identifying the major takeaways, including case studies, and how it will help you succeed in your business role. I will do this. Keep in mind that this is as much a leadership challenge as a technology or management challenge. Let me share a little historical perspective to set the stage for the challenges CIOs face today.

When people look into the history for examples of leadership, the usual names are brought up—Alexander, Caesar, Napoleon, etc.— the list is long. For me though, it is a reluctant leader who resonates most—Xenophon.

Xenophon was a young scholar (student of Socrates) who on a lark went off to war and unexpectedly found himself in command of the recently defeated remnants of an army of Greek mercenaries, primarily Spartans, trapped in the middle of the Persian Empire, surrounded by a significantly (100 times) larger Persian army. He was faced with the challenge to organize these soldiers, motivate them, and get them back to Greece alive. His problem was further complicated by the fact he was an Athenian (Sparta and Athens weren't exactly best buds at this point in time); Greek mercenaries had a tradition of *democratic* principles of command (conducting assemblies to express their opinions and to vote on how things should be done), generally reflected the levels of agreement found among the city states from which they hailed (in other words, very little); and they would have to cross some of the most imposing terrain in the world. Did I mention the natives were not exactly friendly? A further complication was that communications from Greece indicated that the homeland was not real anxious to have them (a group of unemployed prone to violence mercenaries) back either.

Sort of sounds like a contemporary CIO in some ways. CIOs are surrounded by challenges like bring your own technology (more than just BYOD), cloud computing, SaaS, business process as a service, outsourcing, and remote infrastructure management outsourcing (RIMO) suppliers for every element they are responsible for. Similar to the analogy of a Persian army of technology suppliers offering better, faster, cheaper as well as outnumbering the CIO a 1000 to 1. Over time, as the workforce has evolved with both age and familiarity and facility with the technologies available, the work cohorts increasingly focus on choosing what they work on and who they work with, rather than taking directions from who they work for. New technologies such as mobile, social, cloud, business intelligence, and predictive analytics represent as treacherous a terrain as anything Xenophon faced. Recent surveys have shown extremely low satisfaction among users, though probably not as hostile as the Persian natives. Lastly, the survey work I referenced earlier of CEOs showed that less than a third thought their CIOs were better than average and over 70% thought they would be getting IT services from new sources over the next 5 years—not exactly a welcoming homeland either.

Xenophon overcame his challenges as can you. Phil has assembled philosophies, principles, and practices as well as insights from a broad selection of successful CIOs who are weathering and thriving amidst all these changes. Reading *The Strategic CIO* can be your guide much in the same way that Socrates' teachings guided Xenophon.

Phil and I met at the CIO100 Conference in 2012. I was teaching innovation in the context of the future of corporate IT and Phil attended my session. Afterwards, we engaged in a series of intense discussions basically around doing the right things versus doing things right. My view was that the future role of corporate IT was to lead the organization, not to align or supplicate itself to the business. Over the past 20 years, nothing has transformed business as thoroughly, or as frequently, as IT. In the 1990s, advances in IT and the rise of enterprise systems enabled many companies to revamp their operating models by enabling and facilitating business process reengineering as described in the 1993 bestseller *Reengineering the Corporation*. Michael Hammer and James Champy argued for a comprehensive retooling of operating practices—of the processes organizations use to source, produce, and distribute their products and services, which could only really happen through the application of information systems. In the 2000s, IT was at the forefront of new forms of business models like Amazon, eBay, Google, and Facebook, which could not exist without IT and forced businesses and whole industries to be deconstructed, disintermediated, dematerialized, and democratized by the web. Now, we are seeing a global shift of management focus from efficiency and CAPEX ROI/ROA to innovation, problem solving, and creativity focusing on the efficacy of the organization in creating and delivering value to the market in as near real time as possible. This is producing a broad-based and long overdue revolution in management models—in the way companies are led, managed, and organized. This in turn brings a shift in IT focus from transactional record keeping and reporting to social and ecosystem enablement, collaboration, choreography, and orchestration from the furthest customer to the beginning of the value creation chain.

In order to accomplish this shift, the nexus of IT focus must shift from efficiency to efficacy, toward delivering adaptability, flexibility, engagement, and supporting on demand business ecosystems. More importantly, IT should become the source for most product/service, process, and business model innovation in the coming years. It is through IT that companies can begin to move beyond focusing on reducing transaction costs toward accelerating capability building and effectively using that capability to innovate. IT itself needs to move beyond just *faster, better, cheaper* investment models today to offer up new ideas that are forward thinking, feasible, viable, and valuable— to create new value for customers. IT leaders must find new ways to apply existing technologies to enable new business processes and models to create new breakthrough innovative value propositions for customers, to apply new technologies to innovate the creation process for old value propositions; and propose whole new combinations of business models, processes, products and services enabled, facilitated and accelerated by IT that disrupt markets and industries.

Phil agreed but politely suggested that such a role would be difficult, if not impossible, if the organization did not consider IT as a strategic and business-focused asset. Many CIOs have become chief infrastructure officers focusing on developing and managing technology rather than CIOs focused on creating value for the organization and its customers. Some of this is a preference; some of it is learned behavior, because reducing costs and driving efficiency in the infrastructure were the basis for past rewards. Some of it is complacency, which makes people so comfortable with traditional ways of doing things that they are blind to the advantages that can come with change. To become a good chief innovation officer, one first needs to be a great CIO.

This is where Phil's book, *The Strategic CIO*, can be a valuable resource for CIOs who want to transform and work with the C-suite to improve business outcomes and drive value for their company. CIOs who focus on business results and create measurable value will lay the necessary foundation to begin leading the business into the future. The insights, experiences, and lessons learned, coupled with case study examples, will help you transform your IT organization into a strategic powerhouse that leads the company to innovate new and measurable value.

Who more than the CIO best understands the business—all transactions and information and processes flow through or are tied to the systems they deliver to the organization? Who more than the CIO knows the threats and opportunities that the new and emerging technologies present to the enterprise? Combining those two thoughts, who, more than the CIO, should be the CEOs' trusted advisor, confidant, and mentor to the rest of the C-suite as the world turns upside down?

The Strategic CIO will help you to understand and apply the concepts for transforming your IT organization into a strategic asset for your company. The four-phase strategic IT transformation model Phil uses as the framework for his book is an effective model CIOs can use to transform their IT organization to create measurable value. The model focuses on four fundamental principles of a strategic IT organization, each representing a phase of the strategic IT transformation framework. Phil provides numerous case studies for each of these phases.

The major takeaways from this book are the four phases as well as some of the more memorable case study examples to learn from. Following is a quick summary. You can use this as a guide to identify the areas you should reference in your journey to transform your IT organization.

Phase 1: Deliver basic services exceptionally well. This is an important foundation step. You have to get this right to gain the trust of the business so you can collaborate with business teams on projects that result in measurable business outcomes. Whether you have your own data center generating its own power with dedicated communication lines, have partially or totally outsourced your infrastructure, or are heading totally to the clouds—if you cannot deliver basic, relatively simple commodity IT and business services well, procuring, monitoring, managing, and supporting them—then what makes you think you can deliver on demand, complex, generally out of your direct control services of the future? It's just like a Formula 1 team leader getting ready for a race. You will have to have establish credibility that you know how to get the car, all its supplies, and all the team to the track; get through a lap of the track with everything working; and execute a pit stop while you swap tires, engine, transmission, lubricants, fuel, and maybe even the driver successfully, all before you can even begin to talk about race strategy, modifying the car, or even the racing season.

Following are examples from these early chapters that are worth rereading:

- Steve O'Connor (CIO, CSAA Insurance Group), Cynthia McKenzie (former vice president, IT, Fox Entertainment), and Tom Murphy (CIO, University of Pennsylvania) each understand how to deliver basic services exceptionally well. Included in the early chapters are templates, insights, and lessons learned in traversing this difficult, but necessary, course to gain the trust from the business. Their experiences will prove invaluable in developing this core foundation component.
- Operational excellence and effective project governance are critical to delivering basic services, and the frameworks and examples used at CSAA Insurance, Fox Entertainment,

and Georgia Technology Authority will definitely help you understand how to implement these processes within your IT organization.

- How to measure the value of the business services is especially important in building the trust and confidence from business unit leaders. Phil provides an excellent four-step process and accompanying example you can use to implement a measurement process that will clearly demonstrate the business value your IT organization provides to the business.

Phase 2: Understand the business, focus on user experiences, and improve business skills of IT personnel. IT personnel who work on business teams have to understand and speak the language of the business for the collaboration to succeed. Collaboration, orchestration, and choreography across multiple enterprises in a digital business ecosystem will be the key to future enterprise success. Being able to do that internally is a necessary first step, and for that, a lingua franca must be in place. Technology is but a small part of the CIO's future role. To be a mentor to the C-suite and a trusted advisor to the CEO, you must understand the business as well as the value in terms of the business; the stakeholders, singularly and in groups; the market; and the economy as a whole. You must also understand how that value can and should be created with IT enablement:

- Chapter 7 provides examples from CIOs who attained their role from different paths: within IT, within the same industry, and outside the industry. The example of Niel Nickolaisen, CIO at Western Governors University, is interesting. As the business process executive at a major company, he complained so much about IT that the CEO had no recourse but to reassign him to the role. Depending on your previous role, the methods used to learn about the business vary and the examples used are very useful.
- Understanding your organization's culture is an important element in the transformation process. The *Competing Values* $_{TM}$ framework by Kim S. Cameron and Robert E. Quinn that Phil addresses is a perfect tool to help you identify the cultural gaps that, if addressed properly, can accelerate the transformation process.

- One of the most valuable insights in the book is Phil's strategic IT competency model that explores the four key competencies and associated skills IT personnel need in today's info-centric enterprise. Understanding the business, knowledge of the market and competitive environment, and technology prowess represent three key competencies. The fourth is a set of cross-competency skills CIOs and IT personnel need to be able to articulate a vision and communicate in a language the business understands and leadership skills to drive IT/business teams to focus on user experiences as a focal point in identifying innovative value opportunities. Each of these competencies and the associated skills are explored in detail with accompanying examples from CIO and their IT teams. Phil provides a useful tool, instructions, and examples of how you can measure the strategic maturity of your IT organization. Also useful are tips you can use to mitigate any gaps and improve the strategic competencies in your IT organization.

Phase 3: Implement initiatives to improve margin. Phil points out that this is the only immediate credible path for a CIO who wants to create business value for the company. Beyond understanding business, the CIO needs to have a business mindset and use that understanding to identify, plan, and execute on projects that create value for the enterprise. Each of the following five CIO initiatives detailed in this section of the book will provide you with valuable insights you can apply within your company:

1. How *Tom Grooms, CIO at Valspar, successfully worked* with business units to improve processes, reduce IT support costs, and drive initiatives that enabled Valspar to move forward with *an aggressive growth strategy.*
2. How *Randy Spratt, CTO and CIO at McKesson,* the multinational health-care services and IT company, successfully harnessed a company-wide team to develop a unified architecture, which improved *customer service and improved sales.*
3. How Clif Triplett, while CIO at Baker Hughes, drove the development of a product lifecycle management system that

reduced development time for products and services resulting in improved customer service and reduced IT costs.

4. How *Anne Wilms, while CIO at Rohm and Hass,* drove a number of strategic initiatives that increased revenue through an improved pricing system, reduced IT costs, and optimized inventory investment savings millions of dollars, as well as a host of other initiatives.

5. How Steve Heilenman, CIO at CAI Inc., implemented a visibility, control, and optimization strategy to *reduce IT spend by 50%* through reduced legacy support costs and improved project management governance *while at the same time developing a testing solution the company sells to external customers.*

Phase 4: Leverage technology strategically to innovate measurable value. This is where true business value is achieved. This is where CIOs lead major initiatives leveraging information and technology that drive business value. The chapters on Rob Carter, CIO of FedEx, and Filippo Passerini, CIO of Procter and Gamble, provide great insights and examples of how each of these CIOs provides the leadership needed to innovate true value for their respective company. A separate chapter that provides examples of seven CIOs who leverage technology strategically to innovate value will provide you with valuable examples you can apply within your company:

- Chapter 16 on FedEx explains how Rob Carter, CIO, transformed IT by leveraging technology strategy and enabling a business model that allows each of the business units to compete collectively, manage collaboratively, and operate independently. Carter's leadership helped each of the main FedEx core business units be more effective and create innovative value for its customers.

- Chapter 17 on Procter & Gamble is a great example of how a CIO's leadership can change the way the company makes business decisions. Filippo Passerini, group president of Global Business Services and CIO of Procter & Gamble, and his business-focused teams digitized data at Procter & Gamble so business teams accessing a single source of truth make well-informed business decisions using predictive analytics and sophisticated graphic displays that present data in meaningful ways. The use of *digital cockpits* and *business sphere* conference rooms completely changed the way Procter & Gamble business teams make decisions.

- Chapter 18 highlights five CIOs who leveraged technology strategically to innovate value. Each case is from a different industry and provides a different perspective that will help you glean valuable lessons and insights:
  - How the CIO of Build-A-Bear Workshop changed is changing the physical in-store model of customers creating stuffed animals into a digital experience that broadens the reach to customers throughout the entire shopping experience.
  - How the CIO of Express Scripts collaborates with business leaders to help customers improve their health outcomes through enabling technologies that also improved business results, a win for the customer and a win for the company.
  - How the CIO of Lehigh Valley Health Network innovates value in providing health care through integrating technologies with patient services that result in saving lives.
  - How CIOs from Verisk, Lincoln Trust, Penske, and Air Products and Chemicals each find ways to innovate value by leveraging technology.
- Chapter 19 offers an insightful methodology for you to measure strategic maturity, identify gaps, and an approach to develop mitigation plans.
- And, in closing, Chapter 20 provides insights on how companies need to manage differently in the 21st century. Phil provides an approach to consider that integrates agility, speed, and quality in your company's quest to create new products and services. The net result: create customer value, increase margins, and enhance shareholder wealth.

All of which brings us back to Xenophon. He not only successfully led the Spartan army out of Persia but also engaged in a number of successful mercenary expeditions along the way, making both he and the army prosperous. If he were to offer advice to today's CIO, he would say, "There is small risk a general will be regarded with contempt by those he leads, if, whatever he may have to preach, he shows himself best able to perform." Much in the same way my research has shown low expectations on the part of the C-suite for what a CIO can contribute, following Phil's four phases effectively shows that the CIO is *best able to perform*. At that point, you have earned the opportunity and gained the trust to be the C-suite mentor, advisor, and strategist (and not just on technology) for the enterprise on future business models, processes, products, services, and markets and how to organize and manage for them.

If you believe in the transformational power of IT, and all of my research suggests it is real, then you are now in a position to exploit its potential. You can now lead your enterprise to the fact that tomorrow's winning management practices and processes will be as different from what is done today as the web and smartphones are different from plain old telephone service and rotary dial landlines. Then you have to bring all of your imagination and all of you your skills to the challenge of building a *postbureaucratic* organization of collaboration, cooperation, orchestration, and choreography across a socially enabled enterprise operating in a digital business ecosystem assembling capability on demand to deliver innovative value when, where, and how customers want to consume it.

Xenophon also said, "If you consider what are called the virtues in mankind, you will find their growth is assisted by education and cultivation." In this book, Phil has offered education in what to do and, through other CIO's stories, cultivated how to do it. I would further suggest that this book is not only for CIOs but also for CEOs and other C-suite executives and aspiring CIOs. It will provide a challenge and compass for you, having your executive team understand what you should be doing and how you should be performing. It also sets the stage for your future leadership of the enterprise. "When the interests of mankind are at stake, they will obey with joy the man whom they believe to be wiser than themselves. You may prove this on all sides: you may see how the sick man will beg the doctor to tell him what he ought to do, how a whole ship's company will listen to the pilot (Xenophon)."

Let me leave you with one last thought—it won't be easy nor will it all progress linearly from point a to point b. Xenophon made it back to Athens, then was banished from Athens, and then later called back yet again. Expect starts and stops, success and failures, and more than a few side trips to gain experience. But proving you can perform, proving you know the technologies and what they can enable for the business and what the business can extract from the technology, then you can become the chief innovation officer your enterprise needs.

> The true test of a leader is whether his followers will adhere to his cause from their own volition, enduring the most arduous hardships without being forced to do so, and remaining steadfast in the moments of greatest peril (Xenophon).

James A. Stikeleather
Executive Strategist and Chief Innovation Officer
Dell Corporation

Appendix A: Chapter Summaries

Following are the chapter summaries that appear at the beginning of each chapter. I have included this as an appendix to provide you with a quick overview of the book so you can develop your reading plan, and as a reference after you have read the book.

CHAPTER 1: INTRODUCTION

CHANGING ROLE OF THE CIO

A. CHAPTER OBJECTIVE

Provide an overview of the book.

B. KEY MESSAGE

There is no better time to be a chief information officer (CIO). Just look around you! The consumerization of information technology (IT) is dramatically influencing the products and services your company provides to customers, vendors, logistic partners, and business personnel, across the entire value network, to create new markets and competitive opportunities. Some chief executive officers (CEO) and C-suite colleagues may understand the potential of leveraging information for strategic advantage and there is a larger group that does not. The challenge is how to accomplish it.

Your role as a CIO is changing from a technologist to a strategist. The consumerization of IT is revolutionizing how consumers shop, travel, and pay for services. The consumer experience is the focus. On the business side, IT is enabling almost every single business process, which drives and supports customer value. As a result, you, as a CIO, need to be more involved in business discussions than ever before. In fact, strategic CIOs collaborate with C-level peers to develop business strategies and innovate value. The role of a CIO is expanding, and those that truly add business value even oversee and manage key business functions.[2] Today, it is all about business outcome. You, as a CIO, are in the best position to participate and enable new information-rich products and services. The question is *are you and your IT organization up to the challenge?*

- Do you understand the business and competitive environment well enough to help the business achieve significant outcomes?
- Do your IT personnel have the necessary competencies and skills to effectively partner with and participate in business teams?
- Does your IT organization effectively collaborate with business unit executives and employ speed, agility, and quality in responding to their needs?
- Does your CTO understand how to apply the new and emerging technologies for competitive advantage?

C. EXAMPLES

1. A summary of each section and the accompanying chapters.
2. Guide to highlight the value of reading this book for key roles in the enterprise: CEO, CIO, C-suite, business unit executives, business unit and IT directors, managers, and personnel.

3. A template to help you plan your book reading experience. The template provides a listing of each chapter and columns for you to check whether the chapter should be glanced over, reviewed, or read in detail.

CHAPTER 2: SECTION OVERVIEW

HOW TO DELIVER COMMODITY AND BUSINESS SERVICES EXCEPTIONALLY WELL

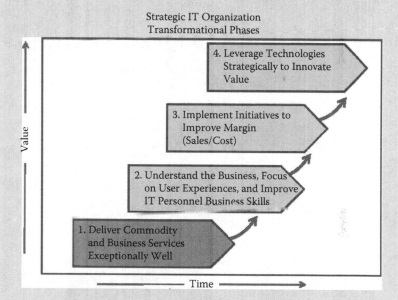

Strategic IT Organization
Transformational Phases

Every chief information officer (CIO) will tell you that delivering services exceptionally well is an important foundation component in building a trust-based working relationship with C-suite executives and business teams. Mostly all the CIOs I interviewed say the same thing. *It is basic blocking and tackling.* When each took on their CIO role at their current company, one of the first priorities was to gain a good understanding from the business how well commodity and business services are delivered. Many found that improvements were required. One would think that this is a no brainer and each IT organization delivers services exceptionally well. Not so. Ask Rob Carter from FedEx. It took Carter 6 years to develop a trust-based relationship with business unit executives.

Today's information-based marketplace is very complex. It is not the same as it was 10 years ago. More third-party solutions, everyone bringing their own devices, and security challenges create an environment where delivery of basic commodity and business services is more complex.

Those of you who are about to embark on a new role as CIO should find this section of the book valuable as it demonstrates the important steps in developing an excellent service delivery model. Examples of success stories from CIOs who successfully accomplished this phase of the transformation will be helpful as you embark on the journey.

If you feel your organization is delivering services exceptionally well to the business, you may want to review the material as a refresher and reassess how the business perceives the delivery of services. You may find the results interesting and be able to head off some potential delivery issues.

Please see Chapter Summary for the following chapters.

CHAPTER 3: HOW TO DELIVER BASIC SERVICES EXCEPTIONALLY WELL

A. CHAPTER OBJECTIVE

1. Explain the importance of delivering basic services exceptionally well in developing a trust-based relationship with C-suite executives and business management personnel.

2. Provide a seven-step framework CIOs utilize to achieve excellence in delivering basic services (commodity and business services) to the business (Figure 3.1).
3. Share insights and experiences from two CIOs in implementing processes to achieve superior delivery of basic services to the business.

B. KEY POINTS

1. Delivering basic services exceptionally well is *table stakes* for building a trust-based relationship with C-suite executives and business personnel.
2. Delivering basic services without disruption builds trust and credibility for the CIO and the IT organization.
3. Assessing, analyzing, and improving the delivery of basic services is a process.

C. EXAMPLES INCLUDING TEMPLATES USED

- CSAA Insurance Group
- Fox Entertainment Group
- University of Pennsylvania

CHAPTER 4: HOW TO EXCEL AT OPERATIONAL STABILITY

A. CHAPTER OBJECTIVE

1. Reinforce the importance of operational stability as a foundation for delivering basic services exceptionally well.
2. Share a framework chief information officers (CIOs) can utilize to achieve operational stability (Figure 4.1).
3. Explore how two CIOs ensure operational stability within their respective companies.

B. KEY POINTS

1. As the CIO or IT Director, your number one issue needs to be the operational stability of the business services you provide the enterprise.
2. A well-thought-out and sound architecture is required to support the business strategy.
3. Don't get caught building an architecture that resembles the physical architecture of the Winchester Mystery House in San Jose, California (see Figure 4.3).
4. Implement an effective change management process.
5. Measure what's important: ensure that uptime, abnormal terminations, performance issues, and defects meet or exceed the service level agreements (SLAs) your business peers require.

C. EXAMPLES

- CSAA Insurance Group
- Fox Entertainment Group

D. KEY TEMPLATE

- See Figure 4.1.

CHAPTER 5: HOW TO SUCCEED AT PROJECT GOVERNANCE

A. CHAPTER OBJECTIVE

1. Discuss the importance of project governance in providing an effective oversight and governance process for all projects and associated portfolios in the business enterprise.

2. Provide a project governance framework CIOs can use to provide an effective governance process within the IT organization.
3. Share a case study of an IT organization that uses an effective governance process tool in managing a diverse set of project portfolios.

B. KEY POINTS

1. A well thought of project governance process will minimize project risk and improve project success.
2. Bad communication, lack of planning, poor quality control, missing interim deliverables, poor budget, and project management contribute to project failures.
3. Your project governance process should include guiding principles, project excellence governance processes and metrics, project portfolios, and a project portfolio management (PPM) tool.
   a. Guiding principles include visible leadership, defined tactics, effective communications, project excellence, and metrics.
4. Project portfolios should be organized by categories and viewable across different categories, characteristics, and strategic alignment. Sustain, operational, and strategic is one category grouping.

C. EXAMPLES

- State of Georgia—Georgia Technology Authority (GTA)

D. FRAMEWORKS

- Governance Framework—Project Excellence

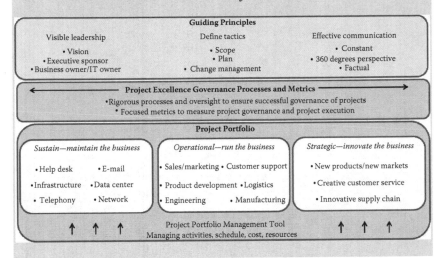

CHAPTER 6: HOW TO IMPROVE THE BUSINESS VALUE OF IT SERVICES

A. CHAPTER OBJECTIVE

1. Reinforce the importance of providing business value through the delivery of IT services
2. Share a framework and associated process for assessing the business value of IT services delivered to the business
3. Examine a process IT organizations can use to assess and identify the maturity of the business value for IT services you deliver to the business

B. KEY POINTS

1. CIOs must communicate the business value IT services provide the business.
2. CIOs need to assess how well IT services provide business value as well as measure how efficiently each IT services is executed.
3. There is a process CIOs can use to measure the effectiveness and efficiency of IT services.

C. EXAMPLES

- Synopsys, Cisco, American Financial

D. TEMPLATES

1. Strategic Framework to Improve Business Value of IT Services

Improve the Business Value of IT Services
A Strategic Framework

 Develop process/ IT services alignment map

 Identify process KPI/key IT services metrics

 Assess process/ IT service maturity

Measure/analyze/ report/revisit/ optimize

- Develop a process/ business services portfolio alignment map

- Develop business services and technical services portfolio

- Identify the key performance indicator metrics (KPI) that measure the effectiveness for each business process

- Identify the costs and performance metrics that measures the efficiency for each business service

- Assess process/IT services maturity

  -Business process

  -IT service

  -Metrics

  -Reporting

- Measure and analyze *process effectiveness* and *services efficiency*

- Identify opportunity areas across the value chain to leverage process performance

CHAPTER 7: SECTION OVERVIEW: UNDERSTAND THE BUSINESS, FOCUS ON USER EXPERIENCES, AND IMPROVE COMPETENCIES AND SKILLS OF IT PERSONNEL

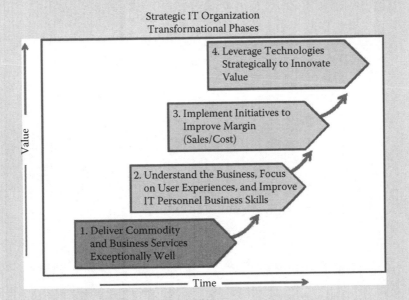

Strategic IT Organization
Transformational Phases

4. Leverage Technologies Strategically to Innovate Value

3. Implement Initiatives to Improve Margin (Sales/Cost)

2. Understand the Business, Focus on User Experiences, and Improve IT Personnel Business Skills

1. Deliver Commodity and Business Services Exceptionally Well

Value

Time

Newly appointed CIOs, who are hired from outside the company, will tell you that assessing service delivery, understanding the business, and IT personnel competencies and skills are three of the most important to dos for the first 100 days on the job. As stated in Chapter 1, the first two phases of the strategic IT transformation phases are most often implemented in parallel.

It is extremely important for the CIO and key IT executives to have a keen understanding of how the business operates on a day-to-day basis, the competitive environment, and where value creation occurs across the value network, which encompasses customers, distribution channels, company personnel, sourcing partners, etc. With this knowledge, CIOs and key IT personnel can identify potential value creation opportunities. For CIOs, it is equally important to assess the organization culture, as well as the competencies and skills of IT personnel to determine gaps that would inhibit the effective partnering with business teams in analyzing, identifying, and implementing solutions that achieve business outcomes.

Please see Chapter Summary for the following chapters.

CHAPTER 8: WHY CIOs NEED TO UNDERSTAND THE BUSINESS TO SUCCEED

A. CHAPTER OBJECTIVE

1. Reinforce for CIOs and key IT personnel the need to understand how the business operates, the value provided to customers, the competitive market, and industry trends.

B. KEY POINTS

1. A strategic CIO will not be successful without a well-based understanding of how the business operates.
2. The depth of understanding includes knowledge of the key processes across the entire value enterprise.
3. CIOs move into the role from the business, within IT, from other companies, in similar or dissimilar industries.
4. CIOs learn about the business in different ways, depending on experience.

C. EXAMPLES

1. CIOs and IT directors share their experiences in learning about the business.
   - Mike McClaskey, CIO, Dish Network
   - Scott Blanchette, CIO, Vanguard Health
   - Steve O'Connor, vice president and CIO, CSAA Insurance Group
   - Niel Nickolaisen, CIO, Western Governor's University
   - Kevin B. Michaelis, vice president, Global IT, and CIO, Air Products and Chemicals
   - Greg Lewis, IT director, Ironclad

2. Training Tomorrow's business leaders and CIOs
   • Dick Brandt—Director, Iacocca Institute—Global Village

CHAPTER 9: THE IMPORTANCE OF UNDERSTANDING YOUR ORGANIZATIONAL CULTURE IN BUILDING EFFECTIVE TEAMS

A. CHAPTER OBJECTIVE

1. Understand how the culture of your organization derives from the underlying values and behaviors personnel exhibit as they work in teams, or independently, on programs, projects, and individual work assignments.
2. Understand what organizational culture is, why it is important, how you measure it, and how you can change it.

B. KEY POINTS

1. A company's business strategies have a direct bearing on the cultural orientation required by the IT organization as well as other business units.
2. To achieve company goals, personnel work together on projects that align to business strategies.
3. Understanding the various cultural orientations, and how they compete with one another, is an important element in successfully achieving desired business outcomes.
4. There are four orientation cultures: collaboration, control, create, and compete.
5. Each dimension includes a set of underlying characteristics exhibited by the organization. The orientation and underlying characteristics compete with one another to achieve specific outcomes. If your organization has an internal focus, such as manufacturing, then the

underlying characteristics focus on collaboration and control. If your organization has an external focus, such as marketing or product development, then the underlying characteristics focus to create value and compete effectively.

6. There is no right or wrong culture orientation. You need to define the one that aligns best with your organizational goals. What is important is to know what your organizational culture orientation is today versus what it needs to be, in order to make the necessary cultural adjustments to successfully deliver business outcomes as defined by your company strategy.

C. EXAMPLES

Four Different Organizational Types

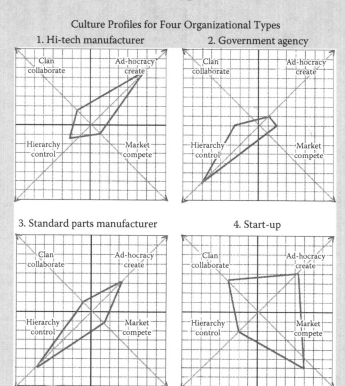

Culture Profiles for Four Organizational Types

D. TEMPLATES

1. Competing Values™ Framework

Collaborate

Focus: Values

Situation: A community united by shared beliefs, competency is closely linked to unique abilities, strong identification with a lifestyle

Purposes: Community and knowledge

Practices: Building teams and developing communities, training, and coaching, creating shared vision and values, harmonious work environment

People: Build trust, helpful, resolves conflict, empowering, good listener, encourages participation

Environment: Harmonious atmosphere, collaborative workplace, informal communication, shared values

Measures: Employee satisfaction, employee turnover, training per employee, competency peer review

Create

Focus: Vision

Situation: Differentiation creates significantly higher margins, a new methodology changes the game, an industry is situated around Blockbuster invention

Purposes: Innovation and growth

Practices: Encouraging radical thinking, launching new ventures, speculating emerging opportunities, launching change initiatives, destroying the old way of doing things

People: Visionary, optimistic, generalist, enthusiastic, quick thinker, expressive

Environment: Stimulating projects, flexible hours, free from everyday constraints, diverse workforce

Measures: Diversity of experiments, new market growth, adoption rate, revenues from new products and services

Control

Focus: Process

Situation: Organization has large and complex scope and scale, government regulations and standards determine business practices, failure is not an option

Purposes: Efficiency and quality

Practices: Implementing large scale technology and systems, applying continuous improvement processes, complying with regulations, adhering to standards

People: Organized, methodical, technical, practical, objective, persistent

Environment: Clear roles, logical objectives, structured work, cohesive work processes

Measures: Budget adherence, milestones achieved, number of failures, regulatory compliance

Compete

Focus: Goals

Situation: Shareholder demands are the primary driver, aggressive competition, markets change from mergers and acquisitions, investors demand quick results

Purposes: Profits and speed

Practices: Managing performance through objectives, investing for increasing rates of return, quickly starting and killing initiatives, quickly confronting problems

People: Goal oriented, assertive, driven, accountable, decisive, competitive

Environment: High pressure, fast moving, quantifiable results, pay for performance

Measures: Gross profit, time to market, return on investment, operating income

Competing Values™ Framework

Flexible — Break through — External — Short-term Performance — Focused — Incremental — Internal — Long-term development

Purpose — Collaborate / Create — Practice — Do things together / Do things first — People — Control / Complete — Do things right / Do things fast

2. Organizational Culture Assessment Template

1. Dominant characteristics	Now	Preferred
A. The organization is a very personal place. It is like an extended family. People seem to share a lot of themselves.	25	25
B. The organization is a very dynamic and entrepreneurial place. People are willing to stick their necks out and take risks.	5	25
C. The organization is very results oriented. A major concern is with getting the job done. People are very competitive and achievement oriented.	15	25
D. The organization is a very controlled and structured place. Formal procedures generally govern what people do. Total	55 / 100	25 / 100

2. Organizational leadership	Now	Preferred
A. The leadership in the organization is generally considered to exemplify mentoring, facilitation, or nurturing.	60	25
B. The leadership in the organization is generally considered to exemplify entrepreneurship, innovation, or risk taking.	5	25
C. The leadership in the organization is generally considered to exemplify a no-nonsense, aggressive, results-oriented focus.	15	25
D. The leadership in the organization is generally considered to exemplify coordinating, organizing, or smooth-running efficiency. Total	20 / 100	25 / 100

3. Management of employees	Now	Preferred
A. The management style in the organization is characterized by teamwork, consensus, and participation.	10	25
B. The management style in the organization is characterized by individual risk taking, innovation, freedom, and uniqueness.	5	25
C. The management style in the organization is characterized by hard-driving competitiveness, high demands, and achievement.	15	25
D. The management style in the organization is characterized by security of employment, conformity, predictability, and stability of relationships.	70	25
Total	100	100

4. Organizational glue	Now	Preferred
A. The glue that holds the organization together is loyalty and mutual trust. Commitment to this organization runs high.	35	25
B. The glue that holds the organization together is commitment to innovation and development. There is an emphasis on being on the cutting edge.	5	25
C. The glue that holds the organization together is the emphasis on achievement and goal accomplishment.	5	25
D. The glue that holds the organization together is formal rules and policies. Maintaining a smooth-running organization is important.	55	25
Total	100	100

5. Strategic emphasis	Now	Preferred
A. The organization emphasizes human development. High trust, openness, and participation persist.	20	25
B. The organization emphasizes acquiring new resources and creating new challenges. Trying new things and prospecting for opportunities are valued.	5	25
C. The organization emphasizes competitive actions and achievement. Hitting stretch targets and winning in the marketplace are dominant.	10	25
D. The organization emphasizes permanence and stability. Efficiency, control, and smooth operations are important.	65	25
Total	100	100

6. Criteria of success	Now	Preferred
A. The organization defines success on the basis of the development of human resources, teamwork, employee commitment, and concern for people.	20	25
B. The organization defines success on the basis of having the most unique or newest products. It is a product leader and innovator.	25	25
C. The organization defines success on the basis of winning in the marketplace and outpacing the competition. Competitive market leadership is key.	10	25
D. The organization defines success on the basis of efficiency. Dependable delivery, smooth scheduling, and low-cost production are critical.	45	25
Total	100	100

Instructions:

The purpose of the Organizational Culture Assessment Instrument is to assess six key dimensions of organizational culture. In completing the instrument, you will be providing a picture of the fundamental assumptions on which our organization operates and the values that characterize it. There are no right or wrong answers for these items, just as there is no right or wrong culture. Be as accurate as you can in responding to the items so that our resulting cultural diagnosis will be as precise as possible. For our purposes, "organization" is AAA Northern California, Nevada & Utah Insurance Exchange.

The OCAI consists of six dimensions. Each dimension has four alternatives. Divide 100 points among these four alternatives, depending on the extent to which each alternative is similar to our organization. Give a higher number of points to the alternative that is most similar to our organization. For example, on Dimension 1, if you think alternative A is very similar to AAA Northern California, Nevada & Utah Insurance Exchange, alternatives B and C are somewhat similar, and alternative D hardly similar at all, you might give 55 points to A, 20 points each to B and C, and 5 points to D. Just be sure your total equals 100 for each Dimension.

Note that responses in the NOW column mean that you are rating our organization as it is *currently*. Complete this rating first. Once you have finished, think of our organization as you think it should ideally be in the future in order to be spectacularly successful. Complete the instrument again, this time responding to the items as if we had achieved extraordinary success. Write these responses in the PREFERRED column. Your responses will thus produce two independent ratings of our organization's culture—one as it currently exists and one as you wish it to be 2–3 years from now.

CHAPTER 10: KEY COMPETENCIES AND SKILLS OF A STRATEGIC IT ORGANIZATION

A. CHAPTER OBJECTIVE

1. Understand the difference between competencies and skills
2. Identify the competencies and skills required by a strategic IT organization

B. KEY POINTS

1. There is a difference between competencies and skills:
   a. Competencies are the effective applications of skills. It is more of an umbrella term that also includes behavior and knowledge.
   b. Skills are specific learned activities that may be part of a broader context.
2. There are 4 competencies and 12 associated skills

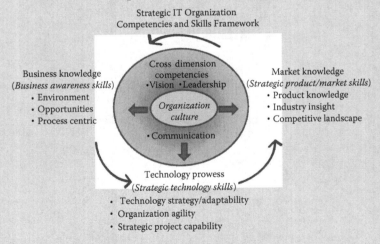

Strategic IT Organization
Competencies and Skills Framework

a. *Business knowledge competency*
   a1. *Business knowledge and environmental skill*
   a2. *Opportunities and challenges skills*
   a3. *Process-centric skills*

   b. *Market knowledge competency*
      b1. *Product knowledge skills*
      b2. *Industry knowledge skills*
      b3. *Competitive landscape skills*
   c. *Technology prowess competency*
      c1. *Technology strategy/adaptability skills*
      c2. *Organization agility skills*
      c3. *Strategic project capability skills*
   d. *Cross-dimensional competency*
      d1. *Vision, leadership, and communication skills*

C. EXAMPLES

1. CIO and IT executive examples for each competency and associated skills
   - Randy Spratt—CIO/CTO, McKesson
   - Harry Lukens—CIO, Lehigh Valley Health Network
   - Steve O'Connor—CIO, CSAA Insurance Group
   - Rosa Sibilsky—business process director, CSAA Insurance Group
   - Debra Martucci—CIO, Synopsys
   - Ravi Naik—CIO, SanDisk
   - Grace Liu—director of finance and human resource (HR) IT, SanDisk
   - Calvin Rhodes—CIO, Georgia Technology Authority (GTA)
   - Sanjib Sahoo—CIO, OptionMonster Holdings

D. TEMPLATES

Strategic IT organization competencies and underlying skills

1. Strategic IT Organization Competency and Best Practices Skills Matrix (Figure 10.1)

STRATEGIC COMPETENCY	ASSOCIATED SKILLS/BEST PRACTICE		CROSS COMPETENCY SKILLS
BUSINESS KNOWLEDGE Business Awareness Skills	1. Business Environment	IT Personnel Understand and Articulate the Enterprise Business Strategy, Objectives, Culture, and Internal Environment	**1. Vision** IT Vision that Aligns with Corporate, Business Units, and IT Organization
	2. Opportunities/ Challenges	IT Organization Understands the Enterprise Business Opportunities to Enhance Customer Value, Revenue, Profitability as Well as Challenges that Impact Enterprise Growth.	
	3. Process Centric	IT Organization Understands How IT Services and Underlying Technologies Align and Enable Enterprise Business Processes that Create/Support Customer Value	
	MARKET		**2. Leadership** CIO Guides the IT Organization in Developing the Skills/ Competencies/Knowledge to Enhance and Develop the IT Services Aligned to Business Needs and Effectively Collaborates with Business Peers to Achieve Business Vision/Financial Objectives/ Market Strategies
MARKET KNOWLEDGE Strategic Product/Market Skills	1. Product Knowledge	Knowledge of How Customer Value is Derived from Enterprise Products/Services	
	2. Industry Knowledge	Understanding of Industry Landscape and Upcoming Trends and their Alignment to Enterprise Products and Services	
	3. Competitive Landscape	Insight into Competitive Environment and the Associated Customer Value Gaps and Opportunities	
	TECHNOLOGY		**3. Communication** IT Personnel Effectively Communicate and Team with Business Personnel to Understand/Uncover Opportunities to Drive Revenue /Reduce Cost
TECHNOLOGY PROWESS Strategic Technology Skills	1. Technology Strategy/ Adaptability	Incorporates a Technology Strategy that Integrates Emerging and Existing Technologies into New and/or Enhanced Customer Value and Revenue Streams.	
	2. Organization Agility	Combined IT/Business Teams Rapidly Respond to Changing Business Needs Utilizing Enabling Technologies to Develop/Enhance Customer Products and Services	
	3. Strategic Project Capability	Increase Capacity to Implement Strategic Project by Reducing Run & Maintain/Enhancement Project Costs/Execution time and Improving IT Personnel Technology/Business Skills	

2. Strategic IT Organization Competencies and Skills Framework (Figure 10.1)

3. Transformation Path to Optimize IT Performance (Figure 10.5)

1. Transparency and control
   - Project selection
   - Resource allocation
   - Project status

2. Alignment and rationalization
   - Process consistency/transparency
   - Predictive analytics to mitigate risk
   - Implement project execution

3. Optimization
   - Leverage learnings
   - Optimize IT investments
   - Increase innovation spend

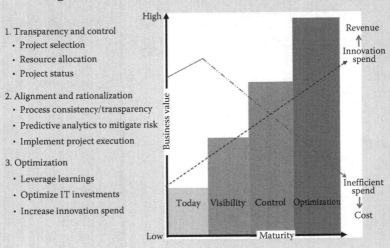

CHAPTER 11: HOW TO MEASURE THE MATURITY OF YOUR STRATEGIC IT ORGANIZATION

A. CHAPTER OBJECTIVE

1. Share a process for measuring the strategic IT competencies and associated skills using a *strategic maturity assessment.*

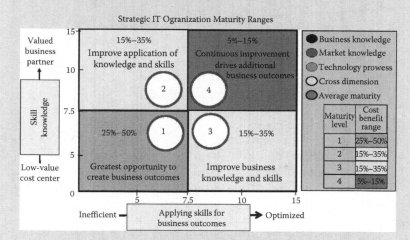

Strategic IT Ogranization Maturity Ranges

B. KEY POINTS

1. IT organizations need to exhibit four strategic competencies and associated skills if they want to effectively partner with business teams to improve business outcomes in the form of increased customer value, improved margins, and enhanced shareholder wealth.

2. What is common among strategic IT organizations is a varying level of knowledge across the four competencies—business, market, technology prowess, and cross dimensional. Knowledge by itself is important. What is more important is how this knowledge is applied using a set of skills to effect business outcomes.

3. A strategic CIO recognizes that to succeed in achieving business outcomes through collaborating with business leaders and teams is not a one-man process. It takes IT personnel using their skills and applying these

skills in collaborative business and IT teams to identify issues, challenges, and solutions that enable business outcomes.

4. A strategic maturity assessment identifies how well IT personnel apply these skills and identifies the gaps in skill maturity that require improvement.

5. You can measure the strategic maturity of your IT organization by following a five-step process:

   a. Assess the level of knowledge and competency of your IT organization.

   b. Plot scores on a maturity index grid.

   c. Assess results to determine gaps.

   d. Develop a plan to improve scores.

   e. Implement a continuous improvement program to achieve positive momentum.

6. There are variations on how to use the strategic IT maturity assessment, from a quick gut check to a more detailed assessment across the IT organization and business:

   a. For items i through vii below: Figure 11.3 provides descriptions of the competencies, skills, and the associated best-in-class practices. Table 11.1 is the Assessment Instrument.

   b. For item viii below: Figure 11.10 provides a template for you to use to capture examples of how your IT organization exhibits the skills.

      i. *Gut check assessment*: The CIO completes the assessment independently based upon his or her observations of IT organization. This provides the CIO with an initial point of reference baseline to determine if further assessments, at a more detailed level, are required.

      ii. *IT leadership assessment*: The CIO completes the assessment of IT leadership to determine their degree of maturity. This provides the CIO with a baseline data for identifying gaps and developing training programs with IT leadership.

iii. *IT personnel assessment conducted by IT leaders as a team*: The IT leadership team performs an assessment, as a team, of the IT organization. This provides the IT leadership team with a perspective of the skill knowledge and application of knowledge for the IT organization, as a whole.

iv. *IT leadership conducts assessment of IT personnel in their organization*: This provides the IT leader, for their organization, a perspective of the skill knowledge and application of knowledge for his or her organization.

v. *Business vice president assessment of IT organization*: This assessment provides the CIO with a perception of how business unit leaders view the skill levels of the IT organization.

vi. *Business unit personnel assessment of IT organization*: This includes business personnel in the IT leadership assessment of their organization (number 3, above). This provides more of a 360-degree perspective on the skills of the IT organization.

vii. *Review results with IT personnel, business vice presidents, and business personnel*: Conduct meetings and town hall meetings to provide results to organization. This helps the entire company view IT in a proactive way as an organization that wants to work with the business to improve business outcomes.

viii. *Adding fields to provide specific examples*: When conducting assessments, you may want to add fields in the template to capture specific examples of where skill knowledge and/or applying skills is deficient or excels as a proof point for the numeric score.

C. EXAMPLES

1. Case example of measuring IT strategic maturity including templates and instructions

D. TEMPLATE EXAMPLES

1. IT Strategic Maturity Assessment—Template (Figures 11.2 and 11.3)
2. Strategic IT Maturity Ranges Framework (Figure 11.4)
3. Strategic IT Organization Maturity Assessment—6-Month Assessment Summary (Figure 11.5 and Table 11.1)
4. Strategic IT Organization Maturity Assessment—6-Month Assessment Scores Summary by Competency (Figure 11.6)
5. Strategic IT Organization Maturity Assessment—6-Month versus 2-Year Assessment Results (Figure 11.8)
6. Strategic IT Organization Maturity Assessment—6-Month versus 2-Year Assessment Results Table (Figure 11.7)
7. Examples of Additional Fields to Add to IT Strategic Maturity Assessment Template (Figure 11.9)

CHAPTER 12: SECTION OVERVIEW: IMPLEMENT INITIATIVES TO IMPROVE MARGIN

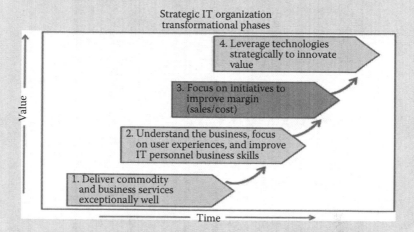

Strategic IT organization transformational phases

Value

4. Leverage technologies strategically to innovate value

3. Focus on initiatives to improve margin (sales/cost)

2. Understand the business, focus on user experiences, and improve IT personnel business skills

1. Deliver commodity and business services exceptionally well

Time

With a solid foundation of delivering services exceptionally well and personnel that understand, communicate, and demonstrate business competencies and skills, the IT organization is positioned to collaborate in business teams that focus on initiatives to drive margin in the form of increased revenues or reduced costs. There is a reason a profit and loss statement and balance sheet are recognized measures of a company's potential worth. This is the basic principle of business. The logical path then is to focus on initiatives that improve the company's revenue, reduce cost, or improve the balance sheet.

If you, as a CIO, want to be recognized as a strategic contributor to the business, you need to work with C-suite executives to evaluate market opportunities that will improve the competitive position of their company. To do so requires the trust from the business that is established by delivering services exceptionally well and demonstrating that your IT personnel can demonstrate business competencies and skills, the first two phases of strategic IT organization transformation phases. How do CIOs successfully focus on initiatives to drive margin. This section of the book demonstrates how five CIOs focused on initiatives to drive margin for their respective company.

Please see Chapter Summary for the following chapters.

CHAPTER 13: HOW STRATEGIC CIOs FOCUS ON INITIATIVES TO IMPROVE MARGIN

A. CHAPTER OBJECTIVE

1. Share examples of strategic CIOs whose journey took them through the first two phases of the IT Strategic Transformation Phases and implemented initiatives that focused on improving margin (phase 3).

2. This chapter will be especially helpful for those of you who are still in phase one or two of your transformation journey and interested in leveraging examples from CIOs who have succeeded at stage three.

B. KEY POINTS

1. Strategic CIOs follow a simple but effective process for transforming their IT organization and implement initiatives that drive margin in the form of increased revenues and/or reduced costs.

C. EXAMPLES

In this chapter, we highlight six strategic CIOs who focus on initiatives that drive margin, through improving revenue and/or reducing costs. Each of these CIOs has broad and deep experience in business and IT at the executive level. Further, each applies these skills in a strategic and focused manner.

1. *Tom Grooms, CIO at Valspar,* joined the chemical coating company after a long career in IT at Medtronic—the medical device company. Although Valspar is in a totally different industry, Grooms took a strategic approach to professionalize the IT organization by working with the business units to improve processes, reduce IT support costs, and drive initiatives that enabled Valspar to move forward with an aggressive growth strategy.

2. *Randy Spratt, chief technology officer (CTO) and CIO at McKesson,* the multinational health-care services and

IT company, is an example of an executive who is both left- and right-brain dominant. He thinks strategically but is just as comfortable at the tactical level designing company-wide architecture. Customers had difficulty integrating McKesson products, due to incompatible architecture, until Spratt harnessed a company-wide team to develop a unified architecture, which improved customer service and improved sales.

3. *Clif Triplett, while CIO at Baker Hughes,* took on some rather large projects. Baker Hughes is an oil industry services company. Triplett turned the IT organization into a world-class organization, developed a common data platform to optimize customer information, and developed a product life cycle management system that reduced development time for products and services. Improved customer service, reduced IT costs, and a transformed IT organization make Triplett a true example of a strategic CIO.

4. *Anne Wilms, former CIO at Rohm and Hass,* embarked on a number of strategic initiatives that increased revenue through an improved pricing system, reduced IT costs, optimized inventory investment savings millions of dollars, and a host of other initiatives.

5. *Steve Heilenman, CIO at CAI,* focused on improving the value of the IT organization while driving down the cost of IT. He succeeded. Over a 5-year period, Heilenman reduced IT costs by about 25% while supporting a business that grew by 50%. The net metric of IT costs as a percentage of revenue is 2%; one-half of the best in class percentage for IT service companies.

6. *Helen Cousins,* former CIO at Lincoln Trust, revitalized and reengineered the major document processes by leveraging technology. This positioned the company for a spin-off of some of its business units and enabled the company to focus on a core competency for future growth.

CHAPTER 14: SECTION OVERVIEW: HOW CIOs LEVERAGE TECHNOLOGY TO INNOVATE VALUE

The section starts with a chapter that explores the significance of leveraging technology strategically and provides examples of where information and associated technologies seamlessly weave into our daily lives. With this foundation, we highlight eight CIOs, in subsequent chapters, who have successfully leveraged technologies strategically to innovate value.

Please see Chapter Summary for the following chapters.

CHAPTER 15: WHY LEVERAGING TECHNOLOGIES STRATEGICALLY TO INNOVATE VALUE IS A GAME CHANGER

A. CHAPTER OBJECTIVE

1. Provide you with examples of strategic CIOs who have navigated through all four of the strategic IT transformation phases and leverage technology strategically to innovate.
2. Provide insights to those of you who are still on their transformation journey but want to understand the strategic value of leveraging technology in innovative ways.

B. KEY POINTS

1. Leveraging technology to innovate value is a recognized global trend exploited by world-class companies.
2. A recent McKinsey global survey of over 1000 chief executive officers (CEOs), chief information officers (CIOs), and other C-level executives supports this trend.

   ...companies are using digital technology more and more to engage with customers and reach them through new channels... and companies are making digital marketing and customer engagement a high strategic priority.[2]

3. An MIT Sloan study of 1600 executives on how they are using digital technologies found that companies must "adopt new technologies effectively or face competitive obsolescence."[3] Leveraging technology is a strategic imperative for every boardroom to embrace or else executives will watch their competitors race ahead in record time.

4. The role of technology in products, services, and processes has never been more important than it is right now. We are the cusp of the *Internet of Everything* (IoE). People will connect in ways we are just beginning to experience:

   a. Wearable technologies enable us to use Google Glass as if it were a laptop computer. Except it is voice activated.

   b. Data will be processed more intelligently than ever before. Instead of just capturing data that accessed for further analysis, predictive analytics will incorporate sophisticated algorithms that evaluate data and help us make faster and more intelligent decisions.

   c. Processes as we know them today will expand to incorporate human behavior. Proactively engaging shoppers is a reality today.

   d. The 2014 Mercedes-Benz S-Class uses 60 onboard computers to control almost every aspect of the vehicle. Mercedes dubs this *intelligent drive*.

   e. 3D printing is changing our lives.

   f. Wearable devices are improving our health care.

   g. *Smart* contact lenses help diabetics control their sugar level.

   h. Digital toothbrushes help improve dental health.

   i. The list is growing every day.

C. EXAMPLES

1. CIO examples of applying technology to innovate value include the following:

- A group of executives meets to analyze marketing trends.
- A father wants to ship a package to his son at college.
- A young child pleads with her mom to take her to a store to build a stuffed animal.
- An elderly man is having difficulty adhering to the doctor's instructions for taking medication.
- A patient in a hospital or at home care, who is concerned about their health outcome.

CHAPTER 16: HOW FEDEX LEVERAGES TECHNOLOGY STRATEGICALLY TO INNOVATE VALUE

OVERVIEW

This chapter describes the evolution of FedEx and its use of technology to innovate value. The chapter is structured as follows:

- Brief history of FedEx
- How Rob Carter, CIO, transformed IT, through a four-stage transformation model, into a strategic organization leveraging technology innovatively
- How Ken Spangler, senior vice president of IT for FedEx Freight and FedEx Ground Systems, leads the IT group and his innovative use of technology that transforms how freight moves through the delivery handling process
- How David Zanca, former senior vice president of Customer Access Solutions, leverages technology to provide a superior service experience to FedEx customers
- How Doug Bonebrake, former IT manager of FedEx Services, uses innovation, in its simplest form, to dramatically improve the quality of IT-developed applications
- What you should remember from this chapter: Summary and key learnings

CHAPTER 17: HOW PROCTER & GAMBLE LEVERAGES TECHNOLOGY STRATEGICALLY TO INNOVATE VALUE

A. CHAPTER OBJECTIVE

This chapter focuses on how P&G leverages technology strategically to innovate value. Filippo Passerini, president of GBS and CIO, is a business-focused executive who understands the P&G business and how to leverage technology to create new business models. The chapter focuses on four key areas: history of P&G, business value of P&Gs Business Services Group, information strategies employed by the CIO and his team to innovate value, and a use-case example of how P&G leverages technology for innovative value.

B. KEY MESSAGES

1. The primary objective of the CIO is to create business value for the enterprise.
2. IT should be used to help business leaders make well-informed decisions.
3. Present data meaningfully to help business leaders focus on analyzing root causes of business challenges.

C. EXAMPLES

1. P&G history and today's competitive environment
2. Passerini's background and how the Business Services Group helps management make well-informed decisions
3. An innovative *what, why, how* business model and *digitize, visualize, and simulate* data strategy to manage, display, and model data

CHAPTER 18: HOW FIVE CIOs FROM DIFFERENT INDUSTRIES LEVERAGE TECHNOLOGY STRATEGICALLY TO INNOVATE VALUE

A. CHAPTER OBJECTIVE:

To share experiences by five CIOs who leverage technology strategically to innovate value.

B. KEY POINTS

1. Understand and anticipate customer needs (Build-A-Bear).
2. Look beyond initial competencies to create new business model (Express Scripts).
3. Leverage the best from each operating division and integrate across the entire enterprise (Penske).
4. Create a true unique differentiator for competitive advantage by leveraging technology (Verisk).
5. Listen and learn about the needs of the business, build a strong team, leverage technology strategically (Lehigh Valley Health Network [LVHN]).

C. EXAMPLES

1. Chief information and interactive officer, Build-A-Bear Workshop
2. Perry Rotella, group executive of Supply Chain Risk Analytics and senior vice president and CIO, Verisk Analytics
3. Gary Wimberly, senior vice president and CIO, Express Script
4. Stephen Pickett, senior vice president of Information Technology and CIO, Penske Corporation
5. Harry Lukens, senior vice president and CIO, Lehigh Valley Health Network

CHAPTER 19: SECTION OVERVIEW: HOW TO MEASURE THE STRATEGIC MATURITY OF YOUR IT ORGANIZATION

A. CHAPTER OBJECTIVE

To define a process for measuring the strategic maturity of your IT organization.

B. KEY POINTS

1. Measuring the strategic maturity of your IT organization is a necessary step to determine how effectively you are leveraging information and technology for competitive advantage.
2. A set of best practices for each transformational phase will help you determine the degree to which your IT organization delivers business value and how efficiently it delivers value.
3. You need to measure each of the four transformation phases across two dimensions:
   a. Business value
   b. Efficiency of delivery
4. Measuring the business value and efficiency for each of the four strategic IT transformation phases will determine the strategic maturity of your IT organization.
5. Understanding the strategic maturity of your IT organization for each transformation phase is a basis for developing a plan to shore up gaps and improve the value IT provides the business and the efficiency of the delivery of value.

C. TEMPLATES USED

1. Strategic IT maturity assessment template (Figure 19.2)
2. IT organization maturity dimensions (Figure 19.3)

CHAPTER 20: FINAL THOUGHTS: AN EXECUTIVE CHALLENGE

CHAPTER OBJECTIVE

The objective of this chapter is to conclude the book with a challenge to the executive suite. Strategic CIOs are now part of the executive team that drives business outcomes to improve customer value, increase revenue, and enhance shareholder wealth. Managing in the twenty-first century requires new thinking. The pace of change is so fast today that management delegates decision making throughout the organization, even those closest to the customer. Unfortunately, personnel don't have all the facts and, as a result, make decisions that create tremendous risks for the company (e.g., JP Morgan's *London Whale* scandal). The result is that decisions not made with all the correct facts, as well as the history of similar decisions and resultant risks, could negatively impact the company. A proactive *early warning* information system is required to coach and mentor decision makers throughout the organization to mitigate risks before they occur; in essence, *instrument the business* to avert risks through a set of early warning indicators, smoke alarms, and mitigating actions to prevent risks before they occur.

- Managing in the twenty-first century requires new approaches than used in the past. The dynamic and ever-changing business landscape requires companies to be agile, flexible, and aware of emerging issues that can quickly turn a profitable and competitively successful company into a potential disaster. Remember the 2012 JP Morgan's London Whale trading scandal that resulted in 6.2 billion dollar trading loss and 920 million billions in penalties. True, JP Morgan has a set of products and services that provide significant revenues.
- However, flaws in supporting processes that enable these products and services did not provide early warning of a potential trading issue. Herein lie the gap and the challenge for the executive suite.

Appendix B: Alphabetical Listing of 156 Executives Interviewed for This Book

NAME	COMPANY	ROLE
Sagar Anisingaraju	Saama Technologies	Chief strategy officer
Lynda Applegate	Harvard	Sarofim-Rock professor of business administration at HBS
Bryce Austin	Wells Fargo	IT-VP, Business Payroll Services
Geoff Avard	Business Strategy and Practice Consulting	Consultant
Malini Balakrishnan	Build with BMC	CIO
Rabbi Laura Baum	Beth Adam Synagogue	Rabbi (and Chief Technology Officer)
Brian Beattie	Synopsys	CFO
Ajay Bhatia	Carsales	CIO
Scott Blanchette	Vanguard Health	CIO
David Bogan	CSC	Former CIO, Managed Services Sector
Doug Bonebrake	FedEx	IT director
John Bowen	Management Envision LLC	President
Dave Bradley	Computer Associates	Former SVP Global Partner Sales at CA Technologies; currently SVP Solution Management and Business Development at R4 Technologies
Dick Brandt	Global Village and Iacocca Institute, Lehigh University	Director
Matthew Broom	Doremus	President, international

(Continued)

NAME	COMPANY	ROLE
Diane Burkert	CSAA Insurance Group	Enterprise Service Deskside Services Executive
Matt Butcher	Karl Storz Endoscopy	CIO
Robert Carter	FedEx	Executive vice president, CIO
Marty Carty	Lifeguard Health Networks	Founder
John Chambers	JCC Executive Partners	President
Giri Chodavarapu	Finisar	CIO
Gener Clater	CAI	Former CIO
Tom Crampton	Trusted Impact	Managing director
Brenda Curiel	Center for Corporate Innovation	Managing director
Tony D'Allesandro	Rogers Corporation	CIO
John Dempsey	Harvey Nash	Executive recruiter
Marcio deOliveira	C1 Bank	CIO
Mike Desosa	SBIT	Consultant
Brian Donovan	Donovan Leadership	President
Chris Dowling	Department of Premier and Cabinet	CIO
John Dubois	Dell	Managing director, Global Business Consulting
Mark Egan	StrataFusion	Partner, IT Transformation and Information Security consulting practices, previously CIO at VMware
Jose Carlos Eiras	The Practical CIO	President
David Evans	Cisco	Chief futurist
Susan Fair	CSC	Principal consultant
Brett Feltingoff	Hexaware Technologies	Director, Sales, Quality Assurance and Testing Services
Cesar Fernandez	PMG	Director of Product and Business Solutions
Ed Ferrara	CareCentrix	VP, IT Infrastructure
David Finnegan	Build-A-Bear Workshop	CIO, (In mid-2014, Dave Finnegan left Build-A-Bear. He is now CIO\VP Technology and Interactive at The Orvis Company.)
Norm Fjeldheim	Qualcomm	CIO
Molly Ford	Salesforce	Director, Radian6
Darren Frearson	Gencom Technology	President and CEO
Tom Fruman	State of Georgia	Director, Enterprise Governance and Planning
Steve Fugale	Villanova University	VP and CIO
Karen Garcia	KHG Consulting	CEO and president

(Continued)

NAME	COMPANY	ROLE
Tom Gill	Plantronics	CIO
Sasan Goodarzi	Intuit	CIO
Tom Grooms	Valspar	CIO
James L. Hanson	Mutual of Omaha Insurance Company	Former CIO
Teresa Hanson	T-Systems	Marketing director
Mike Hedges	Medtronic	CIO
Steve Heilenman	CAI	CIO
Martha Heller	Heller Search Associates	President
Laurie Heltsley	Procter & Gamble	Director, Innovation and Strategic Projects
Bruce Hoechner	Rogers Corporation	President
Bruce Heugel	B. Braun Medical Inc.	CFO/CIO
Tracey Hughes	Q1 Recruitment	VP
James Ivy	SBTI	President
Terry Jacklin	Merck	Executive director, IT
Rebecca Jacoby	Cisco	CIO
Dave Joddock	Boeing	IT director
Adriana Karaboutis	Dell	CIO
Dave Kepler	Dow Chemical	CIO
Stuart Kippelman	Covanta Energy	CIO
Joanne Kossuth	Olin College of Engineering	VP for Operations and CIO
Murali Krishnam	Saama	Practice area leader, Big Data Solutions
Josh Kulberg	The Learning Experience	IT director
R. Lemuel Lasher	CSC	VP (retired 2013)
Michael Lawrey	Telstra	Executive director
Joe LeCompte	PMG	Principal, Consulting Services
David Lee	Dell	VP of Sales, Marketing and Strategy
Hank Leingang	Bechtel, Viacom	Former CIO; currently independent IT leadership consultant
Gene Leonardi	BMC Software	Area director
Greg Lewis	Ironclad Performance Wear	IT director
Grace Liu	SanDisk	Director, Finance and HR IT
Arthur G. Lofton	Northrop Grumman	VP and CIO
Tony Lombardi	Armstrong World Industries	VP, Global Business Services and CIO
Dennis Loughran	Rogers Corporation	CFO
Harry Lukens	Lehigh Valley Health Network	CIO
Duncan MacCallum	Mindfields	Director
Debra Martucci	Synopsys	CIO
Janet Matton	Epworth Healthcare	Nonexecutive director
Jim Mazarakis	WSFS Bank	CIO

(*Continued*)

NAME	COMPANY	ROLE
Mike McClaskey	Dish Network	CIO
Denis McGee	NAB	VP
Pat McGinley	Baker Hughes	IT director
Cindy McKenzie	Fox Entertainment Group	Former VP, Enterprise Application Services. In April 2013, McKenzie joined PricewaterhouseCoopers as managing director, US Entertainment, Media, and Communications practice
James McQuivey	Forrester	VP and principal analyst
John Mercante	The Vanguard Group	CIO
Nader Mherabi	NYU Langone Medical Center	SVP, vice dean, and CIO
Kevin Michaelis	Air Products and Chemicals	CIO
Scott Millis	McAfee	VP, IT Strategy
Suzanne McGann	Medtronic	IT director
Tom Murphy	University of Pa	CIO
Roger Nagel	Lehigh University	Emeritus professor, Harvey Wagner professor of computer science and engineering
Ravi Naik	SanDisk	CIO
Jitender Nankani	Saama	Consulting director
Niel Nickolaisen	Western Governors University	CIO
Cris Nicolli	UXC	Managing director
Claudio Novas	CAI	Director, International Sales
Steve O'Connor	CSAA Insurance Group	CIO
Hank Oelze	State of Georgia	IT manager
Honorio Padron	The Hackett Group	Principal
Georgia Papathomas	Johnson & Johnson	VP and CIO, J&J Pharmaceuticals
Filippo Passerini	Procter & Gamble	President, Global Business Services, and CIO
Ken Piddington	Global Partners	CIO
Bart Perkins	Leverage Partners	Managing partner
Jim Phillips	CAI	Principal consultant
Stephen Pickett	Penske Corporation	CIO
Brian Pollard	Wells Fargo India Solutions	Head of technology
Teresa Reilly	State of Georgia	Director, Enterprise Portfolio Management Office
Calvin Rhodes	State of Georgia	CIO, Georgia Technology Authority
John Rooney	Deloitte Consulting	Principal
Perry Rotella	Verisk	Group executive, Supply Chain Risk Analytics, SVP, and CIO

(Continued)

NAME	COMPANY	ROLE
Sanjib Sahoo	OptionMonster Holdings	CTO
Tony Salvaggio	CAI	CEO
Frank Schettini	PMI Institute	CIO
Mark Settle	BMC Software	CIO
Patti Seybold	Patricia Seybold Group	CEO
Christine Shimizu	Raytheon	VP and CIO of Raytheon Technical Service
Wayne Shurts	Sysco Foods	CIO
Rosa Sibilsky	CSAA Insurance Group	Director, Business Process
Fi Slaven	Former CIO	Executive CIO and management consultant
Dave Smith	CAI	Product manager
Paul Smith	CAI	General manager
Steve Snyder	MCCA	CIO/CTO
Gary Spears	Medtronic	IT director, Sales
Randy Spratt	McKesson	CIO
Leon Sterling	Swinburne University of Technology	Dean, Faculty of ICT
Chris Stevens	Digital Frontier Partners	Managing partner
Holger Stibbe	Baker Hughes	Chief engineer
Jim Stikeleather	Dell	CIO
Mark Sutherlin	Synopsys	Senior business analyst
Joe Tracy	Lehigh Valley Health Network	VP, Telehealth Services
Stephen Tranquillo	Jefferson Hospital	CIO
Clif Triplett	Baker Hughes	CIO (currently managing partner, Steelpointe LLP)
Chris Trott	Telecommunications Industry Ombudsman	Business systems improvement manager
Les Trudzik	ACIL Allen Consulting	Executive director
Greg Valdez	Computer Associates	Former CIO
Ameya Vanjari	TATA Consultancy Services	Global head of delivery, Business and IT Architecture
Dee Waddell	Universal Weather and Aviation	SVP and CIO
Pat Wadors	Plantronics	Director
Dennis Waliczek	USF Logistics	Former CIO
Phil Watson	Fish & Nankivell	Principal
Howard Weber	Geisinger	IT PM
Ron Weber	CSAA Insurance Group	Problem management consultant
Jonathan Weider	NYU Langone Medical Center	Assistant dean for advanced applications
George Westerman	MIT Sloan Center for Digital Research	Research scientist

(Continued)

NAME	COMPANY	ROLE
George White	State of Pennsylvania	CIO
Darrell Williams	Katz, Sapper & Miller	CIO
Anne Wilms	Rohm and Haas	CIO (retired)
Gary Wimberly	Express Scripts	CIO
Glen Wintrich	Dell	Innovation leader
Ben Wood	Clicks IT Recruitment	Managing director
David Zanca	FedEx	SVP, Customer Access Solutions
Shadi Ziaei	CSAA Insurance Group	IT service center manager

Index